DUE	
JE 28 '96	
JY 22 '96	
FEB 27 '97	
DEC 8 '97	
JY 25 '00	
AP 19	
FE 09 '02	

SUMNER PUBLIC LIBRARY
Sumner, Iowa
Telephone 578-3324

WITHDRAWN

RULES

1 Books may be kept two weeks, and are subject to renewal

2. A fine of 5 cents a day will be charged on each book which is not returned according to the above rule. No book will be issued to any person incurring such a fine until it has been paid.

3 All injuries to books beyond reasonable wear and all losses shall be made good to the satisfaction of the Librarian.

4 Each borrower is held responsible for all books drawn on his card and for all fines accruing on the same.

DEMCO

BLOOD ON THE SEA

BLOOD
ON THE
SEA

American Destroyers
Lost in World War II

by
Robert Sinclair Parkin

SARPEDON
New York

Published in the United States in 1996 by
SARPEDON
166 Fifth Avenue
New York, NY 10010

ISBN 1-885119-17-8

Also published in the UK in 1996 by
Spellmount Publishers, Ltd, Staplehurst, Kent

Library of Congress Cataloging-in-Publication Data

Parkin, Robert Sinclair.
  Blood on the sea : American destroyers lost in World War II / by
Robert Sinclair Parkin.
    p. cm.
  Includes bibliographical references and index.
  ISBN 1-885119-17-8
  1. World War, 1939–1945—Naval operations, American.
  2. Destroyers (Warships)—United States—History—20th century.
  3. United States. Navy—History—World War, 1939–1945. 4. United
States—History, Naval—20th century. I. Title.
  D773.P37   1995
  940.54'5973—dc20   95-44042
                                                          CIP

10 9 8 7 6 5 4 3 2 1

MANUFACTURED IN THE UNITED STATES OF AMERICA

This book is dedicated to the
officers and men whose lives were sacrificed while serving
in the seventy-one United States destroyers that were
lost in World War II.

"When at grips with the enemy on the sea, beneath the sea and in the air, no task force commander ever had enough destroyers."

Vice Admiral Walden L. Ainsworth, USN

☆ ☆ ☆

"A destroyer is a lovely ship, probably the nicest fighting ship of all....In the beautiful clean lines of her, in her speed, and roughness, in curious gallantry, she is completely a ship, in the old sense."

John Steinbeck

☆ ☆ ☆

"But here are men who fought in gallant actions, as gallantly as ever heroes fought."

George Lord Gordon Byron

TABLE OF CONTENTS

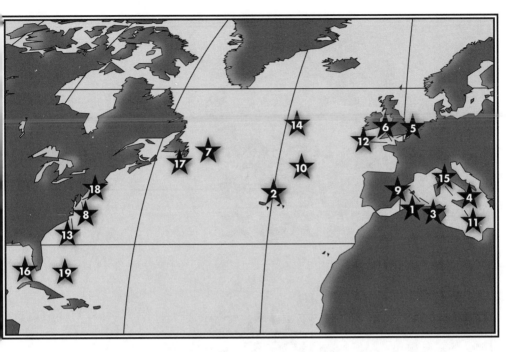

U.S. Destroyer Losses in the West

1.	USS Beatty	air attack	Nov. 6, 1943
2.	USS Borie	surface action	Nov. 1, 1943
3.	USS Bristol	submarine	Oct. 13, 1943
4.	USS Buck	submarine	Oct. 9, 1943
5.	USS Corry	mine	June 6, 1944
6.	USS Glennon	mine	June 8, 1944
7.	USS Ingraham	collision	August 22, 1942
8.	USS Jacob Jones	submarine	Feb. 28, 1942
9.	USS Lansdale	air attack	April 20, 1944
10.	USS Leary	submarine	Dec. 24, 1943
11.	USS Maddox	air attack	July 10, 1943
12.	USS Meredith	mine	June 8, 1944
13.	USS Parrott	collision	May 2, 1944
14.	USS Reuben James	submarine	Oct. 31, 1941
15.	USS Rowan	surface action	Sept. 11, 1943
16.	USS Sturtevant	mine	April 26, 1942
17.	USS Truxtun	grounding	Feb. 18, 1942
18.	USS Turner	accidental explosion	Jan. 3, 1944
19.	USS Warrington	hurricane	Sept. 13, 1944

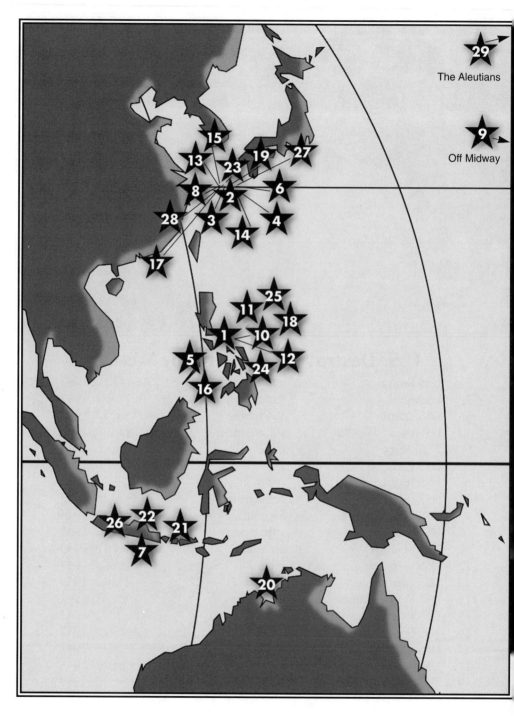

The Aleutians

Off Midway

U.S. Destroyer Losses
in the Far East

1.	USS Abner Read	air attack	Nov. 1, 1944
2.	USS Bush	air attack*	April 6, 1945
3.	USS Callaghan	air attack*	July 29, 1945
4.	USS Colhoun	air attack*	April 6, 1945
5.	USS Cooper	submarine	Dec. 3, 1944
6.	USS Drexler	air attack*	May 28, 1945
7.	USS Edsal	surface action	March 1, 1942
8.	USS Halligan	mine	March 26, 1945
9.	USS Hammann	submarine	June 6, 1942
10.	USS Hoel	surface action	Oct. 25, 1944
11.	USS Hull	typhoon	Dec. 18, 1944
12.	USS Johnston	surface action	Oct. 25, 1944
13.	USS Little	air attack*	May 3, 1945
14.	USS Longshaw	shore fire	May 18, 1945
15.	USS Luce	air attack*	May 4, 1945
16.	USS Mahan	air attack*	Dec. 7, 1944
17.	USS Mannert L. Abele	air attack*	April 12, 1945
18.	USS Monaghan	typhoon	Dec. 18, 1944
19.	USS Morrison	air attack*	May 4, 1945
20.	USS Peary	air attack	Feb. 19, 1942
21.	USS Pillsbury	surface action	March 1, 1942
22.	USS Pope	surface action	March 1, 1942
23.	USS Pringle	air attack*	April 16, 1945
24.	USS Reid	air attack*	Dec. 11, 1944
25.	USS Spence	typhoon	Dec. 18, 1944
26.	USS Stewart	scuttled (captured)	March 2, 1942
27.	USS Twiggs	air attack*	June 16, 1945
28.	USS William D. Porter	air attack*	June 10, 1945
29.	USS Worden	grounding	Jan. 12, 1943

*Kamikazes

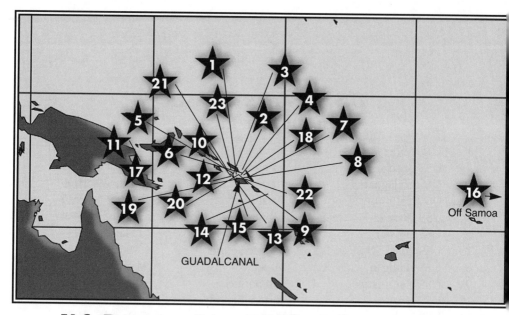

U.S. Destroyer Losses in the Solomon Islands

1.	USS Aaron Ward	air attack	April 7, 1943
2.	USS Barton	surface action	Nov. 13, 1942
3.	USS Benham	surface action	Nov. 15, 1942
4.	USS Blue	surface action	August 22, 1942
5.	USS Brownson	air attack	Dec. 26, 1943
6.	USS Chevalier	surface action	Oct. 7, 1943
7.	USS Cushing	surface action	Nov. 13, 1942
8.	USS DeHaven	air attack	Feb. 1, 1943
9.	USS Duncan	surface action	Oct. 12, 1942
10.	USS Gwin	surface action	July 13, 1943
11.	USS Henley	submarine	Oct. 3, 1943
12.	USS Jarvis	air attack	August 9, 1942
13.	USS Laffey	surface action	Nov. 13, 1942
14.	USS Meredith	air attack	Oct. 15, 1942
15.	USS Monssen	surface action	Nov. 13, 1942
16.	USS O'Brien	submarine	Oct. 19, 1942
17.	USS Perkins	collision	Nov. 29, 1943
18.	USS Porter	submarine	Oct. 26, 1942
19.	USS Preston	surface action	Nov. 15, 1942
20.	USS Sims	air attack	May 7, 1942
21.	USS Strong	submarine	July 5, 1943
22.	USS Tucker	mine	August 4, 1942
23.	USS Walke	surface action	Nov. 15, 1942

AUTHOR'S NOTE

This book is a compilation of historical sketches of the seventy-one U.S. destroyers that were lost in World War II. Of that number, sixty went down as a result of confrontations against enemy sea, land and air forces. The remaining eleven were lost under such tragic circumstances as accidental groundings, severe storms, friendly mines and collisions.

Fortunately, I was able to reach survivors from the majority of these destroyers who were willing to convey their personal experiences. I would like to extend my sincerest thanks and gratitude to those who volunteered their services to assist in completing this work. These "eyewitnesses to history," along with their ship's name, are listed below.

Though many of the engagements described herein were "destroyer battles," many others were combined actions that have gone down in history as turning points in the war. The scope of this work has not allowed complete descriptions of the major battles of the war, however I do hope the accounts that follow will inspire further reading. The experiences of the destroyermen, after all, comprise only one slice of the drama and the heroism put forth by American fighting men in our last global conflict.

Now that we have passed the 50th anniversary of World War II, there is concern that younger generations of Americans will grow up oblivious to the struggles and sacrifices that helped shape the modern world. In today's headlines, which continue to depict a world torn apart by war, America finds itself, for better or worse, more of a bystander than a participant. This was not always the case, and certainly not when the United States simultaneously fought both Germany and Japan. In this work I have simply tried to relate the facts about the valiant ships and gallant men who served their country with more than honor, and deserve to be remembered.

IN ACKNOWLEDGMENT

The following individuals (in ships' alphabetical order) were valuable contributors to this work.

USS *Aaron Ward:* F. Julian Becton, RAdm., USN (Ret), Commanding Officer; Ralph Hutchinson; Thomas McGinnis, CYN, USN (Ret.). USS *Abner Read:* John H. Hoefer, RAdm., USNR (Ret.); William H. Pottberg. USS *Beatty:* John Azzolini; Jackson E. Ellis, BTC, USN (Ret.); Guy E. Hearn Jr., Capt., USN (Ret.); Henry W. Kobolt; Walter Purvis, CMM, USN (Ret.); Robert V. Sasso, CSC, USN (Ret.). USS *Benham:* Alick M. Thomson, Sr. USS *Blue:*

Edward J. Hannan, Sr. USS *Borie:* William Howard; Robert A. Maher. USS *Bristol:* Mrs. Frances Porter, widow of Albert C. Porter. USS *Brownson:* James W. Browne; Ralph Starace. USS *Buck:* George L. Brooks. USS *Bush:* Donald H. Ginrich.

USS *Callaghan:* Frank Dunne. USS *Chevalier:* Burt Hutson; John B. Monroe (President, USS Chevalier Association); Salvatore Pacific; Richard C. Roupe (Historian, USS Chevalier Association). USS *Colhoun:* Raymond Fair; William S. Hurley. USS *Cooper:* George D. Berlinger. USS *Corry:* Grant G. Gullickson, Cdr., USN (Ret.); Robert F. Miller, BT-1, USN (Ret.); Louis Tanga. USS *Cushing:* M.D. Cashman; James E. (Medical Officer); Donald A. Henning, CDR., USN (Ret.). USS *Drexler:* Gene Brick. USS *Duncan:* Warren Craig.

USS *Glennon:* John S. Takacs, John S. USS *Gwin:* John Kosma. USS *Halligan:* Warren R. Buttman, MCPO, USN (Ret.) USS *Hammann:* Clyde A. Connor; Eduard Prezekota, BRCM, USN (Ret.). USS *Hoel:* Mrs. Florence Henritz, widow of Donald T. Henritz (Shipfitter First Class), USN; Glenn H. Parkin. USS *Johnston:* B.J. Chastain. USS *Leary:* Thomas A. Johnson. USS *Little:* Donald S. Humbarger. USS *Longshaw:* Leo E. Scott. USS *LSMR:* Harvey E. Metcalf. USS *Luce:* Richard Flaum; James Gory.

USS *Mahan:* John Meares. USS *Mannert L. Abele:* Herman Rose. USS *Meredith* (DD-434): Edwin A. Downs, Jr., Cdr., USN (Ret.); Rex Musgrave. USS *Meredith* (DD-726): Ernest Graham; Robert Savage, Capt., USN (Ret). USS *Parrott:* Edward Nolan. USS *Pope:* Edward J. Parkin. USS *Porter:* John C. Matthews, Cdr., USN (Ret.). USS *Pringle:* William L. Herman. USS *Reuben James:* Fred Zapasnik. USS *Reid:* William J. Alford; H.M. Blackwell.

USS *Spence:* Alphonse S. Krauchunas; Edward A. Miller. USS *Stewart:* William Kale. USS *Truxtun:* Edward L. Bergeron, ETC, USN (Ret.); B. Dailey, GMGC, USN (Ret.); Mrs. Teresa Newman, widow of Lieutenant Arthur L Newman, USN, ship's Executive Officer; William Shelley.

USS *Twiggs:* Lee Farrow. USS *Warrington:* Eugene E. Archer.

In addition, I wish to extend a special thanks to my wife, Marion, and my sons, Robert Jr. and Eric, for their patience and support. Throughout the long process of writing this book, my enthusiasm would at times begin to flag. Their ongoing encouragement was an invaluable asset.

Robert S. Parkin
1995

Histories of
American Destroyers
that were Lost in World War II
(in chronological order, by date of loss)

USS Reuben James

Launched October 4, 1919
Lost October 31, 1941
South of Iceland

BOATSWAIN'S MATE REUBEN JAMES
(1775–1838)

A veteran of the quasi-war with France (during which time he had been captured), James saved the life of his commanding officer, Captain Stephen Decatur, during the Barbary Wars when he interposed himself between a corsair's slashing scimitar and the unarmed captain. This courageous intervention allowed Decatur to retrieve his pistol and slay his assailant.

Boatswain's Mate James continued to serve under Decatur on board the frigates *Constitution* and *Congress*. During the War of 1812, he served in the frigates *United States* and *President*, the latter captured by four British ships on January 15, 1815. Taken prisoner, James was released after peace was declared and went on to serve in the USS *Guerrière,* again under Captain Decatur.

With the cessation of the war with Britain, the battles against the Barbary States resumed and on June 17, 1815, *Guerrière* engaged with and defeated the Algerian flagship *Mashouda*. This victory was instrumental in ending the conflict between these nations and the United States.

Wounded three times during his wartime service, Boatswain's Mate Reuben James was compelled to retire in 1836 because of declining health and the loss of one leg. He died December 3, 1838, at the U.S. Naval Hospital in Washington, DC.

At the completion of her shakedown trials, the USS *Reuben James* (DD-245), was dispatched to the Mediterranean to serve as part of a U.S. Navy detatchment in Turkish waters. Arriving at Zelinka, Yugoslavia, on

December 8, 1920, *Reuben James* carried out her patrols and training exercises throughout the Mediterranean until July 1922, often assisting the American Relief Administration in delivering goods to the famine- and pestilence-ridden nations of the Balkans and Asia Minor. During this period, Greece and Turkey were at war and the American four-stacker destroyers were frequently called upon to evacuate Greek refugees from towns and cities that were under siege or had been set to the torch by the rampaging Turks.

In late October, *Reuben James* arrived at Le Havre, France, to participate in the ceremonies marking the return of the American Unknown Soldier to the United States. Shortly thereafter, she sailed for the Free City of Danzig, between Germany and Poland, where she assisted the American Relief Administration in its efforts to relieve that isolated city of starvation. Ordered to return to the Mediterranean, she stood out of Danzig on February 3, 1922, and completed her tour of occupation duty in the Middle East until relieved in mid-July.

Upon her return to the United States, the destroyer underwent a shipyard overhaul at the Brooklyn Navy Yard, and between 1922 and 1931 was based at New York. In early 1926, *Reuben James* was ordered to patrol off the eastern coast of Nicaragua in an effort to discourage the landing of arms for revolutionaries who were attempting to overthrow that nation's government. She then resumed operations along the American eastern seaboard and in the Caribbean until she was decommissioned at the Philadelphia Navy Yard in January 1931.

Recommissioned on March 9, 1932, "The Rube," as she was affectionately called by her crew, was present during the Cuban revolution between September 1933 and January 1934, protecting American lives and interests. In October of that year, she was transferred to the Pacific Fleet and conducted her training exercises out of San Diego, California, until she was reassigned to the Atlantic Fleet in January 1939.

With the outbreak of the war in Europe, on September 1, 1939, *Reuben James* was assigned to the "neutrality" patrol, which was intended to prevent the belligerent nations from conducting warlike operations in the neutral waters of the western hemisphere.

By mid-1941, like many destroyers in the Atlantic Fleet, she was assigned to escort British shipping carrying Lend-Lease goods to Great Britain. Fortunately, all of the passages across the North Atlantic were conducted without interference from the Germans—until September 4, 1941, when the destroyer USS *Greer* (DD–145), a near-sister to the *Reuben James*, had a confrontation with a U-boat. At that time, the *Greer* was steaming independently to Iceland with mail and passengers, and its commander, feeling that his ship was threatened, attacked. The U-boat sent out a torpedo. Thus began a three-hour cat-and-mouse game between the two antagonists, during which several depth charges were dropped by the destroyer and the U-boat occasionally fired her torpedoes. Finally, the skirmish ended with the intervention of a British destroyer. *Greer* then proceeded to Iceland without further interference.

It is entirely possible that the U-boat commander mistook *Greer* for one of the American destroyers that had been transferred over to the Royal Navy in the fall of 1940. But the end result was that the "incident" prompted President Roosevelt to issue a proclamation allowing American warships to "shoot on sight" any belligerent aircraft or vessels that interfered with American shipping or shipping under the protection of American escorts.

Then, during the early morning hours of October 17, while escorting convoy SC-48, the American destroyer USS *Kearny* (DD-432) fell victim to a torpedo fired by one of the U-boats in an assaulting wolf pack (12 merchantmen in this convoy were sunk). Struck in the forward boiler room, all the men in that space were instantly killed, the ship suffering a total of 11 dead and 22 wounded. Subsequently, on October 30, the oiler USS *Salinas* was torpedoed. Fortunately, she and *Kearny* were able to steam into port under their own power.

At the time of the *Salinas'* torpedoing, *Reuben James* was one of five U.S. destroyers escorting Convoy HX-156, then plodding through the frigid and tempestuous waters of the North Atlantic. The destroyermen were well aware of the recent torpedoings and knew that, at any moment, they too could be on the receiving end of a hot running "tin fish."

At about 0525 on October 31, *Reuben James'* radioman reported picking up a faint transmission, which was passed on to the escort commander. Ordered to investigate, *Reuben James* was just breaking away from the formation when the thunderbolt struck—a torpedo smashed into her port side forward and ignited the ammunition in her forward magazine.

The tremendous detonation sent a fountain of fire, water and debris bolting skyward, wrenching the destroyer in two as far aft as her number-four stack. Instantly, the forward section of the ship plunged beneath the black, icy depths, taking all hands in that part of the ship down with it, including her commanding officer, Lieutenant Commander H.L. Edwards, and every other officer on board.

The violent concussion catapulted several of the topside watch standers overboard, while, below decks, men were tossed out of their bunks. In the engine rooms, the engineers were knocked off their feet or thrown against hot machinery and bulkheads. Suffering from burns, lacerations and broken bones, the men stumbled dazedly through darkened and rapidly flooding compartments, desperately struggling to reach the main deck. Life rafts and anything else that could float were tossed over the side, into a sea now covered in a thick blanket of bunker "C" fuel oil.

One of the survivors, then-Shipfitter First Class Fred Zapasnik, recalls his experiences at the time the *Reuben James* was torpedoed: "I had just finished sounding the after peak tank, which had been taking on water, and had gone down the after engine room to request permission to pump the space out, when a terrific explosion shook the ship and knocked us off our feet. At the same time, the lights went out, and almost at the same instant another explosion rocked the ship [probably a result of the ship's boilers exploding when the forward section of the ship sank].

"I then tried to make my way up the ladder to reach the maindeck, but a torrent of water cascaded down the hatch and knocked me down to the floorplates. When it stopped, I rushed up the ladder and, since it was still dark, I could not see what had happened. After my eyes adjusted to the darkness, I was horrified to see that there wasn't anything left of the ship forward of the fourth stack, which was lying across the deck right in front of me.

"Then, from a group of men who were assembled by the after deckhouse, someone called out: 'Hey Zap! You're the shipfitter, you better go forward and start shoring up the bulkheads!' I answered back that the whole forward section of the ship was gone and we had better abandon ship. Then another voice piped up asking who the hell gave that order. I then replied: "I did! This ship is going to sink and there aren't any officers; they all must have gone down with the bow!

"We then cut away the life rafts and tossed anything into the water that could float and began to leave the ship. All around us, the sea was covered with a thick, gooey mass of black fuel oil, much of which was ingested by the men, and would eventually result in their deaths. The raft that I reached was so full, I had to cling to the ropes that were hanging from it along with several others.

"Many of the men were praying, others crying and moaning from their wounds and the intense cold that was taking its toll on our bodies. Then someone shouted that we had better start paddling and swim away from the ship or she could pull us down with her when she sunk. Despite their efforts, the men in our raft could not paddle it away fast enough and within a few seconds, the shattered remains of the ship's stern suddenly upended and down she went. But the worst was soon to come.

"It was a foregone conclusion that there wasn't any time to set our depth charges on safe, and when the stern went under they detonated some 50 feet beneath the surface. The severity of the concussion sent up a geyser of water which lifted us and the raft some 20 feet into the air. When we dropped back into the water, it was a swirling, turbulent whirlpool. I was pulled down into the vortex; not knowing which way was up or down, but because of my wearing a life jacket, I soon bobbed to the surface. Actually, we had specific orders that life jackets were to be worn at all times. However, quite a few of the men either refused to wear them because of their bulkiness or they just didn't care. Hence, they would be the first to die.

"No sooner had I recovered from this than another explosion rent the sea, sending up a gusher which, again, hurled me up in the air. After splashing back into the water, I was sucked down into the depths and thought to myself, 'Well, this is it,' and felt for certain that I was a goner and prepared to die. Then suddenly, the water calmed down and, thankfully, I was on the surface again.

"By this time dawn was breaking and I could not help but notice there were not as many men about. One of my closest shipmates, Les Richards, had left our raft and when I asked him why, some forty years later, he replied that he could not stand listening to the moans and the praying any longer, so, he just swam away. And, I'll be damned, if he wasn't the first of the survivors to be rescued by the Niblack [DD-424]!

"When our group was picked up by the Niblack, we were so exhausted and chilled to the bone, we did not have the strength to grasp a hold on the cargo nets that were draped over the sides of the ship, let alone able to climb up them. Without hesitation, several of the destroyer's crew, including a couple of officers, leaped into the icy waters and helped boost us up into the hands of the men on deck or secured lines around the men, so they could be hoisted out of the water.

"When I reached the deck, someone cut my clothes off, tossed them over the side and told me to go take a shower. But in my condition, I could hardly walk. Owing to the numbness brought on by the cold, I had lost all sense of feeling in my legs and I thought they had been blown off. Then two men carried me to the washroom, where they cleaned me up as best they could.

"Most of Niblack's crew had given us their own clothing and gave up their bunks for us as well. Afterwards, we received the sad news that several of our survivors had died after they were rescued; many from internal injuries resulting from the shock of the exploding depth charges; many from the cold and the fuel oil which they had swallowed or had gotten into their lungs. For those of us who survived, our bodies were black-and-blue from the pounding we had received from the detonations."

All told, only 45 men survived the sinking of *Reuben James*. When *Niblack* arrived at Reykjavik, Iceland, the survivors were transferred over to the battleship *Idaho,* where they received medical treatment. From there, they were transferred to the attack cargo ship USS *Algorab* for transportation to New York.

The German submarine responsible for sinking *Reuben James* was the *U-562,* under the command of Lieutenant Captain Eric Topp, who had evaded detection and, like a phantom, slithered away through the dark depths of the North Atlantic. Again, as in the case of the *Kearny*, the *Reuben James* was not his intended target, but had the misfortune to cross into the path of a torpedo that was aimed at one of the merchant ships in the convoy.

Reuben James was the first American warship to be sunk in World War II. The stricken ship sank beneath the surface of the cold North Atlantic over five weeks prior to the Japanese attack on Pearl Harbor.

☆ ☆ ☆

USS *REUBEN JAMES* (DD-245)

Class: Wickes/Clemson.
Builder: New York Shipbuilding Corp., Camden, New Jersey.
Keel laid: April 2, 1919.
Launched: October 4, 1919.
Sponsor: Miss Helen Strauss.
Commissioned: September 24, 1920; Commander G.W. Haines, USN, comdg.
Date of loss: October 31, 1941; Lieutenant Commander H.L. Edwards, USN, comdg.†*
Location: Approximately 300 miles south of Iceland.
Awards: None.

---

* The superscript dagger (†) indicates that the commanding officer perished with his ship or succumbed later as a result of wounds.

USS Truxtun

Launched September 28, 1920
Lost February 18, 1942
Chamber's Cove, Newfoundland

COMMODORE THOMAS TRUXTUN, USN
(1755-1822)

Born in Hempstead, New York, on February 17, 1755, Thomas Truxtun went to sea at the age of twelve and, by the time he turned twenty, was in command of the sloop *Andrew Caldwell*.

During the Revolutionary War, as a privateer, he captured and sank several British merchantmen. Appointed to the rank of Captain in the United States Navy on June 4, 1794, he supervised the construction of the Navy's first frigate, *Constellation*, and upon her completion assumed command of this famous 36-gun vessel. During the quasi-war with France, he defeated and captured the French frigate *L'Insurgente* on February 9, 1799, thereby giving the infant United States Navy its first outstanding victory. A year later, on February 1, 1800, he and *Constellation* emerged victorious after a running broadside-to-broadside engagement against the pride of the French Navy, the 52-gun frigate *La Vengeance*.

Commodore Truxtun resigned his commission from the Navy in 1802. He died in Philadelphia on May 5, 1822.

The career of the USS *Truxtun* (DD-229) spanned 21 years and two days, before she was violently dashed against the rocky shores of Newfoundland during a vicious blizzard.

Assigned to DesRon 3 upon completion of her shakedown trials, *Truxtun* conducted her training operations along the eastern seaboard until June 20, 1922, when she was ordered to serve with the Asiatic Fleet. Based at Manila, she remained in the Far East, protecting American interests there until February 18, 1932, when she stood out from Manila for San Francisco.

After undergoing a shipyard overhaul at the Mare Island Navy Yard, Vallejo, California, Truxtun reported to the destroyer base, San Diego, where she participated in operations with the Pacific Fleet. On April 27, 1939, she departed the west coast for her new homeport at Norfolk, Virginia.

When war was declared in Europe, Truxtun was assigned to the neutrality patrol, serving primarily in the Caribbean and the Gulf of Mexico. In February 1940, she was relieved from this duty to serve as an escort for the cruiser USS Vincennes, which was en route to Casablanca to receive the gold reserves that the French had managed to smuggle out of France for safekeeping in the United States.

After completing this mission, Truxtun resumed her patrolling duties in the Caribbean. Then, on February 7, 1941, she joined DesRon 31, DesDiv 63 at Newport, Rhode Island, and her cruising grounds were shifted from the balmy climes of the tropics to the frigid waters off the New England coast. Soon afterwards, she commenced escorting troop and supply convoys to American bases in Iceland and Greenland, as well as British merchantmen, heavily laden with Lend-Lease goods, bound for the United Kingdom.

On September 12, while patrolling ahead of her convoy, she became enveloped in a blanket of pea-soup fog. A few moments later she was in the clear, only to plunge into another fog bank. At 1904, as she was breaking out of her misty shroud, a surfaced U-boat was seen punching its shark-like bow through a veil of fog on an opposite course. Momentarily stunned by this surprise encounter, both destroyermen and submariners stared at each other as the vessels passed close aboard. By the time the initial shock had worn off, the U-boat had disappeared in the fog and was crash diving.

While Truxtun was turning about to deal with this menace, she sent a message to the convoy commander warning him of the submarine's presence. Other escorts soon converged upon the scene and joined in the hunt for the elusive predator. After probing the depths and dropping depth charges for about an hour, with no results, the escorts gave up and rejoined the convoy.

Truxtun entered the Boston Navy Yard on November 17 for repairs and was there when the Japanese attacked Pearl Harbor. On Christmas Day, the destroyer stood out of Boston, and after escorting a convoy to Iceland, she returned to the United States, arriving at Portland, Maine, in mid-February. On the morning of the 16th, she rendezvoused with the destroyer USS Wilkes and the navy cargo ship USS Pollux off Cape Elizabeth, Maine, and set a zigzag course for the U.S. naval base at Argentia, Newfoundland.

During the early afternoon hours of the 17th, the three ships began to buck heavy seas, gale-force winds and a smattering of snow flurries, which would generate into a howling, arctic blizzard before darkness closed in. Throughout the night, tumultuous seas battered the ships with freezing brine, wailing winds keening through their rigging like demented banshees. Sleet and snow lashed the lookouts and topside watch standers without letup, thus hindering their efforts to peer through the white darkness.

The atmosphere was so dense with snow, freezing rain and sleet, it was short of a miracle that the ships were able to maintain their proper stations. Even the *Wilkes'* radar (she was the only vessel in the group equipped with this new and sometimes unreliable device) was virtually "blacked out." To make matters worse, the division commander, Commander Walter W. Webb, had difficulty reaching the *Truxtun* on the TBS radio circuit and *Pollux* was unable to comprehend the blinker signals sent by the *Wilkes* due to the rolling seas and poor visibility. As a result, none of the crews in these storm-tossed ships had any warning of the catastrophe in which 203 of their officers and shipmates would perish.

By 0330 on the 18th, the ships should have been nearing the entrance to Placentia Bay. However, owing to the erratic currents and the adverse weather, they had been driven off course and were unknowingly steering on a direct heading toward the steep, granite cliffs and rock-strewn shores of the Burin Peninsula, at the southwestern entrance to the bay.

By this time, the three ships had lost all semblance of order. Although *Truxtun* had managed to keep her station, she too had drifted off to port, while *Wilkes* and *Pollux* had fallen behind and were on a more westerly course at least a mile astern of her.

At 0410, tragedy struck. With her lookouts unable to distinguish the difference between the thrashing seas and the booming breakers against the shore, *Truxtun* was catapulted headlong into the base of a 200-foot cliff in Chamber's Cove. The sudden jolt hurled some men to the deck and threw others into bulkheads, hot machinery and other stationary objects. Sleepers were tossed out of their bunks, their sleep-fogged senses unable to comprehend the seriousness of the situation.

Truxtun's captain, Lieutenant Commander Ralph Hickox, believing he had struck an iceberg, immediately ordered his ships' engines reversed at full power. This maneuver, however, only impaled his destroyer on a nest of pinnacle rocks, whose granite jaws held on to the unfortunate vessel with an iron-like grasp. A few moments after *Truxtun* had grounded, *Wilkes* had also plunged ashore, bow first, about two miles away. Then, at 0417, despite her captain's efforts to avoid running aground, the doomed *Pollux* became stranded, broadside, some 1,000 yards to the right of *Wilkes*. Luckily, *Wilkes* would succeed in extricating herself from her precarious position later in the day.

Meanwhile, the grounded *Truxtun* was undergoing relentless punishment as gigantic seas pounded her with battering ram force. Men and loose gear were swept overboard into the swirling, icy surf and foam. Freezing seas were filling her compartments, and black, viscous "C" oil began to seep out of her ruptured bunkers. Topside, men struggled to lower boats and life rafts. Voices shouting orders were lost in the cacophony of howling winds, thundering surf, and groans and shrieks emitted by the destroyer herself as the sharp rocks gnawed through her tortured hull.

A heavy concentration of rocks jutting up through the mass of turbulent water on her starboard side had prevented the lowering of boats on that hand, while the violent seas had stove in the whaleboat's planking on the port side. During the next twenty-four hours, the crews of *Truxtun* and *Pollux* would suffer through one of the most excruciating multiple shipwrecks ever recorded. For a time, the crew of the high-sided *Pollux* could find some refuge from the storm's fury within her superstructure. Not so on the *Truxtun*.

Low of freeboard, with her lower compartments inundated and her main decks constantly awash, she had very little to offer in the way of shelter, except beneath the bridge structure, the galley amidships and the after deckhouse; and these spaces were already filled beyond capacity. For the unfortunate souls who had to remain on the open decks, they held on until the numbing effects of the frigid elements and the pounding seas forced them to let go—washed overboard into the seething tumult.

As a bleak, gray dawn began to lighten the skies, a small, sandy beach, Lawn, was sighted off the port bow and it was decided to make an attempted landing there. Every foot of line and cordage was broken out and carried ashore by two men in a life raft in an effort to rig an apparatus similar to a breeches buoy, using the life raft to convey the crew ashore. On the first try, twelve men were safely brought to land, and later nine more men were landed without difficulty. However, all hopes of saving the remainder of the crew failed when the lines became badly twisted and so slippery with oil that they could not be untangled.

Meanwhile, two men—eighteen-year-old Apprentice Seaman Edward R. Bergeron and Chief Fire Controlman Edward B. Peterson—succeeded in scaling the virtually perpendicular, ice-encrusted, 200-foot cliff, using a knife to chop hand- and footholds in the icy mass, in hopes of seeking some help. Upon reaching the top, both men were astonished to discover a wire fence bordering the cliff and a hay shed a short distance away.

They immediately crawled on all fours toward it, stepped inside and collapsed from sheer exhaustion. Here they found some straw, with which they covered themselves in an attempt to keep warm. After resting for a brief time, Bergeron gathered enough strength to get up and, without any knowledge of where he was headed, and using the fence as a guide, stumbled through a scrub forest, deep snowdrifts and rocky terrain, hoping to locate a town or farm where he might find people to come to the rescue of his shipmates.

After an agonizing trek of two miles, the young seaman staggered into a mining camp at about 0900. The sight of this frozen, oil-smeared apparition tottering groggily into the camp startled the miners, but they sprang into action after they heard Bergeron's shocking report of the shipwreck.

While most of the men broke out all the necessary gear with which to effect a rescue, telephone calls went out to another nearby mine to alert the miners and townspeople of St. Lawrence. Almost every man, woman and young adult turned out and rushed to the site, carrying blankets, food, and clothing. Shopkeepers emptied their shelves of canned goods, coffee, tea, rope, medicines and supplies—anything that could be of use to ease the suffering of the survivors. Where trucks or vehicles could not pass through, horses pulling sleds or slides were employed to carry relief goods to the scene. Also lending a hand were three fisherman, who carried a dory over the rough terrain.

Arriving at the scene of the wrecks, the hardy "Newfies" lowered themselves over the cliff and plunged into the frigid, oil-saturated surf to drag and haul the benumbed men ashore. Those who remained on the cliff lowered ropes to secure to the survivors and hoist them up to the clifftops. All this time, both rescuers and survivors were battling winds of up to 75 miles per hour and waves of up to 50 feet. The blowing snow and sleet was so dense that, quite often, those atop the cliff could not see just what was happening in the turbulent waters beneath them.

As the near-frozen survivors were lifted to safety, they were led or carried to the several fires that had been built, where the women offered what little medication they had on hand and plied the men with hot soups and drink. The most seriously injured were carried to the buildings at the mine, where the women cut away their oil-stained clothing and washed their bodies as well as they could, offering whatever first aid was available. As more and more survivors arrived, those who had been attended to were transported to the homes of the residents of St. Lawrence, who willingly took them in to convalesce until the naval authorities could transport them to the Argentia naval base.

William Shelly, then a First Class Shipfitter, recalled his harrowing experience: "Just after daylight, *Truxtun* had broken in half, with the after section drifting a short ways before it sank. By this time, many of the men had been washed overboard, while others who clung to various parts of the ship had frozen to death. I held on as long as I could, but finally lost my grip when a huge wave hurled me over the side. I tried desperately to swim toward the beach, where I could see several people helping some of my shipmates ashore, but the undertow was pulling me toward a pile of jagged rocks. I thought for certain that my time had come.

"Then, just before the seas were about to slam me into the rocks, I saw a small man standing on a narrow ledge who, by some miracle, managed to grab me just before a giant wave came. He was able to secure me to the line he had descended on. The next thing I remember was waking up, lying on a table in one of the buildings at the mine. In my dazed condition, I saw several women cleaning up the men, who, like myself, were covered with oil. Then, one of the women came over and told me that I had been brought in on a sled.

"The women had to cut off our clothes and did everything they could to revive us and tend to our injuries with what little they had to offer. Sadly, if a man did not show any signs of life, he was set aside. Later I was given a bowl of soup and not long afterwards was wrapped in a blanket and driven into St. Lawrence in a flatbed truck. The driver drove through a street which seemed to be the only road in the village.

"Outside most of the homes were people who would let the driver know how many men they could put up. I was carried into the home of Mrs. Gregory Giovannini. This wonderful and compassionate woman had already taken three other men into her home and, just like she did with the other fellows, she placed me in the bath tub and washed most of the oil off me. She then put me into a bed, and in another bed next to me was our Chief Commissary Steward, George Gaddy. Later, we were given a hearty bowl of stew, the first substantial meal we had that day."

While Bill Shelley was under the care of Mrs. Giovannini, rescue operations were still in progress. By 1300, what remained of *Truxtun* had broken in two and there were still several men clinging to her storm-ravaged bow.

Earlier, an attempt was made to row the dory out in hopes of saving the men from the wreck, but it had overturned, spilling its occupants into the water. As the people stared helplessly, one by one the men on *Truxtun's* bow were washed into the thrashing surf.

By 1400, only four men were left and it was decided to try to take the dory out again. Three men volunteered to paddle the tiny craft out to the wreck, through the heavy surf and the oil—which was as thick as pudding.

When the men finally reached the bow, a line was tossed to the besotted, wretched sailors. Then, a huge wave struck and its sledgehammer force swept the men into the water. Tragically, two of them vanished beneath the roiling foam, but one had fallen into the water next to the dory and managed to grasp hold of the line, while the fourth man had miraculously landed right in the boat. The passage back to shore was almost as precarious as the trip out. One of the rescuers was thrown out of the dory, but luckily was hauled back on board. Sadly, the sailor who had held on to the line died shortly after reaching land.

By now, the rescuers were in as bad a shape as the survivors, and were ready to collapse from utter exhaustion. Then, a man was seen running toward them, shouting excitedly that there was another ship aground at Lawn Head. This, of course, was *Pollux*. Although stunned by this unexpected turn of events, the rescuers trudged wearily to the scene and the rescue of *Pollux's* crew began.

Unfortunately, the details of that rescue are too extensive to include in the story of the *Truxtun*. However, the residents of Lawn and St. Lawrence toiled well into the night, until 0400 on the 19th, with only the aid of flashlights, lanterns and the glow of fires to guide them. A naval rescue party eventually arrived, each man carrying at least 20 pounds of clothing, blankets, medical supplies and food. Also on hand to assist was the ship's doctor from a Canadian patrol boat and three residential nurses.

All told, 168 survivors were pulled from the raging waters. Of these, only three officers and 43 men were from *Truxtun*. Lieutenant Commander Hickcox's remains were found later on board his ship. Of the 203 personnel that were lost, 48 were recovered within a few days after the disaster and were laid to rest at Argentia with full military honors and religious services officiated by military chaplains and civilian clergymen.

Several weeks after the catastrophe, additional bodies were found along the shores and in the many coves of Newfoundland. These were buried in a plot of ground outside St. Lawrence, donated by the parish priest, Father Augustus Thorne.

Although none of the civilian rescuers were killed during this event, many suffered from injuries and frostbite. A few others died of pneumonia several weeks afterward. Upon receiving the news of this tragic event, President Franklin D. Roosevelt sent a personal message to the residents of Lawn and St. Lawrence, thanking them for their magnificent and courageous work in the rescuing and caring for the personnel of the two U.S. Navy ships that had grounded on their shores.

In 1953, the United States government erected a hospital at St. Lawrence designed to serve the communities of the Burin Peninsula (the hospital was officially opened on June 6, 1954). In the lobby, on one wall, *Truxtun's* ensign, salvaged by one of St. Lawrence's townsman, is on display in a glass frame. On the opposite wall hangs a plaque donated by President Dwight D. Eisenhower, which reads as follows: "For the dauntless valor displayed by the people of St. Lawrence and Lawn on 18 February 1942, when during a snowstorm, two ships of the United States Navy were wrecked on the barren and rocky shores of Newfoundland, the intrepid and selfless residents of these two communities, did at great risk to themselves, undertake rescue operations and give aid and comfort to the survivors from both ships.

"The people of the United States in presenting this hospital, desire to express their gratitude for the fortitude and generosity of the people of Newfoundland that night. It is hoped that this hospital will serve as a memorial for the 203 officers and men of the United States Navy who lost their lives in the disaster and as a vital reminder of the inherent courage of mankind."

Although the disaster made headlines in the news, the incident became overshadowed by the war and was soon forgotten. However, it will never be forgotten by the survivors and the rescuers, although, at this writing, the numbers of each are slowly diminishing. In St. Lawrence, to this day, on the anniversary of the disaster memorial services are held on the hospital grounds in remembrance of the American sailors who perished on that fateful night.

☆ ☆ ☆

USS *TRUXTUN* (DD-229)

Class: Wickes/Clemson.
Builder: William Cramp & Sons, Philadelphia, Pennsylvania.
Keel laid: December 3, 1919.
Launched: September 28, 1920.
Sponsor: Miss Isabelle Truxtun Brumbly, great-great-granddaughter of Commodore Thomas Truxtun, USN.

Commissioned: February 16, 1921; Lieutenant Commander M.S. Brown, USN, comdg.

Date of loss: February 18, 1942; Lieutenant Commander Ralph Hickox, USN, comdg.†

Location: Chamber's Cove, Newfoundland.

Awards: None.

USS Peary

Launched April 6, 1920
Lost February 19, 1942
Darwin Harbor, Australia

REAR ADMIRAL ROBERT E. PEARY, USN
(1856–1920)

Well known for his outstanding achievements in Arctic exploration, Robert Edwin Peary was born in Cresson, Pennsylvania, on May 6, 1856. Commissioned Lieutenant in the United States Navy on October 26, 1881, his first Arctic expedition was conducted five years later. In 1887-88, he served as a surveyor for the proposed Nicaraguan Canal, during which time he invented a rolling lock gate intended for it. The pinnacle of Peary's naval career was achieved on December 6, 1909, during his eighth Arctic expedition, when he became the first man to reach the North Pole, after covering a distance of 139 miles in five days.

In between expeditions, he authored several books in which he described his experiences and scientific findings during his Arctic explorations. Revered around the world, he was the recipient of numerous awards from scientific societies in Europe and in the United States. On March 30, 1911, he was promoted to Rear Admiral and given the thanks of Congress. Rear Admiral Peary died in Washington, DC, on February 20, 1920.

The USS *Peary* (DD-226) spent her entire career with the Asiatic Fleet, beginning in 1922. At the time Pearl Harbor was under attack, *Peary* was undergoing repairs at the Cavite Navy Yard, located in Manila Harbor, the Philippines. If not for the courageous action taken by the skipper of the minesweeper USS *Whippoorwill*, in fact, *Peary* would likely have remained dockside in Manila Harbor after that first week of the war, as a burned-out hulk.

On the afternoon of December 10, a flight of about fifty high-altitude Japanese bombers droned over the navy yard, well out of range of the anti-aircraft defenses. After unloading their bombs, it was apparent that the brief but highly accurate attack had virtually pulverized the entire base. In the heat of the holocaust lay the immobile and defenseless *Peary*. Eight of her crewmen had been killed instantly when a bomb exploded forward of her galley. Several more were wounded when flying shards of shrapnel and steel punctured her two forward smokestacks.

The torpedo workshop on the pier where she was moored was a roaring inferno, the intense heat causing the air flasks in the torpedoes to blow up. Firebrands and chunks of flying metal flayed the destroyer, cutting down a number of her crew and starting several small fires. Without power or the means to obtain water, her crew could neither quench the flames nor escape the deluge of flying debris and the scorching heat.

As far as the eye could see, the naval base was enveloped in a sea of fire and roiling smoke, with thundering detonations renting the air. The submarine USS *Sealion* had taken a devastating bomb hit and was sinking alongside her pier. Ahead of *Peary*, two barges were ablaze, with the submarine rescue ship *Pigeon* lying alongside one of them, attempting to douse the flames.

Easing cautiously through the smoky haze, however, came the *Whippoorwill* to lend a hand. When her captain, Lieutenant Commander C.A. Feriter, realized that *Peary* was in serious trouble, he radioed the *Pigeon* that "The 'Whip' is going in to take that destroyer out."

A small motorboat, manned by an officer and three men, had been vainly trying to tow the stricken destroyer away from the pier, but the violent explosions and searing heat made the task difficult. When the *Whippoorwill* arrived, the men in the boat made an attempt to take the minesweeper's tow line to *Peary*, but the fiery blasts prevented the boat from approaching the now burning destroyer.

Feriter then edged his ship's bow against *Peary*'s stern and passed over a 6-inch line. He had begun to pull the destroyer free when a chunk of flying debris severed the line. A second line was secured, but it snapped as the minesweeper began to tow the destroyer from her pier. Feriter then decided to shift his ship alongside and send a man over to see if the mooring lines had been cleared from the pier. When it was verified that the lines were free, the *Whippoorwill*, with *Peary* snugged alongside, backed down and pulled the destroyer out into the bay, the minesweeper's crew hosing her down all the while in an attempt to quell the flames.

Meanwhile, *Peary*'s sister destroyer *Pillsbury* (DD-227), had arrived to assist, and a short time afterward the fires were snuffed out. Damage control parties from both ships clambered on board to clear the wreckage, while pharmacist mates and corpsmen attended to the wounded, who were later transferred to a hospital. Among these was *Peary*'s commanding officer, Commander Harry H. Keith. Subsequently, the destroyer's executive officer, Lieutenant J.M. Bermingham, assumed command. Later, he would be promoted to the rank of Lieutenant Commander.

The battle-scarred and fire-blackened *Peary* remained in Manila Bay with her crew effecting repairs as best as they could until the night of December 26, when she received orders to get underway for Darwin, Australia. Prior to leaving port, she underwent an air attack, but escaped without damage.

On the following morning, she arrived at Campomanes Bay, Negros Island. Later in the day, after having "scrounged" up some green and olive drab paint from a nearby army facility, most of the crew set to work camouflaging the ship while a working party went ashore to gather up palm fronds. Thus bedecked, the disguise must have been effective, for throughout the day several low-flying aircraft passed close by without sighting her. That evening, after sunset, the ship weighed anchor and set out for Ambon Island, a voyage that would prove to be a nerve-wracking experience for all hands.

In the morning, *Peary* was sighted and shadowed by a Japanese four-engined flying boat. Certain that its pilot was radioing his destroyer's presence, Bermingham burned up the air waves calling for assistance from Task Force 5, but there was no response. Bermingham's suspicions proved correct when, at about 1400, three more flying boats appeared and the fight was on.

During the next two hours, Bermingham used every trick in the book in an effort to avoid bombs and torpedoes from his assailants, employing his engines tactically and steering skillfully at the same time. A vicious wall of 30- and 50-caliber machine-gun fire and her 3-inch anti-aircraft gun kept the attackers at bay and, as a result, the planes dropped their torpedoes and bombs prematurely, allowing Bermingham time to evade. Having spent all their ammunition, the enemy retired shortly after 1600. But *Peary* was not out of the woods yet, for just before dusk she would come under another air assault. This time, the attackers would be "friendly."

Just before darkness closed in, three Lockheed Hudson bombers were sighted. Their red, white and blue roundels identified them as either

Australian or British aircraft. As the planes approached *Peary*, she flashed recognition signals, which the leader of the flight acknowledged by waggling his wings. However, one of the pilots, inexplicably, peeled off from the formation and closed in on the destroyer.

In no mood to extend the errant aircraft the benefit of the doubt, *Peary*'s gunners sprayed a fusillade of machine-gun fire at the plane, seemingly without effect. When the aircraft released its bombs, they detonated about 100 yards to port. In his effort to avoid them, Bermingham made a sharp swing to starboard, the maneuver throwing one man over the side. Unable to stop and rescue the seaman, someone tossed a life jacket overboard. The man was last seen swimming toward it and it was hoped that he would be able to swim to Banaking Island, less than a mile away.

By now, all three Hudsons were pouncing on the lone destroyer with a vengeance. Once again, although Bermingham's skillful handling had saved *Peary*, the near misses had taken their toll in underwater and topside damage. One man was dead and several others wounded. With the loss of daylight, the planes withdrew and reported back to their base, there to be informed of their tragic error. Their only explanation was that, owing to the ship's odd color scheme—the new camouflage—they believed that *Peary* was a Japanese destroyer, several of which were known to be operating in the area.

Eventually, the battered and bruised *Peary* and her battle-weary crew arrived at Darwin on January 3, 1942. As a result of her deplorable condition, however, she was considered unfit for combat or to carry out her operations with the American–British–Dutch–Australian (ABDA) naval forces; hence, she was allocated to serve as a convoy escort or patrol vessel outside of Darwin Harbor.

On February 15, *Peary* stood out of Darwin escorting a supply convoy to Timor, an island located some 500 miles northeast of Australia. The convoy was soon sighted by enemy aircraft and, on the following day, the ships were assaulted from the air. The cruiser USS *Houston* and the escorts flayed the skies with a deadly barrage of anti-aircraft fire and succeeded in splashing several of the attackers. Fortunately, none of the ships in the convoy or the escorts were hit. After the enemy broke off the action, a message was received that a carrier force had been sighted within striking distance of the convoy. Therefore, Captain A.H. Rooks, in *Houston*, was ordered to return to Darwin.

Upon the convoy's arrival there on the 18th, *Peary* and *Houston* refueled and made preparations to join up with the ABDA forces in the Java Sea. As they were leaving port, *Peary* made an underwater contact with what she believed to be a submarine. While she carried out her search, *Houston* proceeded on independently. After several hours of probing the waters for the submarine without success, *Peary* returned to port to top off her fuel bunkers.

Then, at 0930, a flight of 18 heavy bombers roared over the horizon, and, with very little opposition, leveled the dock facilities into a mass of burning rubble. Two ammunition ships moored alongside one of the piers were hit and vanished in a huge ball of fire and smoke. For several miles around, buildings were leveled and damaged by the massive explosions. Ships in the harbor rolled from the shock wave and were lashed by flying shards of metal and debris. Close on the heels of this attack, a second wave of bombers winged in to demolish the anti-aircraft batteries and drop incendiary bombs on the already devastated town.

Immediately after this assault, Japanese dive bombers swooped down from the skies and attacked the sitting-duck transports and cargomen. Two bombs sent the transport *Mauna Loa* to the bottom within a few seconds. The army transport *General Meigs* soon joined her, after being hammered by a number of bomb hits and being blown in half by a torpedo. A coastal steamer was sunk while coming to the aid of a Brazilian steamship that was ablaze outside the harbor. Also sent to the bottom were two Australian corvettes and the SS *Admiral Halstead*. Other vessels, too numerous to mention, were severely damaged and burning, with their captains steering them into shallow water to prevent them from sinking.

Caught in this fiery whirlwind, the crews of *Peary* and the ex-destroyer USS *William B. Preston* (AVD-7), fought their hearts out in an effort to reach the open sea. Firing with every anti-aircraft battery that could bear on the aircraft, the two ships side-stepped the falling bombs while, at the same time, their captains were hard-pressed to avoid colliding with the shipping in the congested and smoke-filled harbor.

At 1010, *Preston* was struck by three bombs and, a few moments later, *Peary* found herself on the receiving end of two more. One crashed on her fantail, hurtling her depth charges and several men into the air, slicing off one of her propellers and flooding her engine room. The second bomb, an incendiary, detonated in the galley, leaving the entire area swathed in a pall of smoke and raging fires. Yet, despite these devastating blows, Captain Bermingham succeeded in forging his old four-stacker through the maze of shipping, while his crew bravely fought fires and flooding, and defiantly beat off their assailants.

Then a third bomb struck *Peary*, rupturing her hull plates and causing her fuel to spill out into the harbor. A fourth bomb smashed into her forward magazine, the violent explosion fatally wounding Lieutenant Commander Bermingham and wounding several men nearby.

A fifth bomb, another incendiary, exploded in her after engine room, but still the crippled destroyer—now a mass of smoke and flames, her decks strewn with wreckage, dead and wounded—continued to limp through the din and clangor of battle until 1300, when the feisty four-stacker broke up and sank under a pillar of smoke and steam. Those who witnessed her final moments reported that *Peary*'s men were still firing their machine guns as her shattered hulk slipped beneath the surface.

Lost with the gallant *Peary* were 80 officers and men. The only senior survivor was her gunnery officer, Lieutenant W.J. Catlett. The USS *Peary* was the first destroyer of the Asiatic Fleet to be sunk in World War Two.

☆ ☆ ☆

USS *PEARY* (DD-226)

Class: Wickes/Clemson.
Builder: William Cramp & Sons, Philadelphia, Pennsylvania.
Keel laid: September 9, 1919.
Launched: April 6, 1920.
Sponsor: Mrs. Edward Stafford, daughter of Rear Admiral Robert E. Peary, USN.
Commissioned: October 22, 1920; Lieutenant H.W. Barnes, USN, comdg.
Date of loss: February 19, 1942; Lieutenant Commander J.M. Bermingham, USN, comdg.†
Location: Darwin Harbor, Australia.
Awards: One battle star.

USS Jacob Jones

Launched November 20, 1918
Lost February 28, 1942
Off the Delaware Capes, New Jersey

COMMODORE JACOB JONES, USN
(1768-1850)

Born near Smyrna, Delaware, Jacob Jones was appointed Midshipman on April 10, 1799. During the quasi-war with France, he served on the 32-gun frigate *United States*. During the war with the Barbary pirates, he was serving in the frigate *Philadelphia* when she ran aground and was captured in Tripoli Harbor. Taken prisoner, he was released 20 months later. Upon his return to the United States, he went on to serve in the frigate *Adams* and later in the *Argus*. In command of the sloop-of-war *Wasp* at the outbreak of the War of 1812, he captured the British brig HMS *Dolphin* on October 13, 1812. Five days later, he defeated the HMS *Frolic*, after a fierce broadside engagement off the Delaware Capes, New Jersey. Promoted to the rank of Captain on March 3, 1813, he took command of the captured British frigate HMS *Macedonian*.

After peace was restored with England, he remained in command of the *Macedonian* and joined the Mediterranean Squadron under the command of Commodore Stephen Decatur, participating in securing final peace with the Barbary powers. In 1821, Captain Jones assumed command of the Squadron and, upon his return to the United States in 1824, was appointed to the Board of Naval Commissioners. In 1826, he took command of the U.S. Naval Forces in the Pacific. Commodore Jones died on August 3, 1850, while serving as commandant of the U.S. Naval Asylum in Philadelphia.

On December 4, 1919, the USS *Jacob Jones* (DD-130) stood out of Philadelphia to commence her shakedown trials in the Atlantic and in the Caribbean, prior to being assigned to the Pacific Fleet.

Arriving at the destroyer base at San Diego, California, on January 26, 1920, she operated with the battle force off the West Coast until the summer of 1922. Then, in accordance with the Washington Naval Disarmament Treaty of 1922, the destroyer was decommissioned and placed in reserve at San Diego.

Eight years later, *Jacob Jones* was recommissioned to resume her operations with the Pacific Fleet, but in March 1931, she was reassigned to the Atlantic. Except for one more tour of duty with the Pacific Fleet, *Jacob Jones* continued to serve with the Atlantic destroyer flotillas until the day of her loss.

From October 17, 1936, until late summer 1939, she served as a unit of Squadron 40-T in the western Mediterranean during the Spanish Civil War. During this time, the squadron's primary purpose was to protect American lives and interests and, if necessary, assist in the evacuation of American citizens residing in war-torn Spain. When the squadron was disbanded, *Jacob Jones* returned to the United States, arriving at the Norfolk Navy Yard, Portsmouth, Virginia, on October 14.

After completing a two-month shipyard overhaul, *Jacob Jones* continued to conduct her training exercises along the eastern seaboard and in the Caribbean. With the outbreak of hostilities in Europe, she was assigned to the neutrality patrol, carrying out her operations in Caribbean waters. In November 1941, her patrolling station was shifted to the waters off New England and she was still assigned to this area when the Japanese struck Pearl Harbor.

After the completion of a brief yard period, *Jacob Jones* commenced her duties as a convoy escort, screening shipping through the frigid waters of the North Atlantic. On the night of February 14, 1942, she was one of the escorts shepherding Convoy HX-169 when a vicious winter storm unleashed its fury upon the formation. When a somber, gray dawn began to faintly lighten up the overcast sky, *Jacob Jones* found herself steaming alone on the heaving, mountainous seas. Without benefit of radar, and with her gyrocompass defective, she had unknowingly become detached from the convoy. With her fuel bunkers low, it was decided not to search for the convoy but to proceed on to Hvalfjördur, Iceland.

Despite the difficulties that had plagued her, the ship arrived safely into port on the 19th, and on the 24th rendezvoused with a three-ship convoy headed for Argentia, Newfoundland. Once again, an Arctic storm scattered the ships, however *Jacob Jones* managed to keep station with a Norwegian tanker and escorted her, without incident, to her destination.

On February 22, the four-stacker destroyer cleared New York to take up anti-submarine patrol duties off the New Jersey coast. Shortly after passing the Ambrose lightship, she made an underwater contact, which she believed to be a U-boat. For a period of about five hours, she made repeated depth-charge attacks in the area, until her supply of depth charges was depleted. After her last six "ash cans" were dropped, an oil slick rose to the surface, but no other debris was sighted. Following her return to New York to replenish her depth charges, an investigating team carried out an intensive search throughout the area, but could find no evidence of a sunken submarine.

Five days later, on the 27th, *Jacob Jones* departed New York to carry out patrols between Barnegat Light and Five Fathom Shoals. However, she was later ordered to proceed farther south to take up her patrolling station off the Delaware Capes and Cape May, New Jersey. En route, smoke was seen rising over the horizon and her captain, Lieutenant Commander Hugo D. Black, ordered a change of course to investigate, soon approaching the smoldering wreckage of the oil tanker SS *R.P. Resor*. After an unsuccessful two-hour search for survivors, *Jacob Jones* resumed her southerly course, and at 2000 she radioed her final position.

The sleek, 1,340-ton destroyer sliced her sharp prow through a calm, moonlit sea at a leisurely 15 knots, trailing a long, white, frothy wake behind her. All seemed tranquil and serene until just before 0500, when disaster struck. It will never be determined if the destroyer's sonar operator had even detected the presence of the submarine—but it was there. The *U-578*, which was lurking beneath the cold, dark depths, had been patiently waiting for another target of opportunity. It came in the form of *Jacob Jones*. Within a few short seconds, a spread of three or, possibly, four torpedoes were sent humming toward the oncoming destroyer.

With a shattering roar, the first exploded abaft the bridge on the port side. As a geyser of water, fire and debris bolted skyward, a second detonation occurred in number-one and number-two boiler rooms. Less then a few seconds later, the ill-fated *Jacob Jones* broke in two, the whole forward section of the ship plunging beneath the surface, taking down all hands, including her captain. In quick succession, a third torpedo struck aft, some 40 feet forward of her stern. The warhead exploded in the after living quarters, killing all its occupants, who were making a frantic scramble to reach the main deck.

From out of the smoke- and steam-choked engine rooms stumbled the oil-smeared engineers, many of them suffering from burns and multiple injuries. Once topside, the men soon discovered that the upper decks were a mass of twisted steel and a jungle of ropes and cables, and were slippery with black fuel oil. Yet, despite the presence of noxious smoke and lung-searing steam, Navy discipline was reported to have been excellent in the absence of any officers. Although the assistant engineering officer alone survived the disaster, he was severely wounded and incoherent until his death.

The 35 survivors lowered life rafts and abandoned what had remained of the once proud destroyer. At about 0600, the shattered wreckage of *Jacob Jones* upended and plunged to her watery grave. No sooner had the waters closed over her than her depth charges exploded. The tremendous detonation lifted one life raft into the air and wounded several of the men in it. When the water had calmed down, only a few men were left alive, most of them suffering from injuries.

At about 0800, an army patrol plane sighted the rafts and the pilot sent his report to *Eagle Boat No. 56* of the inshore patrol group. Unfortunately, due to the rising seas and strong winds, the eagle boat managed to save only 12 men and was forced to discontinue the search for any stragglers. Of the 12 who were rescued, one of them died before he could be hospitalized.

Despite a two-day search by ships and aircraft off the southern New Jersey coast, not another soul could be found.

☆ ☆ ☆

USS *JACOB JONES* (DD-130)

Class: Wickes/Clemson.
Builder: New York Shipbuilding Corporation, Camden, New Jersey.
Keel laid: February 21, 1918.
Launched: November 20, 1918.
Sponsor: Mrs. Cazenove Daughton, great-granddaughter of Commodore Jacob
    Jones, USN.
Commissioned: October 20, 1919; Lieutenant Commander P.H. Bastedo, USN,
    comdg.
Date of loss: February 28, 1942; Lieutenant Commander H.D. Black, comdg.†
Location: Off the Delaware Capes, New Jersey.
Awards: None.

USS Edsall

Launched July 20, 1920
Lost March 1, 1942
South of Java, Dutch East Indies

SEAMAN NORMAN E. EDSALL, USN
(1873–1899)

Born on June 3, 1873, in Columbus, Kentucky, Norman Eckley Edsall enlisted in the Navy on June 27, 1898. While serving on the cruiser *Philadelphia,* he joined a landing party under the command of Lieutenant Philip Lansdale, USN, to quell an uprising by the natives near Apia, Samoa. Although the riots were suppressed, Lansdale's party was ambushed while returning to the ship, during which time the lieutenant was seriously wounded. Assisted by Ensign J.R. Monaghan and another seaman, Edsall tried to carry the wounded officer to safety, but they were soon overwhelmed by the natives and killed. Seaman Edsall was buried at Apia, Samoa.

An "Old China Hand," the USS *Edsall* (DD-219) was one of four American destroyers that "went missing" during World War II. Although the final fates of three of the ships were accounted for shortly after the war, it would require seven years of intensive searching before investigators would uncover the exact details of the *Edsall's* loss and the fate of her crew.

Edsall's long and active career began on December 6, 1920, when she departed the Philadelphia Navy Yard to carry out her shakedown trials and training exercises while en route to the destroyer base at San Diego. Arriving there on January 21, 1921, she became a unit of the Pacific destroyer flotillas and carried out her training operations along the West Coast. In December of that year, *Edsall* was reassigned to the Atlantic Fleet and was based at Charleston, South Carolina, until May 1922, when she was ordered to the Middle East. Arriving at Constantinople (now Istanbul), Turkey, she reported to the commandant of the U.S. Naval Detatchment in Turkish Waters. As was previously mentioned in the history of the *Reuben James*, this was a period of political upheaval in the Near East, Russia and the Balkan nations, as well as a full-scale war between Turkey and Greece. Not only were American destroyers on hand to protect American interests, they were also called upon to assist the American Relief Administration in its effort to provide humanitarian supplies. On several occasions, these destroyers and their crews were dispatched to assist in the evacuation of thousands of Greek refugees from the plundering Turkish forces. In one instance, *Edsall* participated in the evacuation of the entire population of Smyrna, when that city was ravaged and set afire by the Turks. On December 14, 1922, the destroyer embarked 607 refugees from the USS *Litchfield* (DD-336) and transported them to Salonika, in Greece. After discharging her passengers, *Edsall* was ordered to return to Smyrna to act as flagship for the U.S. Naval Forces. Later, in October, she took on several more evacuees from this port and carried them to the island of Lesbos.

Prior to returning to the United States, *Edsall* paid repeated visits to ports in Turkey, Palestine, Egypt, Bulgaria, Greece and Russia. In between these visits, she was required to carry out her normal training operations and "show the flag," on occasions of spontaneous uprisings and political unrest.

On January 3, 1925, *Edsall* sailed from the United States, bound for duty with the Asiatic Fleet. Before proceeding on to Shanghai, China, the destroyer participated in fleet maneuvers in the Caribbean and briefly laid over in San Diego and Pearl Harbor.

As in the Middle East, the primary objective of the Asiatic Fleet was to protect American interests, which, in the Orient, had been expanding steadily since acquisition of the Philippines. As a unit of this fleet, *Edsall* witnessed the rise of Chiang Kai-shek during the 1920s and then the retreat of his armies before the onslaught of Japanese forces in the 1930s. Throughout those tumultuous decades, the destroyers were busily engaged whenever either Nationalists, Communists, or simply hordes of bandits placed American and other Western lives in danger. As the 1930s drew to a close, the Japanese invasion had made the eastern coast of the Chinese mainland untenable for operations by the U.S. Navy, so, the majority of Americans having been evacuated, the Asiatic fleet shifted its primary focus to Philippine waters. On several occasions, units of the fleet paid goodwill visits to ports throughout the Dutch East Indies, including Bangkok and

Saigon, before hostilities opened up between the United States and Japan.

Edsall and her division (DesDiv 57), were at anchor in the Dutch oil port of Balikpapan, Borneo, when the Japanese assaulted Pearl Harbor. Immediately, the Asiatic Fleet was placed on a wartime alert. On December 10, when the British battleship *Prince of Wales* and the battle cruiser *Repulse* were sunk by Japanese aircraft off the eastern coast of Malaya, *Edsall* was dispatched to Singapore to embark a British naval officer and four ratings, to assist in the search for survivors. By the time she arrived at the site, all the men who could be found had been rescued; however, *Edsall* remained in the area hoping to locate any stragglers. After a fruitless search, the destroyer returned to Singapore, escorting a Japanese fishing trawler that she had captured en route

By January 1942, the U.S. Asiatic Fleet had teamed up with the combined British, Dutch and Australian naval forces in their efforts to stem the advance of the Japanese juggernaut that was steadily overwhelming the Allied armed forces in the Malay barrier and the Dutch East Indies.

Edsall's primary duties were to escort the shipping of evacuees from Singapore and the Indies to Australia, and to patrol those waters. On January 20, 1942, after a series of these monotonous patrols, *Edsall* came to share the honor of being the first American warship to sink a full-sized submarine following the attack on Pearl Harbor. It happened when *Edsall*, escorting a convoy of evacuees into Darwin Harbor, Australia, reported making a positive underwater sonar contact. Rather than desert his charges, the destroyer's skipper, Lieutenant Joshua J. Nix, radioed his find to the harbor defense authorities, who immediately dispatched three corvettes to investigate. After the ships were safely in port, *Edsall,* in company with the USS *Alden* (DD-211), was ordered to take part in the hunt.

Like beagles on the scent of a fox, the ships sniffed about the area where the submarine was last reported to have been, their sonar beams probing the depths for their elusive quarry. Then, at 1929, the Australian corvette *HMAS Deloraine* hit pay dirt and dashed over the spot, quickly rolling a pattern of depth charges over her stern. The waters boomed, cracked and fountained as they detonated beneath the sea. Close on *Deloraine's* heels raced the *Edsall,* her depth charges at the ready. Again, the waters trembled as her lethal "ash cans" exploded beneath her turbulent wake. Soon afterwards, a rousing cheer reverberated across the decks of the *Edsall,* when a rainbow-hued oil slick, littered with a smattering of wreckage, rose to the surface. However, just to be certain that the submarine's commander wasn't employing any trickery to avoid further punishment, *Deloraine* swept in and issued the coup de grâce with another salvo of depth charges.

Two days later, a team of divers from the submarine tender USS *Holland* boarded the wreckage of the submarine, thus verifying its loss and identifying it as the *I-24*. Consequently, both *Edsall* and *Deloraine* could share the credit of having sunk the submarine, and were authorized to proudly display a painted Rising Sun flag on their bridges.

On February 19, while escorting a convoy to Darwin, *Edsall* sustained damage to one of her propeller shafts when a depth charge prematurely exploded while she was staging an attack against a suspected submarine contact. Unfortunately, owing to the lack of repair facilities and spare parts, the destroyer had no other choice but to continue to carry out her assignments as best as she could.

During the last week in February, *Edsall* was lying in at Tjilatjap, Java, when on the 26th she and the USS *Whipple* (DD-217), were ordered to rendezvous with the aircraft carrier USS *Langley* some 200 miles south of Java. Loaded with 32 P-40 Army fighters, their pilots and mechanics, the carrier's mission was to deliver this vital cargo to bolster what remained of the meager air defenses throughout the Dutch East Indies. At about 0730 on the following day, *Langley* and her escorts were sighted by the Japanese. Then, shortly before 0900, the ships were attacked by nine high-altitude bombers. Ordered to maneuver independently, the ships scattered. With the enemy planes soaring at an altitude of 15,000 feet, they were well out of range of the anti-aircraft fire from the ships' 3-inch batteries and .30- and .50-caliber machine guns. After suffering three aerial attacks, the *Langley,* a slow and ungainly ex-collier, was reduced to a shattered wreck and had to be abandoned, *Edsall* taking on 117 of her survivors.

With the *Langley* not displaying any indication of sinking, the *Whipple* poured nine rounds of 4-inch shells and two torpedoes into her listing hulk. Nevertheless, the crusty old girl seemed reluctant to go under. Certain that another air assault was in the offing, Commander E.M. Crouch, commander of DesDiv 57, in *Whipple,* decided to clear the area. As the destroyers raced over the horizon, smoke could still be seen billowing from the mortally wounded *Langley.* Hence, no one witnessed her final demise. Nor is there any mention of her being observed by the Japanese, prior to her loss.

The destroyers were ordered to proceed to Christmas Island, where a British mining company and a radio station were located. Here, the ships were to join up with the Navy tanker USS *Pecos,* which was en route from Tjilatjap. At 0820, on February 28, the destroyers arrived off the entrance of Flying Fish Cove, where the *Whipple* was met by a representative from the mining company in a small launch, who offered to serve as a pilot. Instead, he was requested to use the launch in transferring the army pilots over to the *Edsall*. As he was discharging the last of the airmen, the *Pecos* arrived.

Shortly afterwards, a flight of Japanese bombers swept into the harbor, ignored the ships and instead blasted the mine's facilities and the radio station. At that point, it was decided to evacuate the harbor as another, stronger, attack would surely follow. At 1105 the ships stood out for Fremantle. During the night, heavy swells battered the ships, but the seas abated before dawn.

During the night passage, however, a message was received ordering *Edsall* to retain the P-40 pilots but transfer *Langley's* other survivors over to the *Pecos*. She (*Edsall*) was then to deliver the valuable airmen to Tjilitjap. At 0815, when the last of the carrier's survivors were received on board the tanker, the three ships parted company.

The *Whipple* proceeded to Cocos Island to refuel, while *Pecos* continued on course to Fremantle. Unfortunately, between 1145 and 1501, she underwent a series of air attacks by "Val" dive bombers from the carriers *Soryu*, *Kaga*, *Hiryu* and *Akagi* and sank at 1530. Although *Whipple* received the tanker's distress call, she arrived too late (1720) to offer any assistance, but did manage to rescue 233 of the survivors.

As for *Edsall*, no word was ever heard from her again. After steaming over the horizon, she, for all practical purposes, vanished from the surface of the earth. *Edsall's* disappearance remained a mystery for seven years after the war had ended. After intensive interrogations, however, naval authorities became satisfied with accounts they had gathered from personnel and war diaries from Japanese Battleship Division Three, which claimed to have witnessed the loss of the *Edsall*. Still, a curtain of doubt remained over what had become of the ill-fated destroyer's survivors. Then, during the early weeks of 1952, the complete story of the *Edsall's* actual demise came to light.

While viewing a strip of movie film taken by a naval officer from the cruiser IJN *Ashigara*, Navy investigators were horrified at the grim scene that unreeled before their eyes. On film was the gallant old four-stacker, *Edsall*, being ripped apart by a torrent of 8-inch shells from the Japanese cruiser. This ghastly discovery consequently directed the investigators to seek out former officers and crewmen from the *Ashigara*, from whom they learned that only eight of the destroyer's crew had been rescued. However, after they were landed (no one knew exactly where), their fates were unknown. In their continuing search to determine the ultimate fate of *Edsall's* survivors, the investigating team was directed to a forgotten prisoner-of-war camp on

Celebes Island, where a group of natives guided them to five graves, barely distinguishable under the matted growth of jungle vegetation. All of the five remains were exhumed and were identified by their I.D. tags as destroyermen from the USS *Edsall.*

☆ ☆ ☆

USS *EDSALL* (DD-219)

Class: Wickes/Clemson.
Builder: William Cramp and Sons, Philadelphia, Pennsylvania.
Keel laid: September 15, 1919.
Launched: July 20, 1920.
Sponsor: Mrs. Bessie E. Bracey; sister of Seaman Norman E. Edsall, USN.
Commissioned: November 20, 1920; Lieutenant Commander A.H. Rice, USN, comdg.
Date of loss: March 1, 1942; Lieutenant Joshua J. Nix, USN, comdg.†
Location: South of Java, Dutch East Indies (today Indonesia).
Awards: Two battle stars.

USS Pope

Launched September 9, 1919
Lost March 1, 1942
Java Sea, Dutch East Indies

COMMODORE JOHN POPE, USN
(1798–1876)

Born on December 17, 1798, in Sandwich, Massachusetts, John Pope was appointed midshipman on May 30, 1816. Prior to the outbreak of the Civil War, he served with distinction in the East Indies, Brazilian, West African and West Indies Squadrons.

During the Civil War, he was in command of the steam sloop, USS *Richmond,* and participated in the search for the Confederate raider, CSS *Sumter,* which had been preying on Union shipping.

On October 12, 1861, he took part in a fierce naval engagement against Confederate warships at the Head of Passages, Mississippi. Unfortunately, due to ill health, Captain Pope was relieved of his command and on 16 July 1862, he was promoted to Commodore and placed on the retirement list. Commodore Pope died at his home in Dorchester, Massachusetts on January 14, 1876.

Completed too late to take part in World War I, the USS *Pope* (DD-225) was assigned to the Asiatic Fleet in 1922. During her twenty years of service in the Far East, she was busily engaged protecting American interests during the periods of civil unrest and anti-foreign demonstrations that were rampant throughout China during the 1920s and 1930s.

When a full scale war broke out between the Republic of China and the Japanese Empire in 1937, *Pope* assisted in the evacuation of Americans from the ports of Tsingtao, Lao Yao and Shanghai, which began on September 19. Between June 14 and August 19, 1939, she was attached to the South China

Patrol Force and took part in the evacuation of Americans and other nationals from ports that were threatened by the swiftly advancing Japanese armies. The destroyer's last Chinese port of call was Swatow, where she observed Japanese warships as they bombarded this port, and witnessed its subsequent surrender.

From late 1939 until December 1941, the Asiatic Fleet patrolled throughout the Philippines, primarily in the northern approaches to the archipelago. After the attack on Pearl Harbor on December 7, 1941, *Pope* and her division (DesDiv 59) departed Manila on December 11, bound for the oil port of Balikpapan, Borneo. From here, she would become a unit of the ABDA naval forces in the Dutch East Indies.

After carrying out several weeks of arduous patrol duties, *Pope* finally had the opportunity to display her mettle as a fighting destroyer, when she and three of her sister destroyers staged a daring attack against an enemy invasion force at Balikpapan, Borneo, during the early morning hours of January 24, 1942.

Pope was part of a strike force made up of six destroyers and the light cruisers USS *Boise* and USS *Marblehead*, which had deployed from Koepang, Timor, three days earlier with the hope of disrupting the landings. Unfortunately, trouble began to plague the group almost from the start of the ' mission, when the *Boise* struck a pinnacle rock as she was entering the Sape Strait. Shortly thereafter, *Marblehead* developed turbine difficulties that cut her speed down to 15 knots. Consequently, two destroyers were detached to escort the cruisers to Wororada Bay, Soembawa.

Despite this handicap, the remaining four destroyers continued to forge through the Sape Strait and by dawn, were on a northerly course, punching their sharp prows through the moderately choppy waters of the Flores Sea. By early afternoon, the old four-pipers, led by the *John D. Ford* (DD-228), flagship of Commander P. H. Talbot, were steaming several miles off the west coast of Celebes Island. In an effort to confuse any enemy aerial observers, Talbot ordered a sharp right turn toward the island. Astern of him, *Pope*, *Parrott* (DD-218) and *Paul Jones* (DD-230), respectively, executed a smart turn into their leader's wake.

When Talbot was assured that there were not any enemy scout planes about, he resumed his northerly course, virtually hugging the Celebes coastline. Then, at about 1900, the column made a swing to port on a heading towards Balikpapan and right into the dragon's mouth. Needless to say, the destroyermen were well aware of the odds that were facing them—at least a dozen modern destroyers, a light cruiser, several armed auxiliaries and the possibility of an aircraft carrier lurking nearby.

Shortly after 0200, on the 24th, the destroyers sighted two burning transports that had been bombed by Dutch aircraft on the previous afternoon. By 0230, the horizon had taken on a fiery, crimson glow; resulting from the Dutch workers setting fire to the oil refineries and fuel storage tanks, which, in turn, had smothered the harbor and it's entrance under a thick blanket of acrid smoke. Meanwhile, the enemy placed a cordon of patrolling destroyers outside the harbor to guard against the infiltration of Allied warships and submarines.

As Talbot's destroyers made their approach to the objective, his voice crackled over the talk between ship's (TBS) radio circuit: "TORPEDO ATTACK . . . USE OWN DISCRETION IN ATTACKING WHEN TARGETS ARE LOCATED. WHEN ALL TORPEDOES ARE EXPENDED, CLOSE IN WITH ALL GUNS. USE INITIATIVE AND DETERMINATION!"

Soon afterwards, the destroyers were shrouded in a heavy mantle of pungent, oily smoke. Talbot then ordered his ships to reduce speed down to a crawl. As the destroyers crept stealthily through the smoke-filled harbor, occasionally they would emerge from their murky shroud, only to find themselves in the clear for a few moments before vanishing into another wall of smoke. The situation became somewhat critical when *Ford* and *Pope* found themselves fully exposed to a Japanese destroyer, which immediately began to challenge them by flashing recognition signals. Fortunately, before Talbot could take evasive action, a thick cloud of smoke rolled over the two destroyers and obscured them from the inquisitive opponent. Apparently, her captain had believed that the destroyers were friendly and did not pursue his investigation further.

The chronometers on the destroyers' bridges were nearing 0250, when they were once again in the clear and, dead ahead of them, silhouetted against the fiery shoreline, sat twelve, fat-bellied cargo ships and transports. It was almost too good to be true. Thus far, Talbot's destroyers had swept through the Makassar Strait in broad daylight without being detected and had eluded the picket destroyers outside of Balikpapan Harbor. Now the wolves were among the sheep, ready for the slaughter. It was a destroyer commander's dream come true!

The ships were lined up in two rows, about five miles from the shore. The first line of shipping, closest to the shoreline, was made up of seven vessels; the second, five. Talbot then ordered his ships to "pour on the coal," and the destroyers leaped ahead, dashing toward the last "Maru" in the first row, on a northeast tack.

When Talbot reached the stern of the cargoman, he made a sharp loop to starboard and raced on a southward course. As the *Parrott,* the third destroyer in the column, began her turn to starboard, she unleashed a brace of three torpedoes from her port side at the cargo vessel. A few seconds later, the *Sumanoura Maru* was blasted by one or, possibly two, of *Parrott's* "tin fish" and was beginning to settle to the bottom.

Meanwhile, as the destroyers were racing down the rear line of vessels, *Ford* let fly with a torpedo salvo at a target, but all missed or were duds. By now, the enemy was alerted not only by the attack upon the *Sumanoura Maru,* but by the creamy wakes from the American torpedoes. Believing his landing force was under submarine attack, the Japanese admiral (RAdm. S. Nishimura) dispatched several more destroyers out of the harbor to deal with the "intruders."

Talbot's destroyers were still racing southward and sweeping astern of the rear line of shipping without hindrance. At 0306, *Pope* launched a salvo of five torpedoes at a transport, with *Parrott* and *Paul Jones* following suit. Although severely damaged, the vessel was salvaged later.

At 0316, *Ford* was approaching the southern end of the anchorage, when Talbot ordered his ships to follow him in between the last two "Marus". Three minutes later, *Pope* and *Parrott* fired one torpedo each at what appeared to be a destroyer. The shots downed *Patrol Boat No.37. Ford* and *Paul Jones* each fired a torpedo at a ship on their port side, but a telltale white froth, seen churning at her stern, indicated that she was still attempting to get underway. Both destroyers dashed past the lumbering vessel; cut across her bow, and, as they skirted down her port side, *Jones* tagged her with a torpedo. However, the damage incurred was not serious enough to sink her.

Now, the veteran destroyers were clipping northward again, parallel to the rear line of shipping. Midway up the line, Talbot made an abrupt turn to port, leading his destroyers into the inner line of vessels. His ships were on their own and each of their skippers could chose his own targets of opportunity. Except for the *Ford,* all of the destroyers had expended their torpedoes and from here on, they would resort to gunfire, as was ordered previously by Commander Talbot.

Pope's skipper, Lieutenant Commander William C. Blinn, pulled out all the stops. Swinging his ship to starboard, he sighted two destroyers and opened fire with his four-inchers. The smoke, which had concealed the Americans, also served the same purpose for the Japanese, however, for right after *Pope* opened fire, a dense pall of smoke had covered the enemy destroyers. No explosions were heard, thus it was assumed the enemy had escaped unharmed.

Pope's gunners then trained their weapons on a transport and raked her from bow to stern. Before she disappeared into a wall of smoke, Pope's crew witnessed a number of explosions taking their toll upon the ship, with several of its crew and chunks of debris hurtling into the air.

Every destroyer had managed to score numerous hits upon their targets. Ford, employing torpedoes and gunfire, had sunk one ship and damaged two others, leaving them in flames. However, she herself did not escape unscathed. Having sustained a shell hit near one of her four-inch batteries, four men were wounded and her ready ammunition had been set on fire. Thanks to the swift action taken by her firefighters, the flames were quickly extinguished and the gun was back in action.

At 0340, Talbot ordered his ships to retire before their luck ran out. One by one, the destroyers fell in behind the Ford and beat a path out of the area at 32 knots, speeding southward to rendezvous with the Marblehead. The retirement down the eastern coast of Borneo was equally as hazardous as the action itself. Provided with charts by the Dutch that were clearly out of date, the destroyers found themselves in danger of running aground on the chain of unmarked reefs and shoals. Worse, all hands were expecting to sight a squadron of enemy destroyers boiling over the horizon in hot pursuit, or to be pounced upon by a flock of aircraft. Unknown to the fleeing destroyermen, however, the Japanese command was still convinced that a group of submarines were responsible for the attack and were continuing to search for the phantoms outside of Balikpapan Harbor.

Thus ended the Battle of Balikpapan, which some historians prefer to call the Battle of Makassar Strait. But, by whatever name, it was the first sea action won by American naval surface warships in World War II and the first surface engagement fought by the United States Navy since the Spanish-American War. During those heady first days of the Japanese onslaught in the Pacific, Pope and her sister ships delivered an important message to the enemy about American courage and resolve.

On the evening of February 18, Pope joined Dutch Admiral Karel Doorman's strike force in an attempt to break up an invasion convoy off the southeastern coast of Bali. The group was composed of two Dutch light cruisers, De Ruyter (Doorman's flagship) and Java, and Dutch destroyers Piet Hien and Kortenaer, along with the USS John D. Ford.

The force stood out of Tjilatjap, Java, at 2200 on the 19th. However, Kortenaer had the misfortune to strike a reef in the narrow channel and had to remain behind. Throughout the night and the following day, the ships raced eastward along the southern coast of Java, reaching the southern tip of Bali at about 2200 that evening. Doorman then ordered his screening destroyers to fall back and form a single column astern of the *Java*, with the *Ford* and *Pope* following in the wake of the *Piet Hien*.

The column of ships then turned to port and charged into the Badoeng Strait, a narrow body of water between Bali and the island of Nusa Besar. The enemy could barely be seen lying close to the Bali shore and to the raiders it was a disappointment, since the bulk of the convoy had long since disembarked its troops and departed, leaving behind a lone cargo ship and two destroyers: *Asashio and Oshio.*

At 2225, *Java* was the first to open fire, with the enemy responding with starshells and gunfire, striking *Java* on her stern and causing minor damage. Then, *Piet Hien's* guns burst to life, and she followed by making a sharp turn to starboard to lay down a smokescreen. This sudden manuever momentarily confused the Americans, however they did manage to follow the Dutchman through his smoke-laden wake. Again, the Dutch destroyer made another turn; this time to port and, as *Ford* executed her turn, her lookouts sighted one of the enemy destroyers and the cargo ship off her port beam. Apparently, all of the destroyers' lookouts had sighted the enemy ships at the same time and all three ships fired as one. Although the cargo ship absorbed the brunt of the barrage, she was not seriously impaired. Somehow, the *Oshio* succeeded in evading the rain of shells that crashed around her. Then suddenly, *Piet Hien* was hammered by a cyclone of shells and blasted by a torpedo from the *Asashio*, which left her dead in the water and sinking.

Now it was for the *Pope* and *Ford* to tangle with the Japanese destroyers and, for the next six minutes, they traded shot for shot, torpedo for torpedo, and maneuvered wildly within the tight confined waters of Badoeng Strait. During this ferocious engagement, both Japanese vessels sustained a number of hits, none of which were serious enough to stop them. *Pope* had fired five torpedoes at the *Oshio,* and all either missed or were duds.

Then, in the confusion of battle, compounded by darkness, the Japanese began to mistake their own ships for Allied vessels and began firing on each other. At this point, the division commander in *Ford*, Lieutenant Commander E.N. Parker, decided to break off the action and retire. As they dashed up through the Lombok Strait, the Japanese destroyers were still firing at one another. The American destroyers soon caught up with the Dutch cruisers and set a course for Surabaya, Java. Thus ended the first phase of the Battle of Badoeng Strait.

During the late afternoon of February 27, 1942, the Battle of the Java Sea exploded, thundering on until the early morning hours of the 28th. As history tells us, this engagement ended in a disastrous defeat for the ABDA naval forces and the eventual surrender of the Dutch East Indies to the Japanese armed forces.

Due to leaky piping in her feed water system, *Pope* was unable to participate in this action. On the 28th, it was decided to dissolve the ABDA forces and plans were put into effect to evacuate the Dutch East Indies. *Pope* and the British destroyer, HMS *Encounter*, were dispatched to escort the damaged British heavy cruiser, HMS *Exeter*, to Colombo, Ceylon (now Sri Lanka). Late that evening, the trio got underway with the hopes of eluding the Japanese on a night run westward through the Java Sea, passing through the Sunda Strait, between Java and Sumatra, into the Indian Ocean. The three ships and their crews were never heard from again, until after the war, when their survivors were released from Japanese prisoner of war camps.

Throughout the night of February 28 and March 1, the battered cruiser and her escorts cut a swath through the Java Sea without making contact with the enemy. Then, shortly after 0800, the masts of two cruisers were sighted looming above the horizon to the southeast. *Exeter's* Captain O.L. Gordon, RN, ordered a slight turn to the northeast, hoping to evade detection. Unfortunately, this maneuver proved fruitless as the enemy had already sighted them and launched scout planes, as the cruisers turned to pursue the lonely fugitives.

The Japanese cruisers were under the command of Rear Admiral T. Takagi, and consisted of the IJNs *Nachi* and *Haguro*, sporting 8-inch guns and escorted by one destroyer. Captain Gordon then ordered another change of course to the north, only to discover more pagoda-type superstructures of Japanese warships rising over the horizon. These were the heavy cruisers IJNs *Ashigara* and *Myoko*, escorted by three destroyers, under the command of Vice Admiral I. Takahashi.

With this avenue of escape cut off, Gordon, in desperation, ordered a sharp turn eastward on a reverse course through the Java Sea. Now there was no safe haven for the three Allied warships, for somewhere up ahead patrolled four more cruisers, as well as a swarm of other miscellaneous warships reported to have been seen boiling down through the Makassar Strait. These included the carrier *Ryujo*, lurking somewhere nearby, her flight deck packed with fighters and dive bombers.

A wild chase ensued that lasted almost two hours before the first shot was fired, by the *Exeter*, but the range was too distant, the enemy answering in turn, also without results. In a desperate effort to confuse the Japanese gunners, the three ships laid down a smokescreen; a futile gesture, since the enemy's scout planes, hovering overhead, were contantly relaying positions back to their mother ships.

It was soon evident that the fleeing Allied vessels were losing the race. *Exeter*, having sustained heavy damage in the Java Sea debacle, could not exceed 26 knots and the enemy cruisers were steadily gaining on her. In addition, her fire control system was out of kilter, therefore when she finally had the opportunity to engage with the enemy, her salvos went wild, missing the cruisers completely.

At about 1050, the Japanese opened fire. With the aid of their spotter aircraft, the gunners laid a pattern of shells about the crippled *Exeter*. These now began to take effect. Shell after shell poured into her, tearing up her decks and superstructure. Up ahead, rainsqualls were sighted and Gordon made an attempt to take shelter, if only temporarily, under the heavy deluges. However, by this time, the ill-fated cruiser was literally aflame from bow to stern and the extensive damage to her engineering plant had reduced her speed drastically. In a last gasp, she launched a spread of torpedoes against her antagonists, the *Pope* also letting fly with four. The long range shots missed. *Pope* then made a sharp turn to port ahead of *Exeter*, and fired the last of her torpedoes at the destroyers on her port hand. Her crew was gratified to witness a fiery explosion fountain at the stern of one destroyer, which retired from the chase trailing a plume of oily smoke behind her.

Then, two destroyers came charging toward the limping *Exeter* with their guns blazing. *Pope* and *Encounter* turned to engage, hoping to divert their attention from *Exeter*. During the slugfest, however, *Exeter* sustained a death-dealing blow of 8-inch shellfire, which demolished her last operating boiler room. Losing all power, the blazing cruiser sloughed to a stop. Gordon then ordered the *Pope* and *Encounter* to make a run for it and gave the order to abandon ship. As the last remnants of her crew were going over the side, the Japanese continued to pound her under. Finally, a torpedo, one of several that were fired at her, found its mark and the fighting *Exeter*, which had fought gallantly against the German pocket battleship *Graf Spee*, off Montevideo, Uruguay, in December 1939, rolled over and sank.

In their life and death struggle to escape the wrath of the Japanese cruisers, *Encounter* and *Pope* sped toward the nearest rainsquall. *Encounter* did not make it. Swamped under a deluge of large and small caliber shells, she soon joined the *Exeter* underneath the waves. *Pope* was now the last Allied warship remaining in the Java Sea.

Surrounded by the enemy on sea and in the air, it can be safely said that no other warship in World War II faced greater odds than those that confronted this old, four-stacker destroyer. Yet, despite almost certain destruction, *Pope's* skipper, Lieutenant Commander William C. Blinn, was not about to surrender.

Blinn was a staunch believer in the age-old adage of the sea: that a ship is not lost unless her captain believes it is so. Evidently, his crew felt the same way and trusted that their commanding officer's leadership would, somehow, pull them through the crisis. True, the men were on the brink of utter exhaustion; they were out of torpedoes and low on ammunition; but they were not short on resolve. They were on the run, but if they had to they were going to slug it out to the very end.

The cruisers' guns rumbled and boomed as *Pope* raced toward the nearest rainsquall, followed shortly by the high pitched whine of projectiles as they closed in and exploded off her port side. The awesome detonations shook the destroyer from truck to keel, causing the brickwork to crumble in number three boiler. Topside, her decks and superstructure were sprayed with brine and shards of shrapnel.

Having safely plunged into the rainsquall, ammunition was hastily transferred to the depleted ready boxes, but all too soon the destroyer was once again under the clear blue skies and it was a relief to see that now none of the cruisers were in sight. Up ahead was another rainsquall and Blinn swiftly ducked into it. If only their luck would hold out, the destroyer could continue to race through the Java Sea, then swing southward by nightfall and sweep through the Lombok Strait to make a dash for the safety of an Australian port. But it was not to be.

As soon as she had emerged from the cloudburst, *Pope* was sighted by one of the scout planes, which relayed the destroyer's position to the pursuing cruisers. Less than a hundred miles away, a flight of dive bombers from the carrier, *Ryujo*, had picked up the signal and were soon bee-lining toward the lone destroyer. At about 1230, the bombers had her in their sights. The *Pope's* gallant and final hour was at hand.

The destroyers' gunners girded themselves to fend off their attackers with their ancient 3-inch anti-aircraft battery and puny .30- and .50-caliber machine guns. Down swooped the bombers from the clear, azure blue skies; their engines screaming. *Pope's* 3-incher snapped and banged away until it's recoil system jammed. As the planes leveled off, the bombs came whistling down. Blinn successfully dodged them, but the near misses rattled *Pope's* framework, inflicting additional damage to her engineering spaces. Her machine guns chattered and spewed the sky with hot lead, but were ineffective against the high-speed aircraft. One of the exploding bombs sprung the plating on her port side, letting the sea into her after living quarters and damaging her port propeller shaft. As a result, the port engine began to vibrate so violently, it had to be shut down, reducing *Pope's* speed to 20 knots.

Soon afterwards, a flight of high altitude bombers came soaring overhead at 3000 feet and released their bombs. At this height, they were easily evaded, but the *Pope* was still in serious trouble. Her repair parties could not stem the flooding in her after compartments and the ship was becoming loggy and difficult to maneuver. With her stern almost underwater, Blinn had no other choice but to make preparations to abandon ship.

Responsible personnel were ordered to gather up all code books and top secret material in weighted-down canvas bags to be tossed overboard. To hasten her sinking, the gunnery department set demolition charges throughout the ship. Lifeboats and rafts were stocked with provisions to enable the men to survive the hardships facing them in the open sea. Then, at 1250, Blinn ordered his crew over the side. All boats and liferafts were lowered and the men left the *Pope* for the last time.

Not long after the crew had abandoned the derelict, the roar of gunfire rolled over the vast expanse of the Java Sea as the *Ashigara* and *Myoko* laid down a barrage of 8-inch shells around the sinking destroyer. Before the demolition charges could do their work, six 8-inch projectiles crashed into the feisty *Pope,* lifting her clear out of the water. Moments later the battered remains of the 1,190-ton destroyer slipped beneath the waves, stern first, under a pall of heavy smoke.

A scout plane from one of the cruisers made a low flying pass over the survivors, during which time an angry seaman with a Browning automatic machine gun, fired upon it. That was all the pilot needed for an excuse to strafe the survivors. For at least twenty minutes, he and another aircraft assailed the helpless men, but by some miracle only one man was wounded. The planes then returned to their cruisers, which sailed on, vanishing over the horizon.

Left alone under the blazing, tropical sun, the men secured the life rafts together and were taken in tow by the motor whaleboats. All attempts to reach the Borneo coast failed after the boats ran out of fuel and, during the following three days, the survivors drifted aimlessly with the erratic currents and winds. Then, on the night of the third day, a Japanese destroyer discovered the bedraggled survivors and picked them up. Amazingly, the officers and crew treated the Americans fairly well. They provided food and administered first aid to the wounded and to those in need of medical treatment from their exposure to the elements.

Two days later, the survivors were disembarked at Makassar City, Celebes Island and interred in the city's jail prior to being transported to a POW camp. Here they met with the survivors from the *Exeter* and *Encounter.* As the war progressed and as the Allies regained their lost territories, a few of the POWs were transported to the Japanese homeland or elsewhere. Of the *Pope's* 149 survivors (only one man was killed before the *Pope* was abandoned, when a demolition charge prematurely detonated in his hand), 28 died of malnutrition and mistreatment by their captors.

Upon his release after the war, Lieutenant Commander Blinn (as of this writing, retired with the rank of Rear Admiral), was promoted to Commander and awarded the Navy Cross, with several of his crew receiving various medals and commendations. Aside from receiving three battle stars, *Pope* was awarded the Presidential Unit Citation for her outstanding performance and achievements in the defense of the Dutch East Indies.

The citation reads in part: "For extraordinary action against the Japanese forces in the Java Sea Campaign in the Southwest Pacific war area from 23 January to 1 March 1942, the USS *Pope*, operating with meager surface forces of the combined United States, British, Dutch and Australian Navies, was contested in combat by Japanese fleets. The *Pope's*, illustrious achievements have added a new luster in the annals of American warfare and upheld the finest traditions of the United States Naval Service."

☆ ☆ ☆

USS *POPE* (DD-225)

Class: Wickes/Clemson.
Builder: William Cramp & Sons, Philadelphia, Pennsylvania.
Keel laid: 9 September 1919.
Launched: 23 March 1920.
Sponsor: Mrs. William S. Benson, great-grandniece of Commodore John Pope, USN.
Commissioned: 17 October 1920; Commander R. S. Galloway, USN, comdg.
Date of loss: 1 March 1942; Lieutenant Commander W. C. Blinn, USN, comdg.
Location: Java Sea, Dutch East Indies.
Awards: Presidential Unit Citation and three battle stars.

USS Stewart

Launched March 4, 1920
Lost March 1, 1942
Surabaya, Java, Dutch East Indies

REAR ADMIRAL CHARLES STEWART, USN
(1778–1869)

Born in Philadelphia, Pennsylvania, Charles Stewart went to sea at the age of 13. Commissioned Lieutenant in the Navy on March 9, 1798, he served on the frigate *United States* during the quasi-war with France until he assumed command of the schooner *Experiment* on July 16, 1800. Soon afterward he captured two French merchantmen and freed several captured American ships.

After serving briefly as captain of the frigate *Chesapeake* in 1801, and service on the *Constellation* in 1802, Stewart sailed to the Mediterranean in command of the brig *Siren*. While serving in these waters, he took part in the burning of the frigate *Philadelphia* in Tripoli Harbor after she had been captured by the Barbary Pirates. He went on to blockade the harbor and distinguished himself in assaults against the Barbary naval forces in August and September 1804.

Placed in command of the frigate *Constitution* during the War of 1812, he aggressively challenged and defeated several British warships. While cruising through the Caribbean on February 20, 1815, he attacked and defeated the HMSs *Levant* and *Cayne*.

After the war, Stewart went on to command the United States' Mediterranean and Pacific Squadrons (1816–24), served as naval commissioner from 1830 to 1832, and was commandant of the Philadelphia Navy Yard. Rear Admiral Stewart retired on July 16, 1862, and died at Bordentown, New Jersey, on November 6, 1869.

After completing a two-year tour of duty with the Atlantic Fleet destroyer flotillas, the USS *Stewart* (DD-224) reported to the U.S. Asiatic Fleet on August 24, 1922.

With China in the throes of civil unrest, including anti-foreign disturbances, *Stewart* and her sister destroyers were dispatched to wherever these tumultuous revolts flared up, in an effort to protect American and other nationals' lives and interests. On one occasion, in January 1925, she transported and disembarked Marines at Shanghai to quell the riots that were rampaging throughout that city. However, there were many occasions when units of the Asiatic Fleet carried out missions of mercy, such as delivering relief goods to victims of the devastating earthquake that virtually leveled the cities of Tokyo and Yokohama in September 1923. For a period of two weeks after that event, *Stewart* and two other American destroyers remained in Yokosuka to provide medical assistance, her crew working diligently with rescue teams in their attempt to render aid to injured and homeless Japanese.

During the late 1930s, conditions in China grew worse for both Americans and other nationals when the war between Japan and China intensified. In late 1939, the last remnants of the American community were evacuated from China to the safety of the Philippines or the United States.

After the war commenced in Europe on September 1, 1939, the Asiatic Fleet began to operate primarily out of Manila and conducted neutrality patrols in Philippine waters. From that time until December 7, 1941, *Stewart* paid goodwill and diplomatic visits to ports in the Dutch East Indies and French Indo-China. On December 8, 1941, the ship and her division were refueling at Tarakan Roads, Borneo, when her crew received the shocking news of the Japanese attack on Pearl Harbor.

Immediately, the American destroyers were placed on a wartime alert, and at 0500 *Stewart's* division, comprised of the *Barker* (DD-213), *Paul Jones* (DD-230) and *Parrott* (DD-218), got underway and raced at 30 knots for the port of Balikpapan, Borneo, arriving there at 0940 on the 9th. The division remained there, carrying out patrols and investigating reports of Japanese vessels in the area until December 16, when the destroyers and other units of the Asiatic Fleet steamed for Makassar City, Celebes Island.

On December 22, *Stewart* departed Makassar City bound for the port of Surabaya, Java, arriving there on the 24th. Signalman Bill Kale noted in his diary that the port was filled with a large number of Allied merchant ships, Dutch warships, several American auxiliary vessels, plus two American cruisers and four American destroyers.

After several weeks of carrying out patrols and escort duties, on February 4, 1942, *Stewart* witnessed an aerial assault against the two U.S cruisers in her strike force. En route to thwart an invasion convoy at Makassar City, the strike force was composed of two Dutch light cruisers, *De Ruyter* (flagship of RAdm. Karel Doorman, RNN) and *Tromp*; three Dutch destroyers, *Van Ghent, Piet Hien* and *Banckert*; American cruisers *Houston* and *Marblehead,* and destroyers *Stewart* (flagship of Commander T.H. Binford), *Barker* (DD-213), *Bulmer* (DD-222) and *John D. Edwards* (DD-216).

Pounced upon by a flight of 27 Japanese bombers, the cruisers proved to be the principal targets for the enemy pilots. *Marblehead* sustained several devastating hits that quickly reduced her to a mass of flaming wreckage, while *Houston* had one of her gun turrets demolished and suffered several hits that virtually crippled her. Owing to the high altitude at which the enemy aircraft were flying, the destroyers were unable to contribute effective gunfire during the attack. With two of his heavy units out of action, Admiral Doorman decided to abort the mission and returned to port, with *Stewart* escorting the damaged *Marblehead* to Tjilatjap, Java.

On February 14, *Stewart* and five of her sister destroyers were part of Doorman's strike force en route to engage Japanese cruisers reported to be steaming off the coast of Sumatra. As luck would have it, Doorman's group came under an air attack that lasted for more than three hours. Although none of his ships sustained serious damage, Doorman considered it foolhardy to press on further and retired. That evening, his ships were again attacked by aircraft as they were passing through Gaspar Strait, resulting in the Australian cruiser HMAS *Hobart* sustaining slight underwater damage.

Then, during the early morning hours of February 20, *Stewart*, in company with the Dutch light cruiser *Tromp* and the American destroyers *Parrott, John D. Edwards* and *Pillsbury*, was sent dashing up Badoeng Strait to disrupt a Japanese landing force on the southern shores of Bali. As mentioned earlier in the history of the *Pope*, Admiral Doorman had intended to break up this landing operation the day before; however, the bulk of the shipping had departed, leaving behind two destroyers and a lone cargoman. After wreaking considerable damage on the two enemy destroyers—inflicted primarily by the *Pope* and *John D. Ford*—Doorman commanded a halt, and retired to Surabaya.

Now the two battered Japanese destroyers and the crippled cargo ship were facing a second wave of attackers. However, the Japanese vessels, barely visible against the darkened backdrop of Bali, had the advantage and sprinted toward the intruders, bearing down upon the *Stewart,* the leading destroyer in the column. *Stewart's* lookouts sighted the creamy bow waves of the oncoming destroyers but U.S. warning shouts only seemed to spur the enemy ships into action; simultaneously, the Japanese switched on their searchlight and let fly with a salvo of torpedoes and gunfire.

Bill Kale describes what occurred next: "I was manning the helm at the time when all hell broke loose. The 'Nipper' turned on his searchlight and let us have it. Shrapnel and shards of steel were banging all around the bridge. I could not duck, since I had to steer the ship. Above the bridge, on the gun director firing platform, one man was killed. Then a second shell burst near the bridge and again, we were showered by shrapnel, of which one piece struck Lieutenant Smiley, our Executive Officer, and ripped out a piece of flesh from his right leg. 'Damn it!' he said. 'One of those sons-abitches got me in the leg!'

"Meanwhile, the 'Nippers' were scoring hit after hit on the after section of the ship. Then a shell hit us below the waterline in the after steering room, tearing a hole in the hull about four feet in diameter and flooding the space." Yet, despite *Stewart's* after steering room being awash, she continued to churn out 30 knots and fight on.

Elsewhere during this melee, *Parrott* and *Pillsbury* nearly collided with each other. Then *Tromp* fired off a barrage of shells against the *Oshio,* mangling her bridge. *Oshio,* in turn, lashed back with a salvo of ten direct hits against the Dutchman's stern. After this exchange, the enemy lost contact and the Dutch strike force leader, Commander J.N. DeMeester, RNN, ordered his ships to retire.

As the ships were leaving the Badoeng Strait, however, they met up with two more enemy destroyers, the *Arishio* and *Michishio.* At 0219, both destroyers opened fire on *Stewart* and *John D. Edwards,* who returned the favor with a volley of gunfire and torpedoes, neither of the adversaries scoring any hits. Then *Michishio* was staggered by a number of hits from *Parrott* and *Tromp,* leaving her dead in the water, 90 of her personnel killed and wounded. Outnumbered and outgunned, *Arashio's* captain broke off the action and DeMeester rapidly cleared out of the area. Shortly afterward, *Parrott's* steering gear malfunctioned, which almost resulted in her running aground on a reef.

With the coming of dawn, the *Stewart's* crew was able to see the havoc that had been wreaked upon the ship. The steam line to the after steering engine had been severed, causing the space to build up with steam and the deck above to become so hot it was virtually impossible to walk on it. The crow's nest had four shrapnel holes. Ensign Alford, who was stationed there during the action, wondered, later, how he had managed to get out of it without a scratch. The main deck was strewn with shrapnel, some as large as a man's fist. Number three stack had two large holes in it. One shell had blown the bow off the port motor whaleboat and it was hanging on one davit, so the men cut it loose and let it drop over the side. A chunk of shrapnel had torn through a blower in the starboard passageway, another piece having gouged a cut about four inches long across one of the torpedo tubes. Also noticed were several other holes in the ship's hull and throughout her superstructure.

By 1000 on the 20th, *Stewart* was entering Surabaya and, since she had suffered the most damage, was placed in a floating dry-dock for repairs. Bill Kale describes what then occurred: "One of the strangest and toughest accidents that could have befallen a ship happened to us. As the drydock was being raised, the shoring collapsed, causing the ship to roll over to port. I was sitting in the bridge, when all of a sudden there was a big crash. All of us on the bridge were thrown off our feet and went tumbling across the space and against the bulkhead. Fortunately, none of the men were seriously injured. The ship was lying at a 37-degree angle and more holes were punctured in her hull, which flooded both engine rooms, the main generator burning out before it could be shut down.

"Our skipper, Lieutenant Commander H.P. Smith, was, to say the least, devastated. After all we had been through and this last action, in which we had narrowly escaped being sunk, this was indeed, the last straw!

"Afterwards, we were transferred to a huge barracks; however, I had lost all my clothing and personal effects since my locker was on the port side of my living quarters, which was completely flooded. Thankfully, some of the men let me borrow their clothes until I could replenish my sea bag.

"Every day we'd go over to the ship in an effort to do some salvage work, but the task soon became impossible since the Japs were staging daily air raids. Then, on the 24th, *Stewart* was struck by three bombs which put her completely out of commission. On the following day our crew was split up, with a third being transferred over to the *Pillsbury*, another third to the *Parrott* and the rest of us were sent over to the *John D. Edwards*."

After the Battle of the Java Sea ended in disaster for the ABDA naval forces, it was decided to evacuate the Dutch East Indies. As for *Stewart*, the Navy had written her off as a total loss. Nevertheless, to prevent the gallant destroyer from falling into enemy hands, demolition charges were placed throughout her compartments and she was blown up along with the drydock next to her. Her name was stricken from the Navy List on March 25, and four months later, her name was assigned to a new destroyer escort (DE-238), which was commissioned on May 31, 1943.

Later in the war, American pilots reported the sighting of an American warship operating well inside Japanese waters. Although its forward stack was trunked, other features raised suspicions that she did seem to sport the lines of an old American four-piper destroyer. However, with more important matters at hand, these reports were considered of little value during the debriefing sessions and were cast aside.

After many fierce battles and the dropping of atomic bombs, World War II finally ended on September 2, 1945. On October 15, a group of naval inspectors in Japan noticed an odd appearing vessel moored in a nest of decrepit, rusted hulks at Hiro Bay, Kure. After boarding her and scouring through her compartments, they realized that this ship was indeed none other than the old USS *Stewart* (DD-224)!

After lying in the mud of Surabaya Harbor for almost a year, the frugal Japanese had raised the damaged destroyer, effected temporary repairs and commissioned her into the Imperial Japanese Navy as *Shokai-tei* 102 (Patrol Boat No. 102). Towed to a naval shipyard in Japan, the former American destroyer was overhauled and her boilers and engines were refurbished. Her 4-inch guns were replaced with 3-inch guns and an anti-aircraft battery. To prevent her from being attacked by her own forces, her outward appearances were necessarily changed. For a time, she carried out operations as an escort vessel with the Japanese Southwest Fleet, and later was attached to a naval group in Korean waters, during which time she was bombed by U.S. Army aircraft at Mokpo Harbor.

In April 1945, she was transferred to the control of the Kure Naval District, serving as a harbor patrol craft. Owing to the shortage of fuel needed to operate her, she was consequently laid up and left to rot along with several other vessels in Kure Harbor.

For all intents and purposes, the old destroyer should have been left to her fate; but on October 20, in an emotional ceremony, the ex-USS *Stewart* was recommissioned into the United States Navy as DD-224. Upon the completion of necessary repairs, DD-224 was manned by a voluntary crew, which, incidentally, nicknamed her: "*RAMP-224*," which stood for "Recovered Allied Military Personnel." Then, with her homeward-bound pennant flying from her truck, old DD-224 stood out of Kure, en route to the home of her birth.

Unfortunately, the long voyage home would prove to be a nightmare for all hands. Continuous breakdowns plagued her engineering personnel and, despite the employment of the latest poisons and insecticides, the ship still crawled with every type of vermin and insect known to man. Layovers in Guam and Pearl Harbor allowed the crew to make repairs; nevertheless, the old girl finally gave up the ghost a short distance from San Francisco and had to call for assistance.

In early March 1946, after 23 years, the ancient but gallant destroyer was home, ignominiously, and, somewhat embarrassingly, passing under the Golden Gate Bridge at the end of a towline. There was some hope that the old destroyer would be restored as a memorial, but this was not to be. On May 23, 1946, DD-224 was decommissioned and, on the following day, was towed out to sea and sunk as target practice for naval aircraft.

☆ ☆ ☆

USS *STEWART* (DD-224)

Class: Wickes/Clemson.
Builder: William Cramp & Sons, Philadelphia, Pennsylvania.
Keel laid: September 9, 1919.
Launched: March 4, 1920.
Sponsor: Mrs. Margaretta S. Stevens, granddaughter of Rear Admiral Charles Stewart, USN.
Commissioned: September 15, 1920; Lieutenant S.G. Lamb, USN, comdg.
Date of loss: March 1, 1942; Lieutenant Commander H. P. Smith, USN, comdg.
Location: Surabaya, Java, Dutch East Indies.
Recaptured: October 15, 1945; Kure, Japan.
Recommissioned: October 29, 1945, as DD-224.
Final disposal: Sunk as a target by aircraft off San Francisco, California.
Awards: Two battle stars.

USS Pillsbury

Launched August 3, 1920
Lost between March 1–4, 1942
Indian Ocean, east of Christmas Island

REAR ADMIRAL JOHN E. PILLSBURY, USN
(1846–1919)

Born on December 15, 1846, in Lowell, Massachusetts, John Elliot Pillsbury was appointed Midshipman in 1862 and commissioned Ensign in 1868. He went on to serve in various types of ships and shore assignments prior to assuming command of the USS *Blake*, a coastal surveying steamer, from 1884 until 1891. During those eight years he performed valuable scientific work in connection with underwater explorations. Employing instruments of his own invention, he discovered the Gulf Stream and its axis in the Florida Straits and off Cape Hatteras, North Carolina.

During the Spanish-American War, he commanded the dynamite cruiser USS *Vesuvius*, and afterwards served as Chief of Staff of the North Atlantic Fleet. He was a member of the National Geographical Society for several years and, upon his retirement from the Navy, became its president and continued as such until his death on December 30, 1919.

The USS *Pillsbury* (DD-227) was assigned to the Asiatic Fleet in 1922 and continued to serve in the Far East until her loss in the Indian Ocean, early in March 1942.

During the first week of December 1941, *Pillsbury* was attached to DesRon 29, DesDiv 58, conducting her operations with units of the Dutch Navy in the East Indies. On December 8, she and her division were refueling at Balikpapan, Borneo, when the stunning news of the Japanese attack on Pearl Harbor was flashed across the world. Ordered to Manila, DesDiv 58 entered port on December 10 during the height of an air attack. During this battle, *Pillsbury* went to the aid of the minesweeper USS *Whippoorwill*, which had towed the fiercely burning and bomb-damaged destroyer *Peary* out into the harbor and assisted in extinguishing her fires.

Following the orders of the Commander of the Asiatic Fleet, Rear Admiral Thomas C. Hart, *Pillsbury* and other units of the fleet departed Manila Harbor on December 27, bound for the Dutch East Indies. Here, the Asiatic Fleet teamed up with the British, Dutch and Australian naval forces, in an effort to make a stand against the advance of the Japanese throughout the Malay barrier.

After serving as a convoy escort and patrolling throughout the Indies between early January and mid-February 1942, *Pillsbury* finally had the opportunity to fire her first shot of the war in anger, when she took part in the Battle of Badoeng Strait.

During the early morning hours of February 20, 1942, *Pillsbury* was part of a second wave of ships scheduled to attack an invasion convoy off the southeastern shore of Bali. In company with USSs *Stewart, Parrott* and *John D. Edwards*, under the command of Commander J.B. de Meester, RNN, in the Dutch light cruiser *Tromp,* the destroyer raced through the southern entrance of the strait and tangled with two Japanese destroyers. Although these had been damaged previously in a hammer-and-tongs confrontation against the American destroyers *Pope* and *John D. Ford*, they were still game for a fight and dashed forward to challenge the intruders. Thus commenced a second free-for-all as the opposing sides fought it out with gunfire and torpedoes.

Stewart, as has been mentioned previously, took quite a thrashing; *Pillsbury* was flayed by shrapnel, which did not result in any apparent damage or casualties. However, while jockeying wildly through the darkened and narrow confines of Badoeng Strait, *Pillsbury* and *Parrott* nearly collided with each other. Once again, the enemy destroyer *Asashio* suffered a severe drubbing, complements of *Pillsbury* and *Parrott. Oshio* had opened fire on the *Tromp* and, in return, her bridge was smothered under a torrent of *Tromp's* gunfire, causing many casualties. Unimpeded by this last barrage, the Japanese destroyer answered back with a hail of shells that scored a number of hits on the cruiser's stern.

The Dutch commander then ordered the group to retire northward through the Lombok Strait. Here, they steamed smack into the path of two more enemy destroyers that were on their way to assist their wounded sisters. Again, another fierce, but short duel began.

Stewart and *John D. Edwards* were shaken by near-misses from the guns of IJNs *Michishio* and *Arashio*, the former being stunned by gunfire from the

Pillsbury that left her staggering. Before she could recover, *John D. Edwards* rocked her with a withering volley from her four-inch batteries. Close astern of her raced the Dutch cruiser *Tromp*, which laid on a murderous barrage of gunfire and completely paralyzed the battle-scarred destroyer. After this exchange, the Allied force beat a path through the strait and made a hasty departure for the port of Surabaya, arriving there later that morning.

On the 22nd, *Pillsbury* and *Parrott* stood out of Surabaya and set a course for Tjilatjap, Java. They were still moored there when the Battle of the Java Sea took place, effecting the demise of the ABDA naval forces. This battle also marked the disbanding of the U.S. Asiatic Fleet, which by this time possessed very few surviving ships.

With the decision to evacuate the Dutch East Indies, *Parrott* departed Tjilatjap on March 1, escorting the minesweepers *Whippoorwill* and *Lark,* the patrol yacht *Isabel* and the island schooner *Lanikai,* to Exmouth, Australia. Later that afternoon, *Pillsbury* got underway for the same destination, escorting the American gunboat *Ashville* and the Australian gunboat *HMAS Yarra*. Like the *Pope* and the *Edsall, Pillsbury,* along with her consorts, sailed over the horizon and into oblivion.

After the war, information was disclosed by Japanese naval officers and ratings who were serving in the cruiser squadrons operating in those waters at the time. The small group of ships had been overtaken by three cruisers from Cruiser Squadron 4 and two destroyers. At times, the informants' statements were somewhat conflicting about dates and the number of ships or types of vessels that were present to witness the final moments of *Pillsbury*. However, they all agreed that the 1,109-ton destroyer put up a gallant fight before she went to her watery grave. Needless to say, the lightly defended gunboats were blown under with very little effort.

It is not clear if all of the crews went down with their ships, for the enemy swiftly retired. Any survivors were left to drown, or drift for days on end under the blazing tropical skies, until succumbing eventually to sharks, thirst or exposure.

☆ ☆ ☆

USS *PILLSBURY* (DD-227)

Class: Wickes/Clemson.
Builder: William Cramp & Sons, Philadelphia, Pennsylvania.
Keel laid: October 23, 1919.
Launched: August 3, 1920.
Sponsor: Miss Helen L. Richardson, granddaughter of Rear Admiral John E.
    Pillsbury, USN.

Commissioned: December 15, 1920; Lieutenant H.W. Barnes, USN, comdg.
Date of loss: Between March 1–4, 1942; Lieutenant Commander H.C. Pound, USN, comdg.†
Location: Indian Ocean; approximately 200 miles east of Christmas Island.
Awards: Two battle stars.

USS Sturtevant

Launched July 29, 1920
Lost April 26, 1942
Off Marquesas Key, Florida

ENSIGN ALBERT D. STURTEVANT, USNRF
(1894–1918)

Born in Washington, DC, on May 2, 1894, Albert D. Sturtevant enlisted in the United States Naval Reserve Force on March 24, 1917. Commissioned Ensign two days later, he underwent flight training at Pensacola, Florida and was designated a naval aviator on May 1. In September of that year, Ensign Sturtevant reported to a U.S. Navy air group that was attached to the Royal Flying Corps at Felixstowe, England.

On February 15, 1918, while flying an escort mission over the English Channel with another aircraft in his unit, he and his companion were attacked by a flight of 12 German aircraft. Despite the great odds, both pilots courageously fought it out with the enemy, until Sturtevant was shot down in flames. For his outstanding heroism in this action, Ensign Sturtevant was posthumously awarded the Navy Cross.

At the completion of her shakedown trials, the USS *Sturtevant* (DD-240) stood out of New York Harbor on November 30, 1920, for occupation duty in the eastern Mediterranean as part of the U.S. Naval Detachment at Constantinople. For six months she was based at Split, on the Dalmatian coast of Yugoslavia. During this time, *Sturtevant* was often called upon to carry out diplomatic missions throughout the Adriatic and Mediterranean Seas, touching such ports as Burgas in Bulgaria, Braila in Romania and Samsun, Turkey.

Sturtevant was also one of several American destroyers assigned to investigate potential ports for the American Relief Administration, from which to

distribute help to the destitute people of that region, including revolutionary Russia (the Bolsheviks accepted humanitarian aid, though grudgingly
and as surreptitiously as possible).

Prior to her return to the United States, *Sturtevant* paid goodwill visits to
Alexandria, Egypt, to the Isle of Rhodes, Greece, and several other Medi-
terranean ports. Following an overhaul at the Brooklyn Navy Yard in 1922,
Sturtevant alternated service between the Atlantic and Pacific fleets before
being temporarily decommissioned at the Philadelphia Navy Yard on
January 13, 1931.

Recommissioned on March 9, 1932, *Sturtevant* was assigned to the
Special Service Squadron at Coco Solo, Panama. During the next two years,
she patrolled throughout the Gulf of Mexico and in Caribbean waters and
assisted in the landing of Marines in Nicaragua, Haiti, Cuba and wherever
American lives and interests were threatened.

In early 1934, *Sturtevant* was homeported at Norfolk, Virginia, from
where she carried out operations with the Atlantic Fleet. In mid-1935, she
transited the Panama Canal and reported for duty with the Pacific Fleet.
However, on November 20 of that year, the destroyer was again decommissioned and placed in reserve at the destroyer base at San Diego.

With the outbreak of the war in Europe in 1939, *Sturtevant* was recommissioned and, after conducting refresher training along the California coast
she was transferred to the Atlantic Fleet. Here, she was assigned to the neutrality patrol, cruising through the Gulf of Mexico and the Caribbean.
During 1941, she was allocated as an escort for British shipping, plying the
U-boat infested waters of the North Atlantic.

After America entered the war, the Norfolk-based *Sturtevant* served as a
convoy escort for shipping along the eastern seaboard until early March
1942, when her homeport was shifted to Key West, Florida. From there, she
escorted shipping through the Caribbean to Panama and back to U.S. ports
along the eastern seaboard.

On April 26, 1942, the *Sturtevant*, now under the command of
Lieutenant Commander C.L. Weigle, cleared out of Key West at 1300 to rendezvous with a convoy near the mouth of the Mississippi River. At 1515, she
was about eight miles south of Marquesas Key, when she was shaken by a
tremendous explosion in her after section that lifted her stern out of the
water. Although the ship did not lose headway, a pillar of yellow smoke was
seen billowing out from the vicinity of her after deckhouse.

Believing he was under submarine attack, Captain Weigle increased
speed and ordered depth charges to be dropped. But before this order could

be carried through, another explosion rocked the destroyer in her amidships area. Then, as the damage-control parties rushed to assess the damage, a third explosion ripped through the twice-wounded *Sturtevant*, breaking her keel, the after section sinking soon afterwards. Curiously, the forward section of the ship remained afloat and stable for several hours, before finally sinking. Resting in shallow water, only her foremast and crow's nest were visible above the surface.

Fortunately, Captain Weigle was able to send out a distress signal before the third explosion had doomed his ship; hence, all hands, except for 15 of the destroyer's crew, were rescued by a group of patrol vessels.

After the tragedy, it was discovered that *Sturtevant* had not been attacked by a U-boat, but had steamed unknowingly into a minefield that had been planted on the previous day. Somewhere down the line, someone had failed to inform Captain Weigle of its presence. Perhaps secrecy was to blame. During the war, both civilian and military personnel, under the threat of disciplinary action, were instructed not to mention the movements of ships, personnel, armaments, etc. Thus, the laying of the minefield may have been considered so secret that not even Captain Weigle had been notified of its presence before leaving port. As a result, the Atlantic Fleet lost its third destroyer.

☆ ☆ ☆

USS *STURTEVANT* (DD-240)

Class: Wickes/Clemson.

William Cramp & Sons, Philadelphia, Pennsylvania.

Keel laid: November 23, 1918.

Launched: July 29, 1920.

Sponsor: Mrs. Curtis R. Smith.

Commissioned: September 21, 1920; Lieutenant Commander E.G. Haas, USN, comdg.

Date of loss: April 26, 1942: Lieutenant Commander C.L. Weigle, USN, comdg.

Location: Off Marquesas Key, Florida.

Awards: None.

USS Sims

Launched April 8, 1939
Lost May 7, 1942
The Coral Sea

REAR ADMIRAL WILLIAM S. SIMS, USN
(1858–1936)

Born in Ontario, Canada, William Sowden Sims was appointed to the U.S. Naval Academy in 1876 and graduated in 1880. After several years at sea, he went on to serve in various posts ashore. These included Naval Attache in St. Petersburg, Russia, aide to President Theodore Roosevelt and President of the Naval War College, Newport, Rhode Island.

After the United States entered World War I, Sims was named commander of American destroyers operating from British naval bases. Advanced to the rank of Vice Admiral in 1917, his title was changed to Commander of the United States Naval Forces operating in European Waters, during which time the North Sea mine barrage was laid under his supervision.

After the war, Admiral Sims was reassigned as President of the War College and served in that capacity until his retirement on October 15, 1922. He died at his home in Boston, Massachusetts, on September 25, 1936.

The lead destroyer of her class, the USS *Sims* (DD-409) reported to the Commandant, Atlantic Destroyer Squadrons (ComDesLant), at Norfolk, Virginia, on August 2, 1940. From there she served on the neutrality patrol, carrying out her operations in the Gulf of Mexico, the Caribbean and in South American waters. In May 1941, she commenced escorting British shipping through the North Atlantic; this lasted until December.

On December 7, *Sims* was undergoing a shipyard overhaul at the Norfolk Navy Yard, Portsmouth, Virginia, and, on the 16th, got underway for San Diego where she became a unit of Task Force 17, which was built around the carrier *Yorktown*. After a short layover in San Diego, the task force proceeded on to Samoa, escorting a convoy embarked with Marines; she arrived there on January 23, 1942.

Two days later the task force departed to carry out air strikes against the Japanese-held islands of Makin, Mili and Jaluit. On the 28th, an enemy bomber sighted the force, winged in and dropped a stick of bombs that splashed harmlessly astern of *Sims*. On the following day, *Yorktown's* aircraft staged an attack against the islands of Makin and Mili, sinking a minesweeper. However, the raid against Jaluit was canceled due to inclement weather.

Between February and May, the Navy was constantly on the move, carrying out hit-and-run strikes against Japanese bases and air fields throughout the Central and South Pacific. During this time, *Sims* took part in the raids against Wake Island and operated in the New Caledonia and Tonga Islands areas. Although these attacks boosted American morale, the Japanese advances through the Pacific could not be stemmed.

During the first week in May 1942, Task Force 17 moved into the Coral Sea to thwart an enemy landing against Port Morseby, New Guinea, and Tulagi, in the Solomon Islands. On the evening of the 6th, the task force, now augmented by the carrier *Lexington* and her group, completed fueling operations and prepared to attack the enemy on the following morning. Meanwhile, *Sims* had been detached to remain with the tanker USS *Neosho*.

On the morning of the 7th, Japanese scouting aircraft were aloft, searching for targets of opportunity. Thanks to a heavily overcast sky, they missed the main body of the task force. Unfortunately, they did sight the ungainly tanker and her lone escort, the *Sims*. The overly excited Japanese pilots reported their find as a cruiser and an aircraft carrier. Their report was all that was needed to spark the fleet carriers *Zuikaku* and *Shokaku* to dispatch 70 fighters and bombers from their flight decks, all bolting toward the ill-fated *Sims* and *Neosho*.

When the first wave of 15 bombers was sighted at 0930, the Americans aboard the two ships braced themselves for the onslaught. Fortunately, these were high-level bombers and their "eggs" were easily evaded. Then 10 more bombers were overhead at about 1038 and, again, neither of the ships was hit. At 1130, however, 36 dive bombers pounced unmercifully upon the two vessels. The sluggish tanker never stood a chance. After suffering seven direct bomb hits, as well as being crashed into by one of her assailants, the *Neosho* was reduced to a mass of burning wreckage. Meanwhile, *Sims* had been zigzagging wildly, her 5-inch guns barking and her .20-mm guns spewing deadly tracers at the swarm of aircraft jumping on her from all sides. Two planes, scorched by her AA guns, burst into flames and tumbled into the sea. But the assault was more than the *Sims* could handle. Bombs splashed and boomed on either side of her, splitting her hull plates open. Three more of her attackers were hit by her gunners and spiraled into the sea close by. Their exploding bombs sprayed the ship with both brine and shrapnel.

Suddenly, it was all over for the *Sims* when three bombs crashed into her amidships section. Exploding in her forward engine room, the gallant ship's keel broke in two. Jackknifing, the *Sims* sank swiftly, stern first, and when her fantail slipped beneath the surface her depth charges detonated. The concussion was so severe that the ship was lifted 15 feet out of the water. Only 14 of her crew survived the battle, and these were picked up by a boat from the *Neosho*, which was ablaze but still afloat.

Eventually, the flames on the tanker were subdued, but *Neosho* was unable to steam under her own power; hence, she drifted about for four days before she was found by the USS *Henley* (DD-409). Considered beyond salvaging, and aware that enemy aircraft and warships were in the area, *Henley* sent the tanker to the bottom with two torpedoes. All told, *Neosho* suffered the loss of 179 personnel, a total larger than necessary because 68 men had prematurely abandoned ship. After drifting aimlessly for ten days on their raft, only four of these men were found, by the USS *Helm* (DD-388).

Though far from the main action in the Battle of the Coral Sea, *Sims* has always been considered a casualty of that battle, which was, after all, the first major naval engagement in which opposing ships never came within sight of each other. Though in this battle the United States was also forced to sacrifice the carrier *Lexington,* and suffered damage to the *Yorktown*, it was here that the seemingly inexorable Japanese drive to the south was stopped. The enemy's next strategic move would be a combined fleet foray to the east— target: Midway.

☆ ☆ ☆

USS *SIMS* (DD-409)

Class: Sims.
Builder: Bath Iron Works, Bath, Maine.
Keel Laid: July 15, 1937.
Launched: April 8, 1939.
Sponsor: Mrs. William S. Sims, widow of Rear Admiral William S. Sims, USN.
Commissioned: August 1, 1939; Lieutenant Commander W.A. Griswold, USN, comdg.

Date of loss: May 7, 1942; Commander W.M. Hyman, USN, comdg.†
Location: Coral Sea.
Awards: Two battle stars.

USS Hammann

Launched February 4, 1939
Lost June 6, 1942
Northeast of Midway Island

ENSIGN CHARLES H. HAMMANN, USN
(1892–1919)

Charles Hazeltine Hammann was born in Baltimore, Maryland, on March 16, 1892, and was appointed to the rank of Ensign, Naval Reserve Flying Corps, on October 14, 1918. Ensign Hammann was awarded the Congressional Medal of Honor for saving the life of a fellow pilot.

While both men were flying seaplanes on patrol off the coast of Italy on August 21, 1918, Hammann's companion's plane developed engine trouble and crashed into the sea. Hammann landed his plane next to the crashed aircraft and took the pilot on board his plane. Although the craft wasn't designed to carry more than one person, Hammann succeeded in flying back to his base safely, despite the constant danger of being attacked by enemy planes. After the war, he remained in the Navy, but was killed in a plane crash while on duty at Langley Field, Virginia, on June 14, 1919.

After having escorted a convoy of British shipping through the North Atlantic, the USS *Hammann* (DD-412) was at anchor in Hvalfjördur, Iceland, on December 7, 1941. At that time, *Hammann* was replenishing stores and fuel in preparation to meet up with another convoy.

On the following day, the destroyer departed Hvalfjördur for the United States, and upon her arrival at the Norfolk Navy Yard, underwent an overhaul that lasted until January 6, 1942. On that date, she and two other destroyers got underway to escort the battleships *New Mexico* and *Mississippi* and the transport *President Hayes* to San Francisco, arriving there on the 22nd. Three days later, *Hammann* and the destroyers *Anderson* (DD-411) and *Morris* (DD-417) left San Francisco escorting a convoy to Pearl Harbor. Shortly thereafter, she and her sister destroyers were outbound for the South Pacific to join up with Task Force 17.

During the first week of May, the Japanese were well established in the Central Pacific and flexing their muscles for a drive into the Solomons and Port Morseby, New Guinea. On the evening of May 3, a report was received that a Japanese convoy embarked with marines was landing on the shores of Guadalcanal and Tulagi. Task Force 17, built around the carriers *Yorktown* and *Lexington*, had already been on the prowl in the Coral Sea in anticipation that the enemy was ready to move south. When this report was received, the task force was finishing refueling, *Yorktown's* tanks being "topped off." Thus, she and her group, composed of four cruisers and six destroyers, were detached to intercept the landings.

At 0700, the group was within 100 miles from the target and, by 0800, *Yorktown's* aircraft were strafing and bombing Florida Island, shooting up landing barges at Tulagi and Gavutu. The strikes continued throughout the day, and by nightfall the Japanese had lost several landing craft, five seaplanes and the destroyer *Kikuzuki*, as well as one destroyer and a minelayer damaged. However, three of the carrier's pilots had not returned. Two had crashed near Henslow Point on Guadalcanal and the other had ditched into the sea. *Hammann* was dispatched to rescue the two pilots on Guadalcanal, while the *Perkins* (DD-337) searched for the third, who unfortunately was never found.

Hammann had better luck, but rescue operations were hampered by increasing darkness and heavy surf. Arriving just before dusk, the destroyer's lookout sighted a parachute on the shore and the whaleboat was lowered. The boat crew was made up of one officer, Ensign P.F. Enright, and five enlisted men.

Unable to make a landing or approach the beach close enough to reach the pilots (Lieutenant E. Scott McCuskey and Ensign John Adams), Coxswain Knapp swam ashore with a line and the pilots were soon hauled on board. Somehow, the boat officer neglected to remind Knapp that the planes had to be destroyed, so one of the pilots had to swim back to shore to burn the planes with a flare from a Very pistol.

By now, darkness had closed in and a rain squall, accompanied by strong winds, caused the boat crew to lose sight of the pilot. Then, to complicate matters further, the line that was secured to the pilot became entangled in the boat's propeller. Boatswain's Mate Jackson then dove into the water with a knife and managed to cut the line free, just in time to prevent the boat from running aground. During this episode, the pilot made it back to the beach and was located by a flare. Jackson once again swam to the shore with the line and both men, exhausted from their ordeal, were hoisted on board and the boat returned to the ship.

On the morning of May 7, the Battle of the Coral Sea erupted. Briefly, both American carriers sustained severe damage, and owing to the fires that ran unchecked throughout *Lexington's* compartments and exploding ammunition, she had to be abandoned. Later, she was sunk by torpedoes from an American destroyer.

During the rescue operations, *Hammann* and the destroyer *Anderson* had to approach the burning carrier cautiously in an effort to avoid running over the men who had been forced to leap into the sea and were cluttered about the fiery hulk. Many of the men were fished out of the water and transported over to other ships in the task force. *Hammann* was then ordered to rescue those on the lee side of the carrier, which was drifting down upon them faster than they could swim away from it. This operation alone was extremely hazardous, for the destroyer could have easily crushed the swimmers between herself and the carrier.

After picking up these men, she transferred them to other ships that were in the area and returned to take on more survivors. By this time, *Lexington's* commander, Captain Frederick C. Sherman, realized his ship was doomed and passed the order to abandon. When she had taken on as many men as she could carry, *Hammann* backed clear of the carrier—and none too soon. Seconds after, a violent explosion vomited a sheet of flame and scattered tons of steel and debris some 300 yards across the water at the exact spot where the *Hammann* had been. Although she did receive a smattering of the debris, no one was seriously injured.

Hammann returned to the "*Lex*" after she had discharged the survivors she carried in order to remove the carrier's executive officer and captain. Over the course of the rescue operations, *Hammann* picked up over 500 men, her crew administering aid and comfort to the wounded. Considering the size of the *Lexington* and the calamitous ordeal her crew had endured, the death toll was light. Out of a crew of over 3,000, only 26 officers and 190 men were killed during the battle. Lost in the sea/air action were 12 of her pilots and flight crews. Miraculously, not one man drowned, but one died later as a result of his wounds.

One month later, *Hammann* took part in the Battle of Midway, in which Japan suffered its first major naval defeat in 350 years and which turned the tide of the Pacific War in America's favor. In the course of this battle, the

Japanese lost four carriers along with the cream of its naval air force. The United States lost the carrier *Yorktown*, a large number of aircraft and the destroyer *Hammann*.

As with the Coral Sea, space here does not permit a full description of the battle. In brief, however, the Japanese began with a heavy attack against the American base on Midway Island, not realizing that heavy U.S. fleet carriers were within striking distance. Consequently the Japanese armada found itself warding off wave after wave of American aircraft, in the process wiping out Torpedo Squadron 8 from *Hornet*. Now aware that U.S. carriers were in the vicinity, the enemy feverishly began to switch the armaments on their aircraft and refuel their planes for a strike on the American fleet. It was just when the enemy flight decks were crammed with planes, bombs, torpedoes and fuel lines that American dive bombers managed to break through the covering screen of Zeros and hit three of the enemy carriers, each of which went up like a Roman candle.

The Japanese had only one carrier left but they launched their few remaining planes at an American fleet that was by now grimly awaiting them. Those planes that managed to get through the American fighter screen ran into a near-solid wall of flak thrown up by the destroyers. Incredibly, and with a harrowing taste of what might have been had all the Japanese carriers been operational, two enemy pilots managed to get through to hit *Yorktown* in their first pass.

After sustaining two bomb hits, one of which disabled her engineering plant, *Yorktown* was able to regain power two hours later. However, a second wave of Japanese swept in and again could not be held at bay, this time tagging the vessel with two torpedoes. Sloughing to a halt, the disabled carrier began to take on a port list. Realizing that the ship's watertight integrity had been weakened from the damage she had suffered in the Battle of the Coral Sea, and, fearing that she could turn turtle at any moment and entomb most of her crew, her captain, Elliott Buckmaster, gave the order to abandon ship.

Now that the battle was over, *Hammann*, along with a number of other destroyers, rushed to the carrier's side and began to remove the crew. However as the day wore on, *Yorktown's* list had not increased and the destroyers *Hughes* and *Gwin* went alongside to put a salvage party on board. When it was reported that the ship might be saved, the destroyers remained there to provide water pressure, thus allowing the crews to fight the fires and pump water and fuel over to the starboard side, managing to alleviate the port list. While salvage operations were being effected, the tug *Viero* took the stricken carrier in tow, in hopes of getting her back to Pearl Harbor.

As the night closed in, the salvage crews were compelled to leave the ship and *Hammann*, along with two other destroyers, screened the carrier throughout the night. On the morning of June 5, *Hammann* went alongside the cruiser *Astoria* to receive Captain Buckmaster and 140 men, and transferred them back to the *Yorktown* to resume salvage operations. *Hammann* remained with the carrier, her fire pumps providing water needed to quell the smoldering fires and continue counter-flooding; she also supplied the salvage parties with sandwiches and coffee.

On the following day, the carrier was still tethered to the straining towline of *Viero* and barely creeping along at eight knots. The fires had been extinguished and she was almost on an even keel, when, at 1534, the destroyermen sighted four creamy-white torpedo wakes streaking toward them and the *Yorktown*. *Hammann*'s gunners opened fire at the oncoming missiles, hoping to detonate them, but their attempt was in vain.

The first torpedo passed under the keel of the *Hammann* and slammed into the carrier. The tremendous explosion lifted and pushed the destroyer away from the *Yorktown*'s side and stove in her hull plating. Seconds later, the second torpedo smashed into *Hammann*'s No. 2 boiler room, broke her keel and shot a column of oil, water, debris and several men into the air. Her captain, Commander Arnold E. True, was hurled across the bridge and suffered a broken rib when he landed against the chart table. *Yorktown* was further blasted by the other two torpedoes, which spelled her doom.

Four minutes after *Hammann* was struck, she plunged to the bottom. Soon afterwards, her depth charges detonated, killing or maiming most of her survivors. The destroyers *Balche* (DD-363) and *Benham* (DD-397) closed in to pick up *Hammann*'s survivors, while other destroyers went in search of the submarine that had daringly penetrated the destroyer screen. Despite severe depth-charge attacks, the wily submarine commander succeeded in evading the hunters.

After the war, it was revealed that the submarine, *I-168*, under the command of Lieutenant Commander Yadachi Tanabe, IJN, was responsible for dealing the death blows to the only two American ships lost in the Battle of Midway. The *Yorktown* remained afloat until 0700 on May 7, when she rolled over and sank.

Meanwhile, *Benham* and *Balche* were racing toward Pearl Harbor with *Hammann*'s wretched survivors as well as those from the *Yorktown*. Out of *Hammann*'s complement of 13 officers and 228 enlisted men, five officers and 71 men were killed as a result of the sinking and the underwater blasting, while 26 others died of their wounds while en route to Pearl Harbor.

☆ ☆ ☆

USS *HAMMANN* (DD-412)

Class: Sims.
Builder: Federal Shipbuilding & Drydock Co., Kearny, New Jersey.
Keel laid: January 17, 1938.
Launched: February 4, 1939.
Sponsor: Miss Lillian Hammann, niece of Ensign Charles H. Hammann, USN.
Commissioned: August 11, 1939; Commander Arnold E. True, USN, comdg.
Date of loss: June 6, 1942; Commander Arnold E. True, USN, comdg.
Location: Northeast of Midway Island.
Awards: Two battle stars.

USS Tucker

Launched February 26, 1936
Lost August 3, 1942
Segond Channel, New Hebrides

CAPTAIN SAMUEL TUCKER, USN
(1747–1833)

Samuel Tucker was born in Marblehead, Massachusetts, on November 1, 1747, and began his naval career as a cabin boy on board the Massachusetts Bay Colony warship *King George.*

During the Revolutionary War, he served brilliantly and with distinction, preying on British shipping while serving as captain of the *Young Phoenix* and the *Franklin.* While in command of the *Hancock,* he transported John Adams across the Atlantic, where he assumed the post of Commissioner to France. Upon his return to the colonies, Captain Tucker assumed command of the *Boston* and continued to harass British merchantmen until the end of the war.

Afterwards, Captain Tucker resigned his commission and went on to command several merchant ships, carrying out trade with various ports in the West Indies and Europe. Upon retiring from the mercantile service, he took up farming in Maine. With the outbreak of the War of 1812, Tucker returned to active naval service and assumed command of a schooner which protected the Maine coast from British privateers. In 1813, he intercepted and captured the British privateer HMS *Crown,* which put an end to the harassment of coastal shipping along the coast of northern New England.

With the end of that war, Captain Tucker changed his residence to Bremen, Massachusetts, and was able to resume his farming. In 1823, he was awarded a comfortable pension from Congress, retroactive to 1818. Later, he became involved in local politics and held various positions of public trust prior to his death at the age of 86 at his home on March 10, 1833.

The USS *Tucker* (DD-374) was one of five destroyers that was moored alongside the destroyer tender *Whitney* at Pearl Harbor when the Japanese struck. Even before the general alarm had sounded, one man was firing a 50-caliber machine gun on the after gun platform at the planes that came swarming in over the naval base on a beeline for the vessels moored at "Battleship Row." Meanwhile, in an effort to get the ship underway, the destroyer's engineers worked feverishly to reassemble machinery that had been torn down for repairs.

After the first wave of planes had retired at about 0810, a second wave of bombers roared in and dropped their loads on the battleships and the airfield on Ford Island. Every ship in the harbor that could fire opened up on the raiders, but only a few were shot down. At 0905, dive bombers screamed down from the skies, heaping additional damage on the now burning and sinking battleships. During the heat of the holocaust, *Tucker's* gunners scored hits against three aircraft and had the satisfaction of seeing one of them crash in flames in a cane field, and another trailing a plume of black smoke as it disappeared over the mountain range.

Like almost every ship in Pearl Harbor on that fateful morning, *Tucker's* captain, her senior officers and most of the crew were ashore on weekend liberty. Before the attack was over, the destroyer was manned and ready, but unable to get underway until later that evening.

From that time until August 1942, *Tucker* was relegated to patrol duties around the approaches to the Hawaiian Islands, also serving as an escort for shipping between Pearl Harbor and West Coast ports and through the South Pacific to ports in Australia and New Zealand.

On August 1, she departed from Suva, Fiji Islands, bound for Espiritu Santo, New Hebrides, escorting the freighter SS *Nira Luckenbach*. On the 4th, as she was approaching her anchorage in the Segond Channel, *Tucker* was shaken by a tremendous explosion in the vicinity of her number one boiler room, which buckled her keel. In an instant, all power was lost and the ship began to jackknife and drift with the current, smothered in a pall of smoke and steam.

From out of the smoke-filled engineering spaces stumbled the burned and shocked engineers. Unfortunately, all hands in number-one boiler room had perished outright. Nearby vessels closed in around the stricken destroyer to receive her survivors. A tug made an attempt to tow her into shallow water; but the effort failed when the *Tucker* suddenly broke in half. The stern section did not sink until the following day, and later the bow was boarded by demolition crews and subsequently scuttled.

Like the *Sturtevant* before her, *Tucker* had stumbled into a newly seeded U.S. minefield and, again, someone failed to pass down this information. The end result was the loss of the *Tucker* and six of her crewmen.

☆ ☆ ☆

USS *TUCKER* (DD-374)

Class: Mahan.
Builder: Norfolk Navy Yard, Portsmouth, Virginia.
Keel laid: August 15, 1943.
Launched: February 26, 1936.
Sponsor: Mrs. Leonard Thorner, a third cousin, twice removed, of Captain Samuel Tucker, USN.
Commissioned: July 23, 1936; Lieutenant Commander G.T. Howard, USN, comdg.
Date of loss: August 3, 1942; Lieutenant Commander W.R. Terrell, USN, comdg.
Location: Segond Channel, New Hebrides.
Awards: One battle star.

USS Jarvis

Launched May 6, 1937
Lost August 9, 1942
South of Guadalcanal

MIDSHIPMAN JAMES C. JARVIS, USN
(1787–1800)

Born in New York, James C. Jarvis was appointed Midshipman at the age of twelve and served in the 38-gun frigate USS *Constellation*, under the command of Commodore Thomas Truxtun. During the famous naval engagement against the 52-gun French frigate *La Vengeance,* on February 2, 1800, Midshipman Jarvis was killed when he refused to leave his battle station, despite its being untenable.

In command of the maintop and with the rigging shot away, a seaman warned Jarvis that the mast was ready to collapse and advised him to leave. However, young Jarvis insisted upon remaining at his station saying, "This is my post! I will not leave it unless ordered to!" Shortly afterwards, the mast toppled over and splashed into the sea, taking Midshipman Jarvis and three other men with it. None of them were ever seen again.

Except for participating in battle maneuvers in the Caribbean and a brief visit to East Coast ports in 1939, the USS *Jarvis* (DD-393) carried out her peacetime operations with the Pacific Fleet. Homeported at San Diego since her commissioning, the destroyer was moved to Pearl Harbor on April 10, 1940, and was there, undergoing repairs, at the time of the Japanese attack.

In spite of the abruptness of the assault, her gunners swiftly manned their battle stations and were soon spraying the skies with their .50-caliber machine guns, splashing four of the raiders. *Jarvis* was in the same predicament as were several other ships under repair that day. Her engines and boilers were dismantled and her decks were cluttered with shipyard workers' paraphenalia: a jumble of cables, air and water hoses, acetylene and oxygen tanks and much more.

While her guns were chattering away, the ship's engineers were desperately trying to reassemble torn-down machinery in an effort to get underway. Yet, during the heat of the action, a crewman was seen calmly walking down the pier to the pumping station where he commenced to pump freshwater into the ship's water tanks.

Also, like many of the ships in the harbor, Jarvis' captain and at least three-quarters of her complement were ashore on weekend liberty. However, by 0945, most of the ship's crew was on board and the destroyer was steaming out of the harbor, despite the fact that her engines and boilers were still partially dismantled. Upon her return to port, repairs were completed and later she was assigned to patrolling duties throughout the Hawaiian Islands. On December 16, she joined up with Task Force 14 to relieve the Marines at Wake Island. The island fell to the enemy, however, before the task force could render assistance.

On January 21, 1942, while operating off the Hawaiian Islands with the carrier Lexington, Jarvis was detached to rendezvous with the navy oiler USS Neches, then en route to Pearl Harbor from San Francisco. On the 23rd, the scheduled date for the meeting, the oiler was nowhere in sight. Several attempts were made to communicate with her, but there was no response. Jarvis then intercepted a message from a patrol aircraft that reported sighting several life rafts and boats and was directing ships to the area. Jarvis sped to the location; arriving at the site at about 1000, she rescued 18 officers and 164 men. The tanker had been torpedoed during the early morning hours of the 23rd and had sunk six hours later.

On January 28, 1942, while patrolling off the island of Molokai, she assisted the ex-destroyer USS Long (DMS-12) in the probable sinking of a submarine. On February 5, the destroyer departed Pearl Harbor, escorting a troop and supply convoy to Brisbane, Australia, arriving there on the 26th. March 7th saw the Jarvis escorting a flock of merchant ships to Nouméa, New Caledonia; from there she proceeded on to Pearl Harbor, escorting the Navy freighter Honolulu en route.

Sorely in need of a refitting and an overhaul, Jarvis sailed for the United States and entered the Mare Island Navy Yard, Vallejo, California, on April 15. After repairs were completed, the destroyer and her crew bade farewell to the United States for the last time on May 9, headed back for Hawaii, where she arrived on the 18th. Three days later, Jarvis, was underway, serving as an escort for a troop convoy en route to Suva, Fiji Island. During the next three months, she was allocated to serve on escort duty throughout the

South Pacific while the United States built up its armed forces and trained for the upcoming thrust against the Japanese, then well entrenched in the Solomons.

On August 7, following a naval and aerial bombardment, the First Marine Division swarmed over the shores of Guadalcanal and Tulagi—the first American amphibious operation in World War II. Offshore, *Jarvis* joined in with other supporting naval units, keeping a sharp surveillance against the intervention of enemy warships and aircraft that were expected to strike back at the invaders.

That afternoon, a wave of Japanese aircraft, composed of some 32 bombers, was repulsed by Marine fighter aircraft and anti-aircraft fire from the screening ships, the enemy losing 14 planes to the Americans' 12. During this action, the destroyer *Mugford* (DD-389) was heavily damaged by a bomb, but none of the Japanese planes were able to reach the transports.

All was tense but quiet until noon on the following day, when a swarm of 30 to 40 torpedo bombers came skimming in low over Savo Sound, determined to sink the offloading ships. Forewarned of this impending attack, the transports and cargo ships were underway and maneuvered about, dodging torpedoes and lashing the attackers with AA fire. One of the planes, reduced to a fiery ball of wreckage, crashed into the transport *George F. Elliot,* causing such severe damage that the ship had to be scuttled later that day.

During the height of this action, *Jarvis* was struck by a torpedo that tore a 50-foot hole in her forward boiler room, killing fourteen men and wounding seven others. Enshrouded in a pall of smoke and billowing steam, the wounded destroyer crawled to a stop. Thanks to her repair parties, the fires were swiftly extinguished, and after the battle was over the destroyer *Dewey* (DD-349) took the *Jarvis* under tow to Lunga Point.

Here, the engineers were able to restore power and the ship was considered seaworthy enough to steam on to Sydney, Australia. Indeed, this was a bold decision for her skipper, Lieutenant Commander William W. Graham, Jr., to take upon himself and his crew, since his ship would have to steam through enemy waters in which she would doubtless prove to be an easy target for a lurking submarine or a swarm of aircraft. Yet, despite these odds, the crew was willing to give it a try.

Since the hull had sprung several leaks, it was decided to remove all excessive topside gear, including her torpedoes, life rafts and boats, in an effort to reduce weight and ensure the stability of the ship. After testing her engines, which performed satisfactorily, Rear Admiral R.K. Turner was notified that the *Jarvis* was ready to steam under her own power. Although Lieutenant Commander Graham had obtained permission from Admiral Turner to get underway, he apparently did not receive the order that he was to stand by for an escort. Hence, just before midnight, *Jarvis* slipped her cable and, unknowingly, skirted past the infamous Battle of Savo Island.

As she limped toward Cape Esperance, a group of Japanese destroyers and cruisers swept past her at a distance of 3,000 yards. Mistaken for a light cruiser, *Jarvis* was fired upon by the IJN *Yunagi*, while another enemy cruiser let fly with a brace of torpedoes. It is quite probable that *Yunagi* succeeded in damaging *Jarvis*, but no one will ever know for certain.

Later, the USS *Blue* (DD-387), then on picket duty—which had missed the enemy warships that had dashed into the sound—sighted the crippled *Jarvis* slogging along at about eight knots. After being assured that the destroyer was friendly, *Blue* returned to her picket station. Not long after, *Jarvis* rounded Cape Esperance and proceeded on her southbound course.

At dawn, she was last seen by a scout aircraft from the carrier *Saratoga*. The pilot's report was indeed a bleak one. The gallant destroyer was trailing a stream of oil in her wake; she was down by the head and barely making progress to the south. The pilot was the last American to set eyes on *Jarvis*, and her fate was unknown until after the war.

According to the war diary of the IJN *Yunagi*, she had damaged a "light cruiser" that was last seen off Cape Esperance attempting to flee on a southerly heading from Guadalcanal. This message was picked up at Rabaul and a flight of Japanese aircraft from the 25th Air Flotilla were ordered to take wing and search for the vessel. The crippled *Jarvis* was sighted shortly before 1300 on August 9. After undergoing a savage raking of machine-gun fire, she was reported to have split in two and sank after being torpedoed. Lacking lifeboats and rafts, Lieutenant Commander Graham and his crew of 247 souls were lost with the ship.

☆ ☆ ☆

USS JARVIS (DD-392)

Class: Craven.
Builder: Puget Sound Navy Yard, Bremerton, Washington.
Keel laid: August 21, 1935.
Launched: May 6, 1937.
Sponsor: Mrs. Thomas T. Craven, wife of Vice Admiral Thomas T. Craven, USN.
Commissioned: October 27, 1937; Lieutenant Commander R.R. Ferguson, USN, comdg.

Date of loss: August 9, 1942; Lieutenant Commander W.W. Graham, USN,
    comdg.†
Location: South of Guadalcanal.
Awards: three battle stars.

USS Ingraham

Launched February 15, 1941
Lost August 22, 1942
North Atlantic

CAPTAIN DUNCAN N. INGRAHAM, USN/CSN
(1802–1891)

Duncan Nathaniel Ingraham was born in Charleston, South Carolina, on December 6, 1802. Appointed Midshipman at the age of ten, he served in the War of 1812 and in the war against Mexico. After many years of distinguished service, he was promoted to the rank of Captain on September 14, 1855.

While commanding the sloop-of-war *St. Louis* in the eastern Mediterranean, he secured the release of Martinoszta, a Hungarian exile who had tried to become American citizen. At the time, Martinoszta had been seized and confined on board the Austrian ship *Hussar.* For his outstanding diplomatic performance in this affair, Ingraham was given thanks from Congress and awarded a gold medal.

Captain Ingraham resigned his commission from the United States Navy on February 4, 1861, to enter the Confederate States Navy. Appointed the rank of Captain, he was placed in command of the Confederate naval forces along the coast of South Carolina throughout most of the Civil War. Captain Ingraham died at his home in Charleston, on October 16, 1891.

A ssigned to the Atlantic Fleet destroyer squadrons upon her acceptance by the Navy, the USS *Ingraham* (DD-444) served continuously on convoy duty in Atlantic waters, from prior to the United States' entry into World War II until her tragic loss on August 22, 1942.

On that date, *Ingraham* was part of Task Force 37, composed of the battleship *New York*, light cruiser *Philadelphia*, the Navy oil tanker *Chemung* and nine destroyers. The task force was escorting Convoy AT-20, which was made up of ten transports en route to the United Kingdom.

Having departed Halifax shortly before noon, the voyage began without incident, but at 1730 the radar operator on the transport *Letitia* detected what appeared to be a surfaced submarine. Both *Ingraham* and the destroyer *Swanson* (DD-443) were ordered to investigate; both ships spent an hour combing the area, but only made contact with a school of blackfish.

As darkness closed in, the vessels began to stray from the formation and, as a result, the destroyers were hard-pressed to lead them to their proper stations. Then, at 2000, the convoy became enshrouded in a pea-soup fog. Before long, the *Letitia* had drifted so far from the group that the USS *Buck* (DD-420) was dispatched to guide her back to the formation. As the destroyer sliced through the thick, gray mist, she cut across the bow of the SS *Awatea*. The huge, black mass of steel crashed into the *Buck's* fantail, dislodging depth charges over the side that detonated beneath her stern and almost blew it off.

The news of this disaster was flashed throughout the convoy and *Ingraham* was ordered to go to *Buck's* assistance. Immediately, Commander Haynsworth swung his destroyer around and sped through the opaque darkness, only to cross in front of the SS *Chemung's* bow. With no time, or even the ability, to swerve away from the warship, the heavily laden tanker plunged into the after section of the *Ingraham,* heeling her over on her beam's end and shoving her ahead as if she were a snow plow. The violent impact catapulted several men overboard.

Then, suddenly, *Ingraham* exploded internally and, just as swiftly, was ablaze from stem to stern. *Chemung's* bow was blown open from the concussion and scorched by the intense heat from the raging fires. Several men in that area suffered burns and injuries from flying debris. As quickly as possible, boats were lowered in an attempt to rescue men from the now fiercely burning destroyer, but the searing heat prevented rescuers from approaching the fiery hulk.

Seemingly in a flash, it was all over as the sizzling wreck suddenly vanished beneath the waves. The *Chemung* lay to, a black shadow, still enveloped in fog, while her boat crews searched the area for survivors from the destroyer. Sadly, only one officer and ten crewmen were found.

What caused *Ingraham* to explode is still a mystery. However, it is probable that her depth charges had detonated below decks after the collision, in turn igniting the ammunition in one of her after magazines. The chain reaction of blasts that followed, throughout the length of the ship, amounted to a swift and certain doom.

☆ ☆ ☆

USS *Ingraham* (DD-444)

Class: Benson/Livermore.
Builder: Charleston Navy Yard, Charleston, South Carolina.
Keel laid: November 15, 1939.
Launched: February 15, 1941.
Sponsor: Mrs. George I. Hutchinson, granddaughter of Captain Duncan N.
    Ingraham, USN / CSN.
Commissioned: July 17, 1941; Lieutenant Commander W.M. Haynsworth,
    USN, comdg.
Date of loss: August 22, 1942; Commander W.M. Haynsworth, USN, comdg.†
Location: North Atlantic.
Awards: None.

USS Blue

Launched on May 27, 1937
Lost on August 22, 1942
Savo Sound, the Solomons

REAR ADMIRAL VICTOR BLUE, USN
(1865–1928)

Born in Richmond County, North Carolina, Victor Blue graduated from the U.S. Naval Academy in 1887. While holding the rank of lieutenant, he was advanced five numbers for his excellent intelligence missions in Cuba during the Spanish-American War. Between 1913 and 1916, he served as Chief of the Bureau of Navigation, and later assumed command of the battleship *New York* during her service with the 6th Battle Squadron in World War I.

Prior to his retirement in 1919, he again held the office of the Chief of the Bureau of Navigation. Rear Admiral Blue died on January 22, 1928.

Upon the completion of her shakedown trials along the eastern seaboard and in Caribbean waters, the USS *Blue* (DD-387) was assigned to the Pacific Fleet in August 1938 and was designated flagship of DesDiv 7, Battle Force. Homeported at the destroyer base at San Diego, the ship carried out her training exercises along the California coast and participated in maneuvers with the Pacific Fleet until April 1940, when her division's homeport was shifted to Pearl Harbor.

Although she was caught up in the holocaustic attack on Pearl Harbor, and with only four junior officers on board (all Ensigns) and a handful of enlisted men, she managed to leave the harbor and succeeded in shooting down four Japanese aircraft.

The senior Ensign, N.S. Asher, suddenly found himself the acting captain of the destroyer and immediately ordered the ship's gunners to commence firing. Less than five minutes after the attack began, her 50-caliber guns were chattering away, followed by the cracking of her 5-inch guns. Forty-seven minutes later, *Blue* was steaming out to sea, her half-warmed engines churning out 25 knots, her guns still blazing away.

Outside the harbor, the cruiser *St. Louis* was sighted maneuvering evasively; she ordered *Blue* to screen her against enemy submarines that were reported to be lying in wait for the ships as they left the harbor. Soon afterwards, *Blue's* sonar operator made an underwater contact and, after two depth-charge attacks, a large oil slick some 200 feet wide rose to the surface, accompanied by huge frothing bubbles. Unfortunately, the loss of the submarine could not be confirmed. Then another sonar contact indicated that a second submarine was close by and probably had the cruiser in its sights. However, another depth charge attack from the *Blue* drove off the submarine and probably damaged her.

After a 30-hour stint at sea, the destroyer re-entered port. Later, Ensign Asher praised the conduct of the crew and lauded the invaluable aid given by the chiefs and the leading petty officers.

Blue was in action again two months later off the Marshall Islands while escorting a task force built around the carrier *Enterprise*. When five twin-engined Japanese aircraft attacked, a lone American fighter swooped in on the raiders, shooting down one that crashed alongside the carrier, while another was seen burning and eventually hit the sea. *Blue* managed to get off four rounds from her 5-inch guns as the remaining aircraft fled, one of which was seen to burst into flames. Two hours later, another attack followed, but the planes were driven off by anti-aircraft fire.

Blue commenced escorting shipping between Pearl Harbor and San Francisco up until early June. During one arrival at Pearl, the furious Battle of Midway was in progress. Hence, she was ordered to refuel and, in company with another destroyer, escort a tanker with orders that read: "Get the tanker through at all costs!" While still en route to their destination, however, the ships were diverted to Midway Island. The outcome of this decisive battle wasn't realized until *Blue* had returned to Pearl.

It wasn't long before *Blue* was being prepared for the invasion of the Solomon Islands. Having escorted a troop convoy to New Zealand, she then participated in amphibious operations off New Zealand prior to the anticipated landings on Guadalcanal and Tulagi.

Although the initial American landings on these islands were virtually unopposed, the ships offloading supplies and troops were hindered by occasional air attacks. It was at this time that the *Jarvis* was blasted by an aerial torpedo, and the *George F. Elliot (AP-12)* had to be scuttled after being severely damaged by a crashing Japanese aircraft.

On the night of August 8–9, while *Blue* was guarding the southwestern approach into Savo Sound, the destroyer *Ralph Talbot* (DD-390) was patrolling off the northwestern side of Savo Island. As luck would have it, both destroyers were steaming on a course opposite the entrance to the sound when a force of Japanese warships composed of five heavy and two light cruisers and one destroyer swept into Savo Sound. Suffice to say, the night action that followed, in which the United States Navy lost three cruisers and the Australian Navy lost the cruiser HMAS *Canberra*, was a serious defeat for the Allied forces. Blamed variously on inexperience, the shortage of ships, inclement weather and improper use of radar surveillance, there was an element of luck involved in the Japanese entering Savo Sound undetected, and additional credit can be given to the designers of that navy's "long-lance" torpedo.

Just shortly after midnight on the 9th, *Blue* left her patrolling sector to investigate a slow moving vessel seen leaving Savo Sound. This ship was none other than the damaged USS *Jarvis*. In the meantime, the ferocious battle of Savo Sound had boomed on. Shortly after daybreak, *Blue* went to the assistance of the destroyer *Patterson* (DD-392), which was alongside the *Canberra*, attempting to fight her fires and rescue her survivors.

During the early morning hours of August 21, *Blue*, in company with the *Henley* (DD-391) and *Helm* (DD-388), was escorting a group of ships into Lengo Channel when her radar operator reported contacting a line of ships, that proved to be American high-speed transports (APDs). Then, just before 0400, her radar made another surface contact and, at the same time, her sonarman picked up the sound of high-speed propeller noises. Almost immediately afterward, two ominous, phosphorescent torpedo wakes were seen spearheading toward the ship. Orders were shouted: "Full speed ahead; full right rudder!" But it was too late.

Struck on the starboard side aft, the tremendous explosion shook the destroyer from truck to keel. Both propeller shafts were damaged and her after steering room wrecked, power being temporarily lost on her main electrical switchboard. Eight men were killed and 22 wounded. Although badly crippled, with her after compartments flooded and her stern almost blown off, her watertight bulkheads and doors prevented the *Blue* from foundering.

At dawn, the *Henley* attempted to tow the destroyer to Lunga Roads, which proved to be a difficult task due to *Blue's* damaged stern ready to break off. At 0709, the towline snapped. A Marine tank lighter, along with ten landing craft, then arrived to take over the task, and the *Henley* was ordered to cover a cargo vessel discharging supplies off Tulagi. Later, *Henley* returned and once more attempted to tow the *Blue*, but again the towline parted. Attempts to tow her alongside also failed and, as the day dragged into the night, other vessels joined in to assist. The struggle to tow the *Blue* to a safe anchorage continued until late into the 22nd.

Rear Admiral Turner then ordered that the destroyer be towed to Tulagi. But before the task could be completed, a dispatch was received that a large Japanese naval force was reported to be oiling down the "Slot" (New Georgia Sound). This distressing news prompted the destroyer division commander, Commander Robert H. Smith, in the *Blue*, to recommend that the *Blue* be scuttled to prevent her from falling into enemy hands. The recommendation was approved by Admiral Turner and at 2100 the watertight doors were opened and the destroyer was left to sink.

In his memoirs, Edward F. Hannah, Jr., describes the final moments of the USS *Blue*: "At about 1800, it was decided to give up the ship. As a member of the damage control party I had assisted in opening all water lines, all watertight doors and shutting down the bilge pumps. Prior to leaving the ship, I checked the officers' and CPO quarters to ensure that none of the crew were left behind.

"While passing through the CPO quarters I picked up two blankets and upon reaching the main deck I found that it was deserted. Then, I heard someone shout from the deck of the *Henley*, which was secured alongside the ship: 'Where the hell is Hannah?' Thus I had attained the dubious honor of having been the last man to leave the ship!

"In an effort to speed the *Blue* to the bottom, *Henley* tried to finish her off with a torpedo, but it missed. Several rounds of 5-inch shells were then fired into her, one of which must have struck her boilers, causing a huge explosion and large cloud of steam. Soon afterwards, the *Blue* began to roll over, with her stern going down first. Then, after a brief pause, her bow shot straight up in the air and she plunged swiftly to the floor of Iron Bottom Sound."

After the war, it was confirmed that *Blue* had been torpedoed by the destroyer IJN *Kawakaze*, which had just disembarked a landing force on Guadalcanal.

☆ ☆ ☆

USS *BLUE* (DD-387)

Class: Craven.
Builder: Norfolk Navy Yard, Portsmouth, Virginia.

Keel laid: September 25, 1935.
Launched: May 27, 1937.
Sponsor: Miss Kate L. Blue, sister of Rear Admiral Victor Blue, USN.
Commissioned: August 14, 1937; Lieutenant Commander J. Wright, USN,
    comdg.
Date of loss: August 22, 1942; Commander H. N. Williams, USN, comdg.
Location: Savo Sound, the Solomons.
Awards: Five battle Stars.

Author's note: A later destroyer, DD-744, was also named in honor of Rear Admiral
Victor Blue's son, Lieutenant Commander John S. Blue, USN, who was killed when his
ship USS *Juneau* (CL-52) was sunk during the Naval Battle of Guadalcanal, November
13, 1942.

USS Duncan

Launched on February 20, 1942
Lost on October 12, 1942
Off Savo Island, the Solomons

COMMANDER SILAS DUNCAN, USN
(1788–1834)

Born in Rockaway, New Jersey, in 1788, Silas Duncan was appointed Midshipman on November 15, 1809. While serving in the gunboat *Enterprise* during the Battle of Lake Champlain, he was sent in a gig to order the gunboat *Allen* to retire. Despite the heavy fusillade of gunfire, and suffering a severe wound, he succeeded in delivering the message to the *Allen's* commander. For his gallantry under intense fire, he received a commendation from the U.S. Congress. During his twenty-five years of U.S. Navy service, he served on the frigates *Hornet, Independence, Guerrière, Ferret* and *Cayne*. Although he had lost his right arm, he continued to serve in the Navy until his death at White Sulphur Springs on September 14, 1834.

Owing to the critical shortage of destroyers during the opening months of the war, the USS *Duncan* (DD-485) was rushed through her shakedown trials and battle-readiness exercises and immediately assigned to escort convoys through the U-boat infested waters of the Atlantic and Caribbean. With the battles against the Japanese growing in magnitude and intensity, however, *Duncan* was shortly reassigned. On August 21, 1942, the destroyer transited the Panama Canal in company with the battleship *South Dakota* and destroyers *Landsdowne* (DD-486) and *Lardner* (DD-487) and set a course for the South Pacific.

Arriving at Espiritu Santo, New Hebrides, on September 14, *Duncan* became a unit of Task Force 17, and, after replenishing stores and fuel, set sail for Guadalcanal as escort for a convoy of supply ships and transports carrying the 7th Marine Regiment. On the following day, tragedy struck, when the American destroyer screen failed to interfere with a counterscreen of Japanese submarines. By the time it was over, the enemy submarines *I-15* and *I-19* had torpedoed the carrier *Wasp*, the destroyer *O'Brien* (DD-415) and the battleship *North Carolina*.

Within a short time, *Wasp* was transformed into an exploding mass of fiery wreckage. *Duncan* and *Lansdowne* were dispatched to rescue the carrier's personnel while other destroyers went in search of the elusive predators. Of the 701 survivors that *Duncan* rescued, 20 were wounded. These were delivered to the base hospital at Espiritu Santo. Meanwhile, *Wasp* was given the coup de grâce from torpedoes fired by the *Landsdowne*. Despite having had her bow partially blown off, *O'Brien* managed to steam under her own power.

During early October, *Duncan* was attached to Task Force 64.2 under Rear Admiral Norman Scott in the heavy cruiser *San Francisco*. On the night of October 11, the task force was patrolling between Cape Esperance and Savo Island, lying in wait for an enemy bombardment and replenishment force, which had been sighted churning down the "Slot" earlier that day.

Steaming in a single column, the task force was led by the destroyer *Farenholt* (DD-491), flagship of Captain R.G. Tobin, ComDesRon 12. Astern of her were *Duncan*, *Laffey* (DD-459), cruisers *San Francisco*, *Boise*, *Salt Lake City* and *Helena*, and destroyers *Buchanan* (DD-484) and *McCalla* (DD-488), respectively.

The time was 2325 when *Helena* made the first radar contact with the enemy. However, for an unknown reason, she allowed 15 minutes to elapse before she reported this. Five minutes later, the pilot in *San Francisco's* scout plane reported sighting the enemy dashing through the hot, humid night, directly into the path of Admiral Scott's force.

The Japanese bombardment group was under the command of Rear Admiral Aritomo Goto in the cruiser *Aoba*, with the cruisers *Furataka* and *Kinugasa* following in his wake. Screening the column on the right was the destroyer *Fubuki* and on the left was the *Murakumo*. Astern of the bombardment force followed the reinforcement group, composed of two seaplane carriers and six destroyers carrying troops and supplies for General Kawaguchi's garrison on Guadalcanal.

Unlike the first Battle of Savo Sound, where confusion reigned supreme—owing to sketchy information and the underestimating of the enemy's strength—the situation now was different. Not only was Scott ready for the expected onslaught, Goto wasn't prepared for a naval engagement; hence, his ships' battle stations were not fully manned. And, at the ready was bombardment ammunition, rather than armor-piercing projectiles. Also in Scott's favor was Goto's lack of radar and his good fortune to cross Goto's "T."

At the time the report was received, Scott's group was approaching the northwestern side of Savo Island and he ordered his ships to reverse course, employing a counter-march maneuver. The tail-end destroyers and the cruisers executed the turn smartly, however, the van destroyers made the swing a few minutes too late. These now had to churn out the knots to race down the starboard flank of the cruisers in an effort to regain their proper spots in the formation. Actually, only *Farenholt* and *Laffey* were bolting on ahead, for when the hairpin turn was executed, *Duncan's* skipper, Lieutenant Commander Edmund B. Taylor, had become confused in the darkness, and assumed that his squadron commander was preparing to attack the enemy force. Thus, *Duncan* plunged headlong and alone into the mouths of the enemy's guns and, eventually, the fire of the American cruisers as well.

The broadside bombardment from Scott's cruisers astounded and bewildered Goto as a cyclone of 6- and 8-inch shells burst and crashed into his flagship. Believing that the ships from his reinforcement group were mistakenly firing on him, he ordered a sharp right turn. In doing so, he exposed his port broadside to the thundering guns of Scott's cruisers and destroyers. Like moving targets in a shooting gallery, Goto's ships marched directly into the path of hot steel.

At the height of this engagement, Scott ordered his cruisers to cease firing when he observed *Farenholt* and *Laffey* dashing down the length of his column and directly into the line of fire of his own ships' guns. Owing to the din and cacophony of the battle, the cruiser captains did not hear the order and continued to lambast the Japanese ships with devastating shellfire.

The outgoing salvos reduced *Aoba's* bridge into a mass of tangled wreckage and mortally wounded Admiral Goto. Unfortunately, *Duncan* had run into this barrage and was struck in her forward fire room. However, just prior to receiving this hit, she had opened fire and let fly with two torpedoes at *Furutaka*, at the same time turning her 5-inch guns upon *Murakumo*. *Murukumo* replied in turn, her projectiles smashing into *Duncan's* gun director. These damaged her forward stack, knocked out her forward fire room and crashed into her No. 2 ammunition-handling room, setting its gunpowder ablaze. Also damaged were her radio coding and radar plotting rooms. In addition, communications were lost from the bridge to all her engineering spaces. After this blow, *Duncan* reeled out of the battle, staggering along in circles, her forecastle and bridge engulfed in flames and roiling smoke.

With one fire room completely demolished, *Duncan's* speed was reduced to 15 knots. Consequently, with all telephone circuits killed, the ship's engineers were unaware of the life-and-death struggle that was taking place above them, and remained at their battle stations. The fires up forward were out of control and consuming everything in their path. Before long, the captain and the bridge personnel found themselves trapped, the flames towering around them on all sides. The only means of escaping the conflagration was to jump overboard.

Although the order was passed to abandon ship, most of the personnel below decks were not aware of it and continued to man their battle stations. Topside, despite the ship still being underway, all hands who acknowledged the order managed to get the wounded into life rafts and away from the fiery vessel.

One officer still aboard, Assistant Gunnery Officer Ensign Frank Andrews, sensed that "something was wrong." Upon leaving his battle station, he was horrified to see the main decks deserted, the entire forward section of the ship smothered in smoke and raging fires, and the ship plunging ahead completely out of control. With the assistance of a chief torpedoman, he was able to regain steering from the after emergency conning station. Believing that the captain had perished in the fires that were consuming the bridge, he sent a man down to the forward engine room to notify the Chief Engineer, Lieutenant H.R. Kabat, of the adverse conditions topside. Finding himself the only senior officer on board, Kabat assumed command and ordered the stricken destroyer to be steered into shallow water to prevent her from sinking.

Unfortunately, this attempt failed when the intense heat forced the engineers out of the forward engine room. In doing so, the distilling plant had to be shut down, thus cutting off the supply of water for her after boilers. Consequently, the water in the reserve feed water tanks was soon depleted and the boilers had to be secured. As the steam pressure dropped, *Duncan* gradually lost headway and sloughed to a halt. Shortly afterwards, the remainder of the crew abandoned the fiery wreck, clinging to anything that could float. As the survivors swam frantically away from the burning ship, her ammunition began to explode, but the fiery *Duncan* continued to remain afloat.

By this time, the battle was over and the Japanese were hightailing it back up the "Slot." Severely damaged was the *Aoba* and, left behind on the bottom of Savo Sound, were the cruiser *Furataka* and the destroyer *Fubuki*.

Meanwhile, the destroyer *McCalla*, having sighted the burning *Duncan*, initially believed her to be an enemy vessel, and approached cautiously. However, when it was verified that the smoke- and flame-shrouded ship was indeed *Duncan*, *McCalla's* captain, Commander W.G. Cooper, eased along-side and sent a salvage party aboard to fight the fires. But with the ship's ammunition exploding, it was feared that *Duncan* could suddenly go under, so all hands were ordered to abandon her. As *McCalla* was pulling away, shouts for help were heard across the darkened seascape. *McCalla's* lifeboats were lowered and made their way toward *Duncan's* first wave of survivors, arriving just in time to thwart a concentrated shark attack against the exhausted men. By daybreak, *McCalla* had succeeded in rescuing all that remained of *Duncan's* men in the water.

Duncan's fire-gutted hulk continued to burn and smolder until just before noon on the 12th, when she vanished beneath the surface under a pillar of smoke and rumbling explosions, about six miles north of Savo Island.

Lost with the *Duncan* during the engagement and its aftermath were 50 members of her crew.

☆ ☆ ☆

USS *DUNCAN* (DD-485)

Class: Benson / Livermore.
Builder: Federal Shipbuilding & Drydock Co., Kearny, New Jersey.
Keel laid: July 31, 1941.
Launched: February 20, 1942.
Sponsor: Mrs. Dorothy G. Thayer, first cousin, three times removed, of
    Commander Silas Duncan, USN.
Commissioned: April 16, 1942; Lieutenant Commander E.B. Taylor, USN,
    comdg.
Date of loss; October 12, 1942; Lieutenant Commander E.B. Taylor, USN,
    comdg.
Location: Off Savo Island, the Solomons.
Awards: One battle star.

USS Meredith

Launched April 24, 1940
Lost October 15, 1942
Near San Cristobal Island, the Solomons

SERGEANT JONATHAN MEREDITH, USMC
(1772–1805)

Jonathan Meredith was born in Bucks County, Pennsylvania, in 1772 and enlisted in the United States Marine Corps on June 6, 1803. On August 3, 1805, while serving in the USS *Vixen*, he saved the life of Lieutenant John Trippe, USN, while engaged in a boarding attack upon a Tripolitan warship. Despite the odds against the Americans in this engagement, they emerged victorious. Unfortunately, four days later, Sergeant Meredith was killed when his ship, *Gunboat No. 3*, blew up during another vicious battle against a Barbary Coast vessel.

A ssigned to the Atlantic Fleet, the USS *Meredith* (DD-434) served on the neutrality patrol along the eastern seaboard and in the Caribbean until mid-September 1941, when she was ordered to serve as a convoy escort. After a long and arduous voyage through the North Atlantic, the destroyer arrived at Hvalfjördur, Iceland, on the 28th. From there, she patrolled the Denmark Strait, where on October 17 she rescued survivors from the torpedoed British merchant ship SS *Empire Wave*. *Meredith* continued to carry out her patrols in those frigid waters until January 31, 1942, when she set sail for the Norfolk Navy Yard, Portsmouth, Virginia. Arriving there in mid-February, she underwent a well-deserved shipyard overhaul.

Upon completion of repairs, *Meredith* found herself assigned to the hard-pressed Pacific Fleet. On April 2, she cleared San Francisco for Pearl Harbor, and shortly afterwards participated in the screen for the aircraft carrier *Hornet* in its famous mission to launch Lieutenant Colonel James Doolittle's sixteen B-25 bombers for their daring bombing raid on the Japanese homeland. After the planes were launched, the task force beat a hasty retreat to Pearl Harbor.

Later, *Meredith* was deployed to the South Pacific and during the next six months was busily engaged in convoy work between Australian ports, Espiritu Santo and Guadalcanal.

On October 12, *Meredith*, in company with the destroyer *Nicholas* (DD-449), departed Espiritu Santo for Guadalcanal, escorting a ragtag convoy made up of two cargo ships, the minesweeper USS *Vireo* and the ex-gunboat USS *Jamestown,* each vessel towing barges carrying ammunition, bombs and aviation gasoline. The small convoy was off San Cristobal Island on the morning of the 15th when it was sighted by a scout plane from the Japanese carrier *Shokaku.* There was very little doubt in the minds of the men that the Japanese pilot had radioed his discovery back to the carrier, and this meant trouble was to come.

The cargo ships and *Jamestown* were ordered to return to Espiritu Santo with the *Nicholas*, while *Meredith* and *Vireo* plodded on to Guadalcanal. Then, at 1050, two aircraft swooped down upon the duo, but were repulsed by *Meredith's* gunners. Shortly after, word was received that two enemy ships were not far off *Meredith's* position. Her captain, Commander Harry E. Hubbard, then ordered *Vireo* to make a run for it; however, the vessel could only make 15 knots and with very little firepower to defend herself, Commander Hubbard decided to take her crew on board his destroyer and sink the *Vireo* to prevent her from being captured by the enemy. Then, before he could do so, a swarm of 27 dive bombers and torpedo planes were sighted closing in on the lone destroyer.

Despite the intense hail of anti-aircraft fire that was thrown up against the attackers, all but three planes got through. Assailed under a rain of bombs, raked by machine-gun fire and tagged by a torpedo, *Meredith* was virtually blown to pieces and sank within twenty minutes. The first bomb hit near No.2 5-inch gun battery and exploded below deck, while another bomb crashed just forward of No. 1 stack. A third bomb exploded near the fantail, with another striking and wrecking the carpenter shop. Lieutenant Charles J. Bates was thrown into the air and landed in a heap on the flying bridge. Picking up a sub-machine gun, he blazed away at six different torpedo planes that were approaching the starboard side of the ship.

Elsewhere, Boatswain's Mate Second Class W.R. Singletary, gun captain of No.2 5-inch gun battery, who had found his gun reduced to scrap, ran to man one of the 20-mm guns on the starboard side, just in time to splash two of the six torpedo bombers as they dropped their steel fish and simultaneously began to strafe the destroyer's decks. Although the torpedoes missed, Meredith's moment had come when six additional torpedo bombers were sighted closing in on her starboard side aft and amidships. Three of their torpedoes passed under Meredith's amidships, while another struck her in the stern, exploding her depth charges and blowing that part of the ship off. Again, the decks of the ship were raked by machine-gun fire that killed most of the Americans left manning the anti-aircraft guns. The remaining number of enemy planes, 18 in all, were dive bombers. One of these was shot down by Fireman First Class Joseph Hoban, who at one time remarked that he would never leave his gun until he shot down an enemy plane. He continued to remain at his post and was last seen, still in the harness of his gun, when Meredith slipped beneath the surface.

On the bridge, Commander Hubbard, blinded, severely burned about his face and hands, and somewhat disoriented, asked Lieutenant Bates what had happened. Only two minutes had passed since the initial attack and, seeing the ship beginning to go down by the bow, Bates notified the captain that his ship was foundering. Hubbard then gave the word to abandon ship.

There wasn't time to lower the whaleboat or the captain's gig and, while the men were cutting the life rafts loose and going over the side, enemy planes swept in again and strafed the men in the water. One of them dropped a bomb, which exploded close to Lieutenant Bates. Although stunned by the explosion, he was not injured. Sitting on a raft, some distance from the ship, he was able to see the final damage inflicted on the destroyer before she went under. The depth-charge racks and part of the stern were gone; one of the propeller shafts was twisted; and the No.4 5-inch gun mount was a mass of twisted wreckage.

After strafing the survivors, the enemy planes withdrew. Then Lieutenant Bates went to the aid of several officers and men who were struggling in the water, pulling them up on his raft.

The abandoned Vireo, meanwhile, had escaped the wrath of the short but savage assault. Later, a raft with an officer and several men on board attempted to paddle toward her. But a strong wind had risen, causing the Vireo to drift away faster than the raft could move. Eventually the raft made it to the minesweeper and the men were picked up on the 21st by the destroyer USS Grayson (DD-435).

Now scattered about the fuel-coated water were the shocked, burned and wounded from Meredith, clinging to bits and pieces of wreckage. Those who were fortunate enough to make it to the rafts and floater nets would still have an excruciating ordeal facing them.

On Lieutenant Bates' raft, all of the officers except the Medical Officer, Lieutenant J.Z. Bowers, were either wounded or incoherent. Bowers took command of the situation and organized the men, allowing six at a time to sit on the sides of the raft to rest. The balance of the room in the rafts was taken up by the most seriously wounded, including *Meredith's* captain, who would be among the first to die. One officer was so delirious that every so often he would jump up and shout, "Ship Ahoy!" and would then sit down. Later that evening he stood up and stepped off the raft, swam away and was never seen again. Provisions for survival were scarce: one raft had its sea ration kits destroyed in the attack and Bates' raft had but one 5-gallon water cask, one box of provisions and a first-aid kit. Over the next three days, each man would receive one-half teaspoon of water each day.

The first morning dawned bright and clear, but every man was covered with oil. Also saturated with oil were the rations, and those who tried them soon vomited. Just before noon they had their first shark casualty, when one of the men hanging on the raft had his leg bitten off. Pulled into the raft, he died shortly after. From then on, sharks could be seen circling about the rafts between 10 to 20 yards away. Despite the men kicking the water and shouting, the sharks managed to kill four more as the day wore on. At about 1500, a B-17 flew over, but it was too high for its pilot or crew to notice the men in the sea.

During the second night, several men became disoriented and would request permission to shut the main steam valves in the engine room or ask if they could go to the scuttlebutt (water fountain) for a drink. A number of men in the water had become so exhausted that they just slipped away, sometimes by losing their bearings in the dark and not having the strength to find their raft again.

The second morning was again bright, clear and very hot. Another B-17 was seen, but it was also too high to see the men. The omnipresent sharks were still close and nipping at the sailors. Around noon, one shark about four feet long leaped into Lieutenant Bates' raft, right over his shoulder, and took a huge bite out of the thigh of one of the men. Bates and another man grasped the shark by its tail and threw it over the side. The poor victim soon became delirious and died some four hours later.

That night, a five-minute shower deluged the men and all leaned back, hoping to get a few drops down their parched throats. Lieutenant Bates had saved a tin from one of the ration kits and managed to collect a small amount of rain water, but a huge wave swamped the raft and brought his effort to naught. As the night wore on, Bates himself began to hallucinate, believing he saw a brightly lit drive-in hamburger stand, with its barbecued hamburgers and malts, drifting by.

Thankfully, on the third day, a Navy PBY Catalina flying boat flew over and dropped a smoke float. Then some of the men stood up and saw two destroyers coming toward them. The lead destroyer was the USS *Grayson*, which eased alongside Lieutenant Bates' raft. Hanging over her sides were cargo nets, but the men were so exhausted and weak that they could not hold on to the netting or climb onto the deck of the ship. Realizing this, some of *Grayson's* crew lowered themselves into the rafts and secured lines about the men so they could be hoisted on board. The second destroyer, *Gwin*, picked up the remainder of the survivors and went in search of stragglers.

All told, aside from being struck by a torpedo, the *Meredith* had taken five direct bomb hits, suffered 10 to 15 near-misses and was severely raked by machine-gun fire. Lost with the *Meredith*, and in the aftermath of her sinking, were 185 officers and men; the *Vireo* lost 51 of her crew.

☆ ☆ ☆

USS *MEREDITH* (DD-434) [I]

Class: Benson/Livermore.
Builder: Boston Navy Yard, Charlestown, Massachusetts.
Keel laid: June 1, 1939.
Launched: April 24, 1940.
Sponsor: Miss Ethel D. Meredith, a great-great-great-granddaughter of
    Sergeant Jonathan Meredith, USMC.
Commissioned: March 1, 1941; Lieutenant Commander W.F. Mendenhall,
    USN, comdg.
Date of loss: October 15, 1942; Commander H.E. Hubbard, USN. comdg.†
Near San Cristobal Island, the Solomons.
Awards: One battle star.

USS O'Brien

Launched October 20, 1939
Lost October 19, 1942
Off Samoa

CAPTAIN GIDEON O'BRIEN
(1744–1818)

Jeremiah O'Brien and his five brothers—Gideon, William, John, Dennis and Joseph—sparked off the first naval engagement of the Revolutionary War when they led a group of volunteers armed with pitchforks, clubs, pistols and rifles and seized the British ships HMSs *Margarita* and *Unity* at Machias, Massachusetts (a city today in Maine), on June 12, 1775.

Gideon assumed command of *Unity*, which he renamed *Machias Liberty,* and went on to capture several British merchant ships between 1777 and into 1780, when he himself was captured by the British. Escaping, he continued to harass British shipping while in command of the *Tiger* and the *Hibernia*, until the end of the war. With the ending of hostilities, he became customs director in Machias and died there on September 3, 1818.

Prior to the attack on Pearl Harbor, the USS *O'Brien* (DD-415) carried out her operations with the Atlantic Fleet on the neutrality patrol and served as a convoy escort for British shipping in the North Atlantic. Upon the completion of a shipyard overhaul, she stood out of Norfolk for San Francisco, in company with her sister destroyer *Mustin* (DD-413), and arrived there on January 31, 1942. Four days afterwards, *O'Brien* cleared San Francisco en route to Pearl Harbor, but misfortune struck when she collided with the USS *Case* (DD-370) and was compelled to return to port for repairs.

After these were completed, *O'Brien* sailed for San Diego, where she picked up a convoy and proceeded on to Pearl Harbor. Upon her arrival, she was designated as flagship of DesDiv 4 and commenced her patrolling duties throughout the Hawaiian Islands. In late March, she escorted the seaplane tender USS *Curtiss,* which had embarked with civilian workers from Midway Island, to Pearl Harbor. After one escort run to the West Coast and back to Pearl, she was dispatched to Pago Pago, Samoa, in mid-April.

On May 26 she assisted in the occupation of Wallis Island, then a Free French possession, and from there returned to Pearl, where she resumed her patrolling duties in Hawaiian waters. Then, on August 17, she joined Task Force 17 and proceeded to the South Pacific to bolster the naval forces operating in the Solomon Islands.

On September 15, *O'Brien* was part of a combined task force built around the carriers *Hornet* and *Wasp,* escorting a troop and supply convoy to Guadalcanal. The Japanese had placed a screen of submarines southeast of the Solomons, however, and that afternoon the Americans suffered one of the most devastating submarine attacks in history. There were nine Japanese vessels strung out in a line, 25 miles apart, and the combined task force entered the jurisdiction of two: the *I-15* and *I-19.*

The main target of the attack, and the first to be struck, was *Wasp,* followed a few minutes later by *O'Brien;* then, almost simultaneously, the battleship *North Carolina* was hit on her port side, 20 feet below her waterline.

Just before *O'Brien* was hit, her lookouts had sighted smoke billowing from *Wasp;* moments later, a torpedo wake was seen heading toward them on the ship's port hand. The destroyer's skipper, Commander Thomas Burrows, ordered a sharp turn to avoid the deadly missile, which barely missed her fantail. However, just as the crew breathed a sigh of relief, another torpedo smashed into her bow, blowing a section of it off, from the keel up to just beneath her anchors.

Fortunately, despite the tremendous shock, none of her crew was injured, and without any inflammables or ammunition stored in that area, the fear of a conflagration was nil. Flooding was swiftly brought under control and weakened bulkheads were shored up. Ordered to Espiritu Santo, she received temporary repairs.

As for the *North Carolina,* she was able to steam under her own power, and arrived safely in port. Unfortunately, the damage inflicted upon *Wasp* was fatal. Hit three times, with fires raging out of control, and exploding ammunition and bombs tearing her guts out, she had to be abandoned and sunk by torpedoes from the USS *Landsdowne* (DD-486).

Though the Japanese submarine *I-15* first reported the death of the *Wasp,* it did not claim to have fired the torpedoes. The *I-15* was sunk six weeks later by a destroyer with the loss of all hands. There is a possibility, in fact, that all the torpedoes fired that day were from the *I-19* and aimed at the *Wasp*; the "long-lancers" that missed simply kept going into the *Hornet's* group, and, by an incredible stroke of luck, hit the *O'Brien* and *North Carolina*. In any case, the *I-19* was lost in the Gilbert Islands in 1943, and her commander, Takaichi Kinashi, was killed while in command of the *I-29* in 1944, in an ambush by U.S. submarines while he was returning from a mission to Germany.

On October 10, *O'Brien* stood out of Espiritu Santo, en route to Pearl Harbor. Three days later, upon entering Suva Harbor, it was discovered that she had developed several additional leaks. On the 16th, she was again underway, but by the 18th, as she was nearing Samoa, the leaks were becoming much more difficult to contain. It was then decided to lighten ship by jettisoning all unnecessary gear and her torpedoes. Then, suddenly, at 0600 on the 19th, the destroyer's bottom virtually dropped out, with her bow and after sections beginning to grind and work themselves separately.

While a distress signal was issued, all of the crew, except for a salvage party, were ordered over the side at 0630. After surveying the damage and with her pumps unable to stem the flooding of her compartments, it was realized that the feisty destroyer was doomed, and attempts to save her were abandoned. Finally, after steaming some 3,000 miles since she was torpedoed, the long-suffering *O'Brien* literally fell apart piecemeal and settled to the bottom just before 0800. Rescue vessels from Samoa were soon upon the scene and picked up her survivors. Fortunately, not one man was lost.

☆ ☆ ☆

USS *O'BRIEN* (DD-415)

Class: Sims.
Builder: Boston Navy Yard, Charlestown, Massachusetts.
Keel laid: May 31, 1938.
Launched: October 20, 1939.
Sponsor: Miss Josephine O'Brien Campbell, great-great-great-granddaughter of
    Captain Gideon O'Brien.
Commissioned: March 2, 1940; Lieutenant Commander C.F. Espe, USN, comdg.
Date of loss: October 19, 1942; Commander T. Burrows, USN, comdg.
Location: Off Samoa.
Awards: One battle star.

USS Porter

Launched December 12, 1935
Lost October 26, 1942
Near Santa Cruz Island, east of the Solomons

(The *Porter* had two namesakes, father and son.)

COMMODORE DAVID PORTER, USN
(1780–1843)

Born in Boston, Massachusetts, on February 1, 1780, Midshipman David Porter was serving in the frigate USS *Constellation* when she engaged with and defeated the French frigate *L'Insurgente* on February 9, 1799. During the war with the Barbary States, he was captured when the frigate *Philadelphia* ran aground in Tripoli Harbor on October 31, 1803.

Upon his release, two years later, he continued to serve with the Mediterranean Squadron as acting captain in the *Constitution*, and later was placed in command of the USS *Lnterprise*. During the War of 1812, he commanded the *Essex* and, on August 13, 1812, captured the first British frigate of the war, the HMS *Alert*.

In 1813, he sailed *Essex* into the Pacific, the first American warship to do so, preying on British shipping and whalers. After having battled a fierce storm, which wreaked severe damage upon *Essex*, he engaged with two British frigates, HMSs *Cherub* and *Phoebe*, off Valparaiso, Chile, on March 28, 1814. After a savage exchange of gunfire, the unequal contest ended in defeat for Captain Porter.

In 1826, Commodore Porter resigned his commission from the Navy and became Commander-in-Chief of the Mexican Navy. He died on March 3, 1843, at Para, Turkey, while serving as U.S. Minister to that country. He is buried at Woodlands Cemetery, in Philadelphia, Pennsylvania.

ADMIRAL DAVID D. PORTER, USN
(1813–1891)

David Dixon Porter, USN, son of Commodore David Porter, was born in Chester, Pennsylvania, on June 8, 1813. He served in the Mediterranean Squadron on board the USS *Constellation* as a Midshipman (1829–31), the frigates *United States* and *Delaware* (1832–34) and, as a Lieutenant, on board the frigate *Congress* (1842–45).

In command of the USS *Spitfire* during the Mexican War, he assisted in the two attacks against Vera Cruz. A firebrand, Porter skyrocketed through the ranks, attaining the rank of Rear Admiral during the first two years of the Civil War. His outstanding accomplishments included the reinforcement of Fort Pickens, Florida; commanding the mortar flotilla under his adopted brother, Admiral David G. Farragut; and the capture of forts St. Philip and Jackson in April 1862. Once again under Admiral Farragut, he carried out operations against Confederate fortifications on the Mississippi River from Vicksburg to New Orleans. While acting as Rear Admiral, he assisted General U.S. Grant in the reduction of Vicksburg, and in late 1863 assumed command of the naval campaigns in the western rivers. Later he was placed in command of the North Atlantic Blockading Squadron and was instrumental in the defeat and capture of Fort Fisher, North Carolina.

For his conspicuous service during the Civil War, Rear Admiral Porter was promoted to the permanent rank of Vice Admiral in 1866. On four occasions during the war, he received votes of thanks from the U.S. Congress. From 1886 until 1889, he served as superintendent of the U.S. Naval Academy, and in 1870 was appointed to the rank of full Admiral, thus becoming the ranking officer in the United States Navy. While serving as Head of the Board of Inspections, Admiral Porter died on February 13, 1891.

At the completion of her shakedown trials, which were conducted in waters off the northern coasts of Europe, the USS *Porter* (DD-355) arrived at St. John's, Newfoundland, in May 1937 to participate in the coronation ceremonies for King George VI of England. Three months later, she was transferred to the Pacific Fleet, and commenced training operations along the West Coast and in Hawaiian waters.

On December 5, 1941, she departed from Pearl Harbor for the United States, thereby missing the devastating Japanese attack on the U.S. Pacific Fleet that brought America into World War II. Ordered to return, she was assigned to patrolling and escort duties throughout the Hawaiian Islands until March 1942. She then returned to the West Coast, where she was assigned to escort coastal convoys between Seattle and San Diego from April to July.

Returning to Pearl Harbor in mid-August, *Porter* resumed her patrolling duties until October 16, when she joined Task Force 16. Deployed to the South Pacific, the Task Force was built around the carrier USS *Enterprise,* the battleship *South Dakota* and eight destroyers. Later, Task Force 16 joined up with Task Force 17, which was built around the carrier *Hornet,* four cruisers and six destroyers. Soon afterwards, both task forces were combined and redesignated as Task Force 61, under the command of Rear Admiral T.C. Kincaid.

The enlarged group was ordered to the Solomon Islands in an effort to strengthen the naval forces at Guadalcanal, where the U.S. Marines and Army were locked in desperate combat against General Kawaguchi's invasion force.

Meanwhile, to the northeast of the Solomons lurked Vice Admiral N. Kondo's Japanese armada, made up of the Second Fleet, with one carrier, two battleships, five cruisers and fourteen destroyers, and the Third Fleet, consisting of three carriers, two battleships, five cruisers and fifteen destroyers. Kondo had been waiting to receive the good news that Kawaguchi's forces had successfully retaken the vital airstrip, so his aircraft could land there. However, despite the overwhelming odds, the Americans stood their ground throughout the night of 24–25 October and well into that afternoon.

By the morning of the 26th, Kondo's fleet was running low on fuel and the commander was compelled to detach some of his ships. It was at about this time that aircraft from *Enterprise* spotted Kondo's ships and zoomed in, attacking the carrier *Zuiho.* The Navy planes raked her decks with machine gun fire and dropped two 500-pound bombs on the carrier's stern. Almost simultaneously, Kondo's scouting aircraft had sighted Kinkaid's force and, in short order, swarms of enemy aircraft were winging their way toward Task Force 61.

Challenged by pilots from the *Enterprise,* a fierce air and sea melee ensued, thus opening the Battle of the Santa Cruz Islands. The blue skies over Task Force 61 were stitched with glowing tracers from the ships' AA batteries, pockmarked with black blossoms of murderous flak and smudged with trails of oily smoke from flaming aircraft as they fell into the sea.

At 0958, *Porter* raced to rescue an American pilot whose plane had crashed a short distance from her. While her crew was fishing the airman out of the water, a torpedo was seen passing just ahead and another astern of the ship. Within a few seconds, another torpedo was sighted churning toward the ship, off her port beam. With *Porter* unable to gain sufficient momentum to avoid this last "fish," it smashed into her two forward engineering spaces, killing one officer and ten men. Enveloped in a pall of smoke and billowing steam, and having lost all power, the wounded destroyer sloughed to a halt.

Commander John C. Matthews (Ret.), then holding the rank of Lieutenant, recalls that despite having lost power, *Porter's* anti-aircraft batteries were still operational. While the repair parties were attempting to fight the damage, her gunners laced the skies with 20-mm shells, hoping to splash the enemy planes which were now concentrating their attacks against *Hornet*. The destroyer *Shaw* (DD-373) closed in on *Porter* to screen her against the possibility of being attacked; however, *Shaw* soon picked up the presence of a submarine on her sonar and went in search of her.

Unfortunately, *Porter* was beginning to founder and going down by the head. With her repair parties unable to curtail the inflow of water into her hull, it was decided to abandon the ship. The *Shaw*, having lost contact with the submarine, came alongside the beleaguered *Porter* and took on her crew.

Meanwhile, *Hornet's* aircraft had caught up with the enemy's Third Fleet and wreaked such severe damage on the carriers *Zuikaku* and *Shokaku* that both of them would be laid up for repairs for nine months. Also severely damaged were one Japanese cruiser and a destroyer. Unfortunately, the *Hornet*, after suffering a number of bomb hits, being crashed by two suicides, struck by several torpedoes and wracked internally by volcanic explosions and uncontrollable fires, had to be abandoned. Yet, despite the conflagration, the doomed carrier still remained afloat. The destroyer *Anderson* (DD-411) attempted to down her with six torpedoes, three of which succeeded in hitting her. Still the dying carrier refused to go under.

The destroyer *Mustin* (DD-413) then teamed up with *Anderson* and together they pumped over 400 rounds of 5-inch shells into the battered and scorched *Hornet*; but still the carrier refused to sink. With Kondo's Third Fleet hovering nearby, it was decided to move on and leave the carrier to her own fate. As it happened, she was found by the Japanese destroyers *Akigumo* and *Makigumo*, who sent her to the bottom with four torpedoes.

As for Task Force 61, the carrier *Enterprise*, the cruiser *San Juan*, the battleship *South Dakota* and the destroyer *Smith* (DD-378) had suffered considerable damage, not counting the loss of 74 aircraft. Joining *Hornet* on the ocean floor was *Porter*, which had to be sunk by a torpedo and gunfire from the USS *Shaw.* Of the nine men who were wounded in the initial torpedoing, four later died.

☆ ☆ ☆

USS *PORTER* (DD-356)

Class: Porter.
Builder: New York Shipbuilding Corp., Camden, New Jersey.
Keel laid: December 18, 1933.
Launched: December 12, 1935.
Sponsor: Miss Carlyle P. Porter.
Commissioned: August 25, 1936; Commander F.B. Royal, USN, comdg.
Date of loss: October 26, 1942; Lieutenant Commander R.G. Roberts, USN, comdg.
Location: Near Santa Cruz Island, east of the Solomons.
Awards: One battle star.

USS Barton

Launched January 31, 1942
Lost November 13, 1942
Off Savo Island, the Solomons

REAR ADMIRAL JOHN K. BARTON, USN
(1853–1921)

John Kennedy Barton was born in Philadelphia, Pennsylvania, on April 7, 1853, and graduated from the U.S. Naval Academy in 1876. After serving in various vessels, he was seriously injured prior to his retirement from active service. However, as a result of his expertise in the field of steam engineering, he was appointed Engineer-in-Chief, and later Chief, of the Bureau of Steam Engineering. Rear Admiral Barton retired on December 23, 1908, and died on December 23, 1921.

Launched at the end of January 1942, the USS *Barton* (DD-599) was dispatched to the Pacific immediately upon completion of her shakedown trials and battle-readiness exercises, in an effort to bolster the destroyer squadrons already at grips with the Japanese in the south. There she took part in the raids against the Buin-Fasi and Tonolai Islands, and the Battle of the Santa Cruz Islands. On October 29, she rescued 17 survivors from a downed air transport that had crashed off Fabre Island.

On the night of November 12, 1942, *Barton* was attached to Task Group 67.4 off Guadalcanal, under the command of Rear Admiral Daniel J. Callaghan, flying his flag on the cruiser *San Francisco*. Earlier that evening, the task group had escorted a convoy of empty transports and cargo vessels southward to Lunga Point and then reversed course to meet an oncoming Japanese bombardment force that had earlier been sighted forging down the "Slot." Under the command of Rear Admiral Hiroki Abe, the enemy force was composed of the battleships *Hiei* (the flagship) and *Kirishima,* the light cruiser *Nagara* and 14 destroyers, steaming in a three-column formation.

Pitted against this juggernaut was Admiral Callaghan's meager force of 13 ships. Steaming in a single column were, respectively: destroyers *Cushing* (DD-376), *Laffey* (DD-459), *Sterett* (DD-407) and *O'Bannon* (DD-450). Following in their wakes were the cruisers *Atlanta, San Francisco, Portland, Helena* and *Juneau*. Bringing up the rear of the van were the destroyers *Aaron Ward* (DD-483), *Barton, Monssen* (DD-436) and *Fletcher* (DD-445).

Under cover of darkness, both American and Japanese battlegroups steamed toward each other, neither aware of the other's proximity. At 0124 on the 13th, *Helena* reported a radar contact with vessels unknown and immediately notified Admiral Callaghan, who ordered a starboard turn. The Americans closed in on the enemy force, which was now rounding the northwestern side of Savo Island.

As the distance between the ships began to narrow, the loquacious Americans were flooding the talk between ships (TBS) radios, with voices reporting various bearings, ranges and tactical data, including requests for information. Fortunately, the enemy's radio operators were not tuned in to this frequency; however, the Japanese gun crews were at battle stations and ready for action.

Approximately 17 minutes after *Helena* made her report, *Cushing* almost collided with one of the enemy's scouting destroyers and veered off course to avoid ramming her. At the same time, she radioed her close encounter and requested permission to fire torpedoes, but her calls were lost in the confusing babel of voices jamming the TBS circuits. Consequently, as *Cushing* made her evasive swing, the destroyers astern of her, as well as the *Atlanta*, broke formation. When Callaghan radioed *Atlanta*, asking what the hell she was doing, he received the reply, "Avoiding our own destroyers!"

In the meantime, the enemy's scouting destroyers had reported the presence of an unknown number of American warships in the area. This news shocked Abe, for he had been assured there were no American combat vessels this close to Guadalcanal. Since this was a preinvasion bombardment force, his armor-piercing shells had been struck below, with bombardment ammunition at the ready in the ships' magazines and turrets.

Then at 0150, a Japanese searchlight stabbed its glaring white finger through the darkened seascape and lit upon the *Atlanta*. Unknowingly, Callaghan had steamed in between two columns of Abe's ships and, within a few short seconds, *Atlanta*'s bridge was saturated with heavy-caliber shells. Two torpedoes then slammed into her, putting out all power, and several more projectiles swamped her bridge, killing Rear Admiral Norman Scott and most of the bridge personnel. Thus began the opening phase of the three-day Naval Battle of Guadalcanal.

Immediately after the enemy fired the first salvo, Admiral Callaghan's voice crackled over the TBS circuit: "Odd ships fire to port, even ships to starboard!" By now, however, the Japanese had broken formation; hence Callagahan's order confused his ships' captains, when the targets were not on their designated flanks.

From that moment on, chaos reigned on either side. Both fleets were scattered hither and yon, firing at one another, and, at times, firing on their own ships. Torpedo wakes criss-crossed the sea's surface, some of which ended in lethal explosions. In their attempts to evade the "tin fish," ships' captains risked the possibility of being rammed or colliding with other vessels. The night was aglow with glaring gunflashes, blinding searchlights, blinking machine-gun fire and burning ships. Each captain took it upon himself to fight his ship the way he saw fit, whenever or wherever a target presented itself. For the American skippers, there were plenty of targets to choose from—but friendly ships kept getting in the way.

Seven minutes into the battle, *Barton* was struck by two torpedoes in quick succession. She had already fired four at a destroyer, but while her guns were blasting away at another vessel, a ship was seen bearing down on her and directly into her line of fire. Not knowing if it was friend or foe, Lieutenant Commander Douglas H. Fox held his fire and, to avoid a collision, ordered his engines reversed at full power. The vessel, which happened to be an American cruiser, missed the destroyer by a cat's whisker.

Just as *Barton* again began to gain forward momentum, the two torpedoes tagged her—in the forward fire room and forward engine room. The tremendous detonation of the torpedoes, combined with her exploding boilers, tore the 2,060-ton destroyer in half and she plunged to the bottom, taking her captain and 90 percent of her crew down with her. Sadly, many of those who survived her sinking were killed or seriously injured when her depth charges detonated some 50 feet below the surface. Then, directly astern of *Barton* came *Monssen*, which plowed through the helpless survivors, increasing *Barton's* casualties to 97 percent.

Over the mangled wreckage of *Barton* and her dead, the vicious sea battle boomed on until 0235, when Admiral Abe decided to "throw in the towel." During those 44 minutes, his flagship had been assailed by 5- and 8-inch shells, peppered by machine guns and 20-mm cannon shells and struck by a number of torpedoes, although a few of them did not explode. The battleship *Hiei* had absorbed enough damage to stagger her, and eventually she lost all power. After transferring his flag to the *Kirishima*, Abe called it a day, leaving his flagship behind with a destroyer standing by to offer assistance.

For the Americans, it was certainly a black Friday the 13th. Every ship in the task group (except *Helena* and *Fletcher*) had suffered serious battle damage. In the heat of the slugfest, *Laffey* joined *Barton* on the floor of "Iron Bottom Sound." *Cushing* and *Monssen* were transformed into incinerators that sank later in the day. *Aaron Ward* was reduced to a shambles, but, by some miracle and the determination of her crew, she was saved. Not so for the *Atlanta*. Badly mauled, she was beyond salvaging and had to be scuttled. The wounded, ill-fated *Juneau* had limped away from the battle in its early stages and was en route to Espiritu Santo for repairs when she was torpedoed by the *I-16*. Only ten members of her crew survived her sinking, and among those lost was her commanding officer, Captain Lyman K. Swensen, and the five Sullivan brothers. Later, one of the survivors from the battle described it as "a barroom brawl with all the lights turned out."

By 1800 that evening, the Japanese were compelled to scuttle the *Hiei*, after it had been further pounded throughout the day by Marine fighters and bombers. Also lost in the battle was Rear Admiral Callaghan, whose last fighting words were, "I want the big ones first!"

☆ ☆ ☆

USS *BARTON* (DD-599)

Class: Benson/Livermore.
Builder: Bethlehem Steel Co., Quincy, Massachusetts.
Keel laid: May 20, 1941.
Launched: January 31, 1942.
Sponsor: Miss Barbara D. Barton, granddaughter of Rear Admiral John K.
    Barton, USN.
Commissioned: May 29, 1942; Lieutenant Commander D.H. Fox, USN,
    comdg.
Date of loss: November 13, 1942; Lieutenant Commander D.H. Fox, comdg.†
Location: Off Savo Island, the Solomons.
Awards: Three battle stars.

USS Laffey

Launched October 30, 1941
Lost November 13, 1942
Off Savo Island, the Solomons

SEAMAN BARTLETT LAFFEY, USN
(1841–1901)

Born in Ireland, Bartlett Laffey enlisted in the United States Navy as a Seaman on March 17, 1862. During a fierce Confederate attack on Yazoo City, Mississippi, on March 5, 1863, Seaman Laffey landed a 12-pound howitzer and its crew in the streets of the city and played a leading role in the battle as the gun crew held its ground against insurmountable odds. Despite heavy and concentrated rifle fire and a hand-to-hand struggle, Laffey and his men succeeded in turning back the determined assault.

For his outstanding courage and leadership, Seaman Laffey was awarded the Congressional Medal of Honor and promoted to Master's Mate. Although he declined the promotion, Laffey remained in the Navy with the rate of Seaman. Seaman Laffey died in the Soldiers' Home at Chelsea, Massachusetts, on March 22, 1901.

The USS *Laffey* (DD-459) joined the South Pacific naval forces on August 28, 1942. On September 15, she was part of the screen for Task Force 16 when it sailed into a cordon of Japanese submarines guarding the approaches to Guadalcanal. In just eight minutes the United States lost the carrier *Wasp* and the destroyer *O'Brien*, with the battleship *North Carolina* badly damaged.

Laffey underwent her baptism of fire during the Battle of Cape Esperance on the night of October 11–12. In this action, she engaged with and sank the destroyer IJN *Fubuki*. Soundly defeated in this action, the enemy broke off the battle, with *Laffey* hot on the heels of another destroyer, *Hatuyuki*. After scoring several hits on the fleeing warship, *Laffey's* skipper, Lieutenant

Commander William D. Hank, gave up the chase and returned to the task group.

Since the Battle of Guadalcanal was briefly described in the story of the USS *Barton,* it will not be necessary to repeat the events that led up the battle. Suffice it to say that in those dark, early morning hours of November 13, the plucky *Laffey* plunged into the fray with her guns blazing. After wreaking severe damage on the cruiser *Nagara* and two destroyers, her lookouts sighted the gigantic silhouette of the battleship *Hiei* bearing down on her, the goliath's 14-inch guns and secondary batteries belching sheets of fire. Captain Hank immediately ordered an evasive turn and at the same time let loose two torpedoes that both struck the battleship. The range was so close, however, that the torpedoes did not have time enough to arm, and bounced off the *Hiei's* armored sides like frolicsome dolphins. As the 31,000-ton behemoth swept past her stern, *Laffey's* fantail was swamped by the froth from her wake.

Then, the massive bulk of the battleship *Kirishima* loomed out of the night, two Japanese destroyers steaming off her port side. The courageous *Laffey* trained her 5-inch batteries on the trio and in return was staggered by a deluge of both large- and small-caliber projectiles that demolished four of her five 5-inch guns. But the actual killing blows came when *Hiei* refocused its attention on the American destroyer with massive 14-inch shells that crashed into her amidships section, wrecking her engineering spaces. Almost simultaneously, *Laffey* was struck by a torpedo on her stern, which flooded her after compartments. Fire, steam and smoke belching out of her ravished hull, the wounded *Laffey* crawled to an agonizing halt and began to take on a dangerous list.

Realizing that his ship was in her death throes, Captain Hank ordered her to be abandoned. Yet, despite the uproar of the battle and the chaotic circumstances, *Laffey's* crew left her in good order. While the men were going over the side, she was struck again on the fantail either by a torpedo or a large-caliber projectile, which detonated her depth charges. This deafening blast injured several men in the water. Immediately afterwards, *Laffey* upended and went to the bottom in a rush, taking down her captain and several of her crew. Sadly, those close to her in the water were also pulled down by the suction of her shattered remains as she plunged to her final resting place.

For his valiant attack against the Japanese battleships, Lieutenant Commander Hank was posthumously awarded the Navy Cross.

☆ ☆ ☆

USS *LAFFEY* (DD-459)

Class: Benson/Livermore.

Builder: Bethlehem Steel Co., San Francisco, California.

Keel laid: January 13, 1941.

Launched: October 30, 1941.

Sponsor: Miss Eleanor G. Forgety, granddaughter of Seaman Bartlett Laffey, USN.

Commissioned: March 31, 1942; Lieutenant Commander W.D. Hank, USN, comdg.

Date of loss: November 13, 1942; Lieutenant Commander W.D. Hank, USN, comdg.†

Location: Off Savo Island, the Solomons.

Awards: Presidential Unit Citation and three battle stars.

USS Monssen

Launched May 16, 1940
Lost November 13, 1942
Off Savo Island, the Solomons

LIEUTENANT MONS MONSSEN, USN
(1867–1930)

Born in Bergen, Norway, on January 20, 1867, Mons Monssen enlisted in the United States Navy on June 3, 1889. In 1904, while serving in the USS *Missouri*, he was promoted to the rank of Warrant Gunner. In October of that year, a gunpowder charge ignited in a 12-inch gun turret during target practice, killing 18 officers and men. Bravely entering the turret with a bucket of water, Gunner Monssen threw water on the flames with his hands until a fire hose could be passed to him. For his courageous action taken in this tragic event, he was awarded the Congressional Medal of Honor and later was promoted to the rank of Lieutenant. Lieutenant Monssen retired from the Navy on December 15, 1925, and died at the Brooklyn Naval Hospital, Brooklyn, New York, on February 10, 1930.

After completing her shakedown trials along the California coast, the USS *Monssen* (DD-436) reported for duty with the Atlantic Fleet destroyer squadrons. Assigned to the neutrality patrol and serving as a convoy escort through the waters of the North Atlantic, she carried out these commitments until she was assigned to the Pacific Fleet on March 1, 1942.

Her wartime operations included the screening of Task Force 16, built around the carrier *Hornet*, which was embarked with Lieutenant Colonel James Doolittle's 16 B-25 bombers that staged the surprise air raid against the Japanese homeland; the Battle of Midway; and supporting the landings on Guadalcanal and Tulagi and escorting reinforcement convoys to Guadalcanal.

On November 12, 1942, *Monssen* was patrolling off Guadalcanal, screening the offloading transports and supply ships, when a flight of enemy air-craft swooped in, hoping to disrupt the landings. Although most of the attackers were splashed by anti-aircraft fire from the ships and Marine fight-er aircraft, one made a suicide dive into the cruiser *San Francisco,* starting fires that killed 30 of her crewmen. *Monssen* was struck by a bomb that dam-aged her fire control radar.

Later that evening, *Monssen* joined up with Task Group 67.4 and es-corted the empty transports to Lunga Point. The task group then reversed course to confront Vice Admiral Hiroki Abe's bombardment force off Savo Island.

During the fierce battle that ensued, *Monssen* was under constant fire from the opening of the first salvo. At the time *Barton* was torpedoed, a deep-running torpedo had skimmed just beneath *Monssen*'s keel, and, in an effort to avoid the torrent of shells that were splashing and booming about her, her captain, Lieutenant Commander C.E. McCombs, maneuvered his ship at full speed, tragically running over what few survivors were left from *Barton.*

Like every American captain in this engagement, McCombs fought his ship on his own terms. Pitting his 1,620-ton destroyer against the 31,000-ton *Hiei,* he raked the battlewagon's decks and superstructure with his 5-inchers and machine-gun fire, and for good measure fired five torpedoes at the monster. Another five torpedoes were unleashed at a target off *Monssen*'s port beam, while other gunners trained their sights and fired upon a destroyer off to starboard.

Since her fire control radar had been damaged during the previous day's air raid, *Monssen* was compelled to fire her main batteries by radio informa-tion. From 0150 to 0220, the vessel swept through the melee without so much as a scratch on her paintwork, when she suddenly found herself brightly illuminated under a cluster of starshells.

Assuming that these were from a friendly ship, McCombs flashed his recognition signals, only to be answered promptly by a hail of heavy shell-fire. A total of 37 projectiles, both large- and small-caliber, crashed into the ship, mangling her bridge, tearing up her decks and demolishing her engi-neering spaces. Her 5-inch gun mounts were uprooted and her torpedo tubes wrecked; even machine-gun mounts were ripped from the deck and their crews slaughtered or hurled overboard.

Quickly reduced to mass a of twisted and mangled scrap, the destroyer lay dead in the water, enveloped in a pall of smoke and billowing steam. Trapped on the shattered bridge, with every department immobilized, and unable to fight the fires, McCombs passed the order to abandon ship. He and his bridge personnel—all of whom were wounded—were forced to jump from the bridge.

By this time, the battle had subsided. Most of *Monssen's* survivors were now in the water, clinging to life rafts and debris and watching helplessly as their ship incinerated herself throughout the night. At daybreak, the destroyer was virtually white hot, although, by some quirk, none of her ammunition had thus far detonated.

Then, miraculously, from out of the fiery wreckage, cries for help were heard. Without hesitation, Boatswain's Mate Second Class, C.C. Storey and two other men, Gunner's Mate Second Class L.F. Sturgeon and Fireman First Class J.G. Hughes, paddled their raft to the blistering derelict and clambered on board her scorched and griddle-hot decks. Despite the possibility of the ship blowing up, the men bravely searched about the area where the voices had come from. In the water, the men virtually held their breaths as the minutes ticked by. Finally, after what seemed up to half an hour, the rescuers emerged from the smoke and haze leading, carrying and dragging eight wounded men who had been trapped in a lower compartment.

Later that day, the survivors were picked up by rescue boats from Guadalcanal. As for *Monssen*, she continued to belch flames and smoke until just before noon, when the intense heat finally touched off her magazines. After the explosion had rumbled across the waters of Savo Sound and the smoke disappeared, the sizzling hulk of the gallant *Monssen* vanished from the face of the earth. Lost with her were 150 of her crew.

☆ ☆ ☆

USS *MONSSEN* (DD-436)

Class: Benson/Livermore.
Builder: Puget Sound Navy Yard, Bremerton, Wa.
Keel laid: July 12, 1939.
Launched: May 16, 1940.
Sponsor: Mrs. Mons Monssen, widow of Lieutenant Mons Monssen, USN.
Commissioned: March 14, 1941; Lieutenant Commander R.N. Smoot, USN, comdg.
Date of loss: November 13, 1942; Lieutenant Commander C.E. McCombs, USN, comdg.
Location: Off Savo Island, the Solomons.
Awards: Four battle stars.

USS Cushing

Launched December 31, 1935
Lost November 13, 942
Off Savo Island, the Solomons

COMMANDER WILLIAM B. CUSHING, USN
(1842–1874)

William Barker Cushing was born on November 24, 1842, in Delafield, Wisconsin. Known for his unsurpassed daring and courage, he was best remembered for his destruction of the Confederate Navy's ironclad ram CSS *Albemarle*.

On the night of October 27, 1864, the twenty-one-year-old lieutenant chugged up the Roanoke River in a small steam launch crammed with 14 officers and men, and with a spar torpedo rigged on its bow. Owing to darkness, fog and drizzle, the small craft and its occupants managed to elude the sentries along the riverbank.

Upon reaching their objective, it was discovered that the iron monster was surrounded by a barrier of logs. Far from being discouraged, Cushing gave the order to forge ahead. As the boat slithered over the logs, he lowered the spar and stood ready to pull the lanyard that would trigger the torpedo.

By now, however, the Confederate guards had been alerted. Musketry from the shore flailed the launch, while the ironclad's crew prepared to repulse the raiders with their 100-pound cannon. Just as the torpedo detonated, the ram's huge guns roared over the heads of the Yankee sailors. Consequently, the combined explosions demolished the launch and killed and wounded several of its crew. Somehow, Lieutenant Cushing and one seaman escaped unharmed.

Following the Civil War, Cushing was promoted to the rank of Commander and went on to serve in several types of ships. While serving as commander of the Washington Navy Yard, Washington, DC, he died on December 17, 1874.

Assigned to the Pacific Fleet, the USS *Cushing* (DD-376) participated in the futile search for the famed aviatrix Amelia Earhart during July 1937. At the time of the attack on Pearl Harbor, *Cushing* was undergoing an overhaul at the Mare Island Navy Yard, Vallejo, California.

After serving as an escort for convoys plying the waters between West Coast ports and Pearl Harbor, the destroyer arrived in the South Pacific in late August 1942, where she screened reinforcement convoys between Espiritu Santo and Guadalcanal. This duty, as well as patrolling around the Solomons, continued until the night of November 13, 1942, when she became embroiled in one of the most vicious sea engagements since the battle off Savo Island on the night of August 9.

Leading the van of Rear Admiral Callaghan's Task Group 67.4, *Cushing* almost collided with one of Vice Admiral H. Abe's scouting destroyers. Unfortunately, her skipper's request to attack the ship with torpedoes was lost due to the cacophony of voices that were jamming the TBS radio circuits. In an effort to avoid colliding with the enemy vessel, Lieutenant Commander E.N. Parker veered away, the ships directly astern of her following suit.

Then at 0150, all hell broke loose when the enemy was the first to open fire. Instantly, the darkened seascape was glowing with gun flashes, probing searchlights, fiery torpedo explosions, burning ships and glaring starshells. A Japanese destroyer was sighted skimming past *Cushing*'s starboard quarter.

Having lost the opportunity to sink a destroyer earlier, *Cushing* now had more targets than she could ask for. Training her sights on the nearest destroyer, she fired off a salvo from her 5-inch guns, thus, possibly, being the first American ship to open fire in the Naval Battle of Guadalcanal.

Sadly, *Cushing*'s crew was unable to observe the punishment she had meted out against her opponent, for immediately afterwards she too was on the receiving end of a maelstrom of hot steel, suffering severe damage in her amidships section. Within a few seconds, all power was lost and half of her engineering plant was in ruins.

With the helmsman straining to steer the ship by hand control, her captain conned his ship as best he could. Flames, smoke and scalding steam poured out of her boiler and engine rooms. At 0154, the battleship *Hiei* was seen plowing through the smoke and haze of the battle, American cruisers and destroyers lashing the giant with their main batteries while the Japanese vessel thundered back with her 14-inchers.

Captain Parker gave the order to turn his ship to the right to enable his torpedomen to fire a brace at the leviathan, now appearing larger with each

United States involvement in World War II began well before Pearl Harbor, as destroyers escorted British shipping across the North Atlantic. The USS *Reuben James* (below) was the first U.S. destroyer lost in the war. A U-boat's torpedo tore her in half on October 31, 1941.

The USS *Kearny* survived a U-boat attack on October 17, 1941. Here, the stricken destroyer is seen being eased alongside a repair ship at Hvalfördur, Iceland.

Iceland became a familiar stop for U.S. destroyermen. Here, an officer and a chief petty officer from the *Meredith* make friends with two young boys in Reykjavik in December 1941.

The USS *Truxtun* takes white water over her bow as she moves in position to serve as plane guard for the carrier *Lexington* off the California coast, April 1937.

The *Truxtun*, along with the USS *Pollux*, slammed into the rocky shores of Newfoundland during a ferocious blizzard on the night of February 18, 1942. Here, a Marine honor guard fires a salute over the graves of some of the men who lost their lives in the disaster.

As a petty officer looks on, a fireman prepares to light off a burner in no.1 boiler in the forward fire room on board a Fletcher class destroyer.

Somewhere in the North Atlantic, a drenched Chief Torpedoman prepares to drop a depth charge over the stern of the USS *Greer*. The *Greer* was the first American warship to duel wit a Nazi U-boat, on September 4, 1941.

The first *Jacob Jones* (above) was the only American destroyer lost in World War I. After being blown under by the U-58, the German commander radioed the destroyer's position prior to leaving the scene, thus allowing rescue ships to pick up her survivors.

eincarnated as DD-130, the next *Jacob Jones* is seen below passing through the Panama Canal. She too fell prey to a U-boat, off New Jersey on February 28, 1942, however no enemy gallantry accompanied her sinking—she was lost with most of her crew.

Above, the USS *Pope* underway somewhere in the South China Sea during the mid-1920s. Her long career was to end March 1, 1942, in the Java Sea.

The USS *Pillsbury* at anchor in a Chinese port (ca. 1927). One of four destroyers who "went missing" in the war, it was later learned she was sunk with all hands by Japanese cruiser and battleship gunfire south of Christmas Island in March 1942.

Hopelessly surrounded by the Japanese, the USS *Pope* found herself the last remaining Allied warship in the Java Sea in March 1942. Here she is seen during her final moments, being ripped apart by shells from the heavy cruisers *Ashigara* and *Myoko*. This photograph was published in the Japanese propaganda booklet "Victory on the March."

The damaged USS *Stewart* was thought to have been scuttled by the retreating Americans in 1942. However, later in the war reports were received of a Japanese ship that closely resembled a U.S. destroyer. The *Stewart* had indeed been repaired by the Japanese, who used her as a patrol vessel. Back in California after the war, her final service was as target practice for U.S. Navy pilots.

The USS *Porter*, shown here in 1937, was lost in October 1942 in the battle of the Santa Cruz Islands.

The USS *Jarvis* was damaged in an air attack off Guadalcanal on August 8, 1942. Attempting to leave the battle area for repairs, she brushed by the Japanese group that was on its way to the infamous battle of Savo Island. It was later learned that the Japanese dispatched aircraft to finish her off.

The USS *Duncan* charged into the nocturnal fray off Savo Island and was caught in a whirlwind of fire from both sides.

The USS O'*Brien* showing torpedo damage on her bow that she sustained while escorting a troop convoy to Guadalcanal.

"Torpedo Alley"—in the famous photograph below, *O'Brien* is shown getting hit by a Japanese submarine's torpedo minutes after the carrier *Wasp* had been fatally wounded. The photo was taken from the battleship *North Carolina*, which itself would be hit seconds later. After a harrowing voyage of over 3,000 miles, *O'Brien* began to break up and is shown at right slipping beneath the surface.

A German U-boat is brought to the surface by a depth charge, May 1943. The German sailor standing on deck disappeared moments after this photo was taken.

A Japanese submarine captured at the end of the war.
Japanese submarines were classified as Ha (under 500
tons), Ro (500–1000 tons) or I-boats. Some I-boats, however, starting at 1000, reached over 4,000 tons, sporting
cruiser-grade guns and catapults for aircraft.

The Japanese battleship *Kirishima*, along with her sister
ship *Hiei*, was lost in the Naval Battle of Guadalcanal,
though not before wreaking havoc on American destroyers
that took them on.

Both the USS *Cushing* (above) and the USS *Preston* (below) presently reside on "Ironbottom Sound." Off Savo Island, *Cushing* grappled point-blank with larger Japanese ships, including the battleship *Hiei*, before being pounded beneath the waves. *Preston* succumbed to a barrage from the cruiser *Nagara*. With all their destroyers fallen or crippled, the American battleships *Washington* and *South Dakota* carried on the fight until the Japanese retired.

After covering a special landing force on Amchitka Island in the Aleutians, the USS *Worden* ran afoul of a nest of pinnacle rocks on January 12, 1943. Despite attempts to pull her off, the destroyer could not be budged. Abandoned in a fierce storm, her remains were not located until the following August.

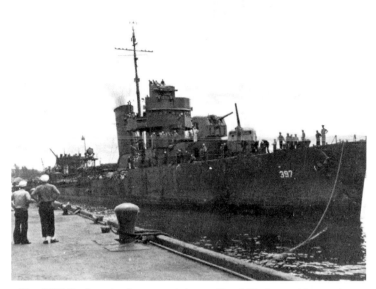

The USS *Benham* is shown arriving at Pearl Harbor with survivors from the *Hammann*, which was sunk at Midway. *Benham* was lost on November 15, 1942, off Savo Island in a battle that one participant described as "a barroom brawl with all the lights turned out."

The USS *Hammann*, which took two torpedos meant for the damaged aircraft carrier *Yorktown* off Midway Island. Though the Americans did not lose a ship during the great victory itself, the Japanese submarine I-168 snuck in later and managed to sink both the destroyer and the carrier.

The charmed life of the USS *Gwin* was terminated by a "long lance" torpedo off Kula Gulf in the Solomons. *Gwin* had fought her way through some of the toughest naval engagements of the war, off Guadalcanal.

Another survivor of the Naval Battle of Guadalcanal, in which she was severely damaged, the USS *Aaron Ward* was back in the Solomons on April 7, 1943, when a massive Japanese air fleet came winging down the "Slot." Though American fighter planes rose to the challenge, several Val dive bombers got through to inflict irreparable damage on the valiant destroyer.

passing second. By the time *Cushing* completed her slow, agonizing turn, the monster was less than 1,000 yards away. Captain Parker did not hesitate. The order to fire was given and six torpedoes went humming toward the lumbering giant. Three of them were seen smashing into her, but the behemoth seemed to shrug them off as if they were harmless firecrackers, continuing to plunge ahead into the wild and deadly melee.

By this point, the severely crippled *Cushing* had lost all headway and was wallowing helplessly in the sea. Below, in the engineering spaces, her engineers struggled to regain steam power, while her damage control parties vainly fought fires and flooding elsewhere throughout the ship. Meanwhile, both enemy and friendly shells were splashing all about her. Torpedoes were seen skirting past her and she was almost rammed by other ships churning through the smoke-hazed night.

Throughout the din and clangor of the battle, *Cushing's* Medical Officer, Lieutenant (j.g.) James E. Cashman, and his assistant corpsman were in the wardroom, busily treating the large number of wounded as best they could, until a large-caliber shell crashed into the compartment's port side. The explosion killed several of the casualties and wounded Dr. Cashman and his aide. Yet, despite their wounds, both men carried on, trying to remove the injured to a safer location. Due to the darkness, however, some of the wounded men could not be found.

Then suddenly, the battered destroyer was locked in tight by a searchlight's beam and torn asunder as a new avalanche of Japanese shells plummeted down. Her bridge was mauled, gun mounts crushed or torn from the deck, and more fires were started, as both men and machinery became hurled into the air.

Reduced to a raging inferno and without any means to contain the conflagration, Captain Parker ordered his ship abandoned, except for himself and a salvage party. The order to abandon was not heard by many of the crew as a result of the damaged intercom. Dr. Cashman was one of these. When he met the captain, he asked to have a water hose brought into the passageway leading to the wardroom in order to extinguish the fires that were raging in that area, but was informed that the ship had lost all power. Then, Cashman, with an assist from several men, was able to round up all the wounded who could be found, put life jackets on them and lowered them into the water.

Even as the men were going over the side, shells were still pouring into the helpless, burning hulk. Then, the bombardment ceased almost as suddenly as it had begun and the assailant raced away into the holocaustic night. Still, Captain Parker had hopes of saving his ship, but without any water pressure to fight the flames that were eating their way through the vessel unchecked, at 0315 even the salvage party went into the water.

By now the furious battle had ended. The *Cushing's* survivors were scattered about the sea, bobbing in life rafts or clinging to whatever debris they could find, as they watched their burning destroyer, now a funeral pyre for 60 of her crewmen, drift away. Of the survivors, 56 had been wounded; 12 of them would die later. The *Cushing* continued to burn and smolder throughout the day until 1700, when her magazines exploded.

After the balloon of smoke had dispersed, *Cushing*—or what was left of her—settled on the floor of "Ironbottom Sound," along with the battered wrecks of other American and Japanese warships that had been sunk since the opening of the Solomons campaign on August 8.

☆ ☆ ☆

USS *CUSHING* (DD-376)

Class: Mahan.

Builder: Puget Sound Navy Yard, Bremerton, Washington.

Keel laid: August 15, 1934.

Launched: December 31, 1935.

Sponsor: Miss Katherine A. Cushing, granddaughter of Commander William B. Cushing, USN.

Commissioned: August 28, 1936; Commander E.T. Short, USN, comdg.

Date of loss: November 13, 1942; Lieutenant Commander E.N. Parker, USN, comdg.

Location: Off Savo Island, the Solomons.

Awards: Two battle stars.

USS Preston

Launched April 22, 1936
Lost November 14, 1942
Off Savo Island, the Solomons

LIEUTENANT SAMUEL W. PRESTON, USN
(1840—1865)

Born in Canada on April 6, 1840, Samuel W. Preston was appointed Midshipman from the State of Illinois on October 4, 1858. Graduating at the head of his class on May 9, 1861, he was named Acting Master six months later and, on August 1, 1862, was promoted to the rank of Lieutenant in the Union Navy.

He went on to serve on various vessels that were attached to the Southern Blockade Squadron throughout most of the Civil War, until he was captured during an attack on Fort Sumter in September 1863. Taken to Libby Prison, Richmond, Virginia, he was released in a prisoner exchange in the fall of 1864. Ordered to the North Atlantic Blockading Squadron soon after his release, he served as Flag Lieutenant to Rear Admiral David D. Porter.

Later, he took part in attacks against Fort Fisher, North Carolina, on December 24–25, 1864. On January 13, 1865, Lieutenant Preston was killed while leading his landing party during the second attack against Fort Fisher.

Assigned to the Pacific Fleet, the USS *Preston* (DD-379) conducted her peacetime operations along the West Coast and occasionally in Hawaiian waters. During the early months of World War II, she served as a convoy escort and carried out patrol duties along the western seaboard.

From June until October 1942, *Preston* conducted patrols throughout the Hawaiian Islands and, at times, rendezvoused with incoming convoys and screened them into Pearl Harbor. On October 15, the destroyer sailed from Pearl Harbor, escorting Task Force 16 to the South Pacific. En route, they joined Task Force 17, at which time both task forces were combined to form Task Force 61, built around the carriers *Enterprise* and *Hornet*.

On the 26th, the planes of the task force tangled with those from the Japanese carriers *Zuikaku* and *Shokaku* off Santa Cruz Island. While American aircraft got through to deliver heavy damage to the Japanese carriers, during this battle, *Hornet* was attacked by 27 aircraft. Suffering from a number of bomb hits, and smashed by two suiciders and several torpedoes, the carrier was transformed into a seething caldron and had to be abandoned. Also lost in the action was the destroyer *Porter*, while the battleship *South Dakota*, the cruiser *San Juan*, the destroyer *Smith* and also the *Enterprise* sustained considerable damage. In this battle, *Preston's* crew enjoyed the satisfaction of splashing two of her attackers and she emerged from the fracas without a scratch.

On the afternoon of November 14, 1942, *Preston* was part of Rear Admiral Willis ("Ching") Lee's Task Force 64, which was racing northward to Savo Sound to intercept a Japanese bombardment force sighted coming down the eastern side of the Solomons.

Under command of Vice Admiral N. Kondo, this force was composed of the heavy cruisers *Atago* (flagship) and *Takao*, the light cruisers *Sendai* and *Nagara*, the battleship *Kirishima* and nine destroyers. Lee's force, steaming in a single column, was led by the destroyer *Walke* (DD-416). Directly astern of her followed the destroyers *Benham* (DD-397), *Preston* and *Gwin* (DD-433), as well as two battleships: Lee's flagship, *Washington*, and *South Dakota*.

Lee, after approaching the southwestern end of Savo Island, steamed on a northeasterly course, circled the island and made a right-hand turn into the sound at 2200. Twelve minutes later, he was well into the sound when Kondo's force made its entrance off the northeastern coast of Savo Island, well astern of Lee.

Owing to the clutter of small islands in the area, Lee's radar was unable to detect the enemy ships and was therefore unaware of Kondo's presence. Although the Japanese did not have the benefit of radar, they were provided with excellent night binoculars and, as a result, *Sendai's* lookouts sighted Lee's force steaming somewhat leisurely through the sound, and immediately reported their finding to Kondo.

Upon receiving this promising news, Kondo divided his fleet into three groups. *Sendai* and a destroyer were to stalk Lee and report his movements. *Nagara* and six destroyers were ordered to steam counterclockwise around Savo Island, the intention being to "box" Lee's ships in the sound or meet them head-on, should Lee decide to circle the island. In the meantime, Kondo deployed his cruiser, *Atago*, *Kirishima* and two destroyers at the northwestern mouth of the sound to wait, hopefully, to polish off any of Lee's ships that might escape from the anticipated battle. However, Kondo was in for an unpleasant surprise, for *Sendai* had erroneously reported Lee's force as only "two cruisers and four destroyers."

The minutes ticked by. Shortly before 2300, Lee ordered his column to turn right and, at 2300, both *Washington's* lookouts and her radar made contact on *Sendai* and her consort, slightly astern of her and off to starboard. After tracking the enemy ships for 17 minutes, the battlewagon's 16-inch guns boomed. *Sendai* and her escort turned tail and fled.

Alerted by the gunflashes and roaring gunfire, *Nagara's* scouting destroyers, *Ayanami* and *Uranami*, dug in their heels and raced toward the sound of the thundering guns, their own guns at the ready and their deadly "long lance" torpedoes trained outboard.

Five minutes later, *Walke* made radar contact on *Nagara* and opened fire. *Preston* and *Benham* joined in and scored several hits on the cruiser. *Gwin* illuminated the night with a salvo of starshells, exposing several enemy ships that had escaped radar detection. The Japanese ships returned fire with a vengeance, *Walke, Benham* and *Preston* absorbing the first hard blows. Of the three, *Preston* was the first to crumble under a vicious storm of 6-inch projectiles from *Nagara*.

The rain of shells poured into *Preston* just as she was preparing to fire her torpedoes. Both fire rooms were wrecked and her after stack was knocked over and tumbled into the sea. The bridge and pilot house were completely demolished and swathed in towering flames. With all power lost, the battered *Preston* lay paralyzed, her fiery hulk a beacon for further Japanese gunnery that now came from both sides. Flayed unmercifully with a cyclone of hot steel, within a few minutes the now easy-target *Preston* was reduced to scrap. Fires were raging out of control and, her hull plating torn open, the dying destroyer began to list heavily to port.

Amid the tangled wreckage lay her dead and wounded, including her mortally wounded captain, Commander Max C. Stormes. At 2336, the ship was abandoned, and not ten minutes later she rolled over on her port side, her fantail well beneath the surface. The sizzling derelict remained afloat for another ten minutes and then sank, stern first, taking her commander and 116 of her crew down with her.

While *Preston* was in her death throes, *Walke, Benham* and *Gwin* were taking severe punishment from large- and small-caliber projectiles. *Walke* had also suffered heavily from a barrage of 6-inch shellfire from the cruiser *Nagara*. Then, losing her bow from a torpedo hit, she sank shortly afterwards. *Benham* had also sustained a torpedo hit, which ripped off her bow. Although she survived the blow, she was living on borrowed time. The spunky *Gwin* had bravely slugged it out against *Sendai* and *Nagara*, before she was clobbered into submission and had to retire. With all of his destroyers knocked out of the engagement, it was up to Lee and his battleships to finish it.

As the crippled *Benham* and *Gwin* limped from the battlefield, the hotly contested engagement roared on in a broadside-to-broadside duel between the battleships and cruisers, while the remaining destroyers fired torpedoes. At 2400, *South Dakota* took a hit on her No.3 16-inch gun turret, and at the same time had an electrical failure, thus rendering her fire control equipment and radar inoperable. Lee ordered her to withdraw, but remained to fight it out single-handedly with Kondo's force from his flagship.

Washington's huge guns and 5-inch batteries slammed into *Kirishima*, sending her reeling out of control and steaming in circles. By 0125, Kondo had had enough and broke off the action, ordering *Sendai* and two destroyers to stand by the maimed battleship, which subsequently had to be scuttled. Also lost by the Japanese was the destroyer *Ayanami*.

The survivors from *Preston* and *Walke* were found shortly after dawn and were picked by the destroyer USS *Meade* (DD-602).

☆ ☆ ☆

USS PRESTON (DD-379)

Class: Mahan.
Builder: Mare Island Navy Yard, Vallejo, California.
Keel laid: October 27, 1934.
Launched: April 22, 1936.
Sponsor: Mrs. Edward H. Campbell.
Commissioned: October 27, 1936; Commander C.D. Swain, USN, comdg.
Date of loss: November 14, 1942; Commander M.C. Stormes, USN, comdg.†
Location: Off Savo Island, the Solomons.
Awards: Two battle stars.

USS Walke

Launched October 20, 1939
Lost November 14, 1942
Off Savo Island, the Solomons

REAR ADMIRAL HENRY A. WALKE, USN.
(1809–1896)

Born on December 24, 1809, in Princess Anne County, Virginia, Henry A. Walke was appointed Midshipman on February 1, 1827. Upon receiving his initial naval training at the Gosport Navy Yard, Virginia, he reported on board the brig USS *Natchez* in July 1828. During the next 18 months, the brig cruised throughout the Caribbean in the campaign to suppress piracy in those waters.

After completing a three-year tour of shore duty at the Philadelphia Navy Yard, Walke was assigned to the 74-gun frigate USS *North Carolina* in January 1836. Joining the Pacific Squadron, the frigate patrolled off the coast of Mexico during a period of strained political relations between that country and the United States. During the Mexican War, he commanded the brig *Vesuvius* and took part in the landings at Vera Cruz and Tuspán.

During the Civil War, Walke served with distinction and rendered valuable service to Union Rear Admiral Andrew H. Foote's ironclad flotillas in the Mississippi River campaign.

While in command of the ironclad gunboat USS *Carondelet*, he engaged with, and defeated the Confederate ironclad CSS *Arkansas* and successfully bombarded Forts Donelson and Henry. Other daring exploits were his running past the batteries of Island No. 10 and passing under the guns of Vicksburg while in command of the ironclad USS *Lafayette*. Later, after a five-hour duel, *Lafayette* successfully silenced the shore batteries at Grand Gulf, Mississippi.

On September 22, 1863, Walke was placed in command of the screw sloop USS *Sacramento* and during the final two years of the Civil War he cruised throughout the South Atlantic in search of Confederate shipping and commerce raiders.

119

After the war, he was promoted to the rank of Commodore and, in 1870, was advanced to the rank of Rear Admiral. Although he was placed on the retirement list on April 21, 1871, he still remained active in naval affairs and was, for a time, Head of the Lighthouse Board. On April 1, 1873, he was detached from this post and devoted his retirement years writing and sketching. His book *Naval Scenes of the Civil War* was published in 1877. He died in Brooklyn, New York, on March 8, 1896.

Assigned to the Atlantic Fleet destroyer squadrons, the USS *Walke* (DD-416) served on the neutrality patrol, and later was busily engaged protecting British shipping against the U-boat menace in the waters of the North Atlantic.

At the time of the infamous attack on Pearl Harbor, *Walke* was en route to Casco Bay, Maine. Her scheduled deployment to meet a convoy was canceled, however, and she was ordered to the Boston Navy Yard instead. After undergoing an overhaul, she reported to the Pacific Fleet and, in early February 1942, she sailed for Pago Pago, Samoa, serving as an escort for Task Force 17.

Constantly on the move, *Walke* operated throughout the South Pacific, taking part in the early raids against the Japanese-held Gilbert and Marshall islands. During the Battle of the Coral Sea, she received credit for splashing five twin-engined bombers. Shortly afterwards, the destroyer experienced turbine difficulties and, much to the delight of her crew, *Walke* spent two weeks at Brisbane, Australia, undergoing temporary repairs alongside a U.S. Navy destroyer tender.

Dispatched to the United States, the destroyer departed Brisbane in mid-July and arrived at the Mare Island Navy Yard, Vallejo, California, on August 2. After repairs were completed, *Walke* stood out of San Francisco escorting the navy oiler USS *Kankakee* to San Pedro. Here, they joined Task Force 15.13, and proceeded on to Nouméa, New Caledonia.

After serving several weeks on monotonous escort and patrol duties, *Walke* was assigned to Rear Admiral Willis A. Lee's Task Force 64. During the early morning hours of November 14, Lee's task force departed Nouméa for the Solomons to intercept Vice Admiral N. Kondo's bombardment force, which was intending to bombard the Marine garrison on Guadalcanal.

As was mentioned in the story of the *Preston*, the confrontation between Lee and Kondo commenced at 2317, when Lee fired on the cruiser *Sendai* and her escorting destroyer. At 2322, *Walke* had sighted and fired upon the heavy cruiser *Nagara*. For a period of two minutes, her 5-inch batteries scored a number of hits upon the cruiser, before she shifted her fire to a destroyer that was seen approaching her starboard bow. At that moment, *Walke* became stunned under a torrent of 8-inch shells that wrecked her forward fire room, smashed her radio room and damaged her No.3 5-inch gun mount. Even as she reeled from the enemy shellfire, a "long lance" torpedo came churning through the dark water to hit her in the bow, tearing it completely off.

By now, fires had broken out forward, billowing steam and smoke were rolling from out of her engineering spaces, and the after bulkheads in the forward fire room and amidships section were beginning to buckle; the ship showed every indication of going down by the head. Her wounded and dying captain, Commander Thomas E. Frazer, ordered the ship abandoned. Unfortunately, only two life rafts could be launched, since the rest, plus the lifeboats, had been completely destroyed during the shelling.

As *Walke*'s survivors struggled in the oil-slicked and debris-cluttered water, the battle continued to explode around them. At 2343, the shattered remains of *Walke* upended and plunged to the floor of "Ironbottom Sound." As the waters closed over her, her depth charges detonated, inflicting additional injuries on the swimmers and killing several more men.

After the battle ended, an enemy submarine passed close by *Walke*'s survivors, but did not stop. Later, a Japanese destroyer discovered the ship's derelict bow, upon which were several men who, by some miracle, had survived the torpedoing and had managed to clear out of its compartments. The destroyer, like the submarine, did not stop to investigate but continued out of the area.

Two of *Walke*'s swimmers, Seaman Dale Land and Machinist's Mate Harold Taylor, managed to get ashore on Guadalcanal Island. Finding the jungle heavy with Japanese soldiers, both alive and dead, the sailors found abandoned weapons and proceeded to fight their way to the American lines. Taylor was killed in an encounter with enemy infantry but Land emerged from the undergrowth on December 5, three weeks after his ship had gone down. Feverish and incoherent, it was not until he was in hospital that he was able to identify himself as a crewman from the *Walke*.

As for the remainder of *Walke*'s battle-weary survivors, these had been rescued on the morning of November 15 by the destroyer *Meade*. Lost with *Walke* were her captain and 76 members of her crew. Six others died later as a result of their wounds.

☆ ☆ ☆

USS *WALKE* (DD-416)

Class: Sims.
Builder: Boston Navy Yard, Charlestown, Massachusetts.
Keel laid: April 23, 1938.
Launched: October 20, 1939.
Sponsor: Mrs. Clarence Dillon, grand-niece of Rear Admiral Henry A. Walke.
Commissioned: April 27, 1940; Lieutenant Commander C.H. Sanders, USN,
    comdg.
Date of loss: November 14, 1942; Commander T.E. Frazer, USN, comdg.†
Location: Off Savo Island, the Solomons.
Awards: Three battle stars.

USS Benham

Launched April 16, 1938
Lost November 15, 1942
Off Guadalcanal, Solomon Islands

REAR ADMIRAL ANDREW E.K. BENHAM, USN
(1832–1905)

Andrew Ellicot Kennedy Benham was born on Staten Island, New York, on April 10, 1832. Appointed Midshipman in 1847, he first served in the East Indian Squadron, then took part in the Paraguay Expedition (1854–55), and subsequently served with the South Atlantic and Gulf Coast Blockading squadrons during the Civil War.

Throughout his naval career, he proved himself an adept officer while in command of various assignments at sea and ashore. In January 1894, he assumed command of the South Atlantic Station at Rio de Janerio, Brazil. At that time, the city was in turmoil due to an uprising of insurgents against the government. After taking command, Benham took action to prevent the rebels from interfering with the unloading and loading of American merchant ships at the wharves and in the harbor. His outstanding performance during this event set a new precedent in international law and he was highly commended by the U.S. Congress.

Rear Admiral Benham retired on April 10, 1894, although on several occasions over the next five years he was recalled to active duty. Rear Admiral Benham died at his home in Lake Mahopac, New York, on August 11, 1905, and is buried at Arlington National Cemetery.

Upon the completion of her shakedown trials, the USS *Benham* (DD-397) joined the Atlantic Fleet destroyer squadrons in the late summer of 1939 and operated off the eastern seaboard and in the Caribbean with the neutrality patrol. In February 1941, *Benham* stood out for San Diego where she commenced carrying out her operations with the Pacific Fleet.

On November 28 she departed Pearl Harbor, screening the aircraft carrier *Enterprise*, flagship of Vice Admiral William F. Halsey, Jr., which was transporting aircraft to the Marines on Wake Island. Upon discharging the aircraft, the task force returned to Pearl. The ships were less than two hours from Pearl Harbor when word was received that the naval base and other military installations on Oahu were under attack by Japanese aircraft. An immediate air search was carried out by the *Enterprise's* pilots, but neither the raiders nor their carriers could be found.

What *Benham's* crew witnessed when she entered Pearl Harbor would never be forgotten. Lining the rails, her crew gazed with shock and horror at the carnage and devastation along Ford Island's "Battleship Row." It appeared that every moored battleship was aflame, belching clouds of smoke and racked by internal explosions. Gliding through the eye-smarting smoky haze, *Benham's* crew could see the overturned hull of *Oklahoma* and, farther on, sunk in the mud, lay the once proud, 26,000-ton *Arizona*, her massive hull broken in half by a single bomb that had ignited her magazines.

After refueling, *Benham* was ordered to sea and spent the night on anti-submarine patrol. On December 19, the destroyer raced to Wake Island with *Enterprise* to land reinforcements for the Marines; however, the island had fallen before the ships arrived and the task force returned to Pearl Harbor.

Benham remained in the Hawaiian Islands conducting ASW patrols and escorting incoming convoys. On January 11, 1942, when the carrier *Saratoga* was torpedoed about 500 miles east of the islands, *Benham*, along with several other destroyers, was dispatched to aid the carrier and escort her into port. Having escorted a number of convoys between the West Coast and Pearl Harbor, *Benham* then took part in escorting the carrier *Hornet*, embarked with Lieutenant Colonel James Doolittle's 16 B-25 bombers that were to strike the first American blow against the Japanese homeland.

Benham resumed her patrol duties in Hawaiian waters until she participated in the Battle of Midway. After the battle, she dashed back to Pearl, carrying the survivors from the destroyer *Hammann*, which had been torpedoed and sunk alongside the carrier *Yorktown*. All hands that could be spared donated their time and services to ease the pain and suffering of that ship's wounded survivors. One man, Mess Attendant Alonza Crawford, Jr., was highly commended by *Benham's* Executive Officer, who stated, "Crawford rendered wonderful work in taking care of the wounded . . . staying up all night and through the following day."

Benham was steadily employed as an escort for *Enterprise's* task force and took part in the initial landings at Guadalcanal on August 8, 1942. When *Enterprise* was seriously damaged in an air attack on August 24, *Benham* was detached from her task force to screen resupply vessels and transports seeking to reinforce the troops ashore.

On November 14, she joined Rear Admiral Willis A. Lee's Task Force 64 and departed Nouméa, New Caledonia, to intercept Vice Admiral N. Kondo's bombardment and reinforcement group, which was sighted steaming toward Guadalcanal. The Japanese intention was to wipe the Americans out of the Solomon Islands; Task Force 64's job was to keep the Japanese fleet at bay.

When the two opponents clashed off Savo Island, the tranquil night was shattered by the roar of thundering guns. Within a few moments, the destroyers *Preston* and *Walke* were hammered to the bottom under an avalanche of large- and small-caliber shells and torpedoes. *Gwin*, after dishing out severe punishment to the cruiser *Nagara*, was thrashed by several hits and forced to retire.

Benham plunged into the fray, opening fire with her 5-inch main batteries, taking aim at *Nagara*. Only a few rounds were fired, when, at 2338, fifteen feet of her bow was blown off by a torpedo, the impact from the blast lifting the *Benham* out of the water. Gunner's Mate Second Class, Aleck M. Thomson, who was close to the point of the explosion, recalls that the geyser of water thrown up by the detonation splashed down on him and his men and knocked them to the deck.

Immediately, all power was lost and, before it could be restored, the decapitated *Benham* was drifting helplessly into the thick of the engagement, occasional shells splashing around her. As stated earlier, the American destroyers were hard hit at the beginning of this battle, and it was now up to Lee's battleships, *South Dakota* and *Washington*, to decide the final outcome.

Meanwhile, *Benham's* damage control parties were busy shoring up her bulkheads. This was, for a time, a touch-and-go operation, but they managed to stem the worst of the flooding. *Gwin* came alongside to assist and prepared to take on *Benham's* crew, should the ship begin to founder. Eventually, her engineers had steam up and she was able to get underway, but just barely under 12 knots, with *Gwin* escorting her from the battlefield.

Throughout the remainder of the night and into the following day, all hands kept a constant vigil about the creaking hull of their crippled destroyer. Then, at about 1500, while the ship was off the western coast of Guadalcanal, the creaks and groans emanating from her tortured hull became more ominous. Suddenly, a sharp crack resounded and vibrated throughout the *Benham's* weakened hull—a positive sign that she was breaking up. Her captain, Lieutenant Commander John B. Taylor, immediately ordered the *Gwin* alongside and *Benham* was abandoned.

Within a short time of abandonment, the drifting derelict split in half with an agonizing screech; nevertheless, both sections still stayed afloat and *Gwin* was compelled to sink the *Benham*'s remains with her 5-inch guns.

Fortunately, not one of *Benham*'s crew was killed during the action; seven men, however, were wounded, all of whom eventually recovered.

☆ ☆ ☆

USS *BENHAM* (DD-397)

Class: Benham.
Builder: Federal Shipbuilding and Drydock Co., Kearny, New Jersey.
Keel laid: September 1, 1936.
Launched: April 16, 1938.
Sponsor: Mrs. Albert I. Dorr, grand-niece of Rear Admiral Andrew E.K. Benham, USN.
Commissioned: February 2, 1939; Lieutenant Commander T.F. Darden, USN, comdg.
Date of loss: November 15, 1942; Lieutenant Commander J.B. Taylor, USN, comdg.
Awards: Five battle stars.

USS Worden

Launched October 27, 1934
Lost January 12, 1943
Off Amchika Island, the Aleutians

REAR ADMIRAL JOHN L. WORDEN, USN
(1818–1897)

John Lorimar Worden was born in Westchester County, New York, on March 12, 1818. Appointed Midshipman on January 10, 1834, he spent his first three years of naval service on board the sloop-of-war USS *Erie*, on the Brazilian Station. At the completion of a seven-month tour of duty in the naval school at Philadelphia, he returned to sea, serving in the Pacific Squadron.

From 1844 to 1846, he was stationed at the United States Naval Observatory, Washington, D.C. During the Mexican War, he served in several vessels, including the stores ship *Southampton*. In 1850, he returned to the Naval Observatory for two years and from there went on to serve seven more years at sea, with the Mediterranean and West Indies Squadrons.

Prior to the outbreak of the Civil War, he was ordered on a secret mission to Pensacola, Florida, in connection with the reinforcement of Fort Pickens. While returning to Washington, he was arrested near Montgomery, Alabama, and held prisoner for seven months. During that time his health began to fail; still, upon his release, he accepted the command of and supervised the construction of the ironclad *Monitor* at Green Point, Long Island.

On March 8, 1862, the *Monitor* entered Hampton Roads, Virginia, to challenge the Confederate Navy's ironclad ram, CSS *Virginia* (ex-USS *Merrimack*). On the following day, the two adversaries confronted each other and a furious hammer-and-tongs battle ensued. For four hours, the ironclads clashed, neither side winning or losing. Shortly before the *Virginia* broke off the action, a shell exploded on the *Monitor's* turret that wounded and temporarily blinded Lieutenant Commander Worden. The *Monitor* then withdrew from the field of combat until First Officer Samuel Green assumed command. By the time the *Monitor* circled back, the *Virginia* had retired.

For his heroism in this action, Lieutenant Commander Worden was awarded a vote of thanks from the U.S. Congress. In late 1862, he placed the ironclad USS *Montauk* in commission and joined the South Atlantic Blockading Squadron. On January 27, he led his ship in the bombardment of Fort McAllisiter, South Carolina, and a month later cruised up the Ogeechee River to destroy the Confederate privateer CSS *Rattlesnake*. Promoted to the rank of Captain on February 3, 1863, Worden went on to take part in several naval operations against Confederate forces. His last action was participating in the bombardment of Charleston, South Carolina, and, shortly afterwards, he was assigned to shore duty, supervising the construction of ironclads.

In 1869, he commenced a five-year tour of duty as Superintendant of the U.S. Naval Academy, during which time he was advanced to the rank of Rear Admiral. During the late 1870s, he was placed in command of the European Squadron, and in 1878 he was appointed a member of the Naval Examining Board and later voted in as President of the Rating Board.

Upon his retirement on December 23, 1886, Congress awarded him full sea pay in his grade for life. Rear Admiral Worden resided in Washington, DC, until his death from pneumonia on October 19, 1897. Rear Admiral Worden was buried at Pawling, New York.

Except for a three-month tour of duty with the Atlantic Fleet in the summer of 1935, the USS *Worden* (DD-352) spent her entire active service with the Pacific Fleet until her loss on January 12, 1943.

Worden was at Pearl Harbor, moored alongside the destroyer tender *Dobbin,* when the Japanese struck. During the attack, she was shaken by several near-misses, but her gunners had the satisfaction of shooting down one of the raiders. Two hours later, the destroyer's engineers were ready to "answer all bells" and *Worden* cleared out of the smoke-filled harbor for the open sea. Shortly afterwards, her sonar operator made an underwater contact. Suspecting it was a submarine, a pattern of depth charges was dropped, without results. Nearby, the cruiser *Detroit* was zigzagging and reported the sighting of a submarine's periscope some distance from her. *Worden* sped to the area, but her sonar did not pick up evidence of a submarine.

Worden remained in Hawaiian waters, conducting anti-submarine patrols until February 5, 1942, when she sailed for Nouméa, New Caledonia. Three days after her arrival, she rescued the crew of the merchant ship SS *Snark*, which had struck a mine on entering port.

Worden continued to serve as an escort for the various task forces that were plying the waters of the South Pacific and also took part in the Battle of Midway. On July 28, she rescued the survivors from an Army transport, No. 42, which had been torpedoed and sunk 75 miles south of New Caledonia. After having seen action during the landings at Guadalcanal and Tulagi and the Battle of the Eastern Solomons, *Worden* sailed for San Francisco for a well-deserved overhaul and leave for her crew.

Upon completion of repairs and alterations, the destroyer underwent a refresher course in gunnery and torpedo exercises prior to her deployment to Dutch Harbor, Alaska, on December 28, 1942. On the night of January 11, *Worden* escorted the Coast Guard transport *Arthur Middleton* into Constantine Harbor, Amchitka Island, to disembark an Army preliminary security unit. Despite the assistance of radar, it required an extremely astute navigator to maneuver through the coal-black night and that rock-infested harbor.

To make matters more difficult, a howling williwaw had swept down from the far regions of the Arctic on the previous day, causing the currents in the surrounding waters to become erratic. However, in spite of these hazards, both ships skirted clear of the pinnacle rocks and anchored until the landing party was able to secure a beachhead.

At 0730, *Worden* weighed anchor and commenced her precarious voyage to the open sea. Well aware of the hazards about them, the ship's lookouts and those not on watch kept a constant vigil, peering through the gray veil of mist that carpeted the bay in the half-light of a cold, stark dawn.

Just as *Worden* seemed to be clear of the bay's groping, granite-like fingers, she was jolted by a tremendous crash. She had run over a submerged rock that tore a huge gash in her hull as if it were tinfoil. The screeching of her hull being slashed open by the hard, immovable obstruction sent shivering spasms up and down the spines of the crew. Before she could be brought to a stop, *Worden* had slithered agonizingly over the rock, only to find herself surrounded by more menacing outcroppings.

The ill-fated ship came to a quivering halt and, by now, her engineering spaces were beginning to flood. Her repair parties rushed into the depths of the rapidly filling engine rooms, sloshing through the frigid water in an attempt to hold back the inrushing sea. Despite the employment of every pump that was available, the flooding could not be contained.

In an effort to prevent his vessel from piling up broadside against the rocks, her captain, Commander William B. Pogue, had the anchors dropped. By now her distress signal had been received by *Worden's* sister ship, *Dewey* (DD-349), which was on her way to the scene.

As the lead-gray morning wore on, the ship was lightened by jettisoning all topside weight, but to no avail. Then the seas, accompanied by stiff, gale force winds, began to rise, tossing the 1,375-ton destroyer about like a toy. Then a mountainous swell shouldered *Worden* on a high crest and slammed her back down on the rocks with such force that her seams split wide open. More and more compartments began to flood and now her fuel bunkers began to tear open. Although *Dewey* arrived, hoping to tow the stricken destroyer out of her trap, the effort failed after two hawsers had snapped.

Realizing that *Worden* could not be saved, Commander Pogue ordered her abandoned. Boats from *Dewey* and *Middleton* were standing by, although buffeting high winds and the turbulent waters made rescue very difficult. Most of *Worden's* life rafts overturned, spilling their occupants into the thrashing, oil-saturated surf. Many of her crew were swept overboard, including Commander Pogue, who was fished out of the frothing seas unconscious. Eventually, all but 14 of *Worden's* crew were rescued.

By noon, the stranded *Worden* was lying almost on her beams end and by 1225 she had split in two. Over the next five days, the williwaw continued to vent its fury. *Middleton* was driven ashore, and when the maelstrom finally abated the wreckage of *Worden* was gone. Not one scrap of her remains could be seen. It wasn't until the following August that her broken and storm-ravished hulk was discovered by a demolition team, which destroyed the wreck with explosives.

☆ ☆ ☆

USS *WORDEN* (DD-352)

Class: Farragut.
Builder: Puget Sound Navy Yard, Bremerton, Washington.
Keel laid: December 29, 1932.
Launched: October 27, 1934.
Sponsor: Mrs. John Halligan, wife of Rear Admiral John Halligan, USN.
Commissioned: January 15, 1935; Commander R.E. Kerr, USN, comdg.
Date of loss: January 12, 1943; Commander W.B. Pogue. USN, comdg.
Location: Off Amchika Island, the Aleutians.
Awards: Four battle stars.

USS DeHaven

Launched June 28, 1942
Lost February 1, 1943
Off Savo Island, the Solomons

LIEUTENANT EDWIN J. DEHAVEN, USN
(1819–1865)

Born in Pennsylvania in 1819, Edwin Jess DeHaven, was appointed Acting Midshipman at the age of ten, and five years later was advanced to Passed Midshipman. In 1839, he was assigned to the USS *Vincennes*, flagship of Captain Charles Wilkes, and took part in his explorations of the Antarctic and islands throughout the Pacific.

In mid-1840, DeHaven assumed command of the USS *Peacock* and proceeded to the waters of the North Pacific, surveying the coasts of North America and in the Puget Sound area. On July 18, 1840, *Peacock* was wrecked in the treacherous waters at the entrance of the Columbia River, her crew being rescued by the USS *Oregon*. DeHaven remained on board *Oregon* until the termination of the expedition in June 1842.

During the war with Mexico, DeHaven was in command of the USS *Somers* when she captured the Mexican schooner *Creole*. In 1850, Lieutenant DeHaven assumed command of the Grinnell Rescue Expedition in an effort to search for Sir John Franklin's exploring party, reported lost somewhere in Greenland. Both of his ships, *Rescue* and *Advanc,* became locked in an ice flow west of Greenland and drifted about for nine months. When they did locate the area where Franklin had camped, there were traces of the campsite, but no remains of his party could be found. In the course of his searching for Franklin's party, DeHaven discovered an island that he named Grinnell Land, in honor of the rescue party's sponsor.

Lieutenant DeHaven was highly commended for his painstaking achievements during his search for the ill-fated explorers and for the valuable scientific data he collected in connection with the winds and currents of the Arctic regions.

After serving for nine years in the Coastal Survey Service,
DeHaven was placed on the retirement list in 1862 because of ill
health. Lieutenant DeHaven died at his home in Philadelphia, on May
1, 1865.

After the completion of her battle-readiness exercises off the coast of New
England, the USS *DeHaven* (DD-469) departed Norfolk, Virginia, for
the South Pacific on November 8, 1942. Arriving at Guadalcanal on
December 7, *DeHaven*, was assigned to escort duty and made several voy-
ages between Guadalcanal and Espiritu Santo, until she was assigned to Task
Group 67.5 on January 20, 1943.

On the night of the 24th, *DeHaven*, in company with two destroyers and
two cruisers, arrived off Kolombangara Island to bombard enemy installations on the Villa-Stanmore Plantations. Afterwards, the ships raced out of
Kula Gulf and were soon chased by an infuriated enemy, primarily a flock of
twin-engine bombers. Thanks to a heavily overcast sky, as well as an occasional rain squall, *DeHaven*'s group could not be found, despite the enemy's
attempt to locate the ships by dropping flares. On February 1, *DeHaven*, in
company with the destroyers *O'Bannon* (DD-450), *Nicholas* (DD-449),
Radford (DD-446) and a seaplane tender, was escorting six landing craft to
establish a beachhead at Morovovo, Guadalcanal. With the assistance of
Marine fighters from Henderson Field, the landings were achieved without
difficulty. However, an enemy scout plane pilot had sighted the activity and
notified his base.

After the landing craft disembarked their troops, *DeHaven* and *Nicholas*
were ordered to escort them back to their station, while *Radford* remained
offshore to provide bombardment if necessary. Meanwhile, a dispatch was
received warning of an impending air attack.

At 1445, *DeHaven*'s crew rushed to their battle stations. While lookouts
scanned the skies and the horizon, gun crews were standing by their
weapons, tensely waiting. In the confines of the sweltering engineering
spaces, the heavily perspiring "black gang" checked their machinery,
watched water levels on their boilers and scores of water, air and steam
gauges, and stood by to "answer all bells."

Throughout other parts of the destroyer, damage control parties closed
watertight doors and hatches and nearby, within easy reach, was all the
equipment needed to fight fires, flooding and shore up bulkheads: axes,
lumber, portable pumps, battle lanterns, fire hoses and more. In the ward-

room and after living spaces, Pharmacist's Mates grimly stood by for casualties that were expected to be certain to arrive. All that could be done was accomplished within a few moments. Now *DeHaven* and her crew were ready.

At about 1457, a swarm of 14 aircraft was sighted off *DeHaven's* starboard beam at a distance of 25,000 yards. At first, it appeared as though the enemy had not seen the tiny convoy and, for a time, the aircraft remained on their original course. Then, suddenly, six aircraft broke away from the formation and streaked toward the destroyers and their charges.

DeHaven's guns, as well as *Nicholas'* and those on the landing craft, opened up. Fiery tracers stabbed into the oncoming flock, with bursts of flak blossoming about the planes. Three of the aircraft were sent spiraling in flames into the sea. The remaining three bolted through the heavy mantle of flak and AA fire and, for some reason, singled out *DeHaven* as their choice target.

Four bombs plunged down upon the destroyer, one of which struck the bridge, killing and wounding all personnel within the structure. Lying dead among the ruins was her captain, Commander Charles E. Tolman. Two bombs smashed on her bow and another exploded below her waterline, splitting open her hull plating.

Severely crippled, *DeHaven* lost all power, came to a halt and began to settle swiftly by the bow. Five minutes after the last bomb had hit, the destroyer's bow was well under, her stern high out of the water. Ensign C.L. Williams, the only officer who was not wounded, realized that *DeHaven* was going down and passed the word to abandon ship. While the personnel belowdecks were scrambling to escape from out of the topsy-turvy hell in the lower compartments, *DeHaven* suddenly upended and plunged to her watery grave, taking 167 members of her crew down with her, to rest forever on the floor of "Iron Bottom Sound."

☆ ☆ ☆

USS DE HAVEN (DD-469)

Class: Fletcher.
Builder: Bath Iron Works, Bath Maine.
Keel laid: September 27, 1941.
Launched: June 28, 1942.
Sponsor: Miss Helen N. DeHaven, granddaughter of Lieutenant Edwin J.
    DeHaven, USN.
Commissioned: September 21, 1942; Commander C.E. Tolman, USN, comdg.

Date of loss: February 1, 1943; Commander C.E. Tolman, USN, comdg.†
Location: Off Savo Island, the Solomons.
Awards: One battle star.

USS Aaron Ward

Launched November 22, 1941
Lost April 7, 1943
Off Tagoma Point, Guadalcanal

REAR ADMIRAL AARON WARD, USN
(1851–1918)

Born in Philadelphia, Pennsylvania, on October 10, 1851, Aaron Ward graduated from the U.S. Naval Academy in 1867. After serving on several types of vessels, Lieutenant Ward was placed in command of the USS *Wasp*, ex-*Columbia*, a yacht that was acquired by the Navy from Mr. J.H. Ladew for service in the Spanish-American War. For his conspicuous gallantry in covering the landings and evacuation of troops at Cabañas, Cuba, and his participation in other actions during the war, Ward was advanced to the rank of Lieutenant Commander.

Rising swiftly through the ranks, he was promoted to Rear Admiral in 1910, and between 1911 and 1912 he commanded the 3rd Battleship Division, Atlantic Fleet. From January 1913 until his retirement on October 10 of that year, he served as Supervisor of New York Harbor. Upon his retirement, Rear Admiral Aaron Ward settled in Roslyn, New York, where he died on July 5, 1918.

Assigned to the Pacific Fleet, the USS *Aaron Ward* (DD-483) arrived at San Diego in early May 1942 and commenced escorting convoys along the West Coast until early August, when she received her orders to proceed to the South Pacific.

Arriving in the Solomons Islands later that month, she joined a rather depleted American fleet that was carrying the brunt of the naval war surrounding the epic battle of Guadalcanal. She continued to operate with this fleet in its brave stand to protect what foothold the fighting Marines had gained on shore.

135

On October 20, *Aaron Ward*'s task force was attacked by a submarine that torpedoed the cruiser *Chester*. While other destroyers searched for the submarine, *Aaron Ward* rushed to the cruiser's side to offer assistance and, if necessary, remove her crew. Fortunately, the cruiser was able to steam under her own power, but the submarine succeeded in evading her attackers.

After serving as a convoy escort between Espiritu Santo and Guadalcanal, and occasionally assisting in shore bombardments against enemy gun emplacements, *Aaron Ward* was assigned to Task Group 67.4, under the command of Rear Admiral Daniel Callaghan.

On the night of November 12, the task group engaged with Vice Admiral Hiroki Abe's bombardment force off Savo Island. During the melee, the American force suffered the loss of four destroyers and the damaging of every ship in the force, except the destroyer *Fletcher* and the cruiser *Helena*.

During the opening phase of the battle, *Aaron Ward* commenced firing on a target some 7,000 yards off her starboard bow. After the tenth round, she had to cease fire when a cruiser crossed into her line of fire. Shortly afterwards, she was nearly rammed by another cruiser. Needless to say, the destroyer had plenty of Japanese targets to choose from, but the risk of mixing with a "friendly" in the dark was also a concern. Throughout the furious and, to say the least, perplexed engagement, *Aaron Ward* seemed to live a charmed life. With ships being sunk and large- and small-caliber shells splashing all around her, not one scrap of steel touched the vessel.

Then, at 0235, about ten minutes before Abe broke off the action, *Aaron Ward*'s luck ran out when she was struck by a heavy-caliber shell that smashed into her gun director and killed all power to her 5-inch guns. Before the gun crews could shift over to manual control, the destroyer was further clobbered by a violent cataclysm of small- and large-caliber shells.

Seven out of eight projectiles crashed into her, demolishing her forward fire room and leaving her without power. Blown overboard were her radar and searchlight platforms; her galley was holed; electric cables were severed and her mainmast went toppling over the side. The eighth shell detonated beneath her waterline, splitting open her hull plating and flooding her forward engine room.

Crawling to a halt, the stricken *Aaron Ward* lay paralyzed. While her repair parties strived to retard the flooding, her engineers labored feverishly to relight her after boilers in an effort to regain steam power. By this time, the vicious battle was over and throughout the remainder of the night *Aaron Ward*'s captain, Lieutenant Commander Orville F. Gregor, and his crew fought a desperate touch-and-go contest against the hungry sea.

Twice, the black gang mustered up enough steam pressure to enable the crippled destroyer to creep a short distance, only to lose steam power when water in her fuel lines snuffed out the fires. Despite the fact that the destroyer was reduced to a helpless derelict, she was still afloat and the hopes of her being saved were further enhanced when the salvage tug USS *Bobolink* arrived at daybreak and took her under tow.

Dawn found Savo Sound littered with both dead and survivors floundering in a sea of oil littered with debris. The wounded ships that were still afloat were lying immobile, smoldering and drifting aimlessly with the wind and tide. Northeast of Savo Island wallowed the shattered, 31,0000-ton battleship IJN *Hiei*, with a destroyer lying alongside. The battlewagon's crew was also struggling to bring the behemoth back to life and were succeeding in that endeavor for, as *Aaron Ward* was being towed to a safe anchorage, *Hiei*'s massive guns came alive. Slowly training outboard, they coughed a salvo of 14-inch shells toward the *Aaron Ward* that, fortunately, splashed harmlessly around her. Towed to Tulagi, the American ship's 57 wounded were hospitalized and, later, the crew attended burial services for 12 of their shipmates.

After effecting temporary repairs, the bloodied but proud *Aaron Ward* was able to steam under her own power and stood out for Pearl Harbor, where she was permanently repaired and lived to fight again.

On February 6, 1943, and under command of a new skipper, Lieutenant Commander F. Julian Becton, *Aaron Ward* put to sea and reported to the South Pacific naval forces. Here, she resumed her escort and patrol duties throughout the Solomons.

On April 7, at about 1200, a message was received that a large swarm of enemy aircraft—composed of 67 "Val" dive bombers and 110 "Zero" fighters—was winging down the "Slot." At that time, *Aaron Ward* was escorting three LCTs from Russell Island to Guadalcanal, when she was ordered to come to the assistance of a landing craft that was experiencing mechanical problems off Lunga Roads. With the vessel under her protection, the destroyer set a course for Lengo Channel. She was soon joined by the Navy salvage tugs *Orlotan* and *Vireo*, along with several smaller craft that had gathered about the destroyer like chicks around a mother hen, hoping to seek protection under the destroyer's anti-aircraft cover.

The oncoming air armada was met by 76 American fighters and a vicious air battle ensued over Savo Sound. Yet, despite the loss of several enemy aircraft, a large number escaped to wreak havoc on the shipping and other targets in the sound. Then, at 1512, three "Vals," their engines screaming, plunged from out of a bank of clouds directly above *Aaron Ward*.

Captain Becton ordered full speed ahead; however, the planes were on top of his destroyer before he could evade, and the bombs came whistling down. Two of them splashed and exploded about 50 yards abroad of her, spraying lethal, jagged, shrapnel across her decks and wounding several of her crew. The third bomb, a 500-pounder, struck the ship itself like a thunderbolt, jarring her from stem to stern. Before the destroyer could recover from this blow, three more dive bombers plummeted down on her. All three of their bombs missed, but detonated less than 15 feet from both sides of the ship. The underwater concussion split open *Aaron Ward*'s hull plating, letting in the sea to both fire rooms. The after bulkhead in the forward fire room ruptured, which consequently caused flooding in the forward engine room. The after engine room was also beginning to fill, and so rapidly that the space had to be abandoned.

With all power lost and without steam pressure to maneuver or fight the several fires that had broken out, portable gasoline powered fire pumps ("handy billies") were employed to douse the flames, and simultaneously used to help pump out flooded compartments. The *Orlatan* and *Vireo* came alongside the now-helpless destroyer to offer assistance and take her under tow.

Despite the use of the portable pumps that were straining to stem the flow of water gushing into her lower compartments, and her damage controlmen attempting to shore up her collapsing bulkheads, as well as forming bucket brigades, the gallant *Aaron Ward* continued to settle by the stern and took on a starboard list. At the same time, her loggy hull was becoming more and more difficult for the sturdy tugs to tow. As her list increased, her exhausted crew were unable to stand upright.

By 2100, it was a foregone conclusion that the fighting *Aaron Ward*'s time had come and her captain, very reluctantly, was compelled to order her abandoned. Dropping their towlines, the tugs came alongside the sinking destroyer and received her crew, of which 59 were wounded.

Almost ten hours after the ship had been disabled, and in spite of the valiant and desperate struggle to save her, the fighting *Aaron Ward* rolled over on her beams' end and slipped quietly beneath the sea at 2135, in 40 fathoms of water, less than three miles off Tagoma Point, Guadalcanal. Lost with the vessel were 27 of her crew.

☆ ☆ ☆

USS *AARON WARD* (DD-484)

Class: Benson/Livermore.
Builder: Federal Shipbuilding and Drydock Co., Kearny, New Jersey.
Keel laid: February 11, 1941.
Launched: November 22, 1941
Sponsor: Miss Hilda Ward, daughter of Rear Admiral Aaron Ward, USN.
Commissioned: March 4, 1942; Lieutenant Commander O.F. Gregor, USN,
    comdg.
Date of loss: April 7, 1943; Lieutenant Commander F.J. Becton, USN, comdg.
Location: Off Tagoma Point, Guadalcanal.
Awards: Four battle stars.

USS Strong

Launched May 17, 1942
Lost July 5, 1943
Off New Georgia Island, the Solomons

REAR ADMIRAL JAMES H. STRONG, USN
(1814–1882)

James Hooker Strong was born on April 16, 1814, in Canandaigua, New York. While studying at the Polytechnic College, Chittenango, New York, he was appointed Midshipman on February 2, 1829. From 1833 to 1835, he served with the Brazilian Squadron on board the USS *Lexington*. After serving on various types of vessels, as well as a tour as commanding officer of the USS *Relief*, he was promoted to the rank of Commander in April 1861.

Between 1861 and 1862, while serving with the South Atlantic Squadron, he assumed command of the USS *Mohawk* and later, the USS *Flag*. From 1863 to 1865, he was commanding officer of the ironclad *Monongahela* and took part in the Battle of Mobile Bay. During this action, he engaged with and defeated the dreaded Confederate ironclad ram CSS *Tennessee*. For his daring initiative and valor, he was highly commended by Admiral David G. Farragut, and advanced to the rank of Captain.

After the war, Captain Strong assumed command of the Brooklyn Navy Yard and later commanded the USS *Canandaigua* in the Mediterranean Squadron. Upon his advancement to Rear Admiral, he served as Commander-in-Chief of the South Atlantic Squadron. Rear Admiral Strong retired on April 25, 1876, and died on November 28, 1882.

The USS *Strong* (DD-467) began her career with the Atlantic Fleet, serving as a convoy escort from mid-September 1942 until December 26. Departing Norfolk on that date, she stood out for the South Pacific and arrived at Nouméa, New Caledonia, on January 27, 1943.

By this time, the Japanese had virtually abandoned Guadalcanal, although they were well entrenched in the northern Solomons and still a formidable power to contend with. The "Tokyo Express" continued to pour in troops, aviation gasoline, food and arms to these strongly held outposts— deliveries made, for the most part, by fast destroyers during the hours of darkness. The job of "derailing" this express train, therefore, was heaped upon the shoulders of the U.S. Navy.

On the night of March 16, *Strong*, in company with the destroyers, *Nicholas*, *Radford* and *Taylor*, steamed up the "Slot" to bombard enemy supply dumps located on the Villa-Stanmore Plantation on Kolombangara Island. Two weeks later, while on anti-submarine patrol, both she and *O'Bannon* caught the enemy submarine *RO-34* on the surface. Both destroyers fired in unison, the *Strong* scoring five direct hits, and sent the sub plunging to the ocean floor.

During the early morning hours of May 7, *Strong* and the destroyers *Chevalier, Taylor* and *O'Bannon* were guarding the minelaying operations in Blackett Strait, between the Kolombangara and Arundel islands. The "miners" were three old four-stacker destroyers, namely, *Breese, Gamble* and *Preble*. Before daybreak, the vessels had completed their mission after laying over 250 of their deadly "eggs." Just as the eastern skies began to lighten, the old destroyers and their escorts kicked up their heels and cleared the area.

On the night of the 8th, four Japanese destroyers came boiling through Blacket Strait, their decks loaded down with troops and supplies, only to plow straight into the newly laid minefield. The first ship to run afoul of these lethal and impartial weapons was the IJN *Oyashio*. Shortly after, the *Kagero* was blasted. Less than an hour later, IJN *Kunashio* got hers and sank in a rush. The *Michishio*, the only one that had the good fortune to come through unscathed, went to the assistance of her crippled sisters.

Ashore, high on a hilltop, an Australian coastwatcher had witnessed this activity in the strait and radioed Guadalcanal of his find. Instantly, a flight of Marine Wildcat fighters were clawing for the sky, their engines snarling. Within a short period of time, they had pounced on the mortally wounded destroyers and dispatched them to the bottom. Again, the lucky *Michishio* made a desperate run for it and escaped, but not before she was brutally assaulted by the Marine fighters.

Under cover of darkness, on the night of May 12, *Strong* participated in another bombardment mission against Kolombangara and, on the 16th, she downed three dive bombers when they attempted an attack against the shipping off Guadalcanal. During the dark morning hours of July 5, *Strong* was attached to Rear Admiral W.L. Ainsworth's task group, which was to cover the U.S. Army landings at Rice Anchorage on the northwestern coast of New Georgia Island. However, unknown to Ainsworth, the enemy had decided to dispatch reinforcements by three destroyers to the Villa-Stanmore Plantations on the same night that the Army landings were scheduled to take place.

At about 0000, as the task group made its approach into Kula Gulf, Ainsworth deployed his group into a single column, *Nicholas* and *Strong* moving up into the van. At 0026, after cautiously entering the gulf, under a heavy cloud cover and infrequent rain squalls, Ainsworth's cruisers commenced hurling shells on the enemy's shore installations. At 0030, while *Strong* and *Nicholas* were firing on Biroko Harbor, the destroyer *Ralph Talbot* reported making radar contact with two vessels approaching the gulf on a northwesterly heading. About ten minutes later, the two unidentified ships were dashing out of the gulf at 25 knots. Just as Ainsworth was preparing to inquire about *Ralph Talbot's* report, *Strong's* Gunnery Officer, J.A. Curran, sighted the ominous wake of a torpedo streaking toward the ship's port side. Unfortunately, his warning came too late for the destroyer to make an evasive turn.

The lethal weapon hit *Strong* at the turn of the bilge between No. 1 fire room and No. 1 engine room and broke her keel. Sloughing to a halt, the vessel began to sag amidships. The entire watch was killed instantly in the forward fire room by the combined blasts from the torpedo and her exploding boilers. Almost immediately afterwards, the forward engine room began to flood, forcing its watch standers to abandon the space. Swathed in a mantle of steam and smoke, the fatally wounded destroyer began to settle

To her assistance came *O'Bannon* and *Chevalier*. Realizing that *Strong* was about to go under, *Chevalier's* captain, Commander E.R. McLean, nudged his destroyer's bow into her side. Without hesitation, her crew dropped nets and lines over her bow and onto the deck of *Strong* to enable her crew to climb on board. Meanwhile, the enemy ashore was firing starshells over the ships and following up with artillery fire, one shell of which hit *Strong*. *O'Bannon* then interposed herself between the enemy guns and her sisters and let fly with every gun that could bear upon the gun emplacement until it was silenced.

A total of 240 men, including the wounded, had climbed on board *Chevalier* before the brazen enemy resumed firing. To prevent his ship from being struck, and the possibility of more men being killed or wounded, Commander McLean was compelled to cease rescue operations and pull away. As he backed off, two more shells crashed into the now listing *Strong* and soon thereafter the destroyer split in two and went under. With a thundering roar, her depth charges then detonated, injuring and killing several of the men in the water. All told, a total of seven officers, including her executive officer, Lieutenant Commander Federick W. Purdy, and 37 bluejackets perished in the loss of *Strong*. Although most of the survivors were rescued by other destroyers in the task group, at least 26 others were listed as missing and, of that number, six made it to the shore, where three later died.

After the war, it was revealed that *Strong* had been torpedoed by one of the two Japanese destroyers that had bolted out of the gulf to avoid contact with the American force. As they fled through the darkness, they each unleashed several torpedoes, one of which had *Strong's* name on it. The weapon employed was the deadly Mark 93 Model ("long lance"), a monster compared to the 21-inch torpedoes then carried on board American destroyers and submarines.

☆ ☆ ☆

USS *STRONG* (DD-467)

Class: Fletcher.
Builder: Bath Iron Works, Bath, Maine.
Keel laid: April 30, 1941.
Launched: May 17, 1942.
Sponsor: Mrs. Hobart Olsen.
Commissioned: August 7, 1942; Commander J.H. Wellings, USN, comdg.
Date of loss: July 5, 1943; Commander J.H. Wellings, USN, comdg.
Location: Off New Georgia Island, the Solomons.
Awards: Two battle stars.

USS Maddox

Launched September 15, 1942
Lost July 10, 1943
Off Gela, Sicily

CAPTAIN WILLIAM A.T. MADDOX, USMC
(1814–1889)

William Alfred Truman Maddox was born in Charles County, Maryland, in 1814. In 1836, he commanded a company of militia volunteers during the Creek and Seminole Indian Wars. On October 14, 1837, he was appointed Second Lieutenant in the United States Marine Corps.

During the war with Mexico, Lieutenant Maddox was serving on board the USS *Cayne* off the coast of California and on July 7, 1846, landed at Monterey with forces under Commodore John Sloat. After a brief skirmish, the Mexican garrison surrendered and the Stars and Stripes were raised in the town's plaza, thus officially proclaiming California an American territory.

Later that month, Lieutenant Maddox himself raised the American flag in San Diego after that town surrendered to his forces. Soon afterwards, he led his mounted riflemen on a 500-mile march to San Luis Obispo, where his troops fought successfully against General Alvarado, capturing 15 officers and a large number of soldiers.

On September 18, he was appointed military commandant of the middle district of California at Monterey. While serving in this capacity, he subdued a Mexican uprising at Monterey, and later was brevited Captain for his gallant and meritorious conduct during the Battle of Santa Clara.

In 1848, Captain Maddox was assigned to duty at the U.S. Marine Barracks, Washington, DC, where in June he suppressed the riots that were running out of control through the streets of the Capital. In 1880, Captain Maddox retired from the Marine Corps and resided in Washington, DC, where he died on January 1, 1889.

Upon joining the Atlantic Fleet destroyer squadrons on January 2, 1943, USS *Maddox* (DD-622) was assigned to escort duty, screening vital convoys through the dangerous waters of the North Atlantic. On the night of January 6, she attacked and drove off a U-boat that was trailing in the wake of the Navy tanker USS *Salamonie*. The destroyer continued to serve as a convoy escort along the eastern seaboard, in the Caribbean and in the Gulf of Mexico, and made one escort voyage to Oran, Algiers.

On the night of May 6, she made an underwater contact and, after dropping several depth charges, a dark shape rose to the surface and quickly vanished again beneath the water. After another depth-charge run, contact was lost, thus raising some doubts as to whether it was a submarine or a whale.

On June 8, 1943, *Maddox* stood out of Norfolk, Virginia for Oran, where she became a unit of Task Force 81, under the command of Rear Admiral J.L. Hall, Jr. The invasion of Sicily (Operation "Husky") was scheduled to take place on July 10, and the American task forces 81, 85 and 86 would be joined by a British task force after they departed from Oran. Composed of some 3,200 Allied ships, landing craft and over 4,000 aircraft, it was, to that time, the largest armada ever assembled.

The Americans were to strike independently at three separate areas along the southern coast of Sicily as follows: Task Force 86 off the towns of Licata ("Joss" attack force); Task Force 81 at Gela ("Dime" attack force); and Task Force 85 at Scolitti ("Cent" attack force).

After bucking choppy seas, the Allied task forces arrived at their designated locations shortly after midnight on the 10th. At 0245, the landing craft spearheaded for the shores and secured a beachhead before the Italians even realized they were under attack. Although shocked by this surprise assault, the enemy recovered swiftly and put up a gallant stand until they were subdued by cruiser and destroyer gunfire.

Throughout the day, the supply ships and screening destroyers were harassed by German fighters and bombers, but these were successfully repulsed. By noon, the Allied forces were well entrenched on the island, and by late afternoon all of the ports were in Allied hands. Casualties were considered to be light on the first day of Operation "Husky"; however, not so on the *Maddox,* which was sunk with a loss of 210 of her crew, including her captain, Lieutenant Commander Eugene S. Sarsfield.

It was 0453 on the 10th, while lending fire support for the landings, when disaster found the *Maddox*. While her guns were firing on the shore and her radar was concentrated landward, a lone German Stuka divebomber swooped in on the stern of the unsuspecting destroyer. At the end of his sudden and cunning approach, the pilot released two bombs. One dropped about 25 yards astern, but the second struck *Maddox* on the starboard propeller guard, igniting the magazine for No.5 five-inch gun mount. Consequently, this explosion triggered off a blast in No.4 magazine, which demolished the after section of the ship.

As men, gear, depth charges, debris and chunks of steel were flung skyward and across the dark seascape, the tremendous explosion split open the bulkhead to the after engine room, rapidly flooding the space. Immediately, the fatally wounded *Maddox* began to plunge to the bottom, stern first. Although her captain passed the word to abandon ship, the vessel was already half submerged and rolling over on her beams end by the time the order was received. The men below decks never had a chance to escape. As *Maddox* slid to her watery grave, just two minutes after she was hit, Captain Sarsfield remained on the bridge directing abandonment operations. He was never seen again. A total of 74 survivors from the destroyer were rescued by a tug that was nearby.

Lieutenant Commander Sarsfield was posthumously awarded the Navy Cross for his extraordinary courage and heroism in standing by to supervise the abandonment of his swiftly sinking ship. Earlier in his career, Sarsfield was highly commended by Secretary of the Navy, Col. Frank Knox for "his leadership, personal courage and ingenuity in solving the many problems arising under adverse conditions," while he was serving as Executive Officer on the destroyer *Kearny* (DD-432), after she had been torpedoed in the North Atlantic on October 17, 1941.

☆ ☆ ☆

USS *MADDOX* (DD-622)

Class: Benson/Livermore.
Builder: Federal Shipbuilding and Drydock Co., Kearny, New Jersey.
Keel laid: May 7, 1942.
Launched: September 15, 1942.
Sponsor: Mrs. Ellen V. B. Wilhout, great-granddaughter of Captain William
    A.T. Maddox, USMC.
Commissioned: October 31, 1942: Lieutenant Commander E.S. Sarsfield,
    USN, comdg.
Date of loss: July 10, 1943; Lieutenant Commander E.S. Sarsfield, USN,
    comdg.†
Location: Off Gela, Sicily.
Awards: Two battle stars.

USS Gwin

Launched May 25, 1940
Lost July 13, 1943
Kula Gulf, Solomon Islands

LIEUTENANT COMMANDER WILLIAM GWIN, USN
(1832–1863)

Born in Columbus, Indiana, on December 6, 1832, William Gwin was appointed Midshipman in 1847. Owing to his outstanding initiative, intense vigor and courageous feats in battle, he rose swiftly through the ranks.

During the Civil War, he commanded several vessels in the western rivers and on the Mississippi. After the fall of Fort Henry, his gunboats swept up the Tennessee River deep into Alabama territory, leaving destruction of Confederate fortifications and terror in his wake. This daring exploit was a major factor in causing the Confederate lines to collapse far behind him in Kentucky.

During the Battle of Shiloh, had it not been for Commander Gwin's two gunboats, USSs *Lexington* and *Tyler*, which lent fire support for General U.S. Grant's troops, a Union disaster might have occurred. For this action, Commander Gwin was highly commended by General Grant.

On December 27, 1862, Lieutenant Commander Gwin was wounded while in command of the gunboat USS *Benton* during the Battle of Haines Bluff on the Yazoo River. Transferred to a hospital ship on the Mississippi River, Gwin died of his wounds on January 3, 1863.

Allocated to the Atlantic destroyer squadrons, the USS *Gwin* (DD-433) served on the neutrality patrol and screened British merchant convoys through the frigid waters of the North Atlantic prior to being assigned to the Pacific Fleet in January 1942. After serving as a convoy escort along the West Coast, *Gwin* stood out from San Francisco on April 3, screening the carrier *Hornet*, which was embarked with Lieutenant Colonel Doolittle and his 16 B-25 bombers whose mission was to bomb the Japanese homeland. The historic launch took place on the morning of April 18, and, as the last bomber lifted from the carrier's flight deck, the task force swiftly retired to Pearl Harbor.

After escorting a Marine reinforcement convoy to Midway, *Gwin* returned to Pearl Harbor, and upon being replenished with stores, fuel and ammunition, raced northward to take part in the Battle of Midway. By the time she arrived, however, the battle was over, the Japanese armada in full retreat.

During the action, the carrier *Yorktown* was severely damaged and had to be abandoned. Upon *Gwin's* arrival, two destroyers were lying alongside the stricken carrier, taking on her survivors. Later, *Gwin* transferred a salvage party over to the carrier to assist in repairs and fighting fires. This task, indeed, was a precarious undertaking, since *Yorktown* had taken on a heavy list to port and could have, at any moment, capsized. Still, the repair parties remained on board until darkness closed in, at which time, the men were compelled to disembark. On the following day (June 6), the Japanese submarine *I-168* sneaked through the cordon of screening destroyers and torpedoed the carrier, also sinking the destroyer *Hammann*, which was lying alongside. However, the *Yorktown* remained afloat until the following day, when she finally rolled over and sank.

Upon her return to Pearl Harbor, *Gwin* was assigned to patrolling duties throughout the Hawaiian Islands and occasionally escorted supply convoys between Pearl and West Coast ports. Then, on July 5, the destroyer departed from Hawaii, en route to the South Pacific, where she went on to participate in the landings at Guadalcanal and Tulagi.

Between August and November, *Gwin* was busily engaged in escort work, plying the waters between Guadalcanal and the New Hebrides. Then, on the night of November 14, the ship was bloodied in the second night of the Naval Battle of Guadalcanal. In company with the battleships *Washington* and *South Dakota,* and the destroyers *Benham, Walke* and *Preston,* she became embroiled in one of the fiercest naval engagements of the war.

Within ten minutes of the first salvo being fired, *Preston* was reduced to scrap and sank under the pounding guns of the cruiser IJN *Nagara*. *Walke's* bow was blown off by a torpedo and she sank shortly thereafter. Then, the fighting *Benham* was brought to a staggering halt, when part of her bow was sheared off by a torpedo.

Gwin, under command of Lieutenant Commander J.B. Fellows, charged into the melee, firing starshells that illuminated an enemy cruiser, the *Sendai*. Although Fellows had intended to attack this cruiser, he veered away to fire instead on *Nagara*, the closest target. Despite the hail of 8-inch shells that were splashing about his destroyer, Fellows, displaying the same courage and initiative as his destroyer's namesake, pressed forward, his guns blazing furiously to score several hits on the cruiser, just before his ship was knocked out of the battle. Struck by two direct hits, one in the forward engine room and the second smashing into her stern, *Gwin's* speed was reduced to a crawl. Nonetheless, her guns continued to fire on *Nagara* until the enemy cruiser was swallowed up in the inky darkness.

With two destroyers sunk and two others damaged, it was up to Admiral Lee's battleships to finish the fight. Meanwhile, *Gwin* had limped from the engagement, and the struggle to save the destroyer began. Repair parties worked feverishly to shore up bulkheads and contain the flooding, while engineers toiled to raise steam for power and propulsion. Once power was restored, *Gwin* eased alongside the crippled *Benham* to lend a helping hand.

Upon regaining steam pressure, *Benham* was able to get underway, but only at a snail's pace. The two cripples were soon on their way, hoping to make it to Nouméa for repairs. Unfortunately, *Benham* was in worse condition than was realized. That afternoon, the destroyer began to break up and *Gwin* came alongside to remove her crew. Shortly after the crew had abandoned her, *Benham* broke in two and had to be dispatched to the bottom by *Gwin's* 5-inch guns.

After effecting temporary repairs at Nouméa, *Gwin* sailed for the Mare Island Navy Yard, Vallejo, California. Repaired and refurbished, *Gwin* returned to the South Pacific theater on April 7, 1943, and resumed her operations throughout the Solomon Islands.

At dawn on June 30, *Gwin* teamed up with the destroyers *Jenkins* (DD-447), *Buchanan* (DD-484), *Farrenholt* (DD-491) and *Radford* (DD-446), to cover the landings at New Georgia and the outlying islands of Rendova and Munda. While providing fire support, *Gwin* was hit by a 4.7-mm shell from a shore battery; it exploded in the after engine room, killing seven of her engineers and causing the ship to lose power. After regaining power, she was relieved from her station by the destroyer *Woodworth* (DD-460) and proceeded to screen the offloading transports.

After the completion of this mission, *Gwin* steamed for Pearl Harbor, where she was hastily repaired and then ordered back to the South Pacific. On June 6, she took part in rescuing the survivors from the cruiser *Helena*, which had been sunk in the Battle of Kula Gulf.

On the night of July 13, *Gwin* was in action once again when she participated in a hammer-and-tongs engagement against Rear Admiral S. Izaki's
reinforcement group off Kolombangara, while attached to Rear Admiral W.L.
Ainsworth's Task Force 36.1. Ainsworth had made radar contact at 0059.
However, Izaki, in his flagship, IJN *Jintsu,* was also aware of Ainsworth's
presence for, unknown to the Americans, the Japanese had developed a
radar detector, thus allowing the enemy admiral to beat Ainsworth to the
punch.

The two opponents clashed at 0108 when Izaki ordered a torpedo
attack. Within a few seconds, 31 lethal "long lance" torpedoes were humming toward the American formation. Then, suddenly, the forward column
of Ainsworth's destroyers was illuminated by *Jintsu's* searchlight and the battle was on. After an awkward beginning, the Americans recovered suffi-
ciently so that soon the *Jintsu* was bludgeoned relentlessly by cruiser and
destroyer gunfire that literally transformed *Izaki's* flagship into a molten
mass of wreckage. After being assailed by several torpedoes, which split her
in two, she plunged to the bottom with a heavy loss of life, including that
of Admiral Izaki.

The American task force, however, did not emerge unscathed. The New
Zealand cruiser HMNZS *Leander* was knocked out of the battle after being
struck by a torpedo, as were the American cruisers *St. Louis* and *Honolulu.*
As for *Gwin,* her charmed life was suddenly terminated when a torpedo
struck her amidships, enveloping her in a terrifying ball of white heat. All
hands in the forward engine room and after fire room, as well as those near
the point of impact, were instantly killed or wounded. Others, who were
trapped in damaged compartments, were drowned by the inrush of water or
were burned by scalding steam and flaming oil.

John S. Kosma, Ship's Baker Third Class, recalls what occurred next: "We
were struck by one of the "long lance" torpedoes that hit us amidships on
the port side, very close to my battle station. All I remember is being hurled
in the air, and when I came to, my close shipmate "Swede" Larson, was dragging me forward to the bow. All the ammunition for the 20- and 40-mm
guns in the area where we had been hit had ignited and was blowing up and
flying in every direction at once. Although the ship was beginning to settle,
some attempts were carried out to try and save her.

"Despite the damage control parties, under the supervision of Ensign
G.E. Stranski, having succeeded in extinguishing the oil and ammunition
fires, they still had a difficult time trying to contain the flooding. Then a
report was received that several aircraft from a nearby airfield were heading

toward us, probably hoping to finish off the cripples. With the ship settling deeper and deeper, our captain, Lt. Commander J.B. Fellows, passed the order to abandon ship."

The destroyer *Ralph Talbot* (DD-390) came alongside to remove the crew of the ill-fated *Gwin*, which soon afterwards rolled over to port. To hasten her death throes, *Ralph Talbot* stood off and fired four torpedoes into her hull. Lost with the valiant ship were two officers and 59 bluejackets.

At the time of *Gwin's* last action, she was the flagship of DesDiv 12, under command of Commander J.M. Higgins, who was her first commanding officer. The loss of *Gwin* also saddened the hearts of the survivors from *Helena,* who would never forget that she was one of the destroyers that had come to their rescue. Afterwards, one of *Gwin's* survivors remarked: "She was a great ship, but we all knew that she was living on borrowed time. I suppose all of us were living on that kind of time in the Solomons."

☆ ☆ ☆

USS *GWIN* (DD-433)

Class: Benson/Livermore.
Builder: Boston Navy Yard, Charlestown, Massachusetts.
Keel laid: June 1, 1939.
Launched: May 25, 1940.
Sponsor: Miss Jesse T. Lippincott, a distant relative of Lieutenant Commander
    William Gwin, USN.
Commissioned: January 15, 1941; Lieutenant Commander J.M. Higgins, USN,
    comdg.
Date of loss; July 13, 1943; Lieutenant Commander J.B. Fellows, USN, comdg.
Location: Kula Gulf, Solomon Islands.
Awards: Five battle stars.

Author's note: A successor to the *Gwin*, DM-33 (ex-DD-772), was: decommissioned April 3, 1958. Sold to the Republic of Turkey October 22, 1971, it was renamed *Mauvenet* (DM-357). On October 2, 1991, she made headlines when she was severely damaged by two Sparrow missiles that had been accidentally fired from the carrier USS *Saratoga*, killing five members of her crew, including her captain. It is assumed that she has been scrapped at this writing.

USS Rowan

Launched May 5, 1938
Lost September 11, 1943
Off Salerno, Italy

VICE ADMIRAL STEPHEN C. ROWAN, USN
(1805–1890)

Born in Dublin, Ireland, Stephen C. Rowan emigrated to the United States at the age of ten. Appointed Midshipman on February 1, 1826, he went on to serve in various ships before becoming the Executive Officer of the USS *Cayne* in 1845.

On July 7 of that year, he participated in the capture of Monterey, California, and later, in the occupation of Los Angeles and San Diego. At the outbreak of the Civil War, he was in command of the USS *Pawnee* and made a gallant attempt to relieve Fort Sumter. When Confederate forces surrounded the Norfolk Navy Yard, he assisted in the burning of the base in an effort to render it useless to them.

In the fall of 1861 he assisted in the capture of the forts at Hatteras Inlet. Then, upon taking command of a small flotilla in the North Carolina sounds, he was instrumental in the capture of Roanoke Island in February 1862. Promoted to the rank of Captain for his gallantry, he later supported Union forces in the capture of Elizabeth City, New Bern and Edenton, North Carolina.

In the summer of 1863, he commanded the USS *New Ironsides* during the blockading of Charleston, South Carolina, and shortly afterwards assumed command of the Federal naval forces in the North Carolina sounds.

After the war, Rowan was advanced to rank of Rear Admiral and, after holding a variety of posts, was commissioned to the rank of Vice Admiral in 1870. His last position was superintendant of the U.S. Naval Observatory, Washington, DC. Vice Admiral Rowan died on March 31, 1890, in Washington.

A ssigned to the Atlantic Fleet, the USS *Rowan* (DD-405) carried out her operations along the eastern seaboard and in Caribbean waters until she was transferred to the Pacific Fleet in June 1940. In May 1941, however, she was reassigned to the Atlantic Fleet, where she served on the neutrality patrol in the Caribbean. Later that year, her patrolling sector was shifted to the northern climes of New England and as far north as Newfoundland.

On November 10, she stood out of Halifax, Nova Scotia, escorting a troop and supply convoy (WS-124) that was embarked with over 20,000 British troops bound for the Middle East via the Cape of Good Hope. By sheer luck, the convoy slipped through the net of U-boat wolfpacks that lurked beneath the waters of the South Atlantic. Then, on December 7, while the convoy was plunging through a severe storm off Capetown, the shocking news of the Japanese attack on Pearl Harbor was flashed around the world. This assault was followed by an attack on the Philippines and several Allied colonies throughout Asia. With the Far East up in flames, the convoy was rerouted to ports in India and then down to Singapore.

Rowan returned to the United States in January 1942 and was promptly assigned to escort convoys through the frigid waters of the North Atlantic. During the first week of May, she was at Hvalfjördur, Iceland, and assigned to Task Force 99, part of the British Home Fleet in Iceland and Scapa Flow, Scotland. In company with other destroyers, *Rowan* patrolled on a line 150 miles east of the Russian-bound convoys in an effort to discourage any German warships bent on raiding the shipping en route to Murmansk and Archangel, U.S.S.R.

On July 2, *Rowan* was detached from Task Force 99 to join the escort group that was screening convoy PQ-17. The Germans were well aware of this convoy prior to its departure from Iceland on June 27, and also knew what it was carrying: over 700,000,000 dollars' worth of war materiel for the beleaguered Soviets. Determined to destroy this Murmansk-bound convoy, the Germans set into motion operation "*Rosselsprung*" (Knight's Move). Consequently, all aircraft, U-boats and surface vessels, including the dreaded 35,000-ton battleship *Tirpitz*, were alerted to deal death and destruction upon this star-crossed convoy.

The convoy was plagued with problems from the start when one of its merchantmen ran aground, and later, when a tanker was so badly damaged by an ice flow that it had to return to port. Once out of the Denmark Strait, the ships were sighted by enemy aircraft and U-boats east of Jan Mayen Island on July 1. Hoping to discourage the Germans from deploying their naval units, Rear Admiral L.H.K. Hamilton, RN, had purposely allowed his powerful Home Fleet to be sighted by scouting aircraft. The ruse seemed to work, for when German observers radioed that the convoy was under the protection of capital ships, cruisers, destroyers and an aircraft carrier, the *Tirpitz* and her escorts were hastily withdrawn and sent back to the shelter of Trondheim, Norway. The Germans then decided to leave the destruction of the convoy to their aircraft and submarines.

By the time *Rowan* caught up with the convoy, it had been sighted by scouting aircraft, which skirted well out of range of the escorting ships' anti-aircraft guns. These planes kept a constant vigil, informing the German authorities of the convoy's movements.

The Germans executed their first aerial assault on the afternoon of July 2, just a short time after *Rowan* had refueled and taken up her screening position. Four torpedo-carrying bombers swooped down out of a cloud bank and dashed toward the lumbering merchantmen, only to fly into a curtain of AA fire. *Rowan*, the first of the escorts to open fire, scorched one of the attackers and sent it flaming into the frigid sea. Consequently, the hot reception caused the pilots to drop their torpedoes prematurely, and as a result all of them missed. Later, four more bombers converged upon the convoy. This time, it seemed as though they had chosen *Rowan* as their primary target. Despite the heavy concentration of AA fire, the Germans dropped their torpedoes, all of them spearheading for the lone destroyer. With remarkably skillful handling, her skipper, Lieutenant Commander H.B. Harrison, deftly combed *Rowan* through their wakes.

On the 3rd, at least 26 German bombers swarmed overhead, randomly dropping their bombs through the heavy cloud cover, and then retired. Thankfully, not one ship in the convoy or its escorts was hit. But the worst was yet to come.

On the 4th, enemy attacks only grew in intensity. First, a single torpedo bomber slashed through a thick barrier of AA fire, succeeded in torpedoing the SS *Christopher Newport*, and then escaped. Just before noon, another enemy attack was repulsed, the Germans losing three aircraft. At about 1645, a further attack was driven off, but not before two more cargomen were sunk; the enemy lost two planes, one shot down by the USS *Wainwright* (DD-419).

Meanwhile, reports had arrived at Admiralty Headquarters, London, that the *Tirpitz* was not at her last reported anchorage. Fearing that the behemoth had broken loose and was en route to demolish the convoy, the Home Fleet was detached from the convoy to search for, and annihilate, this threat. The order to leave the convoy, however, shocked every commander in the force.

This meant that the ships were to scatter and fend for themselves; the death warrant for hundreds of merchant seaman seemed to have been signed, as well as for their armed guard crews and the thousands of tons of vitally needed war materiel.

The convoy still had a long way to go and, worse, except for low cloud cover and occasional fog, there was nowhere to hide, for in these northern latitudes during the summer months the ships were steaming in perpetual daylight. As history tells us, the ships continued under incessant air and U-boat attacks, which resulted in only 11 vessels out of 33 arriving at their designated ports. As it turned out, *Tirpitz* had not put to sea, but had only shifted her berth further inland to Altenfjord.

After escorting a convoy from Murmansk, *Rowan* returned to Iceland, and on the 14th stood out for the United States. Upon the completion of a shipyard overhaul at the Boston Navy Yard, the destroyer resumed her escort duties, screening merchant convoys along the eastern seaboard and through the tropical waters of the Caribbean.

On November 8, she participated in the North African invasion and on the 10th intercepted and engaged with a group of Vichy French destroyers that attempted to interfere with the landings. Two days later, *Rowan* departed the area, escorting empty troop transports back to the United States.

Between December 1942 and into April 1943, the destroyer was busy screening transatlantic convoys and in May joined up with Task Force 80 at Mers-el-Kabir, Algeria. Here, she was assigned to escort incoming convoys and patrol duties, until she left to take part in the invasion of Sicily on July 10, providing shore bombardment.

On September 9, the Allies found that their landings at Salerno, Italy, were meeting much greater resistance than those on Sicily. *Rowan* provided shore bombardment during the difficult first days, and afterwards she screened the transports while the troops stormed the beaches at nearby Paestum. Then, at about 2200 on the 10th, the empty transports formed up and proceeded to depart for Oran. *Rowan* cleared Salerno Harbor at 2300 and, during the next hour, neither her sonar nor radar operators reported any suspicious underwater, surface or aerial contacts. Then, just a few minutes before midnight, *Rowan's* lookouts were stunned to see an eerie, phosphorus torpedo wake streaking toward the ship. The shout "Torpedo!" prompted her captain, Lieutenant Commander R.S. Ford, to take evasive action and sound "General Quarters." Fortunately, the torpedo missed.

Then, fast moving "pips" began to appear on *Rowan's* radar screen, indicating that they could only be E-boats. All guns possible—both 5-inchers and 20- and 40-mm's—opened fire at the German vessels some 2,000 yards distant. Then, as the destroyer made a turn in which to bring all her main batteries to bear upon her targets, she was struck by a torpedo on her port quarter.

Reeling under the terrific impact of the detonation, the ship was further torn asunder as her after 5-inch magazine let go with a thunderous, ear-shattering roar. The whole after section of *Rowan* was thrown upward and out of the water, hurtling men overboard in a lethal shower of shattered steel and debris. Within forty seconds after the devastating hit, the proud destroyer vanished beneath the sea under a pall of smoke and steam.

Those who survived the sinking found themselves thrashing about in a sea coated with globs of viscous fuel oil and strewn with debris and wreckage. The destroyer USS *Bristol* (DD-453) raced to the grisly scene and spent the remaining dark, morning hours searching for and rescuing *Rowan's* pitiful survivors, of which very few had escaped injury. By dawn, *Bristol* had picked up 75 officers and men, including *Rowan's* captain. Despite an extended search throughout the day, no more survivors or bodies could be found. Out of a crew of 273 officers and men, 202 crewmen had perished in the loss of *Rowan* or died later as a result of their wounds.

☆ ☆ ☆

USS *ROWAN* (DD-405)

Class: Benham.
Builder: Norfolk Navy Yard, Portsmouth, Virginia.
Keel laid: June 25, 1937.
Launched: May 5, 1938.
Sponsor: Miss Elizabeth H. Rowan, great-granddaughter of Vice Admiral
    Stephen C. Rowan, USN.
Commissioned: September 23, 1939; Lieutenant Commander H.B. Harrison,
    USN, comdg.
Date of loss: September 11, 1943; Lieutenant Commander R.S. Ford, comdg.
Location: Off Salerno, Italy.
Awards: Five battle stars.

USS Henley

Launched January 12, 1937
Lost October 3, 1943
Off Cape Cretin, New Guinea

CAPTAIN ROBERT HENLEY, USN
(1783-1828)

Robert Henley, a nephew of Martha Custis Washington, was born in Williamsburg, Virginia, on January 5, 1783. Appointed Midshipman on April 8, 1799, he was assigned to the frigate USS *Constellation* and was serving on her when she engaged with and defeated the French frigate *La Vengeance*, on February 2, 1800.

During the War of 1812, he commanded a squadron of gunboats and was instrumental in driving three British frigates from Hampton Roads, Virginia, on June 20, 1813. Promoted to Lieutenant, he reported on board the sloop *Eagle*, which took part in the Battle of Lake Champlain. For his gallant service in this action, he received thanks from the U.S. Congress and was awarded a gold medal.

After peace was declared, he went on to serve in various types of ships, and, upon being promoted to the rank of Captain in 1821, assumed command of the frigate *Hornet*, during which time he assisted in the suppression of piracy in the West Indies. On October 29 of that year, he captured the pirate ship *Moscow* off Santo Domingo.

Between 1822 and 1824, he served as commandant of the naval receiving station at Norfolk, Virginia, and later went on to serve on similar duty at Charleston, South Carolina. After suffering through a brief illness, Captain Robert Henley died on Sullivan's Island, South Carolina, on October 7, 1828.

Assigned to the Pacific Battle Force, the USS Henley (DD-391) conducted her operations primarily along the West Coast until April 14, 1941, when she departed San Diego, California, to become a unit of the destroyer flotilla based at Pearl Harbor.

Henley was moored in East Loch, Pearl Harbor, when the Japanese staged their attack on December 7, 1941. A few moments prior to the assault, a new crew member had mistakenly sounded "General Quarters" instead of "Quarters for Muster." This fortunate error allowed the Henley to be one of the first ships to fire upon the assailants at the beginning of their attack.

As the destroyer slipped her cable, a bomb exploded about 150 yards off her port bow without causing any damage. Once clear of her berth, she steamed through the smoke-filled and wreckage-strewn harbor, her anti-aircraft guns blazing away at the low-flying aircraft. As she was rounding Hospital Point, she scorched a bomber that was bearing in on one of the moored battleships. Although trailing a long, oily plume of smoke, the aircraft dropped its bomb and was last seen winging toward the mountains. Shortly afterwards, another plane darted through *Henley's* line of fire without sustaining any damage.

Once out of the harbor, *Henley's* sonar operator reported an underwater contact, but after a pattern of depth charges was dropped, contact was lost. The destroyer then closed in on one of the cruisers that had escaped the brunt of the attack to screen her from possible submarine danger.

At the time of the Pearl Harbor attack, *Henley's* captain, Lieutenant Commander Robert Hall, and her Executive Officer were on weekend liberty, so the ship's only senior officer on board, Lieutenant F.L. Fleck, had assumed command. Later, Hall and his E.O. managed to board the ex-destroyer *Trever* (DMS-16), which put out to sea; they soon jumped onto a raft that was being towed by *Henley* and were hauled on board.

From December and into April 1942, *Henley* served as a convoy escort between Pearl Harbor and West Coast ports, carried out patrolling duties in Hawaiian waters and screened troop and supply convoys to bases in the South Pacific.

On May 9, she departed Nouméa, New Caledonia, to search for survivors from the USS *Sims* and the navy tanker USS *Neosho* in the wake of the Battle of the Coral Sea. On the 11th, the charred wreckage of the *Neosho* was sighted by a Navy scout plane, some 50 miles from *Henley*. Within the hour, the destroyer came alongside and received her crew, of which 14 were from the ill-fated *Sims*. The *Henley* then stood off and dispatched the derelict tanker to the bottom with gunfire and a torpedo.

After discharging the survivors at Brisbane, Australia, *Henley* and her division, along with several other American destroyers and cruisers, teamed up with the joint American–Australian Task Force 44 to guard the shipping lanes between New Caledonia and Australian and New Zealand ports.

On August 7, *Henley* supported the landings at Guadalcanal and Tulagi, providing shore bombardment and protecting the transports from air and submarine attacks. On the following day, an air attack was repulsed by aircraft and ships' AA fire, *Henley* receiving credit for two kills. Later that evening, *Henley* and several other destroyers departed for Nouméa, screening the empty transports en route.

Two weeks later, *Henley* returned to Guadalcanal, and on the night of August 20–21 she and the USS *Blue* were guarding the approaches to Lengo Channel to intercept the "Tokyo Express," which had been transporting troops and reinforcements to the Japanese army ashore. Shortly before 0400, *Blue* was struck by a torpedo, which almost blew her stern off and killed nine members of her crew. *Henley* dashed to her disabled sister's side and took her under tow. By dawn, several other vessels had taken over the task, while *Henley* was ordered to cover a group of ships that were unloading supplies at Tulagi.

Later, *Henley* returned to take the loggy *Blue* in tow; however, the cable snapped, and, after a second towline had parted, an attempt was made to tow the vessel alongside. By 2100 that evening, the crippled destroyer's situation was becoming critical. Then a dispatch was received that a massive air attack was in the offing. Since time was running out for *Blue,* and there were no proper salvaging facilities in the immediate area, it was decided to scuttle the destroyer. Despite her crew's attempt to open the sea to her compartments, *Blue* remained stubbornly afloat. *Henley* then tried to down her with a torpedo, but it missed. She then turned her five-inchers on her and, after taking nine rounds, *Blue* settled beneath the surface.

Henley continued her operations with Task Force 44 well into 1943. On September 21, she and her division stood out of Buna, New Guinea, escorting a flotilla of landing craft to Finschaven, a short distance north of Buna. On the following morning, while the troops were approaching the shore, a flight of bombers dashed in, hoping to intercept the landings. *Henley's* alert gunners were the first to open fire on the raiders and sent two of them spiraling into the sea. Then three torpedo bombers were sighted closing in on *Henley.* Immediately taken under fire, the pilots dropped their torpedoes prematurely, which allowed the fleet-footed destroyer to take evasive action.

On October 3, *Henley* was steaming in company with the destroyers *Reid* (DD-369) and *Smith* (DD-378), conducting an anti-submarine sweep off Cape Cretin and Finschaven, New Guinea. At 1814, as the destroyers commenced their scouting line formation, *Henley's* captain, Commander Carlton R. Adams, sighted two torpedoes streaking toward the ship's port side—one

headed for the bow, the other for the stern. Immediately ordering his helmsman to make a sharp turn to port, the torpedoes missed by a narrow mar-
gin, the bow shot by some 30 yards and the stern shot by a mere 10. No
sooner had the men wiped the sweat off their brows than another "tin fish"
was seen closing in, but this one was too close to be avoided.

The torpedo struck and blasted a hole in the ship's forward fire room,
killing its entire crew. The boilers blew and, it was immediately realized, the
destroyer's keel was broken. With a fog of scalding steam and smoke roiling
out of her shattered bowels, *Henley* crawled to a stop, her decks already
awash amidships. Captain Adams then passed the order to abandon ship,
and three minutes later, as he was boarding the last life raft, *Henley* slipped
beneath the sea, stern first.

Meanwhile, *Smith* and *Reid* had been scouring the depths, searching for
the perpetrator, later learned to be the *Ro-108*. Despite making contact, and
dropping several patterns of depth charges, the wily submarine commander,
although he must have been badly shaken, escaped.

The destroyers then returned to pick up *Henley's* survivors: 18 officers and 225 men. Of those rescued, eight officers and 44 crewmen were
wounded, two of whom died shortly after. Lost with the gallant *Henley* were
one officer and 14 men.

As for the *Ro-108*, she met her maker on May 26, 1944, as part of what
was probably the greatest submarine-killing spree of the war. As a result of
breaking the Japanese code, the U.S. Navy located a long picket line of IJN
submarines. The destroyer escort USS *England* then rampaged up the line of
submarines, sinking six boats in a row. The fifth of these vessels was the *Ro-
108*, which was presumed lost with all hands.

☆ ☆ ☆

USS *HENLEY* (DD-391)

Class: Craven.
Builder: Mare Island Navy Yard, Vallejo, Calif.
Keel laid: October 28, 1935.
Launched: January 12, 1937.
Sponsor: Miss Beryl Henley Joslin, a collateral descendant of Captain Robert
     Henley, USN
Commissioned: August 14, 1937; Lieutenant Commander H.Y. McCowan,
     USN, comdg.
Date of loss: October 3, 1943; Commander C.R. Adams, USN, comdg.
Location: Off Cape Cretin, New Guinea.
Awards: Four battle stars.

USS Chevalier

Launched April 11, 1942
Lost October 7, 1943
Off Vella Lavella Island, the Solomons

LIEUTENANT COMMANDER
GODFREY DEC. CHEVALIER, USN
(1889–1922)

Godfrey DeCourcelles Chevalier was born in Providence, Rhode Island, on March 7, 1889. Graduating from the Naval Academy in June 1910, he became one of the early pioneers in U.S. naval aviation and was appointed Naval Air Pilot No.7 on November 7, 1915. Three years later, he was promoted to Naval Aviator.

Under the supervision of Rear Admiral Mark L. Bristol, then a staunch advocate of the development of naval aviation, Chevalier assisted in supervising the installation of a catapult on board the battleship *North Dakota* in 1916. Later, he held the distinction of being the first pilot to fly an aircraft launched from this mechanism.

During World War I, Lieutenant Chevalier was placed in command of the U.S. Navy's first naval air station in Europe (Dunkerque, France). For his war service in France, he received the Croix de Guerre with palms and the Chevalier d'Honneur from the French government, as well as the Distinguished Service Medal from the United States government.

In 1922, he was assigned to the *Langley* (CV-1), America's first aircraft carrier, and then to the *Jupiter*, where he supervised this former coal collier's conversion into a carrier. He then chalked up another "first" in his naval career when he landed the first plane on *Jupiter's* flight deck on October 26, 1922.

Nineteen days later, Lieutenant Commander Chevalier was severely burned in a plane crash, and died in the Norfolk Naval Hospital on November 14, 1922.

Prior to reporting to the South Pacific, the USS *Chevalier* (DD-451) was assigned to escort duties along the eastern seaboard and made one transatlantic voyage to Casablanca, escorting a troop convoy en route.

Departing Norfolk, Virginia, on December 17, 1942, the destroyer arrived at Efate, New Hebrides, on January 22 to join Task Force 18, then operating in the Solomon Islands. On the night of the 29th, at about 2200, while the task force was escorting a troop and supply convoy to Guadalcanal, the ships were attacked by a flock of Japanese torpedo planes. Employing flares to illuminate their targets, these succeeded in damaging the cruiser *Chicago* and the destroyer *LaVallette* (DD-448), the cruiser *Louisville* being struck by a dud. Unfortunately, the next day the crippled *Chicago*, then under tow, was sunk by enemy planes that evaded the anti-aircraft barrage thrown up by her escorts.

On the night of May 7, *Chevalier*, in company with four other destroyers, stood guard at the approaches to Blackett Strait and Kula Gulf, while three destroyer minelayers mined these waters in an effort to derail the "Tokyo Express."

Just before dawn on the 8th, four enemy destroyers, loaded with troops and supplies, came dashing into the newly laid minefield. Shortly after, one of the ships struck a mine and went down in a rush, two others sustaining severe damage. While the fourth destroyer was lending assistance to her wounded sisters, they were pounced upon by Marine fighter planes, which polished off the cripples. Although the surviving destroyer had been badly mauled in the assault, she managed to escape.

Between May 11 and 14, *Chevalier*, in company with her task force, participated in the shelling of the Villa-Stanmore Plantation and later covered another minelaying operation in the Kula Gulf. Then, just before midnight on July 4, she again bombarded the Villa-Stanmore Plantation and the beaches in Biroko Harbor. During this operation, two Japanese destroyers randomly fired several torpedoes at the American ships and retired at high speed into the dark night. One of the torpedoes struck the destroyer *Strong* amidships, breaking her keel.

Assuming that the *Strong* could go under at any moment, *Chevalier's* captain, Lieutenant Commander E.R. McLean, deliberately nudged his destroyer's bow into the *Strong's* port side. Immediately, cargo netting and lines were draped over the bow, enabling *Strong's* crew to climb on board. While the men were scrambling aboard, Japanese shore guns opened up. Standing by was the destroyer *O'Bannon*, which turned her 5-inch guns on the batteries and silenced them. However, a short time later, the guns were in action again. This time a dud struck *Strong,* several others splashing and bursting about both destroyers.

By now, 240 of *Strong's* crew had managed to clamber on board the *Chevalier,* but with the enemy's shells crashing about, McLean decided to break off rescue operations to avoid additional casualties and the possibility of losing his ship. In less than a minute after the *Chevalier* had backed away from *Strong,* the destroyer broke in two and plunged to the bottom. As she went under, her depth charges detonated, killing and wounding several of her swimmers. While *Chevalier* retired to deliver *Strong's* survivors to Espiritu Santo, other ships remained behind to pick up whatever survivors could be found.

After this operation, *Chevalier* underwent a brief overhaul and resumed her operations throughout the Solomon Islands. On August 15, she covered the landings on Vella Lavella Island and, on the night of the 17th, she and four other destroyers intercepted four enemy destroyers that were escorting several landing barges. Upon sighting the *Chevalier* and her consorts the enemy turned and fled, with *Chevalier* and her mates in hot pursuit. The tail-end Japanese vessel commenced lobbing shells at the weaving *Chevalier,* with near-misses shaking her from truck to keel. *Chevalier* answered with rapid gunfire and then maneuvered to unleash a torpedo attack. Unfortunately, none of the torpedoes found their mark, but the Japanese skipper had the fight knocked out of him and dashed beyond the area.

Giving up the chase, the destroyers returned to deal out punishment against the landing barges and sank all but one, which was left in flames. Then the deadly foursome met up with two more Japanese landing craft under escort by a lone gunboat. They too were sunk, the gunboat "escorting" them to the bottom.

On the night of August 24–25, *Chevalier's* division was once again called upon to cover a minelaying mission in Blackett Strait. While the "miners" were conducting their hazardous task, the destroyers came under a series of air attacks, but these were easily repulsed. However, during the operation, two of the minelayers, USSs *Preble* and *Montgomery,* were seriously damaged when they collided with each other as they were retiring from the strait. Unfortunately, *Montgomery* sustained underwater damage later that day when a lone bomber plunged out of a bank of low-hanging clouds and dropped a stick of bombs close by her.

On October 5, *Chevalier,* in company with the destroyers *O'Bannon* and *Selfridge,* was churning up the "Slot" to intercept the evacuation of enemy troops from Kolombangara Island. That evening at 2231, *Selfridge,* at the head of the column, sighted a small flotilla of enemy transports and submarine chasers, under the protection of six destroyers.

When the Japanese sighted the three intruders, they interposed their destroyers between their charges and the American destroyers and prepared to engage in battle. The Americans took up the challenge and raced toward the enemy formation at flank speed. At a range of 10,000 yards, the American force made a sharp swing to starboard, opened fire and scored several hits on the enemy's ships, the leading destroyer, *Yagumo*, being demolished under a torrent of 5-inch shells. However, she had already unleashed a spread of torpedoes at the American ships, one of which tagged *Chevalier* in her No. 2 magazine, just forward of the bridge.

The tremendous explosion threw her captain (now Lieutenant Commander) George R. Wilson and all of those on the bridge to the deck, rendering them unconscious. Without anyone to conn her, the wounded destroyer plunged through the darkened sea and a hellscape of flaming gunfire at full speed. Upon regaining consciousness, her dazed captain rose shakily to his feet and staggered out to the wing of the bridge to peer over the splinter shield. To his horror, he discovered that the entire bow had been blown off. Black oil and debris could be seen spewing out of the wreckage as the ship plowed blindly ahead.

With all steerage lost and without any means to communicate with the engineering department, Captain Wilson sent an officer down to the engine room to order the Chief Engineer to halt the engines. Suddenly, the uncontrollable *Chevalier* made a sharp turn to starboard and directly into the path of the *O'Bannon*, which was bearing down on the decapitated destroyer at 30 knots. Despite *O'Bannon's* skipper's efforts to avoid colliding with the damaged *Chevalier* by making a sharp turn to port and reversing his engines, it was too late. The forward momentum of the charging destroyer could not be halted in time and she rammed into the *Chevalier's* starboard side with a sledgehammer blow, heeling the ship almost over on her beams end.

Metal crunched and screeched against metal in a shower of fiery sparks, as *O'Bannon* sliced her sharp prow into her sister's thin hull plating. Once again, *Chevalier's* personnel were thrown off their feet and hurled across her decks, into hot machinery and headlong into bulkheads. The injured cried out in agony as smoke and scalding steam belched out of the ship's innards and the inrush of sea began to flood her lower decks and engineering spaces. Staggering from below came the engineers, the uninjured leading or carrying their less fortunate shipmates to safety.

Since the *O'Bannon* was backing down when she struck her sister, the "bite" was not too deep, but the damage incurred had sealed *Chevalier's* fate. Both of the forward engineering spaces were flooded and No. 2 fire room was taking on water. By now, the ship had a precarious list to starboard, but her captain was determined to save his vessel, and ordered all unnecessary gear to be jettisoned. In an effort to reduce topside weight, her torpedoes were fired in the general direction of the now fiercely burning wreckage of the IJN *Yagumo*. While the struggle to save the destroyer went on, the crew had the satisfaction of seeing the enemy destroyer slide to the bottom after being struck by one of *Chevalier's* torpedoes.

Meanwhile, *O'Bannon* stood by her disabled sister and lowered her boats to pick up wounded and assist in salvage operations, which continued until 0025. Despite an assist from three other destroyers, the *Chevalier* could not be saved. *O'Bannon* then eased alongside to receive her crew and stood off while the destroyer *La Vallette* sank the gallant *Chevalier* with a torpedo and gunfire. Lost with the *Chevalier* were 58 men and one officer.

☆ ☆ ☆

USS *CHEVALIER* (DD-451)

Class: Fletcher.
Builder: Bath Iron Works, Bath, Maine.
Keel laid: April 3, 1941.
Launched: April 11, 1942.
Sponsor: Mrs. Godfrey DeC. Chevalier, widow of Lieutenant Commander Godfrey DeC. Chevalier, USN.
Commissioned: July 20, 1942; Lieutenant Commander E.R. McLean, USN, comdg.
Date of loss: October 7, 1943; Lieutenant Commander G.R. Wilson. USN, comdg.
Location: Off Vella Lavella Island, the Solomons.
Awards: Three battle stars.

USS Buck

Launched May 22, 1939
Lost October 9, 1943
Off Salerno Gulf, Italy

MASTER'S MATE JAMES BUCK, USN
(1808–1865)

James Buck was born in Baltimore, Maryland, in 1808 and enlisted in the Navy in 1852. During the Civil War, Master's Mate Buck was serving in the steamer USS *Brooklyn,* when she took part in the bombardment of Forts Jackson and Philip on the Mississippi. In the heat of the action, Buck was severely wounded, but refused to leave his post and continued to steer the ship for eight hours—throughout the entire engagement. For his courageous and heroic service during this battle, he was awarded the Congressional Medal of Honor. He died at his home in Baltimore, on November 1, 1865.

The last destroyer of the Sims class to be built, the USS *Buck* (DD-420) conducted her shakedown trials in the Atlantic and in Caribbean waters prior to being assigned to the Pacific Fleet. In June 1941, she was reassigned to the Atlantic Fleet for duty with the neutrality patrol. Later that year, she commenced escorting British shipping through the hazardous North Atlantic and continued to carry out this work after the entry of the United States into World War II.

On the night of August 22, 1942, while escorting Convoy AT-20, *Buck's* career was nearly terminated when she was rammed by the troop transport SS *Awatea.* Composed of ten transports and the navy oiler USS *Chemung,* the convoy was under the protection of the battleship, *New York,* the cruiser *Philadelphia* and nine destroyers.

The forenoon and afternoon watches had passed without incident since the convoy departed from Halifax, Nova Scotia, earlier that morning. Then, at about 1730, the ships were "spooked" by a suspected submarine contact, resulting in the transports' captains taking evasive measures. The ships scattered, despite the fact that the destroyers *Swanson* and *Ingraham* had assured the convoy commander it was a false alarm. As a result, the destroyer skippers were busily engaged in rounding up the strays and guiding them to their proper stations.

At 2200, however, a thick mantle of fog rolled in and not long afterwards the ships began to veer off course or lag behind. The SS *Letitia* wandered so far from the convoy that *Buck* was dispatched to search for her and lead her back to the formation. Suddenly, at 2225, from out of the gray, opaque darkness, loomed the huge, black hulk of the SS *Awatea*, not more than 30 yards off *Buck*'s starboard beam. The lookout's warning shout went unheard as the towering, sharp prow of the transport knifed into the destroyer's fantail with an ear-piercing screech.

The sledgehammer impact dislodged a depth charge overboard that detonated and nearly blew the destroyer's stern off. Her men went sprawling to the deck, others being thrown from their bunks, hurled into bulkheads and hot machinery. Several men were injured in the living space where the transport had struck, but how many had been killed outright could not be determined. Tragically, several men were trapped in their bunks, the metal railings wrapped around their bodies. When the *Awatea* disengaged herself, the sea rushed in, filling the space within minutes, thus preventing anyone from entering the compartment to free the trapped men.

George Brooks, then a Chief Machinist's Mate, remembers looking into that gaping hole and hearing the pitiful screams of the living whenever the ship would rise on the swells and submerge beneath the waves.

Immediately after this disaster, another tragic event occurred. *Ingraham*, responding to *Buck*'s distress call, had raced blindly through the fog, directly into the path of *Chemung*, which crashed into her. Within a few seconds of this collision, the destroyer exploded internally and was transformed into a seething cauldron. *Chemung*'s bow was ripped open like a sardine can and scorched, several of her crew suffering burns and injuries from the blast. The heat emitting from the fiery wreckage of *Ingraham* was so intense that the boats from the oiler could not approach the destroyer close enough to effect a rescue. Then, almost in an instant, *Ingraham* went under, smothered in a blanket of smoke and steam that was almost as thick as the fog that had caused the accident.

Meanwhile, on *Buck*, repair parties were attempting to salvage the stern by rigging cables, but this effort failed when the heaving sea began to twist and slam about the vessel. Eventually, the wave action caused the entire section to snap off and it swiftly plunged to the bottom, taking seven men down with it.

At 0510, the damaged *Chemung* closed in and took *Buck* under tow. The USS *Bristol* was detached from the convoy to escort the cripples to Boston, where they underwent repairs. At the completion of these, *Buck* put to sea to resume her escort duties in the Atlantic and in Mediterranean waters.

On July 10, 1943, *Buck* participated in the landings on Sicily and afterwards escorted the empty transports back to Algiers. On August 2, while accompanying a convoy in the Mediterranean, she attacked a submarine with depth charges. After a severe pounding, the Italian submarine *Argento* broached to the surface, her crew hastily abandoning her. Before *Buck's* gunners could blast it to the bottom, the submarine upended and sank. The destroyer then moved in and picked up 46 of her survivors, including her commanding officer.

As the Allies went on to advance up the Italian "boot," *Buck* continued to carry out her escort work, screening troop convoys through the Mediterranean to Italian beachheads. While the supplies and troops were being discharged, destroyers patrolled off the beaches, guarding against the infiltration of E-boats, aircraft and submarines. Then, just after midnight on the night of October 8–9, while *Buck* was on patrol off the mouth of Salerno Gulf, her radar operator reported an unidentified "blip" on his scanner. As *Buck* dashed through the darkness to investigate, she came within range of the *U-616*, whose commander, Captain Lieutenant Siegfried Koitschka, calmly lined the destroyer up in his periscope and unleashed a spread of two torpedoes.

One or, probably, both torpedoes slammed into *Buck's* starboard bow. The effect was devastating. As the wounded *Buck* heeled over to port, a series of explosions followed: her forward magazines were blowing up. Enveloped in a pall of smoke and roaring flames, *Buck* crawled to a stop and began to settle swiftly by the bow. Four minutes later, the ship vanished beneath the sea, her depth charges exploding as her mangled remains plunged to their watery grave.

Wreckage, debris and thick globs of fuel oil bobbed to the surface, the latter smothering the swimmers and gagging their pitiful and desperate cries for help. As the night wore on, more and more men succumbed to the ravages of their wounds, burns and utter exhaustion.

Again we hear from George Brooks, who describes his ordeal at the time the *Buck* was torpedoed and during the aftermath of his ship's loss: "As soon as contact was made with the target, the ship went to General Quarters. It seemed as though I had been in the forward engine room (my battle station) for less than a minute when the ship was jolted by a tremendous explosion. All loose gear went flying about, with most of the men being knocked off their feet and tossed in the air. Almost immediately, we could feel the ship taking a pitch forward and assumed she was on her way down. All of us made a dash for the ladder leading to the main deck.

"I was the last man to leave the engine room and when I reached topside I could see that the whole forward part of the *Buck* was a mass of roaring flames and billowing smoke. A torrent of water was washing over the main deck forward as the ship began to go down by the bow. I then stepped over the side, wearing an inflatable life preserver, though one side didn't inflate.

"Once in the water, I swam as fast as I could from the ship to avoid being dragged down with the suction when she sank. Swimming beside me was Chief Machinist's Mate Baker from the after engine room. Then the ship upended and sank in a rush. I remember asking Baker, 'What the hell do we do now?' However, I don't know if he ever answered me or not, for just then, the depth charges let go. Although we were pounded by the pressure of the underwater detonations, we were, by some miracle, still alive, but unfortunately, Baker died after we were picked up.

"The Navy Special Fuel Oil that had risen to the surface was at least a foot in thickness, and also contributed to the deaths of my shipmates. Thankfully, most of this glutinous muck dispersed later on. So, here we were, drifting about in the darkness—not having any idea of where we were, where everyone was and not knowing for certain how many of us had survived. I do recall there was a life raft on which we tried to place our wounded. Sad to say, some of the men panicked and tried to climb into it all at once, causing it to capsize and toss its occupants into the water. Then and there, I decided to swim away and fend for myself.

"At that time, I did not see any ships or boats nearby and it seemed very doubtful we'd ever be rescued. As dawn approached, there were still several men treading water and swimming about, many of them desperately trying to hold on to the wounded and encouraging them not to give up hope. Then, later that morning, a plane flew over us and soon afterwards we were picked up by the *Plunket* and *Gleaves* and a British landing craft."

All told, 7 officers and 69 men were picked up, of whom 15 were severely burned and wounded. Lost with *Buck* were her commanding officer, Lieutenant Commander M.J. Klein, and 150 members of her crew. As for the *U-616*, she herself was downed on May 14, 1944 by a combination of American destroyers and and RAF planes, with the loss of one man.

☆ ☆ ☆
USS *BUCK* (DD-420)

Class: Sims.
Builder: Philadelphia Navy Yard, Philadelphia, Pennsylvania.
Keel laid: April 6, 1938.
Launched: May 22, 1939.
Sponsor: Mrs. J. Townsend, wife of Rear Admiral Julius Townsend, USN.
Commissioned: May 15, 1940; Lieutenant Commander H.C. Robison, USN, comdg.
Date of loss: October 9, 1943; Lieutenant Commander M.J. Klien, USN, comdg.†
Location: Off Salerno Gulf, Italy.
Awards: Three battle stars.

USS Bristol

Launched July 25, 1941
Lost October 12, 1943
Off Cape Bougaroun, Algeria

REAR ADMIRAL MARK L. BRISTOL, USN
(1868–1939)

Mark Lambert Bristol was born in Glassboro, New Jersey, on April 17, 1868, and graduated from the United States Naval Academy in 1887. After serving brilliantly in the Spanish-American War, on board the USS *Texas*, he was closely associated with the improvement of naval gunnery, as well as the employment of torpedoes in naval warfare.

Promoted to the rank of Captain on July 1, 1913, he was placed in charge of the development of naval aviation, and within three years had established the naval air station at Pensacola, Florida. Here he began a school in free ballooning and acquired the first dirigible for the Navy: a small blimp. In 1916, while serving as commanding officer of the battleship *North Dakota*, he supervised the construction and installation of a catapult for launching aircraft from her deck. Later that year, the first aircraft was successfully launched, piloted by Lieutenant Godfrey De C. Chevalier.

During World War I, Bristol commanded the battleship *Oklahoma*, flagship of Battleship Division 6 in the European theater. In July 1918, he was promoted to the rank of Vice Admiral and made commandant of the U.S. Naval Base at Portsmouth, England.

After the armistice was signed, Vice Admiral Bristol went on to serve as a member of the International Armistice Committee. Between 1920 and 1932, he served as Commandant of the U.S. Naval Detatchment in Mediterranean waters; delegate to the Lausanne Conference; Ambassador to Turkey; and Commander-in-Chief of the Asiatic Fleet. Prior to his retirement on May 1, 1932, he also served as Chairman of the General Board of the Navy Department. Rear Admiral Bristol died in Washington, DC, on May 13, 1939.

On December 7, 1941, the USS *Bristol* (DD-453) was at sea undergoing her shakedown trials when her crew was informed of the Japanese attack on Pearl Harbor. As a result, her battle-readiness training was stepped up and in January 1942 she became a unit of the Atlantic destroyer squadrons and was assigned to escort duty into October of that year.

On April 21, she rescued two boat loads of survivors from the torpedoed freighter SS *Imoden,* and on the night of August 22 took on 11 survivors from the destroyer *Ingraham, which* had accidentally been rammed and sunk by the Navy oiler *Chemung.* She was then detached from her convoy to escort the oiler to Boston. The oiler was towing the destroyer *Buck,* which had itself been damaged in a collision with the troop transport *Awatea.*

On November 8, *Bristol* participated in the landings at Fedala, North Africa, and on the following day she captured the Vichy French trawler *Poitu. Bristol* was then dispatched to intercept a French destroyer that was laying a smoke screen at the African landing sites. Approaching the Frenchman with her guns blazing, *Bristol* scored several direct hits amidships and set the ship afire. Her captain then broke away and promptly ran his ship aground.

Upon her return to the transport anchorage, the destroyer was ordered to fire upon a shore battery on Fedala Point that was laying a withering barrage of gunfire on the reinforcement troops. Within 11 minutes, *Bristol's* 5-inch batteries had silenced the enemy's guns. However, as she was retiring, the guns opened up again; the destroyer returned and reduced the battery to a pile of rubble.

The busy destroyer was in action again when she joined up with the battleship *Massachusetts,* the cruisers *Augusta* and *Brooklyn,* and three other destroyers to intercept six French destroyers that were boiling up the coast with the intention of disrupting the landings. Although the French ships suffered heavily from the torrent of U.S. naval gunfire, the Americans did not escape unscathed from the ten-minute skirmish. All three of the heavy ships sustained major and minor damage, as did the destroyer *Ludlow.* As the French vessels raced for home, they were pounced upon by aircraft from the carrier *Ranger.* Only one of the destroyers made it back to its base.

Although the French surrendered on the 11th, the Germans remained determined to harass the landings and occupation forces. Their U-boats had already taken a toll in shipping, by torpedoing and sinking a transport and an oiler, and damaging the destroyer *Hambelton* (DD-455). On the following night, three more transports were sunk, *Bristol* assisting in rescuing their survivors. Two days later, the attack cargo ship *Electra* was torpedoed and

Bristol was ordered to cover the vessel while salvage operations were being effected. On the 17th, the empty ships formed up and were escorted back to the United States without incident.

For the remainder of 1942 and until July 1, 1943, *Bristol* made several escort voyages through Caribbean waters and to Casablanca. On July 5, she arrived at Bizerte, Tunisia, and on the 6th assisted in repulsing a German air attack.

During the early morning hours of July 10, *Bristol* arrived off the coast of Sicily to join in the pre-invasion shore bombardment of the town of Licata and fought off several enemy aircraft that had swarmed in against the landing sites. During the attack, *Bristol* was shaken, but not damaged, by a stick of bombs that splashed some 50 yards off her port side. Farther down the coast, off Gela, the destroyer *Maddox* was not as fortunate. Damaged by a near-miss and a direct hit, she sank in less than two minutes, taking her commanding officer and over 200 of her crew down with her.

Although the Luftwaffe tried to interfere with the landings, they were more of a deadly nuisance than a threat to Operation "Husky." In between air raids, *Bristol* and her sister destroyers successfully silenced a number of shore batteries. During one bombardment mission, *Bristol* demolished a railway gun and made a direct hit on an ammunition storage building; the latter went up with an earth-shaking blast. Once the landings had been secured, *Bristol* then escorted the empty ships back to Algiers.

Arriving there on the 16th, the destroyer replenished stores, ammunition and fuel and was soon on her way back to Sicily, escorting a reinforcement convoy en route. Several more voyages to Sicily followed until early August. On the 8th, while screening Task Force 88 off Cape Orlando, Sicily, the force was attacked by a flock of German aircraft, one of which was shot down by *Bristol.* Two days later, the destroyer sent two more aircraft spiraling into the sea.

Bristol next took part in the invasion of Salerno, on the Italian mainland. What was expected to be a "piece of cake" would result in one of the bloodiest battles in the European theater. The Germans were ready and waiting and, to compound the situation further, the gulf was strewn with deadly mines. This in itself hampered the naval bombardment ships from approaching their assigned gunfire support stations.

On the morning of September 9, the first two infantry waves spearheaded for the beach, meeting very little resistance. When the third wave landed, however, the huge guns emplaced in the surrounding hills opened up. It was unmitigated slaughter. Withering rifle and automatic weapon fire cut the troops down like a gigantic scythe. German aircraft then swooped in and assailed the invaders and their landing craft. At one point, Panzers lumbered to within 200 yards of the American foxholes, threatening to rampage on the beach itself; farther down, counterattacking Germans broke through and occupied foxholes a stone's throw from the shoreline.

By 1000, the minefields had been safely cleared, thus allowing the destroyers and cruisers to dash into the gulf, using their 8- and 5-inch guns to blast the hillsides. Unfortunately, because several of the shore firing control parties had been knocked out or scattered, the ships' firepower was not as accurate as it had been during the landings on Sicily. But just the same, it kept the enemy at bay, allowing more troops and supplies to land.

Meanwhile, *Bristol*'s guns had successfully sowed a fierce barrage of 5-inch, 20- and 40-mm shells upon a bridge and blown it sky high. Then a shore firing control party raised the destroyer and directed her to fire on a group of tanks that were sighted behind a forested area, not far from the bridge she had just demolished. Within seconds, the destroyer's guns enfiladed the area, forcing the tanks to pull back or scatter. Due to the hilly terrain, however, it was difficult to determine whether any of the tanks had been damaged.

Before noon, the naval guns began to locate the enemy's hidden gun emplacements in the ridges and enclaves, and the effects were devastating. The torrent of hot steel crushed the defenders under tons of rocks and rubble; tanks were blasted to scrap, a railway battery was demolished, machine-gun nests were knocked out of action and mobile guns and artillery batteries blown to shreds. By mid-afternoon, the Germans were in retreat, leaving at least the beaches well in the hands of the Allies. General Lang of the Fifth Army sent the following message to the naval commander, which read in part: "THANK GOD FOR THE FIRE OF THE NAVY SHIPS X PROBABLY COULD NOT HAVE STUCK IT OUT AT BLUE AND YELLOW BEACHES."

Later that evening, *Bristol* stood out of Salerno Gulf, escorting the empty transports back to Algiers. The destroyer *Rowan* joined up with the convoy, but shortly before midnight she was sunk by a torpedo from a German E-boat. *Bristol* raced to the last reported position of the unfortunate destroyer, only to find 75 of her survivors struggling in a sea of oil and debris. After several hours of trying without success to locate any further stragglers, *Bristol* caught up with the convoy and arrived at Algiers on the 14th.

Although the Allies succeeded in broadening their foothold on the Italian mainland, the Germans generally did such a thorough job of demolishing port facilities that for some time all shipping continued to come in and out of Salerno. Throughout the remainder of September and into early October, *Bristol* was engaged in escorting supply convoys to the beachhead and guarding the entrance to the gulf against infiltration by submarines and E-boats. On the night of October 12, *Bristol* was screening a convoy to Oran. The sea was tranquil and the night clear, with a bright, full moon that literally snuffed the winking stars from the sky. Except for the swirling waters swishing and gurgling along her sleek hull and the steady throbbing of her engines, all was quiet on the destroyer.

Shortly before 0400, the watches were changing. On the bridge, the oncoming Officer of the Deck was reading the night orders, and down below, in the confines of the engine and boiler rooms, the engineers were passing down information to their reliefs. Throughout the ship, in other departments, this age-old ritual of the sea was being repeated. Then, this seemingly peaceful interlude came to a shattering end when at 0425 her sonar operator picked up the "whisper" of a torpedo on his listening gear. Ten seconds later, *Bristol* was ripped apart by a violent explosion from the torpedo as it detonated on her port side, in the forward engine room, and broke her keel in two.

Dazed and shocked men scrambled to the safety of the main deck. Others made an attempt to man their battle stations, but it was all over for the stalwart destroyer as she began to buckle amidships and jackknife. Well aware that there was no hope for his ship, her captain, Commander J.A. Glick, passed the order to abandon ship—and none too soon. As her boats and rafts were being lowered and her crew was going over the side, *Bristol* snapped in half, the stern going under almost immediately, the bow remaining afloat for about eight minutes.

Lloyd Matthews, who was manning the sound-powered phones on the 20-mm gun mount just forward of the bridge when the torpedo struck, recalls that the severity of the impact threw him and his mates to the deck. Although stunned, he attempted to communicate with the bridge, but all power had been knocked out. He then ran down to the main deck and helped some men cut a life raft loose, but, lacking a kapok life jacket, Matthews did not leave the ship; besides, he did not believe the ship would sink as he had not received the order to abandon.

When he noticed that the destroyer was beginning to buckle, however, Matthews leaped over the side and swam away from the *Bristol* as fast as he could. For a time, he was confused and had some lapse of memory; then, suddenly, he found he had drifted back to the ship's stern and was floating beneath the port screw. He remembers seeing several black stewards' mates clinging doggedly to the depth-charge racks, refusing to leave the ship.

Matthews then struck out, hoping to find some flotsam to cling to, and found an unconscious man, who had not tied the strings beneath the collar of his life jacket. Matthews tied the man's strings, which probably prevented him from drowning. Then, once again, Matthews suffered a lapse of memory, and when he came to he found himself holding on to a life raft with several men upon it.

After floating about for two hours in a sea of debris and glutinous fuel oil, he and 240 of his shipmates were rescued by two destroyers. The survivors were disembarked at Algiers and hospitalized at an American Army base. Lost with *Bristol* were 52 of her crewmen.

After the war it was learned that the destroyer's stealthy assailant was the *U-371*, commanded by Captain Lieutenant Waldemar Mehl. The U-boat joined Bristol on the bottom of the Mediterranean on May 4, 1944, after being caught by a British destroyer escort, two American destroyer escorts and a French frigate. All but three crewmembers of the submarine were rescued.

☆ ☆ ☆

USS *BRISTOL* (DD-453)

Class: Benson/Livermore.
Builder: Federal Shipbuilding & Drydock Co., Kearny, N.J.
Keel laid: December 2, 1940.
Launched: July 25, 1941.
Sponsor: Mrs. Powell Clayton.
Commissioned: October 22, 1941; Lieutenant Commander C.C. Wood, USN,
     comdg.
Date of loss: October 12, 1943, Commander J.A. Glick, USN, comdg.
Location: Off Cape Bougaroun, Algeria.
Awards: Three battle stars.

USS Borie

Launched October 4, 1919
Lost November 2, 1943
North of the Azores, North Atlantic

SECRETARY OF THE NAVY ADOLPH E. BORIE
(1809–1880)

Born in Philadelphia, Pennsylvania, on November 25, 1809, Adolph Edward Borie graduated from the University of Pennsylvania in 1825. He then became a partner in his father's mercantile company, engaging primarily in the tea and silk trade in the Orient.

In 1843, he was appointed Consul General to Belgium, and from 1848 to 1860 was president of the Bank of Commerce in Philadelphia. Appointed Secretary of the Navy by President Ulysses S. Grant on March 5, 1869, he was compelled to resign four months later due to ill health. However, upon his recovery, he continued to serve in Grant's administration as an advisor, in fact accompanying the former president on a world tour in 1878–79. The honorable Adolph E. Borie died at his home in Philadelphia on February 5, 1880.

Shortly after being placed in commission, the USS *Borie* (DD-215) was assigned to occupation duty in the Middle East with the U.S. Naval Detatchment in Turkish waters and the Black Sea. This lasted until early 1921.

Borie was then assigned to the Asiatic Fleet, and during the following four years was busily engaged protecting American lives and interests in the Far East. Returning to the United States in 1925, *Borie* was assigned to the Atlantic Fleet, where she carried out her operations in Caribbean waters until 1927. She then went on to pay goodwill visits to various ports throughout Europe and the Mediterranean. The destroyer remained as a unit of the Atlantic destroyer squadrons until 1929, when she was reassigned to the Asiatic Fleet. Three years later, she arrived at San Diego and became the flagship of DesRon 2, Pacific Battle Force.

With the outbreak of the war in Europe in 1939, *Borie* was ordered to the East Coast, where she was assigned to the neutrality patrol. Attached to the 15th Naval District, Panama, C.Z., she patrolled through the waters of the Gulf of Mexico and the Caribbean, and guarded the approaches to the Panama Canal.

After December 7, 1941, *Borie* was allocated to serve as a convoy escort, plying the waters along the eastern seaboard and in the Caribbean. On June 16, 1942, she rescued the survivors from the torpedoed merchant ship SS *Merrimac.* In June 1943, *Borie* entered the Norfolk Navy Yard, Portsmouth, Virginia, where she was converted into an anti-submarine vessel. On July 30 she became a unit of the Hunter/Killer (HUK) Group, Task Unit 21.14, built around the escort carrier USS *Card.*

On August 9, the group was steaming several miles off Casablanca when it hemmed in a wolfpack composed of three U-boats, two of which were bagged by *Card's* aircraft. While *Borie* was picking up the survivors, the third submarine fired three torpedoes at her. Luckily, the menacing wakes were sighted in enough time, allowing the destroyer to take evasive action. Two of *Card's* aircraft followed the path of the wakes to their source and gave the U-boat the coup de grâce. In all, *Card's* group, under the command of Captain Arnold J. Isbell, was credited with the sinking of six U-boats after its creation on October 2, 1942. Another U-boat would be downed, this time with *Borie* receiving credit for the kill, but it would be a costly victory.

On October 31, the group was operating some 700 miles north of the Azores. The past three weeks had passed without incident and *Borie's* crew was anxious for some action, or anything, just to break the monotony. Little did they realize that before the day ended, they would become involved in a naval engagement more reminiscent of the War of 1812 than of World War II.

It all began on that Halloween afternoon when one of *Card's* scouting aircraft sighted a surfaced U-boat about 20 miles north of the task group. The U-boat crash-dived, and Captain Isbell then dispatched *Borie* to seek her out and sink her. Throughout the day, the skies had been heavily overcast, the seas choppy and accompanied by brisk, bone-chilling winds. While the *Borie* raced at flank speed toward her quarry, the weather took a turn for the worse, soon to be followed by intermittent rain squalls.

Gray-green seas cascaded over her forecastle as her sharp prow plunged and bucked through 15- to 20-foot swells. Her bridge trembled and shook from the constant pounding, which sent quivering shock waves down the full length of her slim, aging hull, straining every rivet and twisting her framework. Before long, this continuous, sledgehammer punishment began to nibble away at Borie when the impact from one plunge into a heavy, mountainous wave smashed in four portholes on her bridge. One can judge the tremendous power behind this force when one realizes the glass in the ports was 15 inches in diameter and three-quarters of an inch thick.

Now, with the icy winds and freezing seas gushing through the open ports, the bridge crew was chilled to the bone and struggling to keep their balance in ankle-deep water that sloshed from one side of the bridge to the other. Yet, despite these miserable conditions, her captain, Lieutenant Charles H. Hutchins, defiantly forged his ship through the turbulent maelstrom.

Then, just before midnight, a "pip" appeared upon the radar screen . . . and then another! Two U-boats were on the surface, neither of their commanders aware of Borie's presence. Captain Hutchins, ordering his crew to "General Quarters," reduced speed to a crawl and commenced stalking his quarry.

Choosing the nearest target (U-256), Hutchins gave the order to fire. As the 4-inch shells splashed and exploded about the U-boat, she crash-dived, but soon afterwards came under a vicious depth-charge attack. At the time, Hutchins was certain that he had sunk her and confidently sent the following message to the Card: "SCRATCH ONE PIG BOAT—AM SEARCHING FOR MORE." However, after the war, it was revealed that the U-256, under command of Oberleutnant Wilhelm Brauel, had managed to escape the wrath of Borie's depth charge assault.

While Borie was thrashing her prey, the second U-boat (U-405) escaped detection and fled through the dark, heaving seas and blustery rain. Just before 0200 on November 1, however, the all-seeing "eye" of Borie's radar picked up the U-boat's position. Hutchins stealthily closed in on his target, and when his guns were within range the searchlight was switched on. Its long, luminous beam penetrated through the downpour, illuminating the submarine as if she were exposed in broad daylight.

It is very possible that the U-405 was experiencing mechanical problems, since she made no attempt to submerge. As a result, her crew were at their action stations, so that when Borie's searchlight illuminated her, the German gunners were the first to open fire. Fortunately, the shots went wild, missing the destroyer completely. Hutchins then ordered full speed ahead, and during the next hour the antagonists chased one another in circles, firing sporadically on each other whenever the opportunities presented themselves. Owing to the violent pitching and rolling of the ships through the tempestuous waters, and hampered by periodic deluges, none of the shots found their marks. Then the U-boat scored two lucky hits. One shell crashed beneath the destroyers bridge, wrecking her radio room, and the other struck her in the amidship's section. Almost simultaneously, *Borie* scored a devastating blow near the *U-405*'s forward deck gun, damaging it and killing its crew.

Finally, by some strange quirk, Hutchins found himself in a position to ram his foe. The word was quickly passed throughout the ship: "Stand by for a ram!" All hands braced themselves or grasped hold of any stationary object: stanchions, mess tables, range finders, gun tubs. Below deck in the engineering spaces, the men clung to valve wheels and hand rails while simultaneously trying to answer the demands from the bridge to maintain a full head of steam and keep the turbines racing at full power.

As the *Borie* plunged ahead, the *U-405*'s commander (Oberleutnant Rolf-Heinrich Hopmann) fully realized the hazardous predicament he was facing and desperately attempted to avoid the sleek, gray mass that was heading toward him, growing ever larger by the second. Hindered by the heaving seas, the *U-405* was unable to answer her helm quickly enough. The destroyer was boring in ever closer, ready to slice the submarine in two, when a huge swell lifted the destroyer over the U-boat's forward section, just as she dropped into a deep trough. As a result, *Borie* had crashed down upon her adversary's deck, forward of its conning tower. With *Borie*'s turbines churning away at high speed, her forward momentum caused the U-boat to swing toward the American ship's stern, which locked both vessels in a "V" position.

Hutchins attempted to back off, but his destroyer held on to her opponent like an enraged, tenacious bulldog. At that time he didn't realize that his ship had been holed in the forward engine room by the U-405. Meanwhile, both submariners and destroyermen stared at each other in shocked disbelief, momentarily confused as to what to do next. Then, suddenly, as if on cue, the night exploded under the glow of *Borie*'s searchlight.

German seamen poured from out of the conning tower and scrambled across the U-boat's rolling, inundated deck in an effort to man their guns. On the *Borie*, Colt .45s banged away, only to be answered by Lugers snapping back. Twenty-millimeter cannon shells raked the submarine's conning tower, killing and maiming its occupants. One German seaman was seen racing toward the after deck gun to take the place of a fallen shipmate, but was stopped in his tracks when a wrench, thrown by one of Borie's seaman, struck him in the head. Dazed by the blow, the man staggered forward and fell over the side.

Down below in the forward engine room, Bill Howard, then a Fireman First Class, was fervently engaged in assisting the damage control party in its vain attempt to stem the flooding. Yet, despite every effort made to plug the gash with mattresses and the employment of bilge pumps, the ingress of the sea could not be contained. Fortunately, the after engine room was still intact and able to provide power. But with the main machinery in the forward engine room under water, there was nothing left to do but abandon the space.

Meanwhile, the close-quartered skirmish topside was still raging. Those who were not fortunate enough to have a pistol, rifle or sub-machine gun used anything within reach—pots, pans and cutlery from the galley, hammers, empty shell cases, and, believe it or not, potatoes! Later, one of the destroyer's crewman remarked, "We threw everything at the enemy but the galley stove!"

As the battle raged on, both ships ground and gnawed into each other like two live sea monsters, inflicting additional damage upon themselves. The battle came to an abrupt close when a signalman fired a flare from a Very pistol that ignited on the submarine's conning tower. Exploding in a spectacular pyrotechnic display of shooting stars, the intense heat started a flash fire which virtually immolated all of the crew in the structure. Then, suddenly, a huge swell disengaged the ships and, like two groggy boxers, they drifted apart, wallowing in the raging sea.

It can be safely assumed that the U-boatmen, like the *Borie's* crew, were making fervent attempts to salvage their vessel while keeping one eye on their antagonist. With her after engine room still in commission, *Borie* was able to propel herself with one engine. Hutchins attempted to down *U-405* with a torpedo, but it missed. The U-boat was now underway and, although critically damaged, her commander was no less determined than the American to fight it out to the finish.

Once again, a chase ensued with each of the opponents firing on the other. Finally, the submarine actually tried to ram *Borie*, which in turn let fly with a brace of depth charges from her "K" guns, that splashed on both sides of the German. The sea boomed and shook as the lethal charges detonated. The tremendous pressure from the explosions cracked the *U-405's* hull like an eggshell and literally brought her to a sudden halt. As she was settling deeper into the sea, about 20 members of her crew dashed topside and began to toss two-man, yellow life rafts over the side. The men then leaped into the sea and clambered on board the rafts. Shortly afterwards, the spunky *U-405* plunged, stern first, beneath the swirling waters of the Atlantic.

No attempt was made by *Borie* to search for or pick up any survivors, for she herself was in dire straits and her own survival seemed very much in doubt. However, her crew worked feverishly to shore up her weakening bulkheads, plugging holes and pumping out flooded spaces with portable pumps and bucket brigades. Barely able to make headway, the old four-stacker rolled sluggishly in the merciless Atlantic throughout the miserable, rain-soaked night. By now, her men were cold, exhausted and hungry, but continued to fight back the sea and endure the harsh elements. Eventually, the forward bulkhead in the after engine room gave way and flooded the space. Now without power, the fighting *Borie* was reduced to a helpless, drifting derelict.

As a cold, lead-gray dawn slowly pushed back the abysmal, black night, the crew realized the true horror of *Borie's* plight. Her maindeck from amidships to her stern was under water more than above the surface, as each abominable wave endeavored to sink her deeper. Still, the old destroyer managed to recover from each blow—but how much longer she could endure this unrelenting punishment was uncertain. If she were to founder, most of her survivors would probably never be located, for the skies were still heavily overcast and the rain showers gave no indication of abating. The ship's radio room had been damaged during the running fight with the *U-405*, and she was unable even to send out a distress signal when it was discovered that the fuel on hand to operate her emergency radio generator was contaminated with water.

Then, someone on the bridge lit a cigarette with a lighter, an action that spurred the communications officer to pass the word that all lighter fluid be drawn from the ship's store and brought to the bridge. What meager amount was collected, much of which was donated by the crew, was poured into the fuel tank, which worked, but only long enough to send the following message to *Card*: "CAN'T LAST MUCH LONGER . . . AM COMMENCING TO SINK."

Just as all hope was beginning to wane, the Pharmacist's Mate arrived on the bridge with a jug of alcohol, which was poured into the fuel tank and put the radio in operation again. However, instead of sending out a long-worded distress signal, the letter "V" was tapped out over the airwaves. It was soon picked up by one of *Card's* scout planes, and on sighting the beleaguered destroyer, the pilot flashed the news to the carrier. The destroyers *Goff* (DD-247) and *Barry* (DD-248) were then dispatched to come to the assistance of their battle-scarred sister and her gallant crew.

Arriving on the scene just before noon, both destroyers laid to on either side of *Borie* and made preparations to receive her survivors. By now, the waterlogged *Borie* was barely afloat and her battle-weary and forlorn captain was compelled to pass the word to abandon ship. At any moment, his destroyer could slip beneath the waves, with the possibility of taking most of the crew down with her.

Both destroyers closed in on *Borie* with the intention of rigging breeches buoys, but the task became impossible owing to the heaving seas. Ten-inch lines snapped like so much string and lashed back, cracking like huge bull-whips. For the bedraggled crew of the *Borie*, it was either sink or swim— and swim they did. One by one and in groups, *Borie's* crew jumped into the 29-degree waters and struck out for the *Goff* and *Barry*.

Although one of the *Borie's* officers had made it safely to *Goff*, he noticed four men struggling nearby and decided to jump back into the swirling waters to come to their assistance. Sadly, he was killed when *Goff* rolled over on him and pushed him beneath her keel.

Borie's gunnery officer had a close brush with the Grim Reaper after he had safely reached the side of *Goff*. Having gained a hold on the ship's life-line, he lost his grip, fell over the side and was struck on the head by the screw guard. After bobbing to the surface, he found himself adrift, several yards from the ship. He immediately began to swim back, but the heavy swells and the frigid sea, as well as his bulky life jacket, soon sapped all his strength. Utterly exhausted, he passed out. Luckily, the thick collar of his life jacket kept his head above water. When he came to, he found himself being carried belowdecks on board *Barry*.

The rescue operations continued until darkness closed in. Meanwhile, the mortally wounded *Borie* remained stubbornly afloat and was still wallowing about in the mountainous seas on the following morning. Three of *Card's* aircraft were sent to dispatch her to the bottom, but despite being struck by several bombs and set ablaze, the old four piper seemed to be reluctant to go under. It was then decided to finish her off with a torpedo, but as *Barry* prepared to fire, "Old 215" suddenly dipped her stern beneath the surface and, with her bow lifting high out of the water, swiftly and silently plunged to her final resting place.

Ironically, none of *Borie's* crewmen were killed or seriously wounded during the hammer-and-tongs clash with the *U-405*. Instead, it was the sailor's age-old enemy, the sea, that claimed the lives of 27 of her officers and crew. Among those lost were her communications officer and her chief engineer, who had strived to maintain the ship's power and propulsion despite the excessive ingress of the sea into his engineering spaces. He was posthumously awarded the Navy Cross. Lieutenant Hutchins was also awarded the Navy Cross, and *Borie's* executive officer received the Legion of Merit Medal. Two of her engineers were awarded the Silver Star and several other crew members received letters of commendation. The fighting *Borie* herself was awarded the Presidential Unit Citation and three battle stars.

In his article "Stand By for a Ram," Chief Fire Controlman Robert A. Maher lauded both Americans and Germans as: "Two gallant crews engaged in a fierce battle, using every kind of weapon at their disposal. As for the *Borie's* crew, there was no sign of fear or disorder anywhere among the men. Everyone on the ship went about his duty with the utmost confidence. I felt great pride in being a member of her crew and was even more proud by the time the entire action was over."

☆ ☆ ☆

USS *BORIE* (DD-215)

Class: Wickes/Clemson.
Builder: William Cramp & Sons, Philadelphia, Pennsylvania.
Keel laid: April 30, 1919.
Launched: October 4, 1919.
Sponsor: Miss Patty Borie, great grandniece of Adolph E. Borie, Secretary of the Navy
Commissioned: March 24, 1920; Lieutenant Commander E.F. Clement, USN, comdg.
Date of loss: November 2, 1943; Lieutenant C.H. Hutchins, USNR, comdg.
Location: North of the Azores, North Atlantic.
Awards: Presidential Unit Citation and three battle stars.

USS Beatty

Launched December 20, 1941
Lost November 6, 1943
Off Cape Bougaroun, Algeria

REAR ADMIRAL FRANK E. BEATTY, USN
(1853–1926)

Born in Jefferson County, Wisconsin, on November 26, 1853, Frank Edmund Beatty graduated from the Naval Academy in 1875. Upon his promotion to the rank of Captain, he was placed in command of the battleship *Wisconsin*, which took part in the Great White Fleet's round-the-world cruise.

Afterwards, he assumed command of the First Battleship Division, Atlantic Fleet, flying his flag in the *Florida*. While serving as commandant of the Naval Gun Factory at Washington, D.C., Beatty assisted in the improvement of naval artillery practice and developed an electric rangefinder. Prior to his retirement, Captain Beatty served as commandant of the Charleston Navy Yard, in South Carolina. Captain Beatty retired on October 6, 1919, with the rank of Rear Admiral. Residing in Charleston, he died at his home on March 16, 1926.

Assigned to the Atlantic Destroyer Squadrons, the USS *Beatty* (DD-640) carried out her escort duties along the eastern seaboard and in Caribbean waters, before taking part in the North African landings on November 8, 1942. While providing covering fire for the landings off Safi, Morocco, her gunners silenced a gun battery that was firing on a group of landing craft forging toward the beach. With Casablanca and Safi secured by the Allied forces, *Beatty* then escorted the empty transports back to the United States.

After completing a shipyard overhaul, *Beatty* resumed her escort duties and made several voyages to Casablanca until June 25, 1943, when she arrived at Mers-El-Kebir, Algeria. Here, she was assigned to patrol duties, guarding the approaches to this port while the Allies prepared for the upcoming invasion of Sicily.

On July 10, *Beatty* participated in the pre-invasion bombardment of the Sicilian town of Scoglitti. Down the coast, off the town of Gela, the destroyer *Maddox* had been sunk by a German bomber and throughout the day Nazi aircraft continued to harass the landing sites and transport anchorages, contesting the area with naval anti-aircraft gunnery.

By late evening, the Allied forces had occupied the towns of Gela, Scoglitti and Licata, and on the following morning *Beatty* was dispatched to bombard a Sicilian railroad junction. Opening fire at 0738, her 5-inchers reduced the entire area into rubble by 0811. Soon after, *Beatty* received a message from a Shore Fire Control Party that a group of German tanks were sighted grinding toward the landing sites. With the SFCP relaying their location, *Beatty's* gunners, in short order, transformed the once proud Panzers into so much scrap iron. She was then ordered to fire upon a bridge, but with the destroyer running low on ammunition, the task was taken over by the USS *Laub* (DD-613).

By this time, *Beatty's* crew had been at battle stations since the late hours of the 9th. It was now 1140 on the 11th, and with the situation seemingly quieted down, one-quarter of the crew was released from their battle stations for a short rest. But there was little real rest for the destroyer's embattled and bone weary crew, as constant air raid alerts continued to be sounded. Then, at 1900, *Beatty* was dispatched to meet an incoming reinforcement troop convoy and guide it to the transport anchorage.

Later that evening, at about 2330, an aircraft was heard approaching the ship off the starboard bow from the shore. From the sound of its engines, it was a foregone conclusion that the plane was experiencing engine trouble or had sustained some flak damage. Then finally, the low-flying plane was seen through the darkened seascape. Skimming forward of *Beatty's* bow, it crashed into the water on her port side. As *Beatty* skirted past the sinking plane, one of her ship's gunners fired several rounds of 20-mm shells into the wreckage. Almost simultaneously, *Beatty* was illuminated under a string of blinding flares. Believing he was about to come under an air attack, her skipper, Lieutenant Commander F.C. Stelter, ordered full speed ahead and raced out from under the glowing umbrella of light.

When the flares burned out, *Beatty* returned to her patrolling sector. Upon nearing the site where the aircraft had crashed, a life raft was sighted with four men on it. These were found to be the crew from the destroyed plane—and they were Americans. The pilot reported that they had just landed the 15th Paratroopers and had been hit by both friendly and enemy AA fire. Thanks to his skill in handling his aircraft in the crash landing, the pilot had made it possible for his crew to escape and had saved the life of one man who was unconscious. Luckily, the shells from the 20-mm cannon had gone wild so none of the aircraft's crew were killed or wounded. Still, it must be said, the record of coordination between the naval and air arms in the invasion of Sicily was not a good one, and resulted in much worse accidents of "friendly" fire than this.

On July 15, *Beatty* arrived at Oran, and on the 21st set a course for New York, where she entered the Brooklyn Navy Yard for voyage repairs and alterations. Upon completion of her shipyard overhaul and battle-readiness exercises, *Beatty* returned to the Mediterranean. On September 2, while escorting a convoy, she succeeded in repelling an attack by a German bomber. On the 6th, while at anchor at Bizerte, she experienced another air assault against shipping in the harbor, in which neither side sustained any damage. On the following day, the destroyer stood out of port, bound for New York, escorting a convoy en route.

On October 1, Lieutenant Commander W. Outerson relieved Lieutenant Commander F.C. Stelter and assumed command of *Beatty*. Shortly after, the destroyer departed New York, escorting a convoy to Bangor, Ireland, the first leg of a journey from which she would never return.

October 27 found the *Beatty* rendezvousing with Convoy KMF-25-A, made up of troops and supplies to reinforce the Allied forces at Naples, Italy. The voyage had proved to be uneventful until just before sunset on November 6. At about 1800, a flock of German torpedo bombers plunged out of the darkening skies and pounced on the sluggish transports.

The screening destroyers met the onslaught with a barrage of anti-aircraft fire so intense that a few of the pilots dropped their torpedoes prematurely, resulting in them missing their targets. Then two of the attackers approached *Beatty*, flashing recognition signals. Captain Outerson was not easily fooled by this ruse, however, and maneuvered in time to evade their torpedoes. Suddenly, at 1813, as *Beatty* was emerging from out of the smoke screen that had been laid down to obscure the convoy, a torpedo was sighted spearheading toward her starboard side. Unable to dodge in time, *Beatty* took a devastating hit in her after engine room, killing and injuring most of the watch standers. All electrical power was lost and, with her keel broken and both propeller shafts jammed, the stricken *Beatty* lost all headway.

Harold E. Hansen, Chief Gunner's Mate, tells of his experience at the time *Beatty* was torpedoed: "I was at my battle station with the damage control party located amidships. For some reason, I can't recall why, but I decided to check on my gun crew that was manning No.4 5-inch gun mount, when a terrific blast threw me into the air. Upon landing on the maindeck on my hands and knees, and despite my being disoriented and dazed, I could see steam and smoke billowing out from the after engine room, which was just beneath the deck where my battle station was. All of the men in that area were either killed or badly wounded.

"I then ran to my gun mount to take charge of the gun crew in an effort to ward off the attacking planes, but found that the gun had been jarred off its barbette, rendering it inoperable."

The tremendous blast caused other compartments to flood and fires to break out. Damage controlmen and firefighters rushed to the critical areas to retard the flooding and beat back the searing flames. Fortunately, despite *Beatty's* adverse situation, her 20- and 40-mm guns were able to throw up a fierce enough barrage to drive off any further airborne assailants. Not only did the Germans employ torpedoes and bombs in this fight, they also unleashed a flock of radio-controlled glider bombs, of which several barely missed the now paralyzed *Beatty*. With the coming of darkness, the Germans retired and the battle was over. But for the *Beatty's* crew, the battle to save their fighting ship had only begun.

All efforts to raise steam in the forward fire room, primarily to operate the ship's fire and bilge pumps, failed when water in the fuel lines snuffed out the boilers. Although the portable pumps were succeeding in containing the flames, the ingress of the sea into her broken hull could not be staunched. Eventually, the fight to regain buoyancy was lost when the weight of the water proved to be too much of a strain on her weakened framework.

Hour by hour, *Beatty's* list increased. By 2130, she was lying at a 45-degree angle and sagging like a hammock. With both engine rooms and the after fire room inundated, Captain Outerson had no other choice but to order his command abandoned. This was carried out in an orderly manner and without much difficulty. At 2305, while her survivors pulled clear, the dying *Beatty* gave a shuddering lurch, jackknifed and sank under a mantle of smoke and mist, taking seven of her bluejackets down with her.

The survivors were picked up by the destroyers *Laub* and *Parker* (DD-604). One officer and seven men were wounded, of which one died shortly after being rescued.

While the convoy proceeded on its original course, the destroyer *Boyle* (DD-600) remained behind hoping to locate any of *Beatty's* stragglers. Just as she was about to abandon her search, her lookouts heard a faint cry for help across the dark expanse of the sea. As *Boyle* approached the site, a man was seen treading water and was hoisted on board. He identified himself as Samuel Poland, Radarman Third Class, from *Beatty*.

At the time the torpedo had hit the ship, Sam had been running across the 0-1 deck to his battle station, one deck above the point of impact. The violent concussion had flung him up in the air and over the side, accompanied by a 300-pound depth charge, which luckily did not detonate. Despite suffering from a double compound fracture of his left leg, and also thoroughly waterlogged, "Stalwart Sam" recovered from his injuries and lived to fight another day.

☆ ☆ ☆

USS *BEATTY* (DD-640)

Class: Benson/Livermore.
Builder: Charleston Navy Yard, Charleston, South Carolina.
Keel laid: May 1, 1941.
Launched: December 20, 1941.
Sponsor: Mrs. Charles H. Drayton, daughter of Rear Admiral Frank E. Beatty, USN.
Commissioned: May 7, 1942; Lieutenant Commander F.C. Stelter, USN, comdg.
Date of loss: November 6, 1943; Lieutenant Commander W. Outerson, USN, comdg.
Location: Off Cape Bougaroun, Algeria.
Awards: Three battle stars.

USS Perkins

Launched December 31, 1935
Lost November 29, 1943
Off Cape Vogel, New Guinea

COMMODORE GEORGE H. PERKINS, USN
(1835–1899)

Born in Hopkinton, New Hampshire, on October 20, 1835, George Hamilton Perkins was appointed Midshipman in 1851. From 1859 to 1861, he served on the USS *Sumter* as Sailing Master during the suppression of piracy in Caribbean waters.

During the Civil War, he served in the West Gulf Blockading Squadron and under Admiral David G. Farragut in the battles against Forts St. Philip and Jackson. Other outstanding accomplishments included his engaging with and sinking the Confederate screw steamer CSS *Governor Moore* and the capture of three other ships of the Montgomery Flotilla, as well as his boldness when he defiantly walked through the streets of New Orleans, unarmed, and among hostile mobs, to accept the surrender of the city in April 1862.

Three months later, he fought against Port Hudson and Confederate fortifications on the Whitehall River, and during the Battle of Mobile Bay he captured the CSS *Mary Soley* and the ironclad ram *Tennessee*, the flagship of Admiral Franklin Buchanan, CSN. In August 1863, he attacked and captured Confederate Forts Powell, Morgan and Gaines.

With peace restored in 1865, Lieutenant Commander Perkins went on to serve in various types of vessels. In 1871, he was promoted to the rank of Commander and assumed command of the screw gunboat USS *Ashulot*. Advanced to the rank of Captain in 1877, he served as commandant of the Asiatic Station into 1879. Upon his return to the United States, Captain Perkins assumed command of the USS *Hartford* of the Brazilian Squadron. Retiring with the rank of Commodore in 1896, he resided in Boston, Massachusetts, where he died on October 28, 1899.

A Pacific Fleet destroyer from the day of her commissioning, the USS *Perkins* (DD-377) was undergoing a shipyard overhaul at the Mare Island Navy Yard when the Japanese attacked Pearl Harbor. On the 15th, she stood out of San Francisco to escort a convoy to Seattle, Washington, and two days later set a course for Pearl, where she was assigned to patrolling duties off the Hawaiian Islands. On January 15, the destroyer returned to the Mare Island Navy Yard for the installation of new radar equipment.

Back in Pearl Harbor in late January, *Perkins* and her division soon departed for Australia, escorting the cruiser *Chicago* en route. Here they joined up with the "ANZAC" naval forces to guard the shipping lanes between Australian and New Zealand ports.

On May 4, *Perkins* was part of the screen for Task Force 17 built around the aircraft carriers *Lexington* and *Yorktown*. On that date, their aircraft had attacked a Japanese landing force on Tulagi and Guadalcanal, during which three of *Yorktown's* pilots had been shot down. Two crashed at Henslow Point on Guadalcanal, with the third ditching into the sea. *Perkins* and the destroyer *Hammann* were detached from the task force to search for the downed pilots. Although *Hammann* succeeded in rescuing the pilots on Henslow Point, *Perkins* was unable to find the pilot who had crashed into the water.

On the 7th, *Perkins* and her division were dispatched to intercept a troop convoy that was reported heading toward Port Moresby, New Guinea. As the ships were racing through Jomard Pass, they were jumped by a flock of Japanese fighters, several of which were blown out of the sky by the ships' anti-aircraft batteries. At the same time, to the south, the Battle of the Coral Sea exploded. This important, if not decisive, battle resulted in the loss of the *Lexington* and the damaging of the *Yorktown*, the Japanese losing the small carrier *Shoho* and suffering severe damage to their large carriers *Shikaku* and *Zuikaku*. This action also caused the enemy to abort the landings on Port Moresby, which, in turn, virtually halted Japan's further advances into the South Pacific.

Between May and into July 1942, *Perkins* continued to conduct her operations with the Australian and New Zealand naval forces, until she struck an uncharted reef that damaged one of her propellers. After temporary repairs at Auckland, New Zealand, she sailed for Pearl Harbor on July 20, where she received permanent repairs and the installation of 40-mm cannons and newer radar equipment.

From August until late November, *Perkins'* activities were somewhat uneventful. Then, on the night of November 30, while she was assigned to

Rear Admiral C.H. Wright, Task Group 67, she was involved in the Battle of Tassaforanga, off the coast of Guadalcanal.

After firing a brace of torpedoes at a group of Japanese destroyers under the command of Rear Admiral Razio Tanaka, *Perkins* and her sister destroyers were ordered to retire while Admiral Wright engaged the enemy with his cruisers. After a brief exchange of gunfire, in which one Japanese destroyer was sunk, Tanaka ordered his destroyers to fire torpedoes and then swiftly retired. Several of the lethal "long lancers" found their targets, sinking the cruiser *Northhampton* and seriously damaging the *New Orleans*, as well as Admiral Wright's flagship *Minneapolis*. The light cruiser *Honolulu*, which had escaped from the debacle unscathed, made a futile attempt to pursue Tanaka's destroyers, but could not catch up with them.

Throughout December and into late January 1943, *Perkins* resumed her escort duties, and on several occasions was called upon to provide shore bombardment against enemy installations throughout the Solomons, until the Japanese eventually evacuated their troops from Guadalcanal.

In May, after carrying out escort duties and operating with Australian and New Zealand naval forces, she joined in the rehearsal exercises for the proposed invasion of New Guinea. Then, from June into August, *Perkins* and her sister destroyers were kept busy sweeping along the northeastern coast of New Guinea, bombarding Japanese outposts and installations at Finschaven, Lae and Madang. On September 4, she covered the landings of the ANZAC forces in an area between the Buso and Bulu Rivers, and four days later she assisted in the bombardment of Lae. After seven days of this unrelenting punishment, the enemy abandoned the outpost, which was occupied on the following day.

After the fall of Finschaven on October 2, *Perkins* commenced escorting reinforcement convoys to the newly occupied territories without interference. On November 28, *Perkins* sailed from Milne Bay independently, bound for Buna. Later that evening, the skies became overcast with a heavy mantle of low-hanging clouds. At 0145 on the 29th, her radar operator picked up a ship six miles dead ahead and notified the Executive Officer, who was also the ship's navigator. He in turn, tracked the unidentified vessel up to 6,000 yards and went to the bridge to ask the OOD if he had seen the approaching vessel, which, under wartime regulations, was steaming with her lights extinguished.

Before he could answer, however, one of the ships' lookouts bellowed: "Ship! Dead ahead!" A quick glimpse through the inky darkness revealed a huge black shape with a creamy, white mustache curling under its stem, bearing down upon the 1,500-ton *Perkins*. The destroyer's helm was immediately swung to port in an effort to avoid the inevitable collision. But it was too late. The towering, monolithic bulk of the Australian troop transport HMAS *Dundroon* crashed into the American warship's after fire room with a sledgehammer blow—slicing her thin hull plating open like a gigantic butcher's cleaver. The vessel's ponderous weight, combined with her forward momentum, rolled the *Perkins* almost over on her beams' end and broke her keel.

Men and loose gear went flying through the air; steam and smoke billowed out of her mortal wound; the burned and injured screamed in agony. Dazed and shocked men stumbled to the maindeck, the uninjured carrying, leading, pulling or dragging their less fortunate shipmates to safety.

After *Dundroon* came to a stop, she backed away, letting in the sea. The tremendous pressure from the water rushing into the destroyer's hull resulted in the bulkheads to the other engineering spaces splitting open; they filled rapidly. With her back broken, the strain was more than the ill-fated *Perkins* could endure. Settling fast and beginning to jackknife, her captain, Lieutenant Commander G.L. Ketchum, passed the order to abandon ship. At 0225, just twenty-five minutes after *Perkins* was rammed, she broke in two and sank. Out of a complement of 299 officers and men, 11 members of her crew perished with the ship.

☆ ☆ ☆

USS *PERKINS* (DD-377)

Class: Mahan.
Builder: Puget Sound Navy Yard, Bremerton, Washington.
Keel laid: November 15, 1934.
Launched: December 31, 1935.
Sponsor: Mrs. Lars Anderson.
Commissioned: September 18, 1936; Lieutenant Commander S.P. Jenkins, USN, comdg.
Date of loss: November 29, 1943; Lieutenant Commander G.L. Ketchum, USN, comdg.
Location: Off Cape Vogel, New Guinea.
Awards: Four battle stars.

USS Leary

Launched December 18, 1918
Lost December 24, 1943
The North Atlantic

LIEUTENANT CLARENCE F. LEARY, USNRF
(1894–1918)

Clarence Frederick Leary was born in Fowey, England, on January 11, 1894. Emigrating to the United States as a young boy, he joined the United States Naval Reserve Force on June 12, 1918.

While serving as Executive Officer on board the Navy supply ship USS *Carlton Hall*, a fire broke out in one of the ship's holds. Suffering from severe burns and smoke inhalation while attempting to extinguish the flames, Lieutenant Leary died shortly afterwards. For his self-sacrificing valor and bravery, Lieutenant Leary was posthumously awarded the Navy Cross.

The USS *Leary* (DD-158) underwent her shakedown and acceptance trials in Caribbean waters and conducted her training operations along the Atlantic seaboard prior to joining the Pacific Battle Fleet in January 1921. Here, she participated in a large-scale battle exercise throughout the month of February, and in March transited the Panama Canal and reported to the Commandant of the U.S. Naval Base at Guantánamo Bay, Cuba.

After witnessing the bombing of warships by Army bombers, under the supervision of Lieutenant General William "Billy" Mitchell, *Leary* resumed her training exercises in the Caribbean. Then, in accordance with the Naval Disarmament Conference of 1922, *Leary* was decommissioned at the Philadelphia Navy Yard in June of that year.

Recommissioned on May 1, 1930, *Leary* went on to serve alternately with the Atlantic and Pacific fleets, carrying out her normal training operations and taking part in fleet maneuvers.

In April 1937, the destroyer underwent a shipyard overhaul and, under a cloak of extreme security, was equipped with a new and highly secret radio detection and ranging device, commonly known as radar. Having been the first U.S. naval vessel to be fitted out with this instrument, *Leary* also became the first American warship to make radar contact with a surfaced U-boat, while escorting a British merchant convoy in the North Atlantic on November 9, 1941.

With the United States officially drawn into World War II on December 8, 1941, *Leary* continued to serve as a convoy escort, making several transatlantic voyages to Casablanca, Trinidad and various Caribbean ports into the summer of 1943. While undergoing a shipyard overhaul, she was converted into an anti-submarine vessel and later joined Captain Arnold J. Isbell's Task Group 21.41, built around the escort carrier *Card*.

On the night of December 23, 1943, the task group was bucking through a severe North Atlantic storm when, at 0158 on the 24th, *Leary's* radarman made a definite contact with a surfaced U-boat off the destroyer's starboard bow. This was the *U-275*, armed with GNAT acoustic torpedoes, weapons that were specially developed to be used against destroyers. Even while her crew was racing to their battle stations, a torpedo struck *Leary* on her starboard side, detonating in the after engine room and killing all of the men there. With both propeller shafts damaged, *Leary* sloughed to a halt, the old four-piper tossing about helplessly in the black, windswept sea, listing 20 degrees to starboard. Unbeknownst to the Americans, a second enemy vessel, the *U-382*, was on the scene, and it too fired, but missed. In any case, with the frigid seas now cascading into her compartments, *Leary's* captain, Commander James E. Kyes, passed the order to abandon ship.

Thomas J. Johnson, then a Seaman First Class, was at his battle station (No.1 4-gun on the bow), when the torpedo hit the ship, and afterwards recalled: "When I arrived on the well deck [an open deck area located between the forward deck house and the bridge structure], [I saw] our skipper, Commander Kyes, our Executive Officer, Lieutenant Watson, and a black mess attendant, whose life jacket was so badly torn, it never would have kept him afloat for very long. As I was leaving the ship, I saw Commander Kyes hand his own life jacket over to the fellow. Then, as I was swimming away from the ship, another huge explosion wracked the *Leary* and she sank stern first and so quickly, I was certain that our captain never had a chance to leave the ship.

"Later, I came across James E. Stout, Watertender First Class, who was floating among several life jackets, one of which I hung on to. Later we found Mr. Watson sitting astride the bottom of the captain's gig. Both of us clung to the gig until we were picked up by our sister destroyer, *Schenck*"

Lost with *Leary* were Commander Kyes and 97 members of her crew. For sacrificing his own life, Commander Kyes was posthumously awarded the Navy Cross. Thanks to the quick action taken by the captain of the USS *Schenck* (DD-159) and his skillful handling of his ship in the dark and storm-tossed sea, the majority of *Leary's* crew was rescued.

☆   ☆   ☆

USS *LEARY* (DD-158)

Class: Wickes/Clemson.
Builder: New York Shipbuilding Corp., Camden, New Jersey.
Keel laid: March 6, 1918.
Launched: December 18, 1918.
Sponsor: Mrs. Anne Leary, mother of Lieutenant Clarence F. Leary, USNRF.
Commissioned: December 5, 1919; Commander F.C. Martin, USN, comdg.
Date of loss: December 24, 1943; Commander James E. Kyes, USN, comdg.†
Location: North Atlantic.
Awards: One battle star.

USS Brownson

Launched September 24, 1942
Lost December 26, 1943
Off Cape Gloucester, New Britain Island

REAR ADMIRAL WILLARD H. BROWNSON, USN
(1845–1935)

Willard Herbert Brownson was born in Lyons, New York, on July 8, 1845. Entering the U.S. Naval Academy in June 1861, he graduated with high honors in 1865. In 1885, after serving in various types of vessels, he assumed the post of Inspector of Hydrography and later went on to command the USSs Petrel, Dolphin and Detroit, the latter while in Rio de Janeiro, protecting American interests during the Brazilian Revolution of 1893–94. In 1894, he served as commandant of naval cadets at the Naval Academy and in 1896 became a member of the Board of Survey and Inspection.

During the war with Spain, he assumed command of the steamer USS Yankee (formerly the yacht El Norte), which was acquired by the Navy from the president of the Southern Pacific Railway. Advanced to the rank of Captain in 1900, Brownson placed the battleship Alabama in commission and, in 1902, was appointed Superintendent of the U.S. Naval Academy. Six years later, he was appointed commandant of the Asiatic Fleet.

Although he retired in 1907, with the rank of Rear Admiral, he remained active in naval affairs and, at the request of President Theodore Roosevelt, went on to serve as Chief of the Bureau of Navigation. After fulfilling this post, Rear Admiral Brownson settled in Washington, D.C., where he died at eighty-nine years of age on March 16, 1935.

The USS *Brownson* (DD-518) was, for a brief time, attached to the Atlantic Fleet destroyer squadrons prior to reporting to the Pacific Fleet. On August 15, she covered the landings on Kiska in the Aleutian Islands and continued to carry out her operations in the North Pacific until October 21, when she sailed for Pearl Harbor. Upon the completion of a shipyard overhaul, *Brownson* returned to the frigid and windswept waters of the northern Pacific and resumed her patrolling duties there until late November.

Arriving at Pearl Harbor during the first week of December, she underwent another shipyard overhaul. Then, after completing a grilling two-week session of battle-readiness exercises, *Brownson* commenced her operations with the South Pacific naval forces.

On December 26, *Brownson's* division was steaming off Cape Gloucester, New Britain, covering the Allied landings there and guarding the transports and supply ships against interference by enemy air or submarine attacks. At 1419, a flight of over 80 aircraft was sighted swarming toward the landing site. Although several of the planes were intercepted and shot down by a flock of Army P-38 fighters, a large number of planes escaped unscathed and were now winging toward the unloading supply ships and transports.

Brownson and her division formed a single line and increased speed to 25 knots, their crews manning their battle stations and eager for a fight. Upon sighting the oncoming aircraft, the division commander ordered his ships to disperse to meet the expected onslaught. It was during this maneuver that two "Val" dive bombers plunged from out of a low-hanging cloud bank, their engines screaming like banshees, directly astern of *Brownson*. Immediately, her 20- and 40-mm cannons opened up, spitting a hail of fiery tracers and hot lead on her assailants. Several hits were scored on the nearest plane and it went flaming into the sea. The second succeeded in slashing through the curtain of intense anti-aircraft fire to drop two 500-pound bombs from a height of 500 feet and then, like the proverbial "bat out of hell," fled for home.

At 1442, both bombs struck *Brownson* at the base of No. 2 stack. The devastating blow virtually disintegrated the entire ship's midsection from the after torpedo mount to No.3 5-inch gun mount, and demolished the after fire and engine rooms. A dense pall of smoke, steam and roaring flames belched out from her engineering spaces, the searing flames edging closer to number three magazine. The severity of the hit had broken *Brownson's* back, causing her to sag and begin to split in half.

Within a few moments of the hit, *Brownson's* amidships section was underwater, her bow and stern protruding out of the water at a 15- to 20-degree angle. At 1445, the forward section of the destroyer had taken on a prominent list, and began to tear itself from the after part of the ship. Certain that his vessel was beyond saving, and to spare as many lives as possible,

Brownson's captain, Lieutenant Commander J.B. Maher, issued the order to abandon ship. Nine minutes later, the mangled remains of *Brownson* slid beneath the sea, killing two men in the water when her depth charges exploded.

By this time, the enemy had been beaten off by other ships' anti-aircraft fire and Army fighters. Meanwhile, the destroyers *Lamson* (DD-367) and *Daly* (DD-519) had rushed to the site where the *Brownson* had gone down and began to pick up the survivors. One of them, the ship's doctor, Lieutenant C.P. Chandler, who was rescued by the *Daly*, had, throughout the afternoon and into the night, tended to the wounded, despite suffering from a shrapnel wound on his right forearm. For his devotion to duty and to the welfare of his patients, Lieutenant Chandler was awarded the Navy Cross. However, his most honored accolade was expressed by the ship's crew, whose simple but straightforward comment was: "He was one hell of a great Doc!"

Lost with *Brownson* were 108 officers and men.

☆ ☆ ☆

USS *BROWNSON* (DD-518)

Class: Fletcher.
Builder: Bethlehem Steel Shipbuilding Co., Staten Island, New York.
Keel laid: July 19, 1942.
Launched: September 24, 1942.
Sponsor: Mrs. Cleland S. Baxter, granddaughter of Rear Admiral Willard H. Brownson, USN.
Commissioned: February 3, 1943; Lieutenant Commander J.B. Maher, USN, comdg.
Date of loss: December 26, 1943: Lieutenant Commander J.B. Maher, USN, comdg.
Location: Off Cape Gloucester, New Britain Island.
Awards: One battle star.

USS Turner

Launched February 28, 1943
Lost January 3, 1944
Off Sandy Hook, New Jersey

CAPTAIN DANIEL TURNER, USN
(1794–1850)

Daniel Turner was born in Richmond, Staten Island, New York in 1794. Entering the Navy as a Midshipman on January 1, 1808, he attended the New York Naval School prior to reporting on board the frigate USS *Constitution*. On June 8, 1812, he was placed in command of gunboats stationed at the naval base in Norwich, Connecticut.

On March 14, 1813, just two days after being promoted to Lieutenant, Turner was sent to Sackett's Harbor, New York, located on the shores of Lake Erie. Here, he was placed in command of the brig USS *Niagara*, then attached to Commodore Oliver Hazard Perry's squadron. Later, he assumed command of the brig USS *Caledonia*.

During the decisive Battle of Lake Erie, on September 10, 1813, the little brig played an important role when, at the height of the battle, Lieutenant Turner gamely challenged and turned his two long 24-pound guns against three British ships that were in the process of pounding Perry's flagship, *Lawrence,* into splinters. In appreciation for his courageous part in this American victory, Lieutenant Turner was highly praised by Perry and awarded a silver medal by the U.S. Congress and a sword by the State of New York.

Throughout the remainder of the Great Lakes campaign, Lieutenant Turner continued to harass British shipping and supported Army operations around Detroit, as well as blockading the British forces at the Nottawasaga River and Lake Simcoe. On September 6, 1814, he brought his ship, USS *Scorpion,* alongside the American schooner *Tigress.* Unknown to him, unfortunately, the schooner had been captured by the British a few days previously. Hence, he and his crew were imprisoned. Later, he was released in a prisoner exchange.

With peace declared between the United States and Britain, Lieutenant Turner went on to serve in the frigate *Java*, which was captained by his former commander, Commodore Perry. Between 1815 and 1817, *Java* cruised through the Mediterranean in a show of American naval strength, primarily to impress the Barbary powers and intimidate them into honoring their treaties with the United States.

In 1819, after a two-year tour of shore duty, Lieutenant Turner assumed command of the schooner *Nonesuch* and sailed through the Caribbean in an effort to suppress the piracy that was then running unchecked throughout the West Indies. In August of that year, he accompanied Commodore Perry during a goodwill visit to Venezuela, then ruled by President Simón Bolívar. Shortly after their departure from Venezuela, several of Turner's crew, including Commodore Perry, contracted yellow fever. On the 23rd, Perry succumbed to the disease at Trinidad.

Promotions in the Navy were slow during the early 1800s, hence Turner did not attain the rank of Captain until March 3, 1835. Following his advancement to Captain, he was shorebound for several years before taking command of the *Constitution* in 1839. After cruising throughout the Pacific Ocean, Captain Turner was once again assigned to shore duty. From 1843 to 1846, he commanded the Brazilian Squadron, and from there assumed command of the Portsmouth Navy Yard.

On February 4, 1850, while awaiting further orders at the Philadelphia Navy Yard, Captain Turner died suddenly, possibly from a heart attack. He was laid to rest at the Greenmount Cemetery, Baltimore, Maryland.

During the late hours of January 2, 1944, the USS *Turner* (DD-648) dropped anchor in the Ambrose Channel, off Sandy Hook, New Jersey. As a result of wartime security (except in extreme emergencies), all shipping was prohibited from entering port after sunset; therefore, the destroyer was compelled to remain anchored off Sandy Hook until after sunrise on the following morning. After having successfully completed one of her many transatlantic convoy runs, *Turner* was scheduled to enter the Brooklyn Navy Yard for voyage repairs, her crew anxiously looking forward to a well-deserved few days' liberty.

At 0500, the ship's cooks were awakened to prepare a hearty breakfast, the mess cooks and officers' stewards setting up the tables. The heady aroma

of fresh-brewed coffee permeating throughout the ship had already awakened many members of her crew long before reveille had sounded. In anticipation of entering port within a few hours, the usual good-natured banter
passed back and forth between the men as they carried out their pre-break-
fast chores. Then, suddenly, this exultant, high-spirited occasion came to a
shattering end. At 0615, the *Turner* was shaken by a violent explosion.

Rushing to their battle stations, the crew believed the ship had been torpedoed or had been hit by a drifting mine. Actually, the detonation had
occurred in the vicinity of No.2 magazine and handling room, where the
projectiles and powder cases were stored for No.2 5-inch battery. Within a
few seconds, the whole forward section of *Turner* was transformed into an
incinerator that instantly killed her captain, Lieutenant Commander Henry
S. Wygant, his Executive Officer and most of the officers and crewmen who
were performing their morning chores in that location.

At the Sandy Hook Coast Guard Station, Coxswain Fred Williams was
standing anchor watch on board his submarine chaser and happened to
glance out toward the anchored ships in the channel just as *Turner* exploded. Later, he would testify that the ship had actually leaped out of the
water and soon afterwards was enshrouded in flames and billowing smoke.

As he was sounding the general alarm on his ship, he was buffeted by
the tremendous shock wave as it rolled over the vast seascape. Within a few
minutes, the sub chaser was churning at top speed toward the now blazing
destroyer. The explosion had also been heard by the lookout at the Sandy
Hook Lighthouse, who quickly alarmed the harbor authorities.

Meanwhile, on board *Turner*, immediately after the first explosion a second detonation jolted her as the ammunition in No.1 5-inch handling room
exploded, killing all the chief petty officers, whose berthing and messing
quarters were located in that section. Like a searing whirlwind, the flames
leapfrogged swiftly from one compartment to the next. The intense heat
soon ignited her half-filled fuel tanks, which resulted in additional violent
explosions, and caused the engineers to abandon the forward fire room.

The bridge, and the superstructure beneath it, was now swathed in a pillar of fire and a roiling mass of smoke. The 20-mm ready ammunition stored
near the guns began to ignite, their glowing tracers soaring skyward and flying across the waters like Roman candles. Some of these random projectiles
hit the ships anchored nearby. Only two ships dared to approach the now
fiery destroyer in an effort to douse the flames and take off her crew. Like a
floating Vesuvius, more and more violent rumblings could be heard within
the bowels of the ill-starred *Turner*. As the hungry flames swept ever so

swiftly aft, the engineers were forced to abandon their posts to avoid the flesh-searing heat and asphyxiating fumes.

Despite the tons of water the rescue ships sprayed on the ship, the roaring fires could not be contained. The skipper of the aforementioned Coast Guard cutter, Ensign Peter Chase, later testified at the hearings that he noticed that confusion and uncertainty reigned among the few men who were gathered about the after section of the ship, and that there did not appear to be any officers or chief petty officers to issue orders to the bewildered sailors on her smoldering decks. With the ship taking on a heavy list to starboard and fearing that Turner might capsize at any moment, Ensign Chase took it upon himself to order the ship abandoned.

The dying Turner continued to blaze and quake from the thunderous explosions that ripped through her ravished hull until 0745, when her after magazines blew out her bottom plating. Rolling over to starboard, the scorched and fire-blackened derelict began to sink by the stern, beneath a fog of smoke and sizzling steam. Although her stern had touched bottom, her bow remained above water until 0827, when it finally disappeared beneath the surface, taking 15 officers and 138 men down with her.

After the sea had closed over her fire-ravished corpse, the rescue ships closed in and picked up the pitiful remnant of Turner's survivors from the water, many of whom were injured and suffering from severe burns. Among the 165 survivors, only two wounded officers had lived through this tragic event.

The casualties were rushed to the military hospital on Sandy Hook and for the first time in World War II a Coast Guard Sikorsky HSN-1 helicopter played a life-saving role when its pilot, Lieutenant Commander F.A. Erickson, USCG, flew in several cases of blood plasma from New York to Sandy Hook. Consequently, the plasma saved the lives of many of Turner's casualties.

Resting 45 feet below the surface of Ambrose Channel, the wreckage of Turner was considered a navigational hazard; hence, on July 4, 1944, her hulk was blown up.

☆ ☆ ☆

USS TURNER (DD-648)

Class: Benson/Livermore.
Builder: Federal Shipbuilding & Drydock Co., Kearny, New Jersey.
Keel laid: November 15, 1942.
Launched: February 28, 1943.
Sponsor: Mrs. L.E. Denfield, wife of Rear Admiral Louis E. Denfield, USN.

Commissioned: April 15, 1943; Lieutenant Commander H.S. Wygant, USN,
    comdg.
Date of loss: January 3, 1944; Lieutenant Commander H.S. Wygant, USN,
    comdg.†
Location: Off Sandy Hook, New Jersey.
Awards: None.

USS Lansdale

Launched October 30, 1939
Lost April 20, 1944
Off Cape Bengut, Algeria

LIEUTENANT PHILIP VAN HORNE LANSDALE, USN
(1858–1899)

Philip Van Horne Lansdale was born in Washington, DC, on February 15, 1858. Graduating from the Naval Academy as a Passed Midshipman on June 18, 1875, he was promoted to the rank of Ensign on June 1, 1881. After serving on various types of vessels and having seen duty on the Asiatic Station and with the Mediterranean and North Atlantic Squadrons, he was commissioned Lieutenant on May 15, 1883.

On April 1, 1899, while Lieutenant Lansdale was serving on board the cruiser *Philadelphia*, he was sent ashore with a landing party to quell a native uprising at Apia, Samoa, led by Chief Mataafa. Although the disturbance was suppressed, Lieutenant Lansdale's party was ambushed while returning to the ship. Struck by a bullet that shattered his right leg, Lansdale ordered his party to leave him behind. However, Seaman N.E. Edsall, Ensign J.R. Monaghan and another seaman refused to leave, and tried to carry him to safety. When this attempt failed, all four men stood their ground and fought off the hostile natives until they were overwhelmed and killed. Lieutenant Lansdale's remains were transported to San Francisco, where he was interred in Cedar Lawn Cemetery.

Prior to America's entry into World War II, the USS *Lansdale* (DD-426) carried out her operations with the Atlantic Fleet destroyer squadrons on the neutrality patrol and served as a convoy escort for British shipping through the North Atlantic.

During the first year of the war, *Lansdale* continued to serve on escort duty, making several transatlantic voyages without incident. Then, on the night of February 23, 1943, her convoy was attacked by a U-boat wolfpack that succeeded in sinking two oil tankers and damaging two other vessels. Despite a devastating depth-charge attack by the escorts, the U-boats escaped. Two nights later, *Lansdale* sighted and fired on a surfaced U-boat, damaging its conning tower before it crash-dived. Again, in spite of a thrashing depth-charge assault by *Lansdale* and her mates, the enemy eluded his pursuers.

Except for providing shore bombardment and screening duties outside of Anzio, Italy, between early February and March 1, 1944, *Lansdale* was destined to remain on escort duty until the day of her loss.

On the night of April 11, 1944, *Lansdale* was escorting Convoy UGS-37, then en route to Bizerte, Tunisia. Composed of 60 vessels, the convoy was attacked by a flock of German torpedo bombers. Thanks to the vicious hail of anti-aircraft fire thrown up by the escorts, the attack was repulsed, only the destroyer escort *Holder* sustaining severe damage.

Nine days later, *Lansdale* was screening Convoy UGS-38 while throughout the day it was stalked by German aircraft. Consequently, all hands were compelled to remain at their battle stations in anticipation of an attack. It finally came later that evening as the convoy was approaching Cape Bengut. The first wave, composed of nine JU-88s closed in head-on, torpedoing and sinking one freighter. The second wave of seven JU-88s swept through a heavy concentration of AA fire unscathed, and succeeded in sinking two more cargo ships.

Also caught up in this whirlwind attack was *Lansdale*, whose gunners splashed one of the first wave marauders and damaged two others. Meanwhile, a third wave had swarmed in and sandwiched *Lansdale* between itself and the second wave. Assailed on the starboard side by five JU-88's and on the port side by five HE-111s, this was more than the lone *Lansdale* could handle. There just wasn't enough firepower to ward off the vicious attack. As she was being mauled by incessant machine-gun fire, one of her attackers unleashed a torpedo that struck her in the forward fire room.

Under a pall of smoke and steam, the wounded *Lansdale's* rudder jammed at 22 degrees, and with her speed reduced to 13 knots she began to steam in a circle and also started to list. Still, her gunners managed to knock down one more of her attackers. At 2120, *Lansdale* was able to straighten out, but her list had increased to 45 degrees. Coming to an agonizing halt and with her keel broken, she quickly began to settle. Fearing that the ship could roll over at any moment, her captain, Lieutenant Commander D.M. Swift, ordered his ship abandoned—and none too soon.

Just as he stepped off the maindeck, *Lansdale*, already having reached an 80-degree list, broke in two, the stern sinking immediately, followed 20 minutes later by the bow. Lost with *Lansdale* were 47 members of her crew.

In the aftermath of *Lansdale's* sinking, one officer was lost as he swam among the survivors, trying to keep up their morale and encouraging them not to give up. His body was not found when the survivors, 134 of them, were rescued by the destroyer escorts *Newell* and *Menges*. Among the men pulled from the water were two members of the Luftwaffe, who had been shot down by either *Lansdale* or *Newell*.

☆ ☆ ☆

USS *LANSDALE* (DD-426)

Class: Benson/Livermore.
Builder: Boston Navy Yard, Charlestown, Massachusetts.
Keel laid: December 19, 1938.
Launched: October 30, 1939.
Sponsor: Mrs. Ethel S. Lansdale, widow of Lieutenant Philip Van Horne Lansdale, USN.
Commissioned: September 17, 1940: Lieutenant Commander John Conner, USN, comdg.
Date of loss: April 20, 1944; Lieutenant Commander D.M. Swift, USN, comdg.
Location: Off Cape Bengut, Algeria.
Awards: Four battle stars.

USS Parrott

Launched November 25, 1919
Lost May 2, 1944
Hampton Roads, Virginia

LIEUTENANT GEORGE F. PARROTT, USN
(1887–1918)

George Fountain Parrott was born on December 23, 1887. Appointed Midshipman on July 3, 1906, he graduated from the U.S. Naval Academy in 1911. On October 9, 1918, Lieutenant Parrott died while serving in the USS *Shaw* (DD-68), when she was accidentally rammed by the troopship HMS *Acquatania*. Although seriously injured himself, he insisted on helping to remove his wounded shipmates from the damaged compartment. This action exhausted him and eventually resulted in his death.

At the completion of her shakedown and acceptance trials, USS *Parrott* (DD-218) received her orders to report to the destroyer base at San Diego, California. Arriving there on September 7, 1920, she joined the Pacific Fleet destroyer squadrons and carried out training operations along the West Coast until December 1921, when she was reassigned to the Atlantic Fleet.

During the last week of May 1922, *Parrott* was dispatched to the Mediterranean to serve with the U.S. Naval Detachment at Constantinople, Turkey, arriving there on June 12. During this time, Greece and Turkey were at war, and Russia was in the throes of a bloody civil war in the wake of its revolution. Starvation and poverty were still prevalent throughout the Balkans and Asia Minor in the wake of World War I. With American lives and interests in jeopardy, *Parrott* and her sister destroyers were often called upon to "show the flag" in order to discourage any attempts by dissidents to render harm against innocent Americans and other nationals residing in these locales.

The American destroyers were frequently engaged in carrying out missions of mercy. In one instance, *Parrott* participated in the evacuation of thousands of Greek refugees from Smyrna, when the Turks set fire to that city. She also entered several ports in these troubled countries to assist the American Relief Administration in distributing food, clothing and medical teams. Prior to her return to New York in July 1924, *Parrott* served as a communications ship in the eastern Mediterranean and paid goodwill visits to ports in Romania, Tunisia, Italy and France.

In January 1925, *Parrott* was assigned to the Asiatic Fleet. Arriving at Cheefoo, China, on June 14, *Parrott* once again found herself stationed in a country torn by civil war, as well as scores of other tumultuous events that raged throughout the 1920s and 1930s. Time and again, she and her sister destroyers were dispatched to protect or evacuate American citizens in threatened areas along the coast of China. When the Japanese invaded China, most of the American business community decided to evacuate. With relations between Japan and the United States steadily deteriorating, units of the Asiatic Fleet were shifted to Manila, where the fleet commenced its neutrality patrol operations throughout the Philippine Islands.

Occasionally, *Parrott* and other units of the Asiatic Fleet paid goodwill and diplomatic visits to ports in the Dutch East Indies, French Indo-China and Thailand. Attached to Task Force 5 in late November, *Parrott* and her division joined in a combined Allied naval exercise with the Dutch and British navies. Then, on December 8, 1941, while she was anchored at Tarakan Roads, Borneo, word was received of the Japanese attack on Pearl Harbor.

With the Japanese advancing virtually unchecked through Luzon and staging daily air raids on Manila and nearby military bases, the Asiatic Fleet was transferred to the Dutch East Indies to join forces with the Dutch, British and Australian navies. Based at Surabaya, Java, *Parrott* conducted her operations throughout the Indies and often served as a convoy escort.

At 0250 on February 24, 1942, *Parrott*, in company with the destroyers *John D. Ford* (flagship of Commander P.H. Talbot), *Pope* and *Paul Jones,* swept into the Dutch oil port of Balikpapan, Borneo, and participated in the sinking of four transports and the destruction of several other Japanese vessels anchored in the harbor. Thanks to the smoke resulting from the burning oil refineries, the destroyers were able to dash through the group of anchored ships virtually unscathed.

Within the first few minutes of the raid, *Parrott* had fired two torpedoes at one of the ships, but they either missed or were duds. Later, her crew had the satisfaction of witnessing the sinking of the *Somanoura Maru,* after she was struck by one or two of *Parrott's* torpedoes. After sighting the wakes from the destroyers' torpedoes, the Japanese commander, Rear Admiral S. Nishimura, assumed he was under submarine attack and immediately dispatched a group of destroyers out of the harbor to deal with the intruders. While they were pointlessly thrashing the waters with depth charge attacks, the American four-stackers continued to raise havoc among the flock of shipping. Then *Parrott, Pope* and *Paul Jones* fired a brace of torpedoes at a transport and down went the *Tatsukami Maru.*

After the destroyers expended their torpedoes, they raced through the maze of ships, flaying them with their 4-inch and 50-caliber machine guns. Shortly before they retired, however, the *John D. Ford* was slightly damaged by a shell from one of the transports, which caused a fire to break out near one of her 4-inch guns. Quick action taken by her firefighters doused the flames and the gun was soon back in action. Then at 0340, Commander Talbot decided to break off the action, and ordered his ships to retire.

Upon her return to Surabaya, *Parrott* replenished stores, ammunition and fuel and resumed her patrolling duties until the night of February 18, when she stood out of Surabaya to raid a Japanese landing force off the shores of Bali.

Steaming in company with her sister destroyers *Stewart, Pillsbury, John D. Edwards* and the Dutch cruiser *Tromp, Parrott* bolted into the southern entrance of Badoeng Strait, her crew anticipating a repeat of the attack at Balikpapan. A first wave of Dutch and American warships, arriving earlier, had discovered that the main body of transports had already offloaded their troops and had long since departed. The only enemy vessels left were two destroyers and a lone cargo ship. After a brief but brisk slugfest, in which all three enemy ships suffered serious damage, the first wave of Allied ships retired.

The Japanese destroyers *Asashio* and *Oshio* were licking their wounds when *Parrott's* group entered the strait, but they were still game and ready to fight. Within moments, guns cracked and thundered and torpedoes hissed and splashed into the black waters. Searchlights pierced through the darkened seascape, revealing the two enemy destroyers closing in on the *Stewart.* Struck by several shells, *Stewart's* Executive Officer and several of her crew were wounded and one man was killed.

Maneuvering at breakneck speed in these confined waters, *Pillsbury* and *Parrott* nearly collided head-on, missing each other by the thickness of their paintwork. In the heat of the melee, one of *Tromp's* heavy-caliber shells crashed into *Oshio*'s bridge, killing seven men. In turn, the destroyer saturated *Tromp*'s stern with ten direct hits. After this exchange, the enemy broke off the action, probably as a result of serious battle damage and heavy casualties, and the Dutch commander ordered his ships to retire.

Just as the force was departing from Lombok Strait, it ran head-long into two more Japanese destroyers, who had been sailing toward the sound of gunfire. A heated contest raged with both guns and torpedoes before *Pillsbury* and *John D. Edwards* sent the IJN *Michishiro* reeling under a torrent of 4-inch shells. The Japanese ship was further mauled by the *Tromp*'s guns, as the Dutch vessel swept past the cripple. Reduced to a mass of twisted metal, *Michishiro* staggered to a halt. Outnumbered and outgunned, the other destroyer, *Arisiho*, ceased fire and went to the aid of her damaged sister.

The Allied ships then resumed their course for Surabaya. Shortly afterward, *Parrott*'s steering gear malfunctioned, causing her to swing out of the formation and dash toward a menacing pile of reefs. Her engines were immediately thrown into reverse. A lot of sweating and lip biting ensued before her thrashing screws brought her to a halt. Backing down, the destroyer lay to until the problem was rectified and she soon caught up with her group.

On February 28, *Parrott* arrived at Tjilatjap, Java, in company with the British freighter *Seawitch*. Upon the completion of refueling, both ships departed for Freemantle, Australia. While the ships were en route, the Battle of the Java Sea boomed and rumbled across the vast seascape behind them, ending in defeat for the ABDA forces. On the following day, March 1, the American, British, Dutch and Australian forces began preparations to evacuate the Dutch East Indies.

Overhauled in Freemantle, *Parrott* carried out her patrolling duties off the western and northwestern coasts of Australia until May 10, when she stood out for San Francisco via, Melbourne, Sidney, Aipa, Samoa and Pearl Harbor. On June 30, the old war-horse, after almost two decades away from home, passed under the Golden Gate Bridge and entered the Mare Island Navy Yard for a long-awaited overhaul and leave for her crew, many of whom had been serving with the Asiatic Fleet for ten years or more.

With repairs and alterations completed, *Parrott* assumed duties as a convoy escort along the West Coast, occasionally screening convoys to and from Pearl Harbor. On May 21, 1943, *Parrott* was transferred to the Atlantic Fleet, where she was promptly assigned to escort duty. After completing one transatlantic voyage, she became a unit of a "Hunter/Killer" task group formed around the escort carrier USS *Croatan*.

While steaming in the vicinity of the Azores, the *Croatan* received a message that the German submarine *U-161* was known to be operating northeast of those Portuguese isles and was scheduled to rendezvous with the Japanese submarine *I-15*. Unfortunately, the duo could not be located, and the task group set a course for Casablanca.

In early September, *Parrott* entered the Norfolk Navy Yard, at Portsmouth, Virginia, for repairs and was again ready for sea by the end of the month. She was then assigned to another "Hunter/Killer" task group, built around the escort carrier *Block Island*, which departed Norfolk on October 15. On the night of the 25th, *Parrott* was dispatched to investigate a surface radar contact made by the *Block Island*. With the target now on her own radar, *Parrott* came up on the surfaced *U-220* and sprayed her decks and conning tower with a hail of 20-mm cannon fire before the Germans managed to take refuge with a quick dive. Now joined by her old Asiatic companion, *Paul Jones,* she laced the waters with several depth charges, but the wily U-boat commander escaped (only to be downed three days later, by aircraft from the *Block Island*).

Parrott remained with the *Block Island*'s task group until February 4, 1944, when she arrived at the Boston Navy Yard for voyage repairs. Leaving Boston during the last week in February, *Parrott* stood out for the naval operating base at Norfolk. On April 4, she rendezvoused with Convoy UGS-35 and escorted it to Casablanca, arriving there on the 21st. Before joining a stateside-bound convoy, she was dispatched to participate in the bombardment of Cape Spartel, on the coast of Spanish Morocco, which was suspected of harboring Nazi spies.

On May 2, *Parrott* was preparing to get underway from the Norfolk naval base when a thick fog crept in, delaying her departure until later that afternoon. Still on board were most of her Asiatic veterans, including her skipper, Commander J.N. Hughes. With the fog showing every indication of burning off, the *Parrott* sounded her warning whistle and backed out into the waters of Hampton Roads. Suddenly, from out of the swirling whiteness, a huge, towering massif-like shape loomed above the hapless destroyer.

Unable to maneuver in time to avoid the inevitable collision, *Parrott* was struck by the merchant ship SS *John Morton*. The merchantman's sharp prow sliced into the old four-stacker's after fire room with a jolting crash so intense that it hurled Commander Hughes and 14 other men over the side. Three men were killed and seven others injured; three others were reported as missing. Luckily, a Navy tug was close by, which took the injured *Parrott* under tow into shallow water. A few days later, the three missing men's bodies were found within the wreckage of the fire room.

Later, she was towed to the Portsmouth Navy Yard and, after being inspected by the survey board, it was decided that due to her age and the extensive damage incurred, *Parrott* was considered beyond economical repair. Hence, on July 14, the battered but proud destroyer was decommissioned and suffered the indignity of lying in limbo, rusting away until April 5, 1947, when she was purchased by the Marine Salvage Company, Richmond, Virginia, for scrapping.

☆ ☆ ☆

USS *PARROTT* (DD-218)

Class: Wickes/Clemson.
Builder: William Cramp & Sons Shipbuilding Co., Philadelphia, Pennsylvania.
Keel laid: July 23, 1919.
Launched: November 25, 1919.
Sponsor: Miss Julia B. Parrott, sister of Lieutenant George F. Parrott, USN.
Commissioned: May 11, 1920; Lieutenant Commander W.C. Wickham, USN, comdg.
Date of loss: May 2, 1944; Commander J.N. Hughes, USN, comdg.
Location: Hampton Roads, Virginia.
Awards: Two battle stars.

USS Corry

Launched July 28, 1941
Lost on June 6, 1944
Off Normandy, France

LIEUTENANT COMMANDER WILLIAM M. CORRY, USN
(1889–1920)

Born in Quincy, Florida, on October 5, 1889, William Merrill Corry graduated from the Naval Academy on June 3, 1910. Designated Naval Aviator on March 6, 1916, he went on to serve with distinction as commander of the U.S. Naval Air Station at Le Croisic, France, during World War I.

With the ending of the war, Lieutenant Corry remained in Europe in charge of the demobilization of German military aircraft. While serving on the staff of the Commander-in-Chief of the Atlantic Fleet, Lieutenant Commander Corry was injured in a plane crash on October 3, 1920. Although thrown clear, he risked his life in an attempt to pull the pilot from the burning wreckage. Suffering from severe burns, Lieutenant Commander Corry died on October 7, 1920. For his heroism, he was posthumously awarded the Congressional Medal of Honor.

Placed in commission eleven days after the United States was drawn into World War II, the USS *Corry* (DD-463) was rushed through her shakedown trials and battle-readiness exercises. Immediately assigned to escort duty, she conducted her operations through the waters of the Atlantic as far north as Newfoundland and, at times, in the waters of the Caribbean.

On May 21, 1942, *Corry* was dispatched to the mid-Atlantic to rendezvous with the British liner *Queen Elizabeth* and escort her into New York Harbor. Between May 31 and June 23, she was based at Argentia, Newfoundland, whence she carried out her patrolling duties. She then rejoined her division at Newport, Rhode Island on July 1 and from there resumed her escort duties. On July 4, she was detached from her convoy to rescue four bedraggled survivors found adrift on a raft, their cargo ship, SS *Ruty*, having been sunk three days previously by a U-boat.

On November 8, *Corry* participated in the North African landings at Casablanca and Safi. Here she served as an escort and plane guard for the USS *Ranger*. She continued to operate off the coast of Casablanca until the 16th, when she stood out for the United States, escorting the empty transports en route. Arriving at Boston on the 28th, she entered the Charlestown Navy Yard for voyage repairs and the installation of 20-mm cannons.

Corry then resumed her escort duties, a task she would be assigned to until late January 1944. Several of her voyages took her to Iceland, and during the month of October 1943 she was stationed at Scapa Flow, Scotland, attached to the British Home Fleet. While here, she was assigned to patrol duty off the coast of Norway for a period of two weeks.

On February 1, she joined Task Group 21.16, formed around the escort carrier *Block Island*. On March 11, the task group departed Casablanca to search for U-boats known to be lurking north of the Azores. Just before dawn on the 17th, *Corry* was ordered to leave the formation to investigate a report by one of the carrier's aircraft, which had sighted and attacked a surfaced U-boat. As the destroyer approached the site, her radar made contact upon a pod of "bogies," which proved to be decoy balloons that were released by the submarine and which became easy target practice for *Corry's* gunners.

Corry's sonar operator continued to probe the waters for the elusive submarine without success. Despite the arrival of the destroyer escort *Bronstein* to assist in the search, the U-boat could not be found. Then, at 0925, the carrier's patrol aircraft reported the sighting of an oil slick several miles from the two hunters and directed them to that area.

Almost immediately upon their arrival, *Bronstein* made the first definite contact and struck the first blow. The sea tumbled and quaked as the lethal depth charges detonated. The thunderous rumbling had barely ceased when *Corry* swept over the spot and let go with her own deadly barrage. Again, the sea was shaken by the devastating explosions, followed by white geysers spouting skyward from the depths of the Atlantic. Shortly after this thrashing, fragments of debris rose to the surface as well as a rainbow-hued oil slick and a pungent odor of diesel fuel.

Was the U-boat damaged? Or was her commander employing an old trick to avoid a further blasting, hoping that the hunters would believe he had been sunk and leave? But the American skippers were not easily deceived by this ploy and bored in for another assault on their quarry. Three hours later, after undergoing a ferocious pounding, the wounded U-boat broached the surface about 1,250 yards from *Corry*. Wasting no time, the destroyer's captain, Lieutenant Commander George D. Hoffman, ordered full speed ahead.

As the bedazzled U-boatmen were abandoning ship, *Corry*'s 20- and 40-mm cannons and 5-inch guns were blazing, holing the submarine's conning tower and hull. Commander Hoffman had every intention of ramming her, but the U-boat suddenly raised her bow and plunged stern first beneath the surface. *Bronstein* then closed in and rescued two officers and 45 crew members from the boat. The submarine's commander was killed during the action and went down with his ship. The prisoners were then transferred over to the *Block Island* and informed the interrogators that their submarine was the *U-801*.

Two days later, a flight of *Block Island*'s aircraft sank a U-boat; however, one of the planes developed engine trouble and had to ditch. *Corry* was ordered to search for the plane's crew and, if possible, pick up the U-boat's survivors. After covering a distance of 70 miles, *Corry* located and rescued the plane's crew and eight German sailors.

Shortly afterwards the destroyer escort *Bostwick* arrived and made a positive underwater contact. Both ships joined up and blasted the waters with their lethal depth charges—without result. Later, *Corry* discovered a dead seaman adrift not too far from where she had picked up the German survivors. He was soon identified as one of the crew from the U-boat and that afternoon *Corry* held burial services on the fantail and his remains were consigned to the depths.

On April 20, 1944, *Corry* departed Norfolk to escort a convoy to the United Kingdom. She was then assigned to take part in the most crucial operation yet mounted by the Western Allies: the invasion of "Fortress Europe." On D-Day, June 6, *Corry* screened the transports and landing craft embarked with troops and supplies, then en route to the shores of Normandy, France. After leading her charges to their proper anchorages, *Corry* took up her fire support station off Utah Beach. As the landing craft plunged and bucked through the choppy waters, the destroyer's 5-inch main batteries opened fire on the heavily fortified German gun emplacements. At 0633, however, while she was cruising back and forth carrying out this mission, the destroyer struck a mine.

The weapon detonated just above her keel between the forward fire and engine rooms, killing or injuring all hands in those spaces, breaking the destroyer's keel and jamming her rudder hard right. The pressure from the inrushing sea filling the forward engine room caused its after bulkhead to buckle, and then the fire room began to flood. Robert F. Miller, then the vessel's Chief Watertender, and who was at his battle station in the after fire room, tells of his experiences at the time the *Corry* was mined: "I had been at my battle station in the after fire room since 2400 and as we cruised off the Normandy coast, our main batteries were firing on the enemy's shore guns. Occasionally we could hear the chunks of shrapnel striking the ship or when they exploded in the water, but they did not cause any serious damage in the fire room.

"Then, shortly after 0630, the ship was jolted by a tremendous explosion. The shock stung the soles of our feet but none of the guys were knocked down by the blast. At the same time, all the lights went out, but our emergency battle lanterns came on, allowing us to see what we were doing.

"All communications were lost to main engine control [located in the forward engine room], because at that time, we had not realized that the explosion had taken place in that area. Also, we were not aware that the rudder had jammed and that we were steaming in circles. Up to now, both of our boilers were still operating, but then we began to lose feed water pressure, due to the electric booster pump in the after engine room losing its source of power. Eventually, we were forced to shut down No. 4 boiler, hoping to keep steam up in No. 3.

"Then one of the men noticed that water was beginning to flood the space, with the water rising up beneath the floor plates. My First Class Watertender, Hank Passek, went down the starboard side to start the bilge pump and came rushing back, shouting: 'Good God! I can't get to the bilge pump! There's a large hole in the bulkhead and water is pouring in like Niagara Falls!' I then said: 'O.K., but let's try to hang on as long as we can.' I had no sooner said that when my man who controls the feed water valve [the checkman] to the boilers called down saying that he was losing water in No. 3 boiler. I quickly ordered the burner man, who was now standing in water up to his knees, to secure his fires and kept the rest of my men busy shutting down all the machinery and closing various valves so they wouldn't panic. When all was secure, we abandoned the fire room, with the water following us up the ladders. Luckily, none of us were injured. Later, I was picked up by one of the whaleboats from the USS *Fitch*."

Elsewhere on *Corry*, Yeoman 2nd Class Lou Tanga was manning his battle station below in No. 4 5-inch magazine, passing up powder charges to the gun mount, when the ship struck the mine. Fortunately, he had just bent over to pass a powder case to the man above the hatch when the jolt from the explosion slammed the hatch closed. If he had been standing at the time the hatch closed, his skull would have been crushed.

He was certain that the ship was in distress when he felt the deck beneath him taking an extreme pitch downward. Without hesitation, he quickly opened the hatch, scrambled out of the compartment and made it safely to the main deck. Tanga vividly recalls what occurred next: "By this time *Corry* was only three feet above the water and several of the men were placing the lids on the powder charge cans and tossing them overboard so the men would have something to cling to if the ship had to be abandoned.

"It wasn't too long after I had reached topside when the order was passed to abandon ship. Once in the water, which was very cold, I began to swim for the shore, using a church as my guide. Thanks to whoever it was that had the good sense to heave those empty powder charge cans over the side, I was able to hold on to one, since my inflatable life belt didn't work.

"Then one of our sister destroyers, the *Hobson,* swept past me, between myself and the *Corry,* which was now jackknifed and ready to go under. The *Hobson* then came back and stopped to pick me up. One of her crewmen took a chance and dove into the water with a line and dragged me to the ship. Once on deck, I saw that the *Corry* had sunk in shallow water, hence, her superstructure and stacks were still visible." Lou, was one of the lucky survivors, since he had the good fortune to be rescued shortly after he had abandoned ship.

The concussion from the explosion threw captain Hoffman and all hands on the bridge across the deck. The magnetic compass stand and the navigator's desk was torn from the deck, the flagbags being ripped loose. Externally, the starboard wing of the bridge had buckled and the after section of the bridge was bulged in the center. The mast was bent forward and its guy wires severed. With the ship beginning to jackknife, Captain Hoffman ordered a set of signal flags hoisted that read: "THIS SHIP NEEDS HELP." By 0640, the amidships section was underwater and both stacks were beginning to lean toward each other. Well aware that his ship was lost, Commander Hoffman was compelled to order his ship abandoned.

As the crew was going over the side, the damage control officer, Lieutenant (j.g.) John O. Parrott, was conducting a last-minute check to ensure that no one was left behind. As he was passing the forward fire room hatch, he heard a mournful cry for help. Pointing his flashlight into the dark recesses of the flooded and steam-choked space, he saw a man trapped beneath the floor grating, a turbulent swirl of oily water rising about him.

Immediately, and without any thought of the risk he was taking, Lieutenant Parrott plunged into the now topsy-turvy, darkened fire room. After slipping over and under a maze of steam and water piping and through a fog of escaping vapor, he squeezed his body under the grating and pulled the drenched, oil-soaked fireman free. For this self-sacrificing and courageous action, Lieutenant Parrott was awarded the Navy Cross.

Then, all hell broke loose as the German shore batteries began to open fire on *Corry,* several shells exploding about the survivors and flaying them with shrapnel. One life raft was blown out of the water and spilled its occupants into the 57-degree waters. A shell struck one of *Corry's* 40-mm gun tubs and caused the ready ammunition to explode in a pyrotechnic display, the fiery tracers skimming over the heads of the swimmers.

With other destroyers and fire support ships concentrating their fire on the German fortifications during the first critical hours of the D-Day landings, *Corry's* survivors were compelled to endure two hours of unmitigated punishment from the enemy's guns and the harsh elements before they could receive any help.

Throughout their ordeal, the tide and currents had drawn the men and rafts closer to the shore, where they were fired on by the Germans. One raft was swept in a complete circle directly beneath a gun battery, which opened fire on the helpless sailors without mercy, until an exploding projectile lifted it out of the water, thus increasing the death toll and resulted in the wounding of several more men.

Finally, at about 0830, the destroyers *Fitch* and *Hobson* and *PT-99* arrived to pull *Corry's* wretched survivors out of the frigid waters. As they were effecting rescue operations, the destroyers interposed themselves between the enemy's guns and the survivors, firing their 5-inchers away at the shore batteries until these were silenced.

Out of a complement of 19 officers and 265 men, 22 of the *Corry's* crew lost their lives during this action, whether from the mining, drowning or exposure to German shore fire.

☆ ☆ ☆

USS *CORRY* (DD-463)

Class: Benson/Livermore.
Builder: Charleston Navy Yard, Charleston, South Carolina.
Keel laid: October 4, 1940.
Launched: July 28, 1941.
Sponsor: Miss Jean C. Corry, niece of Lieutenant Commander William M.

Corry, USN.
Commissioned: December 18, 1941; Lieutenant Commander E.C. Burchett, USN, comdg.
Date of loss: June 6, 1944; Lieutenant Commander George D. Hoffman, USN, comdg.
Location: Off Normandy, France.
Awards: Four battle stars.

USS Meredith

Launched December 21, 1943
Lost June 9, 1944
Bay of the Seine, Normandy, France

SERGEANT JONATHAN MEREDITH USMC*
(1772–1805)

See history of the USS *Meredith* (DD-434).

The USS *Meredith* (DD-726) was the third U.S. destroyer to be named in honor of Sergeant Jonathan Meredith, USMC.

The first USS *Meredith* (DD-165), a flush-decked four-stacker, was commissioned on January 29, 1919. After three years of active duty, she was decommissioned on June 28, 1922. After lying in reserve for 14 years, she was sold for scrapping on September 28, 1936. The second USS *Meredith* (DD-434), as was previously mentioned, was sunk by Japanese aircraft south of the Solomon Islands on October 15, 1942, with a heavy loss of life.

Upon the completion of her battle readiness training, USS *Meredith* (DD-726) stood out of Boston Harbor on May 8, 1944, bound for Plymouth, England, escorting a convoy en route. Arriving there on the 27th, the destroyer was prepared for the upcoming invasion of Europe, scheduled to take place during the first week of June.

During the early morning hours of June 6, *Meredith* screened the transports and landing craft to Utah Beach and provided pre-invasion shore bombardment in an effort to render the landing sites less hazardous for the Allied soldiers.

With the Allies having secured a foothold on the European continent, *Meredith* was on patrol duty off the Bay of the Seine during the late night hours of the 7th, when a flight of German aircraft came swarming in around the landing sites. These were driven off by anti-aircraft fire from the patrolling ships, but at the time, *Meredith's* captain, Commander George Kneupher, had held his fire since he was unsure whether the planes were friend or foe. Actually, the primary mission of the enemy was to re-seed the waters off the Normandy coast with contact and magnetic mines, a task in which they succeeded, despite the loss of a few planes. More than likely, it was one of these mines that was responsible for damaging the Meredith.

At 0150, while continuing her patrol, a volcanic eruption shattered the Meredith, lifting her out of the water and throwing her forward. The huge blast disemboweled the destroyer in the after fire room, with flames and debris gushing skyward and outward from both sides of the ship. Smoke and flesh-searing superheated steam enveloped the amidships area and, with all power lost, the damaged Meredith crawled to a halt.

The detonation had torn a 65-feet long hole on her port side, which meant that all of the engineering spaces, except for the forward fire room, were flooded or rapidly filling. Twenty minutes after the mining, Meredith took on a 12-degree list and gave every indication of capsizing and plunging to the bottom. The destroyer Jeffers (DD-612) and several other vessels closed in upon the foundering Meredith to offer assistance and receive her survivors. The damage report received by the captain was very grim, and to prevent the ship from drifting toward shallow water, he ordered that the anchors be dropped. With the safety of his crew in mind, Commander Kneupher ordered his men to board the rescue ships, though he himself remained on board throughout the night, while the destroyer escort Bates rode herd on his paralyzed vessel.

At the break of dawn, Commander Kneupher ordered the Jeffers to come alongside, and a salvage party made a thorough inspection of the ship. It was decided that Meredith still had a chance to be saved, providing her two remaining main bulkheads would hold. Jeffers then took the crippled vessel in tow until this task was taken over by a salvage tug. While under tow, the destroyer's list increased two more degrees, but no additional leaks or ruptures were in evidence. Dropping anchor in the Bay of the Seine, the ship was lightened by jettisoning all excessive topside gear, including her torpedoes and depth charges.

The salvage crew then went to work, feverishly shoring up bulkheads, pumping out flooded spaces and plugging up leaks, until 2100 that evening, when the crew from the tug took over salvage operations. Although Meredith's repair parties were exhausted from their labors, their spirits were high with the knowledge that they had removed the list from the ship; they were now confident that she could be saved.

On the following morning (June 9), a flight of German bombers staged a raid on the shipping in the bay. Two 2,000-pound bombs landed close aboard the vulnerable *Meredith*. The detonations struck her with such brutal force that the shock whipped her stern, swinging her sideways, and further damaged her already weakened hull. At first, the damage seemed to be superficial and salvage operations continued. Then, at 1010, and, without any apparent warning, *Meredith* split in two and sank. Fortunately, there were no personnel below decks when she broke up. The tug, which was close by, rushed in and picked up the salvage gang.

Two officers and 33 men lost their lives when *Meredith* ran over the mine. The death toll might have been higher had it not been for the heroism of Chief Machinist's Mate Brady L. Bryan.

Bryan was at his battle station in the after engine room, when the concussion of the explosion caused some object to fly across the room and strike him in the face. Momentarily stunned, and with all lighting extinguished, he staggered to the nearest escape ladder and out of the smoke- and steam-choked room, which was rapidly flooding.

Upon reaching the maindeck, he dazedly made his way aft to the stern, where several men were gathered about, some as confused as he was. Still somewhat numb, he realized that none of his crew was among the group. "My God!" he said to himself. "My men must still be trapped below!" Grabbing hold of a battle lantern, he retraced his steps back to the engine room hatch, pointed the light into the darkened space and, to his horror, saw that the compartment was inundated just four feet from the overhead. Probing the lamp further, he saw four injured men struggling about in the debris-strewn and oil-scummed water.

He immediately climbed down into the muck and led his shipmates to safety. All of them were suffering from burns, lacerations, broken limbs and contusions. Not satisfied with saving his men's lives, he further assisted in taking charge of their evacuation to the *Jeffers* and personally saw to their welfare until they were transferred to the naval hospital in Plymouth. All the men made a full recovery. For his courage and deep concern for his men, Chief Bryan was highly commended by Commander Kneupher and was awarded the Navy Cross.

The battered wreckage of *Meredith* remained in her watery grave until August 5, 1960, when she was raised by the St. Francois Recherches of France, and scrapped.

☆ ☆ ☆

USS *MEREDITH* (DD-726) [II]

Class: Allen M. Sumner.
Builder: Bath Iron Works, Bath, Maine.
Keel laid: July 26, 1943.
Launched: December 21, 1943.
Sponsor: Mrs. William Kepper.
Commissioned: March 14, 1944; Commander George Kneupher, USN, comdg.
Date of loss: June 9, 1944; Commander George Kneupher, USN, comdg.
Location: Bay of the Seine, Normandy, France.
Awards: One battle star.

USS Glennon

Launched August 26, 1942
Lost June 10, 1944
Off Quinéville, Normandy, France

REAR ADMIRAL JAMES H. GLENNON, USN
(1857–1940)

James Henry Glennon was born on February 11, 1857, at French Gulf, California, and was appointed Cadet Midshipman on September 14, 1874, going on to serve in the USSs *Lackawanna*, *Alaska* and *Pensacola*. Promoted to Lieutenant in 1881, he reported on board the *Ranger* and continued to serve on her until 1885. From there, he went on to the *Constellation*, into 1888.

Following a tour of shore duty and serving on various types of ships, Lieutenant Glennon was ordered to the battleship *Massachusetts*, shortly before hostilities commenced between the United States and Spain. He was in command of *Massachusetts'* forward gun turret during the Battle of Santiago, Cuba, on July 4, 1898, when she assisted the *Texas* in sinking the cruiser *Reina Mercedes*.

Advanced to the rank of Lieutenant Commander shortly after this action, he was ordered to the gunboat *Vicksburg*, serving as her Executive Officer and navigator. *Vicksburg* then joined the Asiatic Fleet to participate in the U.S. Army's mopping-up operations against the Philippine insurgents and the eventual capture of their leader, Emilio Aguinaldo, in March 1901.

During the next 11 years, Glennon went on to serve in various ships, and in 1912 served as President of the Board of Naval Ordnance, working diligently with the Joint Army-Navy Board on smokeless powder. Promoted to Captain, he was appointed Commandant of the Washington Navy Yard and Superintendant of the Naval Gun Factory from 1915 into early 1917.

Owing to his fluency in the Russian language, he was soon relieved from this post to carry out a special mission to Russia, under the auspices of Navy Secretary Elihu Root. Tragically, that nation was

225

not only involved in World War I, but was also on the brink of a bloody revolution. In Sevastopol, mutiny was running rampant among the warships anchored in that port. With the backing of several American destroyers, whose guns were aimed at the Russian ships, Captain Glennon, single-handedly, and at great risk to his life, boarded the warships, confronted the mutinous crews and convinced their leaders to assemble at the town hall. After a long, heated debate, he eventually persuaded the unruly crews to restore authority to their ships' officers.

Glennon went on to assume command of Battleship Division 5, flying his flag in the *Connecticut.* For his meritorious service in this command, he was awarded the Navy Cross and was highly commended for his training of midshipmen and thousands of recruits for duty as armed guard crews for merchant ships

Captain Glennon became commandant of the 13th Naval District in September 1918, and in January 1919, assumed command of the 3rd Naval District, New York. Upon reaching the mandatory age of retirement, Captain Glennon retired with the rank of Rear Admiral on February 1, 1921. Residing in Washington, DC, Rear Admiral James H. Glennon died on May 29, 1940, at the age of eighty-three.

F rom the onset of her active wartime career, the USS *Glennon* (DD-620) was assigned to escort duty and made several successful Atlantic crossings as well as taking part in the landings at Sicily.

On May 5, 1944, *Glennon* stood out of New York Harbor with a task group that arrived at Belfast, Ireland, on the 14th. From there, she was assigned to the gigantic armada the Allies were assembling for the D-Day invasion. During the night of June 5, she joined Assault Force "U," a unit of the Western Naval Force, and arrived at the Bay of the Seine on the Normandy coast of France. Upon leaving her group, she commenced bombarding the German shore fortifications with her 5-inch main batteries and, for a time, it seemed that *Glennon* and her crew were living a charmed life. Unlike several Allied vessels, which had been mined and later assailed by shellfire and bombers, *Glennon* emerged from the first two days of Operation "Overlord" unscathed from the wrath of the enemy.

Then, at 0830, on the 8th, as she was returning to her fire support station, *Glennon* was shaken by a tremendous explosion when a mine detonated on her stern. The explosion lifted her stern out of the water and hurled several of her crew up into the bone-chilling bay. Also torn loose was a depth charge, which was thrown 50 feet into the air and landed on the after bank of torpedo tubes abaft the after smokestack. The shock and damage incurred from the mine caused the ship to lose all power, flooded her after compartments and warped both propeller shafts, all of which brought the destroyer to a halt.

One of *Glennon*'s men, William G. Takacs, recalls: "A few of my shipmates and myself had just finished breakfast and had gone aft to have cigarettes before going below to our living quarters. Three of us were standing by the entrance leading to the living quarters, when suddenly a terrific explosion lifted the fantail out of the water. I was tossed in the air and landed on my hands and knees as did my shipmates. Somewhat stunned, we soon regained our composure and realized that except for a few bruises and scratches we were not seriously injured.

"Then, looking aft and not more than 12 to 15 feet from us, we saw a huge, jagged split opening completely across the width of the ship and exposing the lower living spaces. We then wondered if we would have to abandon ship, but soon after the explosion, our captain, Commander C.A. Johnson, passed the word that help was on the way and he did not intend to abandon ship.

"Meanwhile, the repair parties were busy shoring up bulkheads, attempting to pump out our flooded compartments and gathering up our wounded and the dead. The pharmacist's mates were on the scene almost as soon as the explosion occurred and were occupied in rendering first aid and comfort to our wounded shipmates."

Help came very quickly when two British minesweepers, HMSs *Staff* and *Threat,* closed in to offer assistance to the disabled *Glennon*. While *Threat* was picking up the men in the water, *Staff* took the destroyer under tow. On shore, the Germans began to open fire on the wounded ship, but a barrage of 8-inch gunfire from an American cruiser soon silenced the enemy battery. Then, tragically, at 0920, the destroyer escort USS *Rich* also approached the *Glennon* to offer assistance, but despite Commander Johnson's warning that there were mines in the area, it was too late. Abruptly, *Rich* was blown out of the water when she struck three mines. Within a few seconds, the vessel broke into three parts and disappeared beneath the surface under a pall of smoke and steam. Of her crew of 215 officers and men, 27 were killed, 73 wounded and 62 were listed as missing.

By now, repair parties were losing the battle to save the *Glennon*. Unable to stem the influx of the sea, the destroyer's stern touched bottom, thus making it impossible for her to be towed any farther. Despite the efforts of both British vessels, *Glennon* could not be budged. Much to their regret, and that of *Glennon's* crew, the tugs had to abandon the operation.

Takacs recalls that later in the day most of the ship's crew was removed by PT boats and transferred to an American LST that had many G.I. casualties from the land fighting on board. As a result, many of the crewmen and medics were on the brink of collapsing from exhaustion and were themselves in dire need of assistance. Without hesitation, *Glennon's* crew pitched in, helping the medical teams to bandage and render comfort to the wounded and lend a hand wherever they were needed. They also took over many other duties on board the ship, such as standing watches and working in the galley and mess decks.

Eventually, *Glennon's* wounded were transferred to a hospital in Portsmouth, England. Later, the well and fit were taken to a British Army barracks, where their ragged and oil-stained clothing was discarded and they were issued British Army uniforms. This was soon followed by a march to the mess hall where, Takacs remembers, they were served the most delicious lamb stew they had ever tasted, topped off with strong tea laced with rum. They were so well treated by the Tommies, who were salty veterans of several campaigns, from Narvik to Greece and the desert operations against General Rommel, that Takcas has never forgotten the kindness extended to him and his shipmates.

Back on *Glennon*, Commander Johnson and his skeleton crew were still hopeful that the ship could be saved, and the work still went on in an attempt to salvage her. In the meantime, the Germans were feverishly effecting repairs on their shore batteries and, at dawn (June 10th), they commenced firing on the immobile destroyer.

The first salvo missed, but the second smashed into her after engine room and knocked out all electrical power. Some of the shells splashed in the water around her bow, one holing her forecastle. Unable to return fire, Commander Johnson had no other choice but to discontinue salvage operations and order his ship abandoned. While the crew was scrambling over the side and onto the decks of the rescue craft that had rushed to *Glennon's* side, the enemy found the proper range and began to pound the destroyer to pieces.

After the Germans had ceased fire, *Glennon's* executive officer and several responsible personnel boarded the wreck to examine the damage. They also removed her code books and demolished any top-secret equipment and material could prove beneficial to the Nazi forces. After surveying the battle damage, it was determined that *Glennon* had absorbed well over 12 direct hits, and had also suffered a score of near-misses that had opened her seams beneath the waterline, thus flooding the compartments belowdecks. Taking on a port list, which increased throughout the day, the valiant and battle-ravished *Glennon* finally rolled over on her beams' end at 2145 and settled to the bottom of the Bay of the Seine, near Quinéville, France.

The initial mine explosion resulted in the deaths of 25 men. Of *Glennon's* 267 survivors, 38 had been wounded.

☆ ☆ ☆

USS *GLENNON* (DD-620)

Class: Benson/Livermore.
Builder: Federal Shipbuilding & Drydock Co., Kearny, New Jersey.
Keel laid: March 25, 1942.
Launched: August 26, 1942.
Sponsor: Miss Jeanne L. Glennon, granddaughter of Rear Admiral James H. Glennon, USN.
Commissioned: October 8, 1942; Lieutenant Commander Floyd C. Camp, USN, comdg.
Date of loss: June 10, 1944; Commander C.A. Johnson, USN, comdg.
Location: Off Quinéville, Normandy, France.
Awards: Two battle stars.

USS Warrington

Launched May 15, 1937
Lost September 13, 1944
North of the Bahama Islands

COMMODORE LEWIS WARRINGTON, USN
(1782–1851)

Lewis Warrington was born in Williamsburg, Virginia, on November 3, 1782. While studying at William and Mary College he was accepted into the United States Navy on January 6, 1800, as a Cadet Midshipman. Assigned to the frigate USS *Chesapeake*, he sailed to the Caribbean during the last year of the quasi-war with France, where he took part in the capture of the French privateer *La Jeune Créole*, on January 1, 1801.

With the ending of hostilities against France, Warrington was assigned to the frigate *President*, which sailed for the Mediterranean to fight against the Barbary powers. During the next five years, Warrington continued to serve with the Mediterranean Squadron and saw duty on the schooner *Vixen* and the frigate *Enterprise*.

With the outbreak of the War of 1812, Warrington served as First Lieutenant on board the frigate *Congress*. During her first war cruise, *Congress* captured nine prizes off the East Coast. On her second cruise, she captured two more vessels along the eastern seaboard and two others off the coast of Brazil. On March 12, 1814, Warrington assumed command of the sloop-of-war *Peacock* and on April 29 engaged with and defeated the British brig HMS *Epervier* off Cape Canaveral, Florida. For his extraordinary performance in this action, he was awarded a gold medal from the U.S. Congress and a gold-hilted sword from his home state.

In June of that year, Warrington sailed the *Peacock* north to Newfoundland and then voyaged across the North Atlantic, searching for British shipping. After skirting the coasts of Ireland, France and Spain, he recrossed the Atlantic and cruised throughout the Caribbean, arriving at New York on October 29. During this five-

230

month sortie, *Peacock* took 14 British vessels, of which nine were sunk, three were burned and the remainder retained as prizes.

Still in command of the *Peacock*, Warrington sailed from New York on January 23, 1815, and steered a course for the Indian Ocean via the Cape of Good Hope. On June 30, as he was passing through the Sunda Strait in the Dutch East Indies, he intercepted and captured the British East India Company merchantman HMS *Nautilus*. However, when he was informed by her captain that the war was over, Warrington allowed the *Nautilus* to go on her way and sailed for home.

Between 1816 and 1826, Commander Warrington served as commanding officer of the frigate *Macedonian,* was advanced to the rank of Captain and commanded the frigates *Java* and *Guerrière,* respectively, in the Mediterranean Squadron. Returning home in 1826, he reported for duty at the Norfolk Navy Yard and, later, was placed in command of the West Indies Squadron during the latter stages of the suppression of piracy in Caribbean waters.

Upon his return to the United States, he commenced a tour of shore duty that lasted for 25 years. He served temporarily as Secretary of the Navy when then-Secretary Thomas W. Gilmer died of his wounds after a new Navy cannon, the "Peacemaker," exploded during a firing demonstration on the deck of the USS *Princeton.*

Promoted to Commodore in 1846, Warrington became Chief of the Bureau of Ordnance, an office he held until his death on October 12, 1851.

The USS *Warrington* (DD-383) was assigned to the Atlantic Destroyer Squadrons upon the completion of her shakedown and acceptance trials, until June 1939. On the 9th of that month, she was host to the King and Queen of England, and, with the Union Jack hoisted at the fore, she steamed from Fort Hancock, New Jersey, up the Hudson River to Manhattan. There the British royalty were disembarked, later to be transported to President Franklin D. Roosevelt's estate at Hyde Park, New York.

Warrington was transferred to the Pacific Fleet later that month and reported to the destroyer base at San Diego, arriving on July 3. During the next two years, the destroyer carried out her training operations and participated in fleet maneuvers along the West Coast and in Hawaiian waters.

On April 7, 1941, she transited the Panama Canal and rejoined the Atlantic Fleet Destroyer Squadrons. Assigned to the neutrality patrol, she and her division cruised off the coast of Brazil and the approaches to the Panama Canal with the cruisers *Memphis* and *Cincinnati*. In mid-November, *Warrington* entered the Charleston Navy Yard, South Carolina, for an overhaul and was still there when the Japanese struck at Pearl Harbor.

On the following day, *Warrington* stood out for Norfolk, where she was ordered to rendezvous with the British battleship *Duke of York* and escort her to the Naval Base at Hampton Roads, Virginia. Three weeks later, she received orders to report to the Southeast Pacific Fleet based at Balboa, Panama. With this fleet, she served on patrol duty guarding the approaches to the Panama Canal and occasionally served as a gunnery training ship and as a target vessel for U.S. submariners prior to reporting for operations in the western Pacific.

This assignment was terminated in mid-June 1943, when she set sail for the South Pacific, escorting a convoy of supply ships to U.S. Army and Marine outposts throughout the Solomon Islands. From then on she was busily engaged escorting resupply ships and transports from New Zealand and Australian ports to the Solomons. During the landings at Bougainville, on November 8, she was credited with splashing two Japanese aircraft while covering the infantry transports. On June 5, she participated in the bombardment of Biak Island, north of New Guinea, however this assignment put the destroyer near the end of her tether after her long Pacific tour, and she was ordered out of the battle area to New York.

Upon the completion of shipyard repairs at the Brooklyn Navy Yard, *Warrington* was assigned to patrol duty off the New England coast until late August. On September 10, she stood out of Norfolk in company with the stores ship *Hyades*, en route to Panama. For a day and a half, both ships sailed through the calm, subtropical waters, under perfect weather conditions. Then, just before noon on the 12th, a dark, ominous bank of clouds began to loom over the horizon. By 1300 the seas, stirred by gusty winds, began to rise. Shortly after 1400, a message was received that a hurricane was in the making. Within a short time, the *Warrington*'s crew had the ship rigged for heavy weather, her hatches and doors closed and all loose gear lashed down.

Two hours later, *Warrington* was taking heavy, green seas over her bow and was buffeted by gale-force winds. One tremendous swell jolted the 1,850-ton destroyer with such terrific momentum that it caused the battens securing the 5-inch shells in the forward handling rooms to snap. Consequently, all available hands were rushed to the spaces and spent some anxious moments chasing the wildly rolling shells in an effort to return them to their racks and secure them with new battens.

By 1800, the skies were black, the seas mountainous, and the ship was being lashed by wind-driven rain. Hoping to avoid as much damage to his ship as possible, *Warrington's* captain, Lieutenant Commander Samuel F. Quarles, reduced speed to four knots in an attempt to alleviate any further punishment from the raging tempest. In the past, *Warrington,* her skipper and crew had weathered many a storm without mishap and, thus far, the destroyer was riding out this blow fairly well.

However, as the stormy night wore on, the velocity of the maelstrom increased with unmitigated fury. By midnight, both ships were driven off course and radar contact with the 4,000-ton *Hyades* was lost. The force of the winds had risen to over 130 knots, the turbulent seas bringing the destroyer virtually to a standstill. At about 0200 on the 13th, the storm-battered ship was in deep trouble. Despite all the precautions taken to secure *Warrington* for heavy weather, the incessant pounding of the sea was beginning to tear her apart piecemeal.

Stanchions were wrenched from the deck; rivets began to pop; her superstructure was buckled and stoved in; the port side bulwarks were sprung in two sections; water seeped and poured into her open seams. Several of her engineering personnel were drenched when a huge wave slammed against the ventilator ducts and poured a gusher of water into her engine rooms. More often than not, *Warrington's* amidships would be submerged in a huge wave with her bow and stern protruding from out of either side of the monstrous swells, causing the ship to "hog" and placing additional stress on her framework. It was during one of these inundations, when the seas again poured down the ducts leading to the engine rooms, that the electrical circuit boards became flooded, causing a complete loss of power. With her means of propulsion gone, the beleaguered *Warrington* lost way and wallowed helplessly in the troughs of the raging tempest.

Fortunately, the destroyer's engineers soon restored all power and *Warrington* was again turned into the heaving swells. Her captain then sent out a message to *Hyades*, informing her of his precarious situation and requesting that she stand by in the event that his ship should founder. Apparently *Hyades* was in serious straits herself or the signal did not get through; *Warrington* did not receive any response from the stores ship. In desperation, Quarles sent out the following signal: "IN DISTRESS X . . . NEED ASSISTANCE X . . . ENGINEERING SPACES FLOODED X . . . FIGHTING WINDS OF HURRICANE FORCE X."

As the message was being sent, a gigantic wave smashed against the destroyer's port side and another deluge of sea water cascaded down through the ducts, shorting out her power panels completely. Sloshing through knee-deep water, the engineers strived to raise steam and repair parties labored continuously to plug holes and pump out the ship's flooded compartments. But the ingress of the sea was more than the puny portable pumps could handle. Topside, the crew attempted to lighten ship by jettisoning all loose gear and wreckage, but to no avail.

Lying dead in this nightmarish vortex, *Warrington* was tossed about like a cork. Her crew was hard-pressed to keep a secure footing on her slanting decks, causing many of the men to lose their equilibrium like punch-drunk boxers. Consequently, many of them were hurled or thrown, uncontrollably, against stanchions, bulkheads and other protuberances found on shipboard. Then another sea slammed into her, toppling her mainmast and knocking her single stack askew.

Come the dawn, *Warrington*, by some miracle, was still afloat, and much to the amazement of her captain, not one man had been washed overboard. However, with her decks littered with debris, her superstructure buckled and stoved in, her foremast nowhere in evidence, and her stack uprooted and expected to topple over at any time, one would have believed that the ship had just emerged from a hotly contested naval engagement. Then, as a group of men were in the process of clearing the decks of residue, two were washed overboard. Both had grasped hold of a length of line that was trailing over the side; one man held on, but the other lost his grip and vanished beneath the violent, convulsive waters.

By noon, *Warrington* had reached the point of foundering and it was taking longer and longer to recover from each succeeding wave. Realizing that the ship's time was running out, Captain Quarles dispatched his last signal over the emergency radio just after 1200. This time, his distress call was heard and he was assured that help was on the way. The *Hyades,* which thus far had survived the storm, had also heard this call, but unfortunately, owing to the adverse weather conditions, she was unable to pinpoint the destroyer's location, which was approximately 300 miles north of Crooked Island Passage.

At 1230, the ship took a heavy roll to starboard and passed beyond the point of no return. Ten minutes later, all hands were called topside, and at 1250 Captain Quarles ordered *Warrington* abandoned. While the crew was going over the side, Quarles entered his sea cabin to retrieve a pillow and, as he stepped across the slanting deck and onto the wing of the bridge, *Warrington* rolled completely over on her starboard side. Simultaneously, a huge wave rose up and lifted him off the ship. As he was attempting to swim away from the capsizing destroyer, he was pulled under by the suction, but soon bobbed to the surface unharmed and was hauled aboard a life raft.

Through the deluge of rain, salt spray and violent winds, Warrington's survivors watched somberly and with heavy hearts as their proud ship slowly dipped her stern under and her bow rose toward the dismal gray sky. Then, all at once, it was over. Her bow pointing straight up, Warrington slipped swiftly and silently beneath the tempestuous Atlantic.

Having spent most of its fury, the storm began to abate just a few hours after Warrington had been swallowed by the hungry sea. Nevertheless, the waves were still running high, which resulted in the survivors becoming separated; many of them were never found. Captain Quarles and three men were all that remained aboard his raft on the morning of the 14th, as a result of its having overturned several times during the night. Later that day, two of the men died from having ingested a large amount of sea water. The two remaining survivors were further plagued by a school of sharks that glided close to the raft and often butted their snouts against it, almost flipping it over.

Lieutenant Eugene E. Archer recalls leaving the Warrington and reaching a raft occupied by several men with a group of survivors clinging to the sides. Throughout the remainder of the day and during the night many of the men, he recalls, slipped away from the raft and were never seen again. By morning, only 26 were left. On the morning of the 15th, a mere 15 survivors remained.

As the day passed, the sea moderated and the winds calmed, thereby allowing aircraft to join in the search for Warrington's survivors. Captain Quarles and his remaining companion were elated to sight a PBY Catalina seaplane flying some distance away, but unfortunately it was too far for its pilot to see the life raft. Then, a lone merchant ship was seen approaching them at about 4,000 yards. Yet, despite waving their shirts and shouting, the vessel passed them by.

Another long, miserable night passed. However, on the morning of the 15th, the two bedraggled and weakened men were relieved and astonished to see more rafts and survivors a short distance from them. Unfortunately, the remnants of Warrington's survivors would spend the remainder of this grueling day, and another agonizing night, drifting aimlessly about the vast expanse of the Atlantic.

On the morning of the 16th, the men were half crazed from thirst. Several had died from exposure or were dying as a result of their injuries or having drunk sea water to ease their parched throats. Needless to say, there was very little hope that they would ever be found. Then at 0900, the cargoman *Hyades* was sighted heading toward the exhausted and demoralized survivors. Since *Hyades* was the first ship to reach the scene, she was able to pick up 61 men, one of whom later died. Also coming to the rescue were seven destroyer escorts and the baby flattop *Croatan* and her task group, which rescued eight more men.

A total of 152 officers and men were lost with the *Warrington* or died in the aftermath of her sinking. Pilots, in their exhaustive search for stragglers across the vast stretch of water, reported sighting 100 lifeless bodies bobbing on the surface of the inhospitable Atlantic.

Following an investigation and an inquest, Lieutenant Commander Quarles was absolved of all blame for the tragic loss of his ship and those who had perished with her.

☆ ☆ ☆

USS *WARRINGTON* (DD-383)

Builder: Federal Shipbuilding & Drydock Co., Kearny, New Jersey.
Keel laid: October 10, 1935.
Launched: May 15, 1937.
Sponsor: Miss Kathleen E. Chubb, great-great-granddaughter of Commodore Lewis Warrington, USN.
Commissioned: February 9, 1938; Commander L.W. Wood, USN, comdg.
Date of loss: September 13, 1944; Lieutenant Commander S.F. Quarles, USN, comdg.
Location: North of the Bahama Islands.
Awards: Two battle stars.

USS Hoel

Launched December 19, 1942
Lost October 25, 1944
Off Samar Island, the Philippines

ACTING LIEUTENANT COMMANDER WILLIAM R. HOEL, USN
(1825–18 ?)

Born in Ohio on March 7, 1825, William R. Hoel was a Mississippi riverboat pilot prior to entering the U.S. Navy on October 19, 1861. He was wounded on February 6, 1862, during the attack and capture of Fort Henry while serving as First Master on board the gunboat USS *Cincinnati*. Upon recovering from his injuries, he piloted the gunboat *Carondelet* during its bold dash up the Mississippi on March 4, passing under the Confederate gun batteries on Island No. 10 to reach Major General John Pope's army at New Madrid. The vessel's daring run through the fusillade of Confederate gunfire enabled the Federal troops to cross the river and capture this key island and its stores of arms and ammunition, thereby opening the Mississippi for Federal gunboat operations.

For his courageous action during this operation, First Master Hoel was highly commended by Flag Officer Andrew H. Foote, and received personal thanks from the Secretary of the Navy, Gideon Welles. He was promoted to the rank of Acting Volunteer Lieutenant on April 29.

He then went on to serve as captain of the *Pittsburgh* in the bombardment of Vicksburg on October 29, 1862. While serving in Rear Admiral David D. Porter's West Gulf Flotilla, he came to the assistance of Porter's flagship, *Benton* when she was disabled by shore guns from the Confederate batteries on Grand Gulf. Interposing the *Pittsburgh* between Porter's ship and the thundering Confederate cannon, Hoel opened fire, causing such severe damage to the fortifications that later General Grant was able to safely cross the Mississippi River to continue the long campaign against Vicksburg that led to its eventual capture.

Advanced to the rank of Acting Lieutenant Commander on November 10, 1864, Hoel left the *Pittsburgh* on March 1, 1865, and assumed command of the USS *Vindicator.* He was honorably discharged on July 7, 1865.

From November 1943 until mid-October 1944, the USS *Hoel* (DD-553) operated with various task forces, taking part in the strikes against the Gilbert, Marshall, Caroline and Palau Islands. On October 12, 1944, she joined Rear Admiral Thomas L. Sprague's Escort Carrier Group (TG 77.4) and made preparations for the invasion of Leyte in the Philippines. The force was composed of three units, each comprised of a group of escort carriers and screened by destroyers and destroyer escorts. Owing to their radio identification calls as "Taffy," they were affectionately referred to as the "Three Taffys" (Taffy-1, Taffy-2 and Taffy-3).

On October 18, the task groups encountered a typhoon, just two days prior to the landings on Leyte. After riding out the tempest, the Three Taffys cruised off the Island of Samar, while their aircraft provided air cover for the invasion forces.

Taffy-3, under Rear Admiral Clifton A.F. Sprague, who was carrying his flag in the escort carrier *Fanshaw Bay*, was composed of the *St. Lô*, *White Plains* and *Kalinin Bay*, and screened by the destroyers *Hoel*, *Johnston* (DD-557) and *Heerman* (DD-532). Later, the group would be augmented by two more escort carriers, the *Kitkun Bay* and *Gambier Bay*, and seven destroyer escorts.

In retaliation against the landings, Imperial Naval Headquarters in Tokyo dispatched an armada of warships to Leyte Gulf to disrupt the invasion. Two Japanese fleets were to penetrate the gulf at its southern entrance through the Surigao Strait: the Southern Fleet, under Vice Admiral T. Nishimura, and the Fifth Fleet under Vice Admiral Shima. A larger body, the Second Fleet, under Vice Admiral T. Kurita, was to race east-bound across the Sibuyan Sea, pass through the San Bernardino Strait, down the eastern coast of Samar and dash into Leyte Gulf.

Also deployed was a fourth group of ships (under the command of Vice Admiral J. Ozawa), composed of four carriers, a battleship, two cruisers and eight destroyers, which were to serve as a decoy, hoping to lure the U.S. Fleet away from the Leyte area. As history tells us, fighting Rear Admiral William F. Halsey, Jr., fearing the potential of the carriers' aircraft, snapped at the lure hook, line and sinker, thus leaving the eastern door to Leyte Gulf partially open.

Fortunately, the American submarines *Dace* and *Darter* were on patrol west of Palawan Island and reported their sightings of a fleet of ships— Kurita's Second—racing on a northern course on the night of October 23. They promptly torpedoed and sank Kurita's flagship, the heavy cruiser *Atago*, plus the heavy cruiser *Maya*, and damaged the heavy cruiser *Takao*, resulting in its having to be detached from the group and towed back to North Borneo.

On the 24th, Kurita's Second Fleet was further assailed by carrier aircraft in the Sibuyan Sea. From early afternoon until sunset, the Japanese force underwent a severe thrashing. After losing his 63,000-ton super-battleship *Mushashi* (sister ship of the dreaded giantess *Yamato*, now Kurita's flagship), a destroyer, and with one cruiser severely damaged, Kurita decided to turn tail and flee for Singapore. As far as U.S. naval intelligence was concerned, his threat had been eliminated. However, Tokyo had other ideas. Kurita was ordered to turn back and continue on to Leyte Gulf.

Owing to the lack of space, and due to its complexity, the Battle of Leyte Gulf cannot be described here in its entirety. However . . .

While the battle in Surigao Strait was in its violent stages, Kurita's body of ships was approaching the Pacific side (Philippine Sea) of the San Bernardino Strait. Once he was clear of the strait, his big guns were boiling southward along the eastern coast of Samar, and by 0600 he was halfway between the entrance of Leyte Gulf and the exit from San Bernardino Strait. With Halsey lured away in hot pursuit of Ozawa's decoy force, the approaches to Leyte Gulf were open—that is, except for Admiral Sprague's meager Taffy-3.

At 0645, a scout plane sighted Kurita's fleet and sent Sprague the following message: "ENEMY SURFACE FORCE OF 4 BATTLESHIPS; 7 CRUISERS AND 11 DESTROYERS SIGHTED 20 MILES NORTH OF YOUR TASK GROUP AND CLOSING AT 30 KNOTS." Needless to say, Sprague was astounded by this report and demanded verification, since Halsey's fleet was supposed to be guarding the northern approaches to Leyte Gulf. The answer was not long in arriving. The ships were positively verified as Japanese, easily identifiable by their tall, pagoda-styled superstructures.

Sprague immediately turned his baby flattops into the wind in an attempt to launch his aircraft. Then, at a distance of 17 miles a forest of masts began to sprout over the northern horizon. Almost simultaneously, Kurita's huge guns began to roar. Unable to launch enough planes in time to repulse the oncoming juggernaut, Sprague had no other choice but to run and call for assistance, of which none was readily available. After the night's engagement in Surigao Strait, Rear Admiral Jesse Oldendorf's ships were low on ammunition and fuel and would not be able to come to Taffy-3's assistance until late in the afternoon. And Taffys 1 and 2 were over one hundred miles away with their aircraft pursuing the remnants of Shima's fleet.

As the thin-skinned flattops and their escorts dashed southward, Kurita's battleships' guns thundered, their 14-inch projectiles splashing, detonating and fountaining ever closer to the beleaguered fugitives (for some odd reason, the giant battleship *Yamato*, did not contribute any firepower with her large 18-inch guns). For a brief spell, a providential rain squall shielded the carriers, but, by the same token, also screened the enemy's ships from air attack. After plunging through the downpour, Kurita split his force into three columns. Down the port flank of the carriers came the cruisers. On the starbord side raced the destroyers and, churning down the center, the formidable battlewagons.

As the gap swiftly closed, Sprague's voice was heard over the TBS radio circuits: "SMALL BOYS . . . SMALL BOYS [destroyers and destroyer escorts] . . .ON MY STARBOARD QUARTER INTERPOSE WITH SMOKE BETWEEN MEN [carriers] AND ENEMY SHIPS!" Without any qualms, the "small boys" bravely concurred. Black, curling smoke poured out of their stacks to serve as a screen for the vulnerable flattops, as the destroyers themselves then pressed forward to slug it out with the goliaths.

One of the first ships to jump into the seething caldron was the 2,100-ton destroyer *Hoel*. Breaking away from the formation, her skipper, Commander Leon S. Kintberger, charged forward at flank speed toward the 32,000-ton battleship IJN *Kongo*, lashing her with his puny 5-inch guns. Almost simultaneously, a 14-inch shell from the battleship crashed into *Hoel's* fire control director just above her bridge. Undeterred, Commander Kintberger continued to plunge toward his adversary, maneuvering skillfully in an effort to avoid the heavy-caliber shells that were splashing and detonating about his ship. At a distance of 9,000 yards, *Hoel* peeled off and at 0727 a school of "tin fish" were sent churning toward *Kongo*. The battleship's captain, sighting the spread of torpedoes, reeled away and in doing so, lost ground in his pursuit of the carriers.

Less than a minute after firing her torpedoes, *Hoel* was struck by another 14-incher, which wrecked her after engine room, placing the entire space out of commission. Right on the heels of this hit, a third 14-inch shell blasted her stern and damaged two of her after 5-inch guns. Unknown to the gun crew in No. 4 gun mount, the gun barrel had been sheared off, and when the gun was fired it backfired, blowing up the mount and causing the

he "Greyhounds of the Sea" were present at every pitched naval battle and invasion in World War II. Here a destroyer stands guard over amphibious landing craft off Tarawa.

A flight of Japanese bombers going in for the attack.

With her hull plating sprung from the underwater blast of a crashing Kamikaze, the USS *William D. Porter* (above) heels over to starboard as the "pall bearers" come alongside. While her crew watches from the bow of a rescue ship (below), the *William D. Porter* begins to roll over and sink. She was the only destroyer sunk by Kamikazes that did not suffer a fatality.

The USS *Mahan* during her sea trials in 1936. While covering a landing at Ormoc Bay in the Philippines on December 7, 1944, *Mahan* was hit by three Kamikazes.

The USS *Monaghan* is in the foreground, posing for a shot for Fox Movietone News off San Diego in 1936. *Monaghan,* along with the USS *Hull* (below) and the USS *Spence,* was lost in the monstrous typhoon off the Philippines in December 1944.

The USS *Borie* is shown here badly damaged and wallowing in a choppy sea following her legendary victory over the U-405. *Borie* had rammed the U-boat and, while the ships were attached, both German and American crews had fought at close quarters in a battle reminiscent of John Paul Jones.

U-boats were often the prey of American destroyers, however they could be hunters as well. The USS *Bristol* (above) fell to the U-371 while escorting a convoy to Oran, Algeria, following the landings at Salerno. The USS *Leary* (below) was stalked by the U-275 in the North Atlantic on Christmas Eve, 1943. She was hit by a GNAT acoustic torpedo that had been specially developed to use on destroyers.

bove, the USS *Meredith* during shakedown trials off e coast of New England. ie photo at right shows me of the mine damage at crippled *Meredith* off ormandy on D-Day. Air acks inflicted further mage on the destroyer, hich broke in two and nk (below) on June 9, 944.

This incredible photo shows the battle off Samar Island in the Philippines after Admiral Sprague ordered the "small boys" to take on the approaching Japanese juggernaut. In and around the smokescreen put down by the destroyers, the

splashes made by Japanese gunfire can clearly be seen. The destroyers *Hoel* and *Johnston*, as well as the destroyer escort *Samuel B. Roberts*, were lost in this gallant action that prevented a major American defeat.

The USS *Parrott* served for two decades with the Asiatic Fleet. Ironically, after fighting courageously through the 1942 debacle in the Dutch East Indies, she was lost in Hampton Roads, Virginia, in a collision with a merchant ship.

The USS *Glennon*, at the right, with her stern blown off by a mine near Normandy beach on June 8, 1944. Her fate was sealed when German gun crews on shore found the range.

The USS *Warrington* was lost in a hurricane north of the Bahamas in September 1944, after seven years of service.

The USS *Abner Read* is shown here with her stern blown off, after striking a mine off Kiska in the Aleutians. When repairs were completed, she went back on duty with the Pacific Fleet.

Beneath a sky pockmarked with flak, a pillar of smoke marks the gravesite of *Abner Read*, in Leyte Gulf on November 1, 1944. *Abner Read* was the first U.S. warship to fall victim to the "Divine Wind," also known as Kamikazes.

An American destroyer battles a Pacific typhoon, of the type that claimed the *Monaghan*, *Hull* and *Spence* in the Philippine Sea in December 1944.

The USS *Cooper* was in the process of shooting up a Japanese reinforcement convoy on December 2, 1944, off Leyte in the Philippines when a "long lance" torpedo found its mark.

A Kamikaze fails to successfully negotiate the anti-aircraft fire thrown up by American ships.

After striking a mine off Okinawa that killed all hands in the forward section of the ship, including the captain, the USS *Halligan* drifted aimlessly for several hours before piling up on a reef. Her hull was finally donated to the Ryukus government for scrapping in 1957.

The USS *Longshaw*, shown above after her launching in mid-1943, ran aground on Okinawa beneath a battery of Japanese shore guns. Below, death and destruction rain down as some of her crew help to lead their wounded shipmates to safety. Note the lower extremities of one crewmen suspended in the mass of wreckage at the mid-upper right of the photo.

Getting "the bow blown off" is not just an expression. Pictured here is the USS *Selfridge*, which was badly damaged in the Battle of Vella Lavella. *Selfridge* is one of the American destroyer that survived the war.

deaths of all but one man. Also damaged in this last hit was her electrical steering apparatus. Shifting over to hand steering and with *Hoel's* only two remaining main batteries operating manually, and bolting ahead on one engine, Commander Kintberger prepared to launch another torpedo attack—this time against the cruiser *Haguro*.

After skillfully dodging the cruiser's shellfire, Kintberger closed in and let fly with his remaining supply of torpedoes at a distance of 6,000 yards. A rousing cheer went up as the crew witnessed three huge columns of fire, smoke and debris spout skyward along *Haguro's* water-line. With all of *Hoel's* torpedoes expended and her speed drastically reduced, Commander Kintberger decided it was time to get out of there. However, this task proved to be much harder than getting in, because the destroyer was now surrounded. On her port beam loomed the battleships; off to starboard were the cruisers; and, within shooting range, swarmed the Japanese destroyers. During the next hour, despite *Hoel's* frantic maneuvering, she was hammered time and again by large- and small-caliber shells, in addition to several armor-piercing projectiles that passed through the ship without exploding. Her decks were ripped up and her bridge reduced to a shambles. Topside and belowdecks, she was a floating charnel house.

The dead and wounded lay about in grotesque attitudes, their life's blood staining the decks and running into the scuppers. Near-misses and direct hits continued to hole her and split her hull plating beneath the waterline. Still, the feisty destroyer surged on ahead, caroming about while her gallant gun crews fired their 5-inchers manually whenever a target of opportunity presented itself. Not only was *Hoel* taking a thrashing; the other "small boys" were also taking a severe beating, as well as dishing it out. But this sacrifice had, in effect, drawn the enemy's fire and attention away from Sprague's carriers.

Finally, at 0830 and after sustaining over 40 direct hits, and several near-misses beneath the waterline, an 8-inch shell smashed into the *Hoel's* only operating engine room, bringing her to a staggering halt. Under a shroud of roiling smoke, billowing clouds of steam and tongues of flame leaping from her innards, the battered *Hoel* took on a heavy list to port and began to settle by the stern. With the valiant destroyer's time running out, Commander Kintberger was compelled to order his ship abandoned. Even as the fighting *Hoel* was sliding down to her final resting place and her survivors were going over the side, the enemy continued to pour shell after shell into the battle-ravaged hulk. After absorbing several more hits, the smoldering wreckage capsized and sank at 0855 in 4,000 fathoms.

Out of a crew of 273 officers and men, only 86 personnel, including her captain, had survived. The majority of her fighting crew perished in the thick of the action, while others died later of their wounds, from shark attacks, or were drowned while awaiting rescue—which only arrived some 50 hours after *Hoel* was sunk. Commander Kintberger praised his officers and men highly when he described the courageous devotion of his crew in his battle report which read, in part: "Fully cognizant of the inevitable result of engaging against such vastly superior forces, these men performed their assigned duties coolly and efficiently until their ship was shot out from under them."

☆ ☆ ☆

USS *HOEL* (DD-533)

Class: Fletcher.
Builder: Bethlehem Steel Shipbuilding Co., San Francisco, California.
Keel laid: June 4, 1942.
Launched: December 19, 1942
Sponsor: Mrs. Charles B. Crane, granddaughter of Acting Lieutenant
    Commander William R. Hoel, USN
Commissioned: July 29, 1943; Commander W.D. Thomas, USN, comdg.
Date of loss: October 25, 1944; Commander L.S. Kintberger, USN, comdg.
Location: Off Samar Island, the Philippines.
Awards: Presidential Unit Citation; Philippine Republic Presidential Citation
    and five battle stars.

USS Johnston

Launched March 25, 1943
Lost October 25, 1944
Off Samar Island, the Philippines

ACTING LIEUTENANT JOHN V. JOHNSTON, USN
(18?–1912)

Born in Cincinnati, Ohio, John Vincent Johnston entered the U.S. Navy in September 1861 and was assigned to the gunboat *St. Louis* as First Master. His exploits during the Civil War included directing gunboat attacks against Fort Henry on the Tennessee River on February 6, 1862, and leading a combined army and naval attack on the Confederates' Island No. 10 the following April. In this action, he succeeded in spiking the fort's guns, for which he was highly commended and advanced to the rank of Acting Lieutenant.

After participating in the bombardments of Vicksburg, Johnston was placed in command of the gunboat *Forest Rose*, to patrol the Mississippi River and its tributaries. On February 15, 1864, while still in command of the *Forest Rose*, he successfully repelled a band of Confederate raiders, thus saving the Federal garrison of the town of Waterproof, Louisiana. Lieutenant Johnston resigned from the Union Navy on June 23, 1864. Residing in St. Louis, Missouri, he died at his home there on April 23, 1912.

Upon his placing the USS *Johnston* (DD-557) in commission, her commanding officer, Commander Ernest E. Evans, ended his introductory speech with the following words: "The *Johnston* is going to be a fighting ship. I intend to go in harm's way and anyone who doesn't want to go had better get off this ship right now!"

Commander Evans, an Oklahoman of Cherokee descent and proud of his Native American heritage, was a fighting man and hard taskmaster who was highly admired and respected by his fellow officers and men. Stockily built, he possessed a dark complexion, wiry black hair, a round, cheerful face, dark brown eyes and a voice that, in an emergency, could boom over the sound of thundering gunfire. While under his command, the *Johnston* was awarded the Presidential Unit Citation and went on to win six battle stars. Her first five were awarded for her participation in the mopping-up operations in the northern Solomons, her participation in strikes against the Marshall, Gilbert and Marianas islands, and the sinking of the Japanese submarine I-176.

On the morning of October 25, 1944, *Johnston* was screening Rear Admiral Clifton C.A. Sprague's task force, Taffy-3, off Samar Island in the Philippines. Threatened with an assault by battleships, cruisers and destroyers under the command of Vice Admiral T. Kurita, IJN, *Johnston*, like the USS *Hoel* and several other "small boys," was quick to respond to Admiral Sprague's desperate plea to intercept the oncoming Japanese juggernaut.

Johnston, the destroyer nearest the enemy's big guns, was the first to respond. Turning away from the formation, Commander Evans drove his destroyer headlong into the mouths of the battleships' 14-inch guns, trailing a heavy, black smoke screen in her wake. Later, her gunnery officer, Lieutenant R.C. Hagen, remarked: "We felt like David without a slingshot!"

Scores of shells began to splash and spout on all sides of the charging destroyer, flaying her with shards of jagged shrapnel and dousing her decks with brine as she knifed through the water toward her target, the cruiser IJN *Kumano*. When his 5-inch guns were within point-blank range, Commander Evans gave the order to fire. Within less than five minutes, *Johnston*'s gunners had poured 200 shells into the cruiser, and for good measure let fly with a salvo of torpedoes into the blazing wreckage. *Johnston* then circled around, ducking into her own smoke screen. Breaking out from her curtain of smoke one minute later, her crew gained the satisfaction of seeing the battered *Kumano* dead in the water and listing heavily.

Suddenly, *Johnston* was struck by three 14-inch projectiles and, in rapid succession, hammered by three 6-inch shells. Lieutenant Hagen described the devastating blows as comparable to a "puppy being smacked by a truck."

The hits had damaged the destroyer's after engine room, knocking out the power to her three after 5-inch batteries and wrecking her gyro compass. Her bridge was showered with shrapnel that killed two officers and wounded Commander Evans himself as well as several personnel close by. Even though he was riddled with shrapnel and had lost two fingers, Evans refused to leave the bridge for medical attention. Nearby was a rain squall and Evans ordered the helmsman to steer into it. The torrential downpour helped douse the numerous fires that had sprouted up about the ship and allowed her damage control parties to effect repairs and clear the decks of wreckage and debris.

Then Admiral Sprague ordered the "small boys" to attack with torpedoes. Although Johnston had expended all of hers and was hindered by the loss of one engine, Evans burst from out of the mini-Niagara in hopes of lending fire support with his two remaining 5-inch guns. In doing so, his destroyer almost collided with the USS Heerman, whose captain, Commander C.A. Hathaway, was appalled at the sight of Johnston's damage. Later, he reported, "It was obvious the Johnston was badly damaged and could not make the speed that we could. The radar was hanging down on her yardarm and Commander Evans flashed a message stating that he had only one engine, no gyro and no radar. There was little doubt that the ship could not survive much longer."

The time was 0815. With the seascape shrouded in smoke, Commander Evans, fearing that his gunners might accidentally fire on friendly ships, ordered his gunnery officer, Lt. Hagen, not to fire blindly into the haze. However, at 0820, the battleship Kongo plunged out of the veil of smoke not more than 7,000 yards off Johnston's port beam. Immediately, the spunky destroyer pounded the giant with 30 5-inch shells. Kongo, in turn, responded with a torrent of 14-inch projectiles, nine of which struck Johnston.

Evans then noticed that the baby flattop Gambier Bay was under heavy fire from a cruiser. Lieutenant Hagen later wrote in his report: "Commander Evans then gave me the most courageous order I've ever heard: 'Commence firing on that cruiser and draw her away from that carrier!' After a short slugfest with the cruiser, and scoring four direct hits upon her, Commander Evans broke off the action and bravely turned his attention to a swarm of destroyers that were now seen converging upon the lone Gambier Bay."

Disabled as she was, the fighting Johnston literally outfought the Japanese destroyers. After pounding the lead destroyer until its guns were silenced, a second destroyer was reduced to a virtual mass of molten wreckage and left dead in the water. As a result of Johnston's valiant attack, all the torpedoes that had been fired by the enemy destroyers missed the carrier. However, despite Johnston's daring intervention, the carrier was raked by 8-inch shells beneath the water line and was sunk. The enemy cruisers also managed to get in close enough to slam four 8-inch shells into the Fanshaw Bay and scored fifteen hits on the Kalinin Bay.

Now out for blood, the Japanese destroyer captains vented their fury against Johnston. Five and 6-inch shells slammed into the American destroyer, adding to what was already appearing to be mortal damage. With her bridge reduced to a shambles and rendered untenable, Evans shifted the con to the after steering station. Racing aft, he reached the hatch above the after steering room and shouted steering instructions to the men below. By now, fires were cropping up all over the ship. Ammunition stores were beginning to explode, killing and wounding men by the score. Now only one of her 5-inch mounts was still in commission, its gun captain shouting: "More shells! Dammit! We need more shells!" *Johnston* was now reduced to a battered, fire-gutted wreck, smoke and steam billowing from every opening and gash in her hull and superstructure.

In spite of *Johnston's* captain and crew having fought with valor to prevent the enemy from reaching the carriers, the overwhelming odds were catching up with her. Lieutenant Hagen remarked after the bloody engagement, "We were now in a position where all the gallantry and guts in the world could not save us. But we figured that help for the carriers was on the way and every minute's delay would count."

By 0900, *Johnston* was losing way and becoming loggy. Moments later, a 5-inch shell crashed into her forward engine room, which brought the pugnacious destroyer to a shuddering halt. Wallowing helplessly in the sea, it was a matter of time before the enemy destroyers would close in about the ship and finish her off with a vengeance. Like a lone covered wagon on the Western plains, *Johnston* became surrounded by the Japanese, who continued to pound her battle-ravaged remains with unrelenting gunfire.

Fifteen minutes later, Commander Evans ordered his embattled but proud ship abandoned. Still, the Japanese destroyers continued to flay *Johnston* and her men as they were going over the side. Finally, at 1010, the fighting *Johnston* rolled over on her beams and was given the coup de grâce by an enemy destroyer. As the survivors thrashed about in the water, one of the Japanese ships was seen approaching, causing fear among the men since they assumed they were about to be strafed. However, much to the Americans' astonishment, the Japanese commander was seen to come to attention and salute the dying *Johnston* as she slipped beneath the surface.

Lost with the *Johnston* were 187 of her crew, of whom 50 were killed during the initial engagement. Forty-five died on the rafts or in the water as a result of their wounds, exposure to the elements or as victims of sharks. Ninety-two officers and men, including Commander Evans, who was known to be alive after the ship's loss, were never seen again.

As for the battle itself, to the astonishment of the beleaguered Americans, Admiral Kurita, with victory seemingly in his hands, broke off the action and fled northward. Owing to the aggressive action taken by the destroyers and destroyer escorts and the damage they had inflicted on his ships, he believed he had tangled with Essex Class carriers, escorted by 30-knot cruisers and destroyers!

Before he retired, however, his ships also sank the *Samuel B. Roberts* (DE-413), as well as *Hoel*, and damaged *Heerman* and several destroyer escorts. Only the USS *Raymond* (DE-341) escaped from the fracas without a scratch. Sadly, the carrier *St. Lô* was sunk later by a suicide aircraft.

About 48 hours after the battle ended, rescue ships arrived to pick up the last of the survivors from the *Johnston, Hoel* and *Samuel B. Roberts.* Commander Evans was posthumously awarded the Congressional Medal of Honor for his courageous contribution to the decisive battle of Leyte Gulf. He was affectionately, and with much admiration, called the "The Chief" by his crew. Said one officer: "The Johnston was a fighting ship, but Commander Evans was the heart and soul of her."

☆ ☆ ☆

USS *JOHNSTON* (DD-557)

Class: Fletcher.
Builder: Seattle Tacoma Shipbuilding Co., Seattle, Washington.
Keel laid: May 6, 1942.
Launched: March 25, 1943.
Sponsor: Mrs. Marie S. Klinger, great-niece of Acting Lieutenant John V. Johnston, USN.
Commissioned: October 27, 1943; Commander E.E. Evans, USN, comdg.
Date of loss: October 25, 1944; Commander E.E. Evans, USN, comdg.†
Location: Off Samar Island, the Philippines.
Awards: Presidential Unit Citation and six battle stars.

USS Abner Read

Launched August 18, 1942
Lost November 1, 1944
Leyte Gulf, the Philippines

COMMANDER ABNER READ, USN
(1821–1863)

Abner Read was born in Ohio on April 5, 1821. During the Civil War he served under Admiral David G. Farragut as commander of the West Gulf Blockading Squadron while captain, respectively, of the USSs *New London* and *Monongahela.* For his outstanding leadership and bravery during the Mississippi River campaign, Read was highly commended by Farragut. On July 12, 1863, Commander Read died from wounds he received during a fierce engagement against Confederate forces below Donaldson, Louisiana.

After the completion of her shakedown trials and battle-readiness exercises, the USS *Abner Read* (DD-526) reported to the Commander, Destroyers, Pacific Fleet (ComDesPac) and was promptly assigned to duty in the waters of the North Pacific.

Here, she participated in the Aleutian campaign, covering the landings on Attu from May 13–22, 1943, and carrying out a bombardment mission on Kiska July 22–31. On August 15, the destroyer returned to Kiska to provide shore bombardment for the landings of American and Canadian troops. This was accomplished without battle casualties because the Japanese had evacuated the island two weeks prior to the landings.

On the 18th, *Abner Read* was on anti-submarine patrol off Kiska when, at 0150, she was staggered by a tremendous mine explosion on her stern that nearly broke her in two. The brunt of the detonation damaged her propeller shafts and lifted her fantail clear out of the water while her bow was pushed beneath.

William J. Pottberg, then a Radio Technician First Class, recalls: "After the explosion pushed the bow down, the stern then fell back with such force that some of our bunks were lifted from their brackets, causing them to collapse and spill their occupants on the deck. Consequently, many of the men were injured, suffering from broken bones, lacerations and contusions."

In the after living quarters, the wounded moaned for assistance and the dead lay about like broken and discarded mannequins. In the darkened and smoke-choked compartments, the survivors stumbled and groped blindly through a jungle of severed cables and sloshed about in ankle-deep water. With the aid of battle lanterns, however, they were able to locate some of their wounded shipmates and guide or carry them to the maindeck.

The situation topside was just as adverse as it was below, for the explosion had damaged the FS (a compound of sulfur trioxide and chlorosulphonic acid) chemical tank, used to generate smoke screens. This compound, when exposed to water or moisture in the air, releases a gas that, if inhaled, can be highly toxic. Consequently, the lethal fumes wafting across the ship rendered most of the crew virtually incapacitated. In his report, her captain, Commander T. Burrows, wrote: "The FS smoke was the most depressing single effect of the disaster that the men had to cope with. It blinded them, but worse yet, it strangled them. It appeared to immobilize their respiratory muscles so they could not breathe in or out. After a few whiffs of smoke, their mental outlook became one of forlorn abandon. Some leaned fruitlessly over the lifelines, gasping for air. There was no escaping from the smoke." Shortly after the detonation, Commander Burrows sent out a distress signal and the destroyer *Bancroft* (DD-598), along with the salvage tug *Ute,* were dispatched to come to the crippled destroyer's assistance. Although both of *Abner Read*'s anchors had been dropped, their flukes could not take hold owing to the solid-rock ocean bottom in that area. Hence, the disabled vessel was left to the mercy of the tide and currents as it drifted closer to the jagged coast of Kiska.

Meanwhile, an offshore breeze continued to drift across the seas, blowing the FS smoke across the ship's decks and into her engineering spaces and lower compartments. Fortunately, however, the nearly severed fantail began to work itself loose, and suddenly it broke away from the ship.

Prior to its breaking away, several men had climbed atop No.5 5-inch gun mount in a desperate attempt to escape the noxious fumes. When the stern separated from the hull, these men were still on board. Fortunately, the stern did not sink immediately, allowing them enough time to abandon it and swim to what was left of the ship. Not long after, the fantail plunged to the bottom, snuffing out the toxic FS fumes. Luckily, none of the ship's engineering spaces, with their vital machinery, were damaged as a result of the explosion. The ship still had the power to allow repairs without too much difficulty.

At 0300, *Bancroft* joined the floundering *Abner Read* and took the disabled vessel in tow until the *Ute* arrived. After completing the long, slow voyage to Adak, Alaska, where *Abner Read* received more temporary repairs, she was towed to the Bremerton Navy Yard in Washington State. Seventy-one members of her crew had been lost in the disaster, 34 others suffering serious and minor injuries, as well as complications caused from FS smoke inhalation.

Her repairs completed, *Abner Read* returned to active duty on December 2 and went on to serve as a training ship out of San Francisco prior to returning to the war zone on February 28, 1944. After taking part in the operations against New Guinea throughout the summer and fall of 1944, the destroyer was assigned to Rear Admiral W.L. Wyler's Task Group 77.1 to cover the landings on Leyte, in the Philippines, on October 20.

On November 1, Admiral Wyler's task group was guarding the eastern entrance to Leyte Gulf, and although most of the Japanese fleet was by now lying on the bottom of the sea surrounding the Philippine Islands, land-based aircraft still posed a serious threat to the Navy and Army forces. Throughout the night of October 30, the task group was constantly alerted by air attacks—attacks that never materialized, hence the crews were exhausted and bleary-eyed owing to lack of sleep.

Then, at 0916, radar contact was made with a flock of "bogies," closing in upon the task group. Still, the Japanese made no attempt to strike. Instead, they skirted the outer perimeter of the task group, well out of range of the ships' AA batteries. Gun crews, CIC teams and lookouts tracked the aircraft, tensely awaiting the onslaught that was certain to come.

At 0950, the first wave of torpedo bombers came racing in, skimming low over the water. Every gun that could bear on the attackers opened up. Flak from 5-inch shells blossomed about the raiders, exploding shrapnel that sent several planes spiraling in flames and smoke into the sea. A curtain of 20- and 40-mm shells blazed across the waters, striking the aircraft and setting them afire, yet still the enemy pressed in. The Australian cruiser HMAS *Stropshire* damaged a fighter that afterwards disappeared into the clouds. When next seen, it was plunging from the cloud bank in flames, only to crash off the starboard side of the USS *Claxton* (DD-571). Its exploding bombs sprayed her decks with shards of lethal metal, killing five of her crewmen and wounding 23 others, while the impact of the blast caused considerable underwater damage.

The destroyer *Killen* (DD-593) was struck by a bomb that started several fires and caused her to lose all power. However, before she was knocked out of the fight, she succeeded in downing four of her assailants. USS *Ammen* (DD-522) was crashed into by a suicider, which knocked out her power and killed and wounded several of her crew. Shortly afterwards, the raiders broke off the action, leaving a large number of aircraft scattered on the floor of Leyte Gulf and the remains of one plane, a mass of tangled and charred wreckage, scattered across the decks of the *Ammen*.

While the crew of *Claxton* was clearing up its wreckage and effecting repairs, *Abner Read* screened the damaged vessel and stood by to offer assistance. Meanwhile, the crippled *Ammen* and *Killen* were being escorted to a safe anchorage.

After a lull that lasted until 1339, another gaggle of "bandits" was detected closing in at a distance of 11 miles. From out of the flock, a lone dive bomber singled out *Abner Read* and slashed into the ship's deadly mantle of AA fire. Despite being aflame and trailing a plume of black smoke, the plane continued to bore in and released its bomb, which dropped into the destroyer's after stack and exploded in her boiler room. The Japanese pilot then terminated his dive on the base of the after stack at about the same time as his bomb detonated in the after boiler room.

Flaming gasoline splashed across the destroyer's deck and super-structure, cremating gun crews and other personnel where they stood. The tremendous blast blew men over the side and riddled many others with debris. The initial detonation had blown out the ship's bottom and severed her fire mains, thereby preventing the firefighters from quelling the gasoline inferno. With flames running unchecked throughout the after section of the ship, the intense heat set the gunpowder cases ablaze, which in turn caused the 5-inch ammunition to explode. These volcanic detonations jolted *Abner Read* from bow to stern, the internal pressure opening her compartments to the sea. In less than 30 minutes the ship's stern was nearly swamped. Every method used to douse the raging fires and retard the flooding failed when power was lost in the forward engine room; and there was no time to rig up additional firefighting equipment.

As still another series of explosions rocked his ship, her captain, Commander A.M. Purdy, at last admitted defeat and ordered the destroyer abandoned. A few moments after her commander left the ship, *Abner Read* suddenly raised her bow and plunged beneath the waves. As her fiery wreckage slipped under, her fires ignited the fuel that had been leaking out of her bunkers. The result: a pillar of black smoke and fire blazing over her gravesite for several hours after she sank. Thus it was that *Abner Read* became the first American destroyer to be sunk deliberately by a suicide aircraft—a forerunner of the dreaded Kamikaze ("Divine Wind") pilots, who would strike terror among the U.S. and British fleets during the Okinawan campaign some six months later.

Lost with *Abner Read* were three officers and 19 men. Among her 187 survivors, rescued by *Claxton,* one officer and 55 men were wounded. While rescue operations were in progress, the sea/air battle continued to rage, with the USS *Richard P. Leary* (DD-664) being damaged by another suicider.

☆ ☆ ☆

USS *ABNER READ* (DD-526)

Class: Fletcher.
Builder: Bethlehem Steel Shipbuilding Co., San Francisco, California.
Keel laid: October 30, 1941.
Launched: August 18, 1942.
Sponsor: Mrs. John W. Gates, wife of Captain John W. Gates, USN (Ret.).
Commissioned: February 5, 1943; Commander T. Burrows, USN, comdg.
Date of loss: November 1, 1944; Commander A.M. Purdy, USN, comdg.
Location: Leyte Gulf, the Philippines.
Awards: Four battle stars.

USS Cooper

Launched February 9, 1944
Lost December 2, 1944
Ormoc Bay, Leyte, The Philippines

LIEUTENANT ELMER G. COOPER, USN
(1905–1938)

Elmer Glenn Cooper was born in Monticello, Arkansas, on May 9, 1905. Graduating from the Naval Academy in June 1927, he served with various air groups as a naval pilot. Lieutenant Cooper was killed while on a training flight off the coast of southern California on February 2, 1938, when his aircraft developed engine trouble and crashed into the sea.

Upon joining the Third Fleet in the Western Pacific in early November 1944, the USS *Cooper* (DD-695) took part in several strikes against Japanese installations throughout the Philippine Islands. On November 19, she was detached from her task force to rescue a pilot whose plane had crashed about 100 miles from Luzon. With the aid of several aircraft flying over the downed pilot, *Cooper* was able to find him without difficulty. With the planes running low on fuel, however, they were forced to return to their carriers, leaving *Cooper* without air cover.

Just before dusk, a lone Japanese torpedo bomber was sighted sweeping over the horizon barely above the waves with every intention of stabbing the destroyer with its torpedo. Running into a wall of heavy AA fire from *Cooper*, however, its pilot had second thoughts and retreated post-haste into the darkening sky. Later that night, *Cooper* rejoined her task force, which by this time was en route to Ulithi.

Although Army forces had gained a strong foothold on Leyte, the enemy was still being supplied with reinforcements by barges and destroyer transports under cover of darkness at Ormoc Bay on the western coast of the island. In an effort to hinder and discourage the landing of troops and supplies, the Navy carried out three missions to sweep the bay clear of enemy shipping. Nonetheless, despite suffering heavy losses in ships, personnel and supplies, the enemy remained determined to continue their seaborne resupply.

During the late hours of December 1, a fourth mission, composed of *Cooper*, in company with her division flagship, *Allen M. Sumner* (DD-692), and *Moale* (DD-691), departed Dulac, Leyte, and steamed for Ormoc Bay. Prior to arriving at their destination, the trio endured several enemy air attacks, although neither ships nor planes suffered casualties or damage. At 2330, as the vessels entered the bay, three more planes came sweeping in. Two of the attackers were splashed by *Cooper* and *Moale*, and the third marauder took such a pasting that he broke off the attack and fled into the darkness.

At 0002, *Cooper's* radar operator reported making contact with a lone vessel. Shortly afterwards, the scanner picked up several more. To their surprise, the destroyermen found themselves in the midst of a train of Japanese ships and barges preparing to offload troops and cargo. Immediately *Cooper's* captain, Commander M.A. Peterson, gave the order to open fire, using every gun that could bear. The tranquil night was soon illuminated with flashes and shattered by the roar of gunfire. *Cooper's* gunners commenced lambasting 5-inch shells into a destroyer, IJN *Kuwa*, that was packed to the gunwales with troops and supplies. Eight minutes later, the Japanese vessel was reduced to a mass of twisted, mangled wreckage, burning furiously from bow to stern. Satisfied that the ship was done for, Commander Peterson turned his guns on a destroyer escort, and was having equal success until *Moale* cut across his line of fire.

Then, in the light of winking automatic gunfire and beads of glowing tracer shells, *Cooper* trained her sights on another vessel. The 5-inch mounts again swung into action and their crews blasted away, oblivious, in this night engagement, to the fact that *Cooper* had only seconds left to live. A "long lance" torpedo, fired by an unknown Japanese ship, was skimming just below the surface straight toward its intended target. Abruptly, it crashed through the darkness into *Cooper's* starboard side and its thunderous impact broke the destroyer in two. There had been no warning before the torpedo hit, and there was no time after to postpone disaster. Within half a minute, even as her guns were still firing at the enemy ship, *Cooper* went to the bottom, taking 191 members of her crew down with her.

While her survivors were struggling in a sea of debris and thick globs of viscous fuel oil, the violent skirmish continued to roar around them. Also swimming close by were Japanese sailors and soldiers from the ships *Cooper* had sunk. According to *Cooper's* survivors, the Japanese acted friendly and did not attempt to harm them.

One of *Cooper's* survivors, George D. Berlinger, then a Gunner's Mate Third Class, and nine of his shipmates (one of whom was an officer) managed to reach the shore on a life raft. Thanks to the kindness of the Filipinos, they were well fed, the wounded being tended to and hidden in the hills until rescued.

After the battle, the two remaining American destroyers cleared the scene and ran through a gauntlet of shore fire, patrol boats and, for good measure, submarines. Both ships sustained minor damage, *Moale* losing two men, 22 others being wounded. En route to Dulac, the ships were further assaulted by aircraft, but these did not cause any damage.

Although the division commander, Commander J.C. Zahm, was compelled to leave *Cooper's* survivors behind, he had not forgotten them. His dispatch set into motion a flight of PBY Catalina flying boats, which were winging to the area before dawn. Arriving on the scene, the plane crews began the remarkable feat of fishing *Cooper's* men out of the water, at the same time as Filipino guerrillas onshore kept the enemy occupied. By sunset, all of *Cooper's* survivors were rescued and on their way to the nearest naval base. One of the PBYs was crammed with 56 men, a cargo 3,000 pounds heavier than the aircraft was designed to carry.

☆　☆　☆

USS *COOPER* (DD-695)

Class: Allen M. Sumner.
Builder: Federal Shipbuilding & Drydock Co., Kearny, New Jersey.
Keel laid: September 30, 1943.
Launched: February 9, 1944.
Sponsor: Mrs. Elmer G. Cooper, widow of Lieutenant Elmer G. Cooper, USN.
Commissioned: March 27, 1944; Commander J.W. Schmidt, USN, comdg.
Date of loss: December 2, 1944; Commander M.A. Peterson, USN, comdg.
Location: Ormoc Bay, Leyte, the Philippines.
Awards: One battle star.

USS Mahan

Launched October 15, 1935
Lost December 7, 1944
Leyte Gulf, the Philippines

REAR ADMIRAL ALFRED T. MAHAN, USN
(1840–1914)

Born on September 27, 1840, at West Point, New York, Alfred Thayer Mahan graduated from the Naval Academy in 1859. During the Civil War, he served with the South Atlantic and Western Gulf Squadrons. From 1886 into 1889, he was President of the Naval War College at Newport, Rhode Island, and later served in this post again, from 1892 to 1893.

His publication *The Influence of Sea Power Upon History*, as well as other scholarly books and articles, were widely admired and had a major impact on geopolitical thought, as well as on modern strategic theory.

Although Mahan retired from active service in 1896, he was recalled to duty during the Spanish-American War to serve on the Naval Strategy Board. Following the war, he served in several important offices: delegate to the First Peace Conference at The Hague, Holland; member of the Board of Visitors at the Naval Academy, 1903; member of the Senate Committee on Merchant Marine, 1904; and member of the Commission on the Reorganization of the Navy Department. He often lectured at the Naval War College. Rear Admiral Mahan died at his home in Washington, DC, on December 1, 1914.

At the completion of her shakedown trials, during which time she conducted goodwill tours to South American ports between December 1936 and January 1937, the USS *Mahan* (DD-364) carried out training operations with the Atlantic Fleet until the following July. She then reported to the destroyer base at San Diego and commenced her operations with the

Pacific Fleet. During the first week of December 1941, *Mahan* arrived at her new base of operations, at Pearl Harbor.

At the time of the Japanese attack, *Mahan* was on patrol duty with Task Force 12. Dispatched to search for the Japanese armada that had just devastated the U.S. battle fleet, the task force was unable to locate the enemy, and shortly returned to Pearl.

Between December 1941 and into October 1942, *Mahan's* primary function was to patrol Hawaiian waters and escort vital convoys to and from West Coast ports. After the completion of a shipyard overhaul at the Mare Island Navy Yard, the destroyer was assigned to escort duty along the West Coast as plane guard for aircraft carriers; later, she resumed her patrol duties off the Hawaiian Islands.

On October 16, *Mahan* departed Pearl Harbor for the South Pacific with Task Force 61. On the 22nd, while in company with the USS *Lamson* (DD-367), she carried out an attack on a group of Japanese patrol boats south of the Gilbert Islands, sinking two. On the 27th, while steaming north of the Santa Cruz Islands, the task force was attacked by enemy aircraft, during which time *Mahan* splashed four of the raiders. Unfortunately, after her fine performance in this clash, *Mahan* collided with the battleship *South Dakota* on the following day and seriously damaged her bow. After temporary repairs were effected at Nouméa, New Caledonia, *Mahan* stood out for Pearl Harbor, where she was given a new bow.

Upon her second arrival in the South Pacific, on January 9, 1943, *Mahan* was promptly assigned to escort duty, plying the waters between the New Hebrides, New Caledonia and the Fijis until mid-March. Shortly afterwards, she made another escort run to Guadalcanal and then returned to New Caledonia in April. Next, she teamed up with a combined American and Australian naval force and commenced her operations against enemy strongholds in the New Guinea campaign. Continuously active during the next three months, *Mahan* took part in the landings at Nassau Bay on July 9, bombarded Finschaven on the 22nd and 23rd, and bombarded the beaches at Lae in support of the landings there from September 4 to 8. On the 22nd she supported the invasion of Australian troops at Finschaven and succeeded in shooting down three enemy aircraft during this action.

During the months of October and November, *Mahan* was busily engaged in patrol duties off New Guinea. In December, she took part in the bombardment of Japanese installations on New Britain, and on the 26th covered the landings at Cape Gloucester on that island. Following this operation, the destroyer was replenished, and later participated in the bombardment of Gali, on New Guinea.

After a brief period of rest and recreation for her crew at Sidney, Australia, *Mahan* resumed her escort duties throughout the South and Central Pacific into late February 1944, when she bombarded enemy positions on Los Negros Island. After almost two years in the war zone, the veteran destroyer proceeded to San Francisco in the spring for a well-deserved overhaul and leave for her crew.

Returning to Pearl Harbor in July, *Mahan* commenced her battle-readiness exercises in Hawaiian waters prior to departing for the war zone on August 15. Assigned to escort duty, she screened convoys to the newly occupied islands of Enewetok, Jaluit, Guam, Saipan and Ulithi. Based at Hollandia, New Guinea, *Mahan* began escorting resupply convoys to Leyte and carried out anti-submarine patrols off New Guinea until the end of November.

On December 7, 1944, while the landings at Ormoc Bay were in progress, *Mahan,* in company with the USS *Smith* (DD-378), was on patrol between Leyte and Ponson Island when they were attacked by a flock of enemy aircraft. At about 0948, *Mahan's* gunners opened fire on a flight of nine bombers, escorted by four Zero fighters. While the destroyers' gunners hammered away at their assailants, three Army P-38 fighters arrived on the scene, shooting down three Zeros and damaging two bombers. In spite of this intervention, the remaining aircraft, in a concentrated suicide attack, pressed in, skimming low across the water, and penetrated *Mahan's* curtain of AA fire.

Three of the attackers crashed headlong into the destroyer in quick succession, the violent impact of the blows and exploding bombs sending the *Mahan* reeling. Burning gasoline saturated her decks and superstructure, setting ready ammunition ablaze. Unable to contain the conflagration, the fires soon spread to No. 2 magazine, causing the 5-inch ammunition there to explode.

Thirteen minutes after the third plane had struck, *Mahan* was aflame virtually from stem to stern. Rocked by violent explosions and showing every indication of sinking, her captain, Commander E.G. Campbell, ordered his ship abandoned. The destroyers USS *Lamson* and *Walke* (DD-723) moved in to rescue her survivors, of whom 13 were seriously wounded or burned. Considering the damage incurred, and the fires that had consumed the ship, it was a miracle that only one officer and five men were killed.

Nothing could be done to save the fiery and now-exploding destroyer, so *Walke* was compelled to send the fighting *Mahan* to the bottom with gunfire and a torpedo.

In his battle report, Commander Campbell highly commended his crew, issuing the following statement: "The strain of standing there and battling back as one after another of the bombers came roaring in, was terrific. Even so, not a single man left his post or jumped overboard to escape what at times looked like inevitable death. . . . The fact that four of the nine planes were shot down; that no one abandoned ship until the word was given; that the entire engineering force stayed by their stations throughout the action, in spite of no information . . . that the damage control parties continued to function . . . that gun captains shifted promptly to local [hand] control when the main battery director was disabled . . . and that the ship was abandoned in an orderly manner all testify to the high state of discipline and courage displayed by the entire crew."

☆ ☆ ☆

USS *MAHAN* (DD-364)

Class: Mahan.
Builder: United Dry Docks, Inc., Staten Island, New York.
Keel laid: June 12, 1934.
Launched: October 15, 1935.
Sponsor: Miss Kathleen H. Mahan, great-granddaughter of Rear Admiral
    Alfred T. Mahan, USN.
Commissioned: September 18, 1936; Commander J.B. Waller, USN, comdg.
Date of loss: December 7, 1944; Commander E.G. Campbell, USN, comdg.
Location: Leyte Gulf, the Philippines.
Awards: Five battle stars.

USS Reid

Launched January 11, 1936
Lost December 11, 1944
Off Limasawa Island, The Philippines

SHIP'S MASTER SAMUEL C. REID, USN
(1783–1861)

Samuel Chester Reid was born in Norwich, Connecticut, on August 24, 1783. Entering the U.S. Navy in 1794, he reported on board the USS *Baltimore*, then under the command of Commodore Thomas Truxtun. In 1803, he became master of the brig *Merchant*.

During the War of 1812, while in command of the privateer *General Armstrong*, he gallantly challenged a group of British gunboats that were en route to New Orleans. Outnumbered and outgunned, Reid was ultimately compelled to scuttle his vessel, but his intervention delayed the shipment of vitally needed arms and ammunition to the British forces, thus aiding General Andrew Jackson's defense of New Orleans. In 1844, Reid was promoted to the rank of Ship's Master and retired soon afterwards. Residing in New York City, he died at his home on January 28, 1861.

Between 1937 and December 7, 1941, the USS *Reid* (DD-369) served alternately with the Atlantic and Pacific fleets. Anchored in Pearl Harbor on the morning of the Japanese attack, *Reid*'s gunners responded with heavy AA fire against the Japanese attackers but did not score any hits. For the remainder of December, *Reid* was allocated to patrol duty in Hawaiian waters; then, in the first week of January, she departed for the West Coast, serving as a convoy escort en route.

Although *Reid* was primarily engaged in escort and patrol duties on the American West Coast, in the North Pacific and in the waters of the South and Central Pacific, she did manage to chalk up an impressive war record. In between these long, arduous assignments she aided in 13 major landings and participated in 18 bombardment missions; sank the submarine RO-61 (capturing eight of her crew); and was credited for shooting down 12 aircraft. All told, Reid had fired over 10,000 rounds of 5-inch shells against Japanese forces on shore and in the air, before she, herself, was finally blown to the bottom by two suicide aircraft.

Death came to Reid and 150 of her crew on December 11, 1944, while she was escorting a reinforcement convoy to Ormoc Bay. As the ships were cruising off Limasaw Island, near the western end of Surigao Strait, a swarm of Japanese fighters was sighted bearing in on the convoy. Despite the heavy concentration of AA fire thrown up by the defensive screen of destroyers, the enemy planes continued to hurtle in with a vengeance. Two of them were struck and crashed into the sea in flames, while others locked in on Reid and the USS Caldwell (DD-605). Racing down through a murderous wall of 20- and 40-mm cannon fire and 5-inch projectiles, four more "bandits" were splashed, four others being damaged by Reid's gunners. Then five more aircraft prepared to crash-dive onto the destroyers, four of which ganged up on Reid.

The first suicider screamed in, snagged its wing on the starboard whaleboat, and went careening forward to crash against the ship's hull, just above the waterline abreast of No.2 magazine. The explosion blew a huge hole in the destroyer's side and set her ammunition ablaze. Seconds later, another aircraft plunged into her No.3 5-inch gun mount aft, then spun around and crashed into a 40-mm gun tub, detonating with a thundering blast. A flaming shower of burning gasoline splashed across Reid's decks, burning and scorching every sailor in its path and causing ready 20- and 40-mm ammunition to explode in a lethal pyrotechnic display.

Within two minutes of first being struck, the damaged Reid was on her way to a watery grave. Shaken by violent internal explosions and unchecked flames gutting her bridge and superstructure, Reid began to settle swiftly by the stern, thus compelling her skipper, Commander S.A. McCornock, to order his ship abandoned. Of her crew, 150 men, including her captain, managed to clear Reid's decks before she slipped to the bottom. Reid did not die quietly, however. Seemingly as if in protest, after she had vanished beneath the waves, the sea shook and rumbled violently as her ammunition continued to detonate throughout her battered, fiery hulk.

☆ ☆ ☆

USS *REID* (DD-369)

Class: Mahan.

Builder: Federal Shipbuilding & Drydock Co., Kearny, New Jersey.

Keel laid: June 25, 1934.

Launched: January 11, 1936.

Sponsor: Mrs. Beatrice R. Power, a collateral descendant of Ship's Master Samuel C. Reid, USN.

Commissioned: November 2, 1936; Captain Robert B. Carney, USN, comdg.

Date of loss: December 11, 1944; Commander S.A. McCornock, USN, comdg.

Location: Off Limasawa Island, the Philippines.

Awards: Seven battle stars.

USS Spence

Launched October 27, 1942
Lost December 18, 1944
Philippine Sea

CAPTAIN ROBERT T. SPENCE, USN
(1785–1826)

Robert T. Spence was born in Portsmouth, New Hampshire in 1785, and was appointed Midshipman in 1800. During the war with the Barbary powers, Spence served in the brig *Siren*, with Commodore Edward Preble's Mediterranean Squadron. He was then serving in a captured gunboat when it engaged with a corsair warship; despite his ship's being struck in the magazine, Spence's crew continued to fire their guns until the captured vessel sank beneath their feet.

In 1807, Spence was advanced to the rank of Lieutenant and, in 1813, to the rank of Master Commandant. During the War of 1812, he commanded the naval station at Baltimore, Maryland, where he supervised the construction and equipping of the schooner USS *Ontario*. He was highly commended for his quick thinking, and for putting into motion the laying of obstructions in Baltimore Harbor to impede the advance of a fleet of British warships there.

Spence continued to serve as commandant of the Baltimore Naval Station until July 1819, when he assumed command of the brig USS *Cayne*. With this ship, he cruised throughout the Caribbean in an effort to abolish piracy and, later, along the southern and Gulf coasts, to suppress the African slave trade.

In July 1823, Captain Spence returned to shore duty and resumed his post as commandant of the Baltimore Naval Station. He continued to serve in this capacity until his death in September 1826.

Prior to being assigned to the Pacific Fleet, the USS *Spence* (DD-512) was attached to the Atlantic Fleet and made several escort voyages to Casablanca, as well as conducting operations in Caribbean waters. On July 25,

1943, *Spence* stood out of San Francisco, bound for the Pacific war zone via Pearl Harbor. Here, she commenced a refresher course in battle-readiness exercises before proceeding on to the South Pacific.

Arriving at Tulagi during the last week of September, *Spence* joined DesRon 23 ("The Little Beavers"), under the command of Captain Arleigh "31-Knot" Burke, and was designated flagship of DesDiv 46, under Commander B.L. Austin. On the night of October 1, DesDiv 46 engaged a fleet of Japanese landing barges between the Vella Lavella and Kolombangara islands, sinking 20 of them. Then, on November 1, *Spence* and her division covered the landings on the Treasury Islands and at Torokina, Bougainville. During the early morning hours of November 2, her division joined up with DesDiv 45—Captain Arleigh Burke in the USS *Charles Ausburne* (DD-570)—and Task Force 39, under the command of Rear Admiral Aaron "Tip" Merrill, to intercept a Japanese bombardment force composed of two light and two heavy cruisers, along with six troop-carrying destroyers under the command of Rear Admiral Sentaro Omori.

When the enemy was sighted approaching Empress of Augusta Bay, at 0221, all hell broke loose as Burke's destroyers fired a brace of 25 torpedoes at the enemy ships, which at the same time had changed course. As a result, all of the destroyers' torpedoes missed. However, as the IJN *Sendai* was making her turn, she was wracked by a murderous salvo of 6-inch shells that virtually disemboweled her. Now, utter confusion reigned within the enemy force. In an effort to avoid a fate similar to *Sendai*'s, the destroyers *Samidare* and *Shiratsuyu* collided with each other, and Omori's flagship, *Myoko*, mistakenly rammed into the destroyer *Hatsukaze,* slicing off her bow.

In the heat of the action, the destroyer *Foote* (DD-511) was knocked out of the battle when she was stung in the stern by a torpedo at 0308. Then, while racing at 30 knots through the ink-black night, *Spence* and the destroyer *Thatcher* (DD-514) sideswiped each other, causing *Spence* to miss the opportunity to fire a salvo of torpedoes at a cruiser. Soon after, at 0320, *Spence* was struck by a shell on the bow, just below the waterline, which holed her fuel tank, causing her to lose fires in her forward boilers and cut down her speed. Thanks to the quick action taken by her boiler room personnel, however, fuel oil suction was shifted over to the standby tank. With fires restored to her boilers, the destroyer was ready to plunge back into the fight.

Despite being slightly hampered by this wound, the feisty *Spence* and her fighting crew were still seeking out targets of opportunity. The fire-gutted *Sendai* loomed in her sights and, with an assist from the USS *Converse* (DD-

509), *Spence* let fly with four torpedoes at the fiery wreck. The crew was rewarded when four columns of fire, water and debris were observed fountaining skyward along the battered cruiser's waterline. Still, however, the Japanese vessel remained afloat.

After this action, *Spence, Converse* and *Thatcher* broke away to pursue the damaged *Samidare* and *Shiratsuyu*, which were now retiring from the battle. By 0350, the destroyers had caught up with the fugitives and jockeyed into position for a torpedo attack. Within a few minutes, a swarm of "tin fish" were humming toward the Japanese destroyers, but all failed to hit the fleeing targets. In return, the enemy answered in kind with gunfire and torpedoes that also missed.

Unfortunately, *Spence* was running low on fuel and was forced to retire to rejoin Burke's division. At 0425, as she was approaching DesDiv 45, she was mistaken for an enemy destroyer and became shaken by a rain of shells that splashed all around her. Over the TBS, Commander Austin shouted to Burke: "WE'VE JUST HAD A CLOSE MISS! HOPE YOU ARE NOT SHOOTING AT US!" Burke's reply was a classic in Navy humor: "SORRY, BUT YOU'LL HAVE TO EXCUSE THE NEXT FOUR SALVOS ALREADY ON THEIR WAY!" Luckily, Austin was able to avoid the oncoming salvos by a cat's whisker, and, in so doing, had the good fortune to sight the damaged *Hatsukaze*. After pouring several projectiles into the cripple and reducing her to a flaming wreck, Austin was compelled to cease fire because of a shortage of ammunition; hence, he called upon Burke's division to polish her off.

With the enemy badly bloodied and in full retreat, the Battle of Empress of Augusta Bay was over. However, as the victors were leaving the area, they were pounced upon by a flight of some 70 to 80 vengeful aircraft, of which 20 were shot down. Nevertheless, the Japanese pilots scored two hits on the cruiser *Montpelier.*

On the afternoon of the 10th, the crew of *Spence* were witnesses to a grisly episode when she went to investigate the sighting of a float with seven men on it. At first they appeared to be dead, but when the destroyer closed in, the men stood up and spoke in Japanese. One of them, apparently an officer, broke out a 7.7 machine pistol and, in quick succession, each man put the muzzle of the weapon in his mouth and pulled the trigger, blowing out the back of his skull. When one of the men seemed reluctant to join in this suicide pact, he was held by two others while the officer performed the morbid task. After the final two Japanese had killed themselves, the officer made a seemingly fanatical speech, then turned the gun upon himself and toppled into the sea, by now swarming with hungry sharks. The shocking incident was over in less than five minutes.

After effecting temporary repairs, *Spence* was committed to carrying out patrols and escort work until her squadron was in action again against Japanese shipping in St. George Channel during the early morning hours of November 25. During this fracas, the "Little Beavers" sank three out of five enemy destroyers. *Spence* continued to carry out her operations from the Port Purvis-Kula Gulf area from November into late January 1944. On February 5, she took part in the bombardment of enemy supply dumps on the Hahela Plantation on Buka Island, and on the following day sank a barge. On the night of the 9th, *Spence's* guns pounded enemy outposts on Tiaraka and Teopasino, Bougainvile. This was followed by a raid against Kavieng and Cape St. George, New Ireland on the 18th, and, on the 22nd, she assisted in the sinking of a 5,000-ton merchant ship and two landing barges. On June 19–20, the fighting *Spence* took part in the famous "Marianas Turkey Shoot" in the Philippine Sea and, prior to deploying to San Francisco, she assisted in the strikes against the Marianas Islands.

Arriving at the Hunter's Point Naval Shipyard on August 18, *Spence* underwent a complete and well-deserved overhaul, her crew enjoying several weeks of leave before returning to the war zone. On October 5, she departed from San Francisco, arriving at Eniwetok on the 31st. From then until mid-December, as a unit of Task Group 38.1, she screened the carriers while their aircraft assaulted enemy positions on Luzon and airfields throughout the Philippines.

During the second week of December, *Spence* was screening Admiral Halsey's Third Fleet, east of Luzon. On the 16th, all air operations were canceled to allow the fleet to refuel on the following day. Since the ships had depleted most of their fuel supply, their tanks had been ballasted with sea water in order to stabilize them. As they were approaching the fueling rendezvous, the ships commenced deballasting and so were riding high in the water. Having also recently been installed with additional anti-aircraft weapons and radar scanners, the ships were now much more "tender" than when they were first commissioned.

Upon reaching the fueling area, the vessels with less fuel on board—primarily the destroyers—were given first priority. *Spence*, having only 15 percent of fuel remaining, maneuvered toward the battleship *New Jersey*. However, by this time, the seas had begun to rise, making the destroyer's approach difficult. After the hoses had been passed over, the water sluicing between the ships became so turbulent that the destroyer's helmsman was hard-pressed to prevent the bobbing, corkscrewing ship from slamming against the side of the battlewagon. Heavy swells heaved the 2,150-ton *Spence* about like a child's toy, inundating the fueling gangs. Then the *Spence* veered away from *New Jersey*, yanking the fuel hoses from out of the fueling trunks and snapping the heavy mooring lines as if they were string. When messages began filtering in that other destroyers and destroyer escorts were experiencing similar problems, Halsey postponed all fueling operations and ordered the fleet on a northwest tack, as the gale was coming in from the east. Little did the men of the Third Fleet realize that they were in for something more than a gale.

Later that afternoon, the storm changed direction, and so did Halsey, this time to the southwest. Before dusk, the seas were becoming mountainous, with fierce, howling winds and driving sheets of rain. By now, there was no doubt in anyone's mind that they were heading into a full blown typhoon.

Throughout the tempestuous night, the barometer had been dropping steadily. At 0700, more attempts were made to refuel the oil-thirsty destroyers, but the raging seas made the task impossible. Then, at 0800, the barometer virtually dropped out of sight and by 1000 the storm was venting its full fury upon the fleet.

The destroyers *Dewey* (DD-349) and *Aylwin* (DD-355) had taken 70 and 75-degree rolls, respectively. Even the escort carriers were taking precarious rolls. On board the *Cowpens* and *Monterey*, the tie-down lines securing the aircraft had snapped, letting several planes crash into each other, puncturing their fuel tanks and starting gasoline fires.

On board the frail, tender destroyers, it was unmitigated hell. It was impossible for the men to stand or walk without holding on to something for support, and by this time many of them were suffering from cuts, contusions, broken limbs and burns. The serving of hot meals was simply out of the question. Men off watch took to their bunks, their arms and legs wrapped around their bunk railings so they would not be thrown out of their berths. Superstructures were buckled; boat davits and ladders were twisted as if they were made of soft clay. Many whaleboats had been reduced to splinters or torn off their davits. Radar antennas were warped or knocked askew, thus rendering them useless, and those that were operable were "blacked out," unable to detect other ships because of the density of salt spray and wind-driven rain. Communications between ships was practically lost, and without the benefit of radar to locate each other, many of the ships plunged virtually blind through the raging tempest.

By 1400, the storm had all but spent its wrath. The winds began to decrease in velocity and the tumultuous seas began to ease. By 1600, the barometer was on the rise, and the winds were dropping to about 30 knots. Before nightfall, word was received that as many as four ships had been swallowed up by the storm. A search was begun before darkness set in.

During the next three days the fleet conducted, in the words of Admiral Halsey, "the most exhaustive search in naval history." As communications gradually became restored, ships began reporting in. Then, three days after the typhoon, came a shocking report from the destroyer escort *Tabberer* that she had just rescued several survivors from *Spence* and the destroyer *Hull* (DD-345) and that both vessels had capsized in the vicious storm. Soon after, a message came through from the USS *Brown* (DD-546) and the destroyer escort *Swearer* that they had picked up several men from *Spence,* plus men from the USS *Monaghan* (DD-354), which, likewise, had succumbed to the storm.

One of the survivors from *Spence,* then-Seaman First Class Edward Miller, from Clark, New Jersey, recalls his horrendous ordeal during the storm and in the wake of *Spence's* loss: "Since the *Spence* was the lowest on fuel, she had first refueling priority. When we came alongside the *New Jersey,* the seas were already running high and rain, as well as brisk winds, had already begun to lash the ships. After experiencing much difficulty in getting the fuel hoses on board, the battleship had just commenced pumping when a huge swell caused us to pull away, in turn pulling the hoses out and spewing hundreds of gallons of oil all over the ship and the fueling parties.

"It was decided by Admiral Halsey to change course and, hopefully, resume fueling operations early the next morning. As the night progressed, the seas and winds seemed to get worse, making it difficult for any of us to get any sleep. The next morning, we attempted refueling from an oiler, but by now we realized that we were in the midst of a violent typhoon, and again we stopped trying after we were slammed into the side of the tanker, jolting several men off their feet and causing several injuries.

"That morning I had the 0800 to 1200 watch in the main battery gun director, located directly above the bridge. On watch with me in that cramped space were two fire controlmen and an officer. By now, the storm had really increased in velocity. The seas were like mountains and the winds had reached well over 100 knots, blowing the tops off the waves in a foamy, horizontal spray, as if a giant was blowing the froth from an overfilled beer mug.

"Then, a huge wave smashed us broadside and poured down into one of the engine rooms, knocking out power to the main generator and causing us to lose steering control. Now we were lying dead in the water, the engineers vainly trying to restart the generator. Unfortunately, we were now caught in the trough and, as we rose on the first swell, we leaned so far over I thought we were going to capsize right then and there. But, thank God, when we reached the crest of the wave, the ship righted herself. All during that time, the *Spence* quivered and shook from bow to stern. We could also hear the din and clangor of loose gear crashing about belowdecks. Again, as if we were riding on a roller coaster, we rose up on the second swell and down on the other side. Then, as we were lifted up on the third wave, the ship just rolled over on her port side and kept going.

"At the time, we did not have any life jackets on, since the access hatch leading to the director was so small you could not enter or leave it while wearing a bulky kapok. For that reason, we would leave them on the deck outside the hatch, where they could easily be reached if we needed them. Unfortunately, when the ship capsized, the life jackets were washed into the sea and floated away. In the meantime, after I had left the director, I was hurled into the water and pulled beneath the surface—for just how long, I don't recall. But suddenly, I rose to the surface and found myself less than five feet away from the overturned hull of the *Spence*. And, thankfully, close by was a life jacket! After putting it on, I could see several men in the water and, as swiftly as possible, we tried to swim away from the ship.

"Strewn about us was a smattering of debris and a couple of life rafts and floater nets with a few fellows on or clinging to them. While we were close to the ship, her hull gave us some protection from the onslaught of the storm, but less than ten feet away our faces and other exposed parts of our bodies were stung and lashed by the wind and rain. The latter felt like sharp needles being jabbed into our flesh.

"I then saw a length of timber that was at least 12 feet long, with seven or eight guys clinging to it. I managed to swim over to it and hung on. What I remember clearly was that one fellow had one arm wrapped around the plank; on his other arm was a small item that resembled a life ring. At the time, I was puzzled to see such a small life-saving device, since I'd never seen anything like it on board ship. Then I realized that the poor guy must have been suffering from hemorrhoids, and the ring must have been issued to him by our pharmacist's mate.

"Up to now, the seas were still high and rough, with the winds showing no signs of abating. Then suddenly, we rose up upon the crest of a wave and the wind lifted us up bodily, blew us across the surface, and caused all of us to lose our hold on that piece of timber. I don't know what happened next, but when I regained my equilibrium I had that ring in my hand and there wasn't a soul anywhere near me.

"Next, from out of nowhere, a black fellow by the name of David L. Moore, First Class Steward's Mate, a 9-year Navy veteran, came drifting close to me and we managed to stay together. Shortly afterwards, another man joined us, a gunner's mate by the name of Larry Collier, from Kansas. Looking back, I seem to recall that none of the men in the water displayed any signs of panic, nor was there any sort of cries or frantic shouting. At the time, I lived in Linden, New Jersey, and one of my shipmates was an old school chum of mine. Although he did get off the ship, I never saw him again. Meanwhile, we three stayed together, despite being tossed about. We never did see the ship go down after she was capsized, but we could hear muffled explosions throughout her hull due to the boilers blowing up.

"Normally, whenever a ship sinks, the sea is usually saturated with a heavy, dense blanket of fuel oil, which in most instances can result in the deaths of the men from ingesting it or getting it into their lungs. However, the ship was so low on fuel that there wasn't too much of it in the water and what there was quickly dispersed by the strong winds and sea. Still, there was enough around to cover us and our clothing.

"After darkness fell, the seas began to calm down and the skies began to clear. The stars were so bright, we felt that we could reach out and touch them. On the following morning, the sea was almost as calm a pond and the sun came up strong and clear."

For the next three days, Miller and his companions drifted alone on the vast expanse of the Philippine Sea. During that time several aircraft were seen, but none came close enough to sight the men. However, just when all hope seemed lost, they were sighted by a plane which dropped a flare and a dye marker. Within an hour they were rescued by the USS *Swearer*.

Another survivor, the supply and disbursing officer, Lieutenant (j.g.) Alphonso S. Krauchunas, the only officer to survive the disaster, chronicled the tragedy and his experiences after his rescue:

"At 1030 on the 18th, in an effort to seek relief from the rolling and pitching, I decided to flake out in my bunk. As I lay in my berth, I could feel the ship shudder and groan as she fought bravely against the fury of the maelstrom. Then, at about 1100, the Chief Engineer, Lieutenant (j.g.) Larry Sundin, entered my berthing space, saying: 'You had better get topside, Al! We're taking water down the stacks!' I just could not believe it, and figured he was pushing the panic button so I ignored his warning. But within a few seconds after he had left the wardroom, the lights began to flicker and finally went out. Immediately, the emergency lighting came on and I raced like hell to reach the maindeck.

"Then the ship took a sharp, snap roll that threw me off my feet. Getting up on my hands and knees, I scrambled on all fours along the passageway toward the watertight door that led to the maindeck, which someone had not closed. Just as I was exiting through the doorway, another wave rolled the *Spence* over on her side. A wall of water gushing into the passageway almost swept me back into the wardroom. Luckily, I had been able to grasp hold of a railing on the bulkhead and held on. In the meantime, I could feel the ship heeling over—now almost upside down! Completely underwater, I still managed to cling on to the railing, and, like a flag in a gale, I was whipped about as tons of water tried to pull me back into the wardroom. Luckily, another wave had lifted the ship momentarily, thus allowing the area where I was trapped to be free of water. After taking four or five deep gulps of air, I scrambled with all my might and whatever strength I could muster to escape through the access door before the ship rolled back over again.

"I was unable to recall what happened from then on, until I regained consciousness in the sea, vomiting several times as a result of swallowing some oil and saltwater.

"So, there I was, bobbing about in the swirling, tempestuous waters, without a life jacket, gazing about and looking for something to cling on to, with the overturned *Spence* right next to me. Several life jackets that had been washed off the ship were floating about and one of the men, Chief Watertender George Johnson, passed one on to me; he then disappeared. I tied it around my legs to give me more buoyancy. Then I was tossed against the hull of the *Spence* and through her thin-skinned hull plating, I could faintly hear the pitiful screams and cries from the poor souls who were trapped within her hull.

"At this point, I was concerned about getting caught in the suction of the ship, should she sink, so I made every effort to swim away from her. By now, the velocity of the winds must have reached well over 100 knots. Then, I saw another fortunate crew member, Water Tender Third Class Charles F. Wohlleb, who had managed to escape from the after fire room and, together, we made our way toward a group of some 18 to 20 men on board a floater net. With the seas running at least 30 to 40 feet in height, many of the men on the net had been thrown off it. Some were in such a weakened state they could not hold on. And those who were not wearing life jackets had either been washed away or gone down beneath the thrashing sea in spite of efforts made by their shipmates to save them. Probably because of the trauma they had suffered as a result of the ship's capsizing, many of the men did not seem to make any effort to survive.

"Sometime later, a large canvas bag was seen floating near by. Much to our delight and relief, it contained a 20-man rubber life raft. After it was inflated, with the CO cylinders, three men and myself climbed on board; however, I did not trust the stability of the craft and decided to return to the floater net. The raft and the three men on board it were never seen again.

"By 1400, it seemed that the worst of the typhoon was over. Before darkness had closed in, the seas and wind had calmed down to the point where there was very little wave action and just a slight breeze. Remaining on the netting were myself, two other officers and six enlisted men. By the following day, one of the officers, Lieutenant (j.g.) John Whalen, and Seaman First Class James Heater, had died."

Under circumstances very similar to the ordeal that Ed Miller and his shipmates had endured, Lieutenant Krauchunas and his men also drifted aimlessly about the sea for three days under the searing, tropical sun and cold nights, barely surviving on a swallow of water every three hours. Before long, the men began to hallucinate, as did Lieutenant Krauchunas. On the second night, one of the men left the netting unnoticed, swam a short distance and returned. When asked why he had left, he said he had seen a Coca-Cola sign all lit up by a grocery store. On the following day a can of vegetable shortening was seen floating nearby and was retrieved by Chief Wohlleb, who opened it with a hatchet. Its contents were used to protect the men's exposed bodies against the prolonged, searing rays of the sun.

During the daylight hours, several aircraft were seen, but none came close enough to see the wretched survivors. One morning, Ensign George Poer was found to be missing and was never seen again. Now there were only six men left. On the following night, a baby flattop was sighted approaching the survivors. None of their frantic shouts were heard by the carrier's lookouts and the vessel continued steaming on into the dark night. Then just before dawn they were rescued by the destroyer escort USS *Swearer*, which later that day picked up Ed Miller and his shipmates.

All told, a total of nine survivors from *Spence* were rescued by *Swearer*, 14 others being picked up by *Tabberer*. The last of *Spence*'s survivors to be picked up was William E. Keith, Seaman Second Class, rescued by the destroyer *Gatling* (DD-671). Upon being hoisted on board, he was in such a deranged state that he attempted to jump over the side, believing he had been taken off a torpedo, which he intended to ride to Japan to blow up the city of Tokyo.

On January 2, 1945, Lieutenant Krauchunas was transferred to the receiving ship USS *Sturgis*, where he joined the remaining 23 survivors from *Spence*. Each man was asked to write down the names of any person they had seen in the water at any time after *Spence* had capsized. Only 23 other names were mentioned that were known to have gotten off the ship. A total of 294 others had either been trapped within the hull of the destroyer, had drowned or had otherwise reached the limit of their ability to survive.

☆ ☆ ☆

USS *SPENCE* (DD-512)

Class: Fletcher.

Builder: Bath Iron Works, Bath, Maine.

Keel laid: May 18, 1942.

Launched: October 27, 1942.

Sponsor: Mrs. Eban Learned.

Commissioned: January 8, 1943; Lieutenant Commander H.J. Armstrong, USN, comdg.

Date of loss; December 18, 1944; Lieutenant Commander J.P. Andrea, USN, comdg.†

Location: Philippine Sea.

Awards: Presidential Unit Citation and eight battle stars.

USS Monaghan

Launched January 9, 1935
Lost December 18, 1944
Philippine Sea

ENSIGN JOHN R. MONAGHAN, USN
(1873–1899)

John R. Monaghan was born on March 26, 1873, in Chawelah, Washington. Upon graduating from the Naval Academy in June 1891, he reported on board the monitor USS *Monadnock* and later was ordered to the gunboat *Alert*.

Ensign Monaghan was serving on board the cruiser *Philadelphia* while she was in Apia, Samoa, during a native uprising in the spring of 1899. On April 1, he joined a landing party led by Lieutenant Van Horne Lansdale, in an effort to restore order among the natives. After the Samoans were disbanded, the small band of sailors was ambushed while returning to the ship, during which time Lieutenant Lansdale was wounded in the leg. Ensign Monagahn and two seamen, one being Norman E. Edsall, attempted to carry their wounded officer back to the ship. Despite his orders to leave him behind, they stood by him until they ran out of ammunition and were overpowered by the natives and killed.

Upon being accepted by the Navy, the USS *Monaghan* (DD-354) reported to the Commandant of Destroyer Squadrons, Atlantic Fleet, carrying out her training operations along the eastern seaboard, in Caribbean waters and in the North Atlantic. During the closing months of 1939 she was transferred to the Pacific Fleet

Anchored at Pearl Harbor and assigned as the ready-duty destroyer on December 7, 1941, *Monaghan* was preparing to get underway in the early morning to investigate a report of the sinking of a submarine outside the harbor by the destroyer *Ward* (DD-139). However, before she could slip her cable, all hell broke loose when scores of Japanese aircraft came winging in to blast the stationary American fleet in a surprise attack. *Monaghan* was underway at 0827, steaming out of the harbor, her guns spraying the skies with AA fire. Unfortunately, her crew did not enjoy the satisfaction of shooting down any of the raiders, but an alert lookout sighted a periscope, suspected to be a midget submarine attempting to sneak into the harbor during the main attack. Immediately the destroyer's captain turned his ship toward the intruder, struck it with a glancing blow, dropped two depth charges and sank it.

Having escaped the naval base unscathed, *Monaghan* remained on antisubmarine patrol duty for a week, guarding the approaches to Pearl Harbor. After replenishing her fuel supply, she joined up with a task force built around the carrier *Lexington*, which was delivering aircraft to the defenders of Wake Island. While returning to Pearl, *Monaghan* and her sister destroyers *Dale* (DD-353) and *Aylwin* (DD-355) made contact with a submarine. After several depth charges were dropped, an oil slick was sighted, followed by the submarine broaching the surface, only to sink immediately afterwards.

Monaghan operated in Hawaiian waters for a short time before she commenced escorting shipping between West Coast ports and Hawaii. This assignment continued until April 15, when she departed the Hawaiians for the South Pacific with her task force, again built around *Lexington*. Here she took part in the Battle of the Coral Sea and was later dispatched to search for the survivors from the destroyer *Sims* and the oiler USS *Neosho*. Due to an error in reporting their position, *Monaghan* was unable to locate them. However, the bomb-damaged *Neosho*, with 14 of *Sims'* survivors on board, was found by the USS *Henley*. Considered beyond salvage, the wreck was sunk by gunfire and torpedoes.

Upon her arrival at Pearl Harbor on May 26, *Monaghan* was promptly replenished with stores, ammunition and fuel, and two days later was underway to join in the decisive Battle of Midway. Screening the carrier *Enterprise* during this action, *Monaghan* was called upon to rescue several of the carrier's pilots who had been forced to ditch into the sea.

During the battle, the carrier *Yorktown* suffered several bomb hits that rendered her untenable. During salvage operations, *Monaghan* came alongside the stricken carrier to assist in fighting her fires and to take on her wounded. Unfortunately, two days after the battle (June 6), the Japanese submarine *I-168* penetrated the destroyer screen and sent four torpedoes streaking toward *Yorktown*. One struck the destroyer *Hammann*, which was alongside the carrier rendering assistance, and she sank in less than four minutes. The remaining torpedoes spelled *Yorktown's* doom, and she sank on the following morning.

In mid-June, *Monaghan* stood out of Pearl Harbor for operations in the North Pacific and off the Aleutian Islands. While on patrol she was damaged in a collision while steaming in a heavy fog. After effecting temporary repairs at Dutch Harbor, she steamed back to Pearl and, after permanent repairs were completed, escorted a convoy to the West Coast. Back in the South Pacific in mid-November, she had the misfortune to strike an underwater obstruction while entering Nouméa Harbor; which damaged her starboard propeller. Compelled to return to Pearl Harbor, she limped into port on one screw and was laid up for repairs until February 21, 1943.

Monaghan was back in the Aleutians in early March, where she became a unit of Task Group 16.6, built around the cruisers *Richmond* and *Salt Lake City*. On the 26th, the task group engaged with Vice Admiral Moshiro Hosogaya's battleship and cruiser force in a hotly contested battle off the Kormandorski Islands. What was unique about this battle, in World War II, was that no aircraft or submarines were involved. In other words, it was a real old-fashioned naval gun duel, fought in broad daylight, in a calm sea and at close quarters. Cruisers, battleships and destroyers traded shot for shot, torpedo for torpedo, zigzagging, feinting, and laying smoke screens in a slugfest that thundered on from 0840 until shortly after 1200.

Although the Americans were outnumbered and outgunned and, despite the *Salt Lake City's* having been crippled by two enemy projectiles, *Monaghan* and the destroyers *Bailey* (DD-492) and *Coghlan* (DD-606) charged headlong into the fray, firing their 5-inchers and letting fly with a brace of torpedoes at the enemy warships. After the war, a commander who had served on Hosogaya's flagship remarked: "I do not know how a ship could live through the concentration of firepower that was brought to bear upon the leading destroyer. . . . All three ships were literally smothered with shell splashes."

During the action, *Bailey* was hammered by three 8-inch shells. Temporarily knocked out of the fight, her repair parties had her back in operation and she was game to rejoin her sisters, only to be struck by a fourth 8-incher. Luckily, it was a dud and the spunky destroyer doggedly resumed her assault upon her opponents in spite of the maelstrom of bursting shells that were falling about her. When the destroyers reached the distance at which their torpedoes could be launched, all three of them flung a salvo of five and continued to flay their adversaries with their 5-inch batteries. Thanks to the alertness of the Japanese lookouts, the deadly fish were sighted streaking toward their ships, thus allowing their captains to take evasive action. All of the torpedoes missed.

Just before 1200, *Salt Lake City* regained power and commenced firing her 8-inchers at the enemy's ships. However, Hosogaya's vessels were running low on fuel and at 1204, to the astonishment of the Americans, he suddenly broke off the action, regrouped his fleet and hastily withdrew.

Having emerged from this action unharmed, *Monaghan* continued to carry out her operations in the Aleutian theater, serving on patrol duty and as an escort for incoming convoys en route to Dutch Harbor. On several occasions she was called upon to bombard enemy positions on Kiska and Attu islands. Then, during the early morning hours of June 22, *Monagahn's* radar made contact with an unidentified vessel off the southern coast of Kiska.

Ordering his ship to "General Quarters," and with the ship's radar locked in upon the target, her captain, Lieutenant Commander P.H. Horn, warily approached his quarry to about 2,500 yards. There were no American submarines known to be operating in the area, so the destroyer's guns were at the ready. As it happened, they had come upon the *I-7*.

At 0230, Captain Horn gave the order to fire. Tongues of orange-yellow flames belched out of *Monaghan's* 5-inch gun batteries, lighting up the jet-black seascape. In return, the destroyer was peppered with machine-gun bullets that pinged and clattered against her bridge and hull. For over ten minutes, both antagonists dueled each other, neither side sustaining serious damages. This was followed by a cat-and-mouse game as the opponents each attempted to jockey into an advantageous position.

At 0310, *Monaghan* opened fire again at a distance of 2,030 yards. The Japanese commander, utilizing *Monaghan's* gun flashes as a guide, scored a hit on her port bow with a 5.5-inch shell well above the waterline. Once again, a fierce gun duel ensued for another eight minutes until the *I-7* was staggered by a direct hit from one of the destroyer's 5-inchers. Still, the submarine's commander was determined to fight it out. However, Captain Horn broke off the action when he noticed that the *I-7* was on a heading toward the rocky shores of Kiska. Later, the submarine was discovered hard aground between two pinnacle rocks known as "The Twins," where her crew had demolished the vital machinery before abandoning her.

For the remainder of 1943, *Monaghan* carried out her operations in Hawaiian waters, serving as plane guard for incoming carriers and escorting a number of convoys from Hawaii to the West Coast. On several occasions she escorted shipping to the South Pacific and, in mid-November, covered the landings at Tarawa, prior to her returning to the U.S. coast.

Between February and late July, 1944, *Monaghan* was constantly on the move, taking part in the landings and strikes against New Guinea and the Marshall and Caroline islands, and on escort duty throughout the South and Central Pacific. In late July, the destroyer entered the Puget Sound Navy Yard, Washington, for a long-awaited overhaul and leave for her crew. After conducting her operations out of San Diego and undergoing a period of battle-readiness exercises, *Monaghan* stood out of San Diego for the war zone on November 11.

During the first two weeks of December, *Monaghan* was screening the Third Fleet, then operating in the Philippine Sea, while its carrier's aircraft staged their raids against choice Japanese airfields, important bases and staging areas throughout the Philippines. On the 17th, the fleet was scheduled to refuel; however, heavy seas and gusty winds made it difficult to carry out this task. Hence, fueling operations were postponed until the following day. During the night, the storm increased in velocity and fury, thereby making the second attempt utterly impossible. By 0800 on the following morning, the fleet was enmeshed in one of the fiercest typhoons ever recorded.

Being critically low on fuel, *Monaghan* was tossed about like a toy ship in the tempest. Similar to *Spence*, the actual time of her loss was never determined. Here, in part, is the testimony of one of her survivors, Watertender Second Class Joseph C. McCrane: "After a rough night with hardly getting any sleep, I climbed out of my bunk at about 0630 and went topside only to discover that the storm was worse than any of us had realized. The sea was so rough and the winds so strong, it was almost impossible to keep your balance, and it was extremely dangerous just to walk on the maindeck.

"My assistant, Third Class Watertender Len Bryan, and I went forward to sound the fuel tanks and found that we had between 29,000 to 30,000 gallons remaining. At about 1030, I was ordered to pump ballast into the two empty fuel tanks back aft. Since ballasting would take some time, I decided to wait in the engineer's living quarters. But by now the ship was rolling and pitching so heavily that the men agreed to go topside and take shelter in the after 5-inch gun mount. There were already several men in the mount and one of them was praying. The ship was taking anywhere from 60- to 70-degree rolls, and each time she rolled over on her beams end, the guy would cry out, 'Please dear Lord, bring her back! Don't let us down now!'

"We must have taken at least seven or eight heavy rolls to starboard when the ship finally rolled over on her side. As she was going over, the men tried to open the port door—this being difficult to accomplish due to its weight and the winds blowing against it. But eventually, we did get it open and managed to crawl out. Thankfully, none of the men had panicked, nor was there any confusion among them. They did the best they could to help their shipmates, especially Gunner's Mate Joe Guio who, without any thought for his own safety, was standing outside the hatch pulling everyone out."

Eventually, McCrane was thrown off the ship and into the swirling, churning tempest. In spite of the heaving seas, he succeeded in reaching a life raft with several men on board. Not long afterwards, a shocked, exhausted and nearly naked Joe Guio was hauled aboard. McCrane held on to him to keep him warm, and shortly afterwards the man lapsed into unconsciousness. Upon his awakening later, Guio asked if anyone could see anything. He thanked the man who had pulled him out of the water and then turned to McCrane, thanking him for keeping him warm. Later, McCrane testified at the inquest, "He laid his head back on my shoulder and dozed off. About 30 minutes later, a strange feeling came over me and I tried to wake him up, only to discover that he had died. I then told the other fellows about it and we decided to hold him a little longer before burying him. Twenty minutes later, we held our first burial at sea. We all said the Lord's Prayer as we lowered him into the sea."

For the next three days, the men in McCrane's raft were plagued by sharks, and two more died from exposure and their injuries. One poor soul was so delirious that he thought he saw land and houses; he jumped into the water and swam away into the darkness, never to return. At one time, an onion was seen floating close to the raft. As the men paddled toward it an 8-foot shark was seen hovering close to the morsel; the sailors decided that the creature could have it. Several times, ships and aircraft came within sight, but the survivors were not discovered.

At last, two search planes spotted the lone raft with its ragged and exhausted occupants. Within an hour of the sighting, the destroyer *Brown* had come to their rescue and the men were hauled to safety and carried below for medical treatment. There were six of them: the only survivors from the USS *Monaghan*.

☆ ☆ ☆

USS *MONAGHAN* (DD-354)

Class: Farragut.
Builder: Boston Navy Yard, Charlestown, Massachusetts.
Keel laid: November 21, 1933.
Launched: January 9, 1935.
Sponsor: Miss Mary F. Monaghan, niece of Ensign John R. Monagahn, USN.
Commissioned: April 19, 1935; Commander R.R. Thomson, USN, comdg.

Date of loss: December 18, 1944; Lieutenant Commander F.B. Garrett, USN,
    comdg.†
Location: Philippine Sea.
Awards: Twelve battle stars.

USS Hull

Launched January 31, 1934
Lost December 18, 1944
Philippine Sea

COMMODORE ISAAC HULL, USN
(1773–1834)

Born in Derby, Connecticut, on March 9, 1773, Isaac Hull was appointed Lieutenant in the U.S. Navy on March 9, 1798. During the quasi-war with France, while Executive Officer on the USS *Constitution,* he led a raiding party against a French fort at Porto Plata, Santo Domingo, where he and his men spiked its guns and made off with a prize vessel.

After several outstanding exploits during the war with the Barbary pirates, Hull further distinguished himself during the War of 1812 while in command of the *Constitution.* As he was cruising along the coast of New Jersey in July 1812, he was sighted by four British frigates, commanded by Admiral Blake, which commenced to pursue the lone American frigate. However, the winds failed, thus becalming Hull and the British warships.

The intrepid Hull then ordered two boats lowered with the ship's anchors on board. After rowing several yards ahead of the ship, the anchors were dropped. The ship's crew then hauled the vessel along on its anchors, away from the British. This backbreaking and Herculean feat continued for three days before the British sighted the cat's paws rippling across the sea. When the wind came up, Hull, already having his sails set, managed to escape.

On August 9, Captain Hull engaged with the British frigate HMS *Guerrière* in one of the classic sea battles of the war. When *Constitution* emerged victorious, she rightfully earned the nickname "Old Ironsides," after British cannonballs were seen to bounce off her hull without causing any severe damage.

Promoted to the rank of Commodore in 1823, Hull assumed command of the Washington and Boston navy yards, respectively, and went on to command both the Pacific and Mediterranean Squadrons. Upon retiring from active service, Commodore Hull made his home in Philadelphia and died there on February 13, 1843.

On completion of her shakedown trials, during which time she paid goodwill visits to ports in the British Isles, Portugal and the Azores, the USS *Hull* (DD-350) reported to the Commandant of the Pacific Fleet. Homeported at the destroyer base, San Diego, she participated in fleet maneuvers with the battle force and conducted her training operations along the California coast and in Hawaiian and Alaskan waters. On October 12, 1941, *Hull's* home port was shifted to Pearl Harbor and, at the time of the Japanese attack, she was moored alongside the destroyer tender *Dobbin*.

During the raid, *Hull* contributed her share of firepower against the attackers while her engineers labored to raise steam in an effort to get underway. Escaping from the cataclysmic raid unscathed, the destroyer joined up with several ships outside the harbor, hoping to engage with submarines that had been reported trying to enter the harbor

During the grim weeks that followed the attack, *Hull* took part in the hit-and-run strikes against the Japanese-held islands of Jaluit and Makin. Upon her return to Pearl Harbor in March, she was allocated to escorting shipping between Hawaii and West Coast ports for a period of three months.

On August 7, 1942, *Hull* covered the landings on Guadalcanal and Tulagi. On the following day, the Japanese retaliated with an all-out air assault against the invasion forces, but the fierce AA fire thrown up by the warships took its toll in aircraft, of which several were splashed by *Hull's* well-trained gunners. However, during one of the raids, the transport *George F. Elliot* was seriously bomb-damaged and crashed by a suicide plane. Her repair parties being unable to contain the fires or effect repairs, *Hull* was compelled to sink the fiery wreck later that evening.

Hull was then consigned to escort duty, screening resupply convoys between Espiritu Santo and Guadalcanal prior to returning to Pearl on October 20. Returning to the South Pacific in mid-November, *Hull* spent the remainder of the year operating with the battleship *Colorado*, safeguarding the vital supply lines between the United States, Australia and New Zealand. In early January 1943, she escorted a convoy to San Francisco, and upon her arrival entered the Mare Island Navy Yard, Vallejo, California, for alterations and repairs.

At the completion of her yard overhaul and battle-readiness exercises,

Hull went on to conduct her operations in the North Pacific. Arriving at Adak on April 16, 1943, she and her division operated with battleships and cruisers in these northern waters and took part in several bombardments on Attu and Kiska islands. On August 15, she covered the landings at Kiska, which were met without resistance from the Japanese. Upon "taking" the island, the landing force was astonished to discover that the enemy had successfully evacuated their troops two weeks earlier by submarines.

Following this assignment, *Hull's* operations were shifted to the South and Central Pacific, at which time she participated in the bombardments and landings on the Gilbert, Caroline and Marshall islands. On November 20, after the taking part in covering the landings on Makin, *Hull* escorted the empty cargo and troop ships to Pearl Harbor and from there stood out for San Francisco, arriving on December 21.

Throughout the remainder of December and into mid-January 1943, *Hull* participated in amphibious training exercises out of San Diego prior to returning to Pearl Harbor and then to the Central Pacific. On March 18, she bombarded the Mille Atoll, Truk, on April 29–30, and took part in the famous "Marianas Turkey Shoot" on June 19.

On August 25, *Hull* entered the Bremerton Navy Yard in Washington State for repairs and went on to carry out her training operations off the West Coast before returning to Pearl Harbor on October 23. From there, she covered a convoy to the Philippines, later joining up with Rear Admiral Halsey's Third Fleet, which was carrying out air strikes against Japanese airfields and military concentrations in the northern Philippines.

As was previously mentioned in the histories of *Spence* and *Monaghan*, *Hull* was one of the destroyers consumed by the ferocious typhoon of December 17–18. After sustaining a savage battering from the demonic sea and fierce winds, the doomed *Hull*, having lost steering control, became "locked in irons" in a monstrous trough. Despite every attempt by her captain, Lieutenant Commander James E. Marks, to keep her afloat, a strong gust of wind, recorded at 110 knots, finally leaned her well over on her beams end to 80 degrees. She never recovered.

Here, in part, *Hull's* captain, J.E. Marks, describes the terrifying situation that he and his crew had to contend with: "The seas were monstrous, the winds having reached well over 100 knots. I had served on several destroyers during my naval career and had witnessed many severe storms, primarily while on convoy duty in the North Atlantic, and believe that no wind or sea could have been worse than what I was now experiencing.

"As the seas grew worse, the motor whaleboat's bow was stove in and, later, was ripped from its davits and tossed into the sea. Several depth charges were yanked from the 'K' guns and were rolling across the deck, eventually dropping overboard. Because of the velocity of the wind, the smokestacks were under a terrific strain. At times, I felt that the bridge, which was taking such extreme punishment from the tons of water bashing the whole structure, would be torn off the ship.

"Shortly before 1200, the ship had withstood what I estimated to be the worst punishment that any storm could offer. She had just rolled over to 70 degrees, but thankfully recovered when a gust momentarily ceased. But now, the wind had reached up to 110 knots, its enormous force laying the *Hull* steadily on her starboard side and holding her down. The sea was beginning to surge in torrents into the ship's upper structure. I continued to remain on the bridge until the water flooded up to me, before stepping into the sea as she rolled over.

"Then I heard and could feel the concussion from the ship's boilers exploding, but did not feel any ill effects from the blasting. I then concentrated every effort to survive. What with the wind whipping the sea into a froth and the air full of salt spray and driving rain, I could hardly see but a few feet around me. Actually, I felt like a pea in pot of boiling water, being thrown and tossed up and down beneath the waves and being smashed about by their turbulence."

Three days later, Commander Marks, seven officers and 55 enlisted men were rescued by the USS *Tabberer*. Sadly, the remainder of *Hull's* crew were never found.

☆ ☆ ☆

USS *HULL* (DD-350)

Class: Farragut.
Builder: New York Navy Yard, Brooklyn, New York.
Keel laid: July 3, 1933.
Launched: January 31, 1934.
Sponsor: Miss Paricia L. Platt.
Commissioned: January 11, 1935; Commander R.S. Wentworth, USN, comdg.
Date of loss: December 18, 1944; Lieutenant Commander J.E. Marks, USN, comdg.
Location: Philippine Sea.
Awards: Ten battle stars

USS Halligan
Launched March 19, 1943
Lost March 26, 1945
Off Okinawa

REAR ADMIRAL JOHN HALLIGAN, USN
(1876–1934)

John Halligan was born in South Boston, Massachusetts, on May 4, 1876. Graduating from the Naval Academy at the head of his class in 1898, he reported on board the armored cruiser *Brooklyn* and continued to serve on her during the Spanish-American War. In World War I, he served as chief of staff to the Commander of U.S. Naval Forces in France. As a result of his outstanding performance in this assignment, he was awarded the Distinguished Service Medal.

After the armistice, he went on to serve as commanding officer of the battleship *Ohio,* and in 1925 became Chief of the Bureau of Engineering. Other assignments included commanding officer of the aircraft carrier *Saratoga* and Assistant to the Chief of Naval Operations in 1930. Later that year, he was promoted to the rank of Rear Admiral. In 1933, he served as Commander of Aircraft, and from there was commissioned Commandant of the 13th Naval District. While serving in this office, Rear Admiral Halligan died at Bremerton, Washington, after a brief illness, on December 11, 1934.

At the completion of her shakedown trials, the USS *Halligan* (DD-584) was one of several destroyers assigned to escort the battleship *Iowa,* which was embarked with President Franklin D. Roosevelt and other important officials to and from the historic Tehran Conference. At the completion of this mission, *Halligan* arrived at the Charleston Navy Yard on December 17, and four days later sailed for San Diego to join the Pacific Fleet.

When not engaged in escort work and patrol duty, *Halligan* participated in five major operations, including the landings and occupation of the Marshall and Marianas Islands, covering the landings at Leyte and Lingayen

Gulf (Philippine Islands) and at Iwo Jima. During her activities in the Philippines, she repelled a number of air attacks and was credited with the splashing of three Japanese aircraft. While lending fire support off Iwo Jima, her 5-inch batteries silenced a gun emplacement that had pinned down a detatchment of Marines.

After a brief respite from the war zone, *Halligan* departed Ulithi on March 21, 1945, in company with a bombardment force en route to Okinawa to soften up the enemy's defenses prior to the landings that were scheduled for April 1. Arriving at her fire support station off the southwestern coast of Okinawa on the 25th, she provided cover for the minesweepers while they performed their hazardous tasks close to the shore. Late in the afternoon on the following day, *Halligan* was ordered to patrol independently seven miles farther south. Then, just before she arrived at her patrolling station, tragedy struck when the destroyer rolled over a mine that detonated beneath her forward magazines.

The violent detonation blew upward and outward, sending a column of smoke, scalding steam, fire and water skyward some 200 feet in the air and across the seascape. Seaman First Class Harvey E. Metcalf, who was on board the *LSMR-194*, recalls that the *Halligan* had just crossed his ship's bow when a few seconds later she blew up. Before he and his shipmates were thrown to the deck from the tremendous shock wave, he witnessed several *Halligan* crewmen being flung up in the air and into the sea.

The severity of the explosion rent the length of *Halligan*, tossing the men about, throwing them off their feet and causing serious injuries, burns, contusions and broken bones. Finally, when the smoke had cleared, the entire forward section of the ship, including the bridge, the forward fire room and part of the forward engine room had completely disintegrated. Also missing were all hands who had been at their battle stations in that area, including her captain, Lieutenant Commander E.T. Grace.

Only two officers survived the disaster, one being Ensign R.L. Gardner, who did not suffer injuries, and the other the assistant engineering officer, Ensign B. Jameyson, who had, by some twist of fate, managed to escape the carnage and wreckage of the forward engine room a few seconds after the explosion. Unfortunately, he was suffering from burns on his face and had a broken arm.

A few seconds after the earthquake-like blast, Ensign Gardner, then at his battle station in one of the after 5-inch guns, made an attempt to communicate with the bridge. When the phone talker reported that there was nothing but silence in response to his calls, Gardner went forward to investigate. Seeing nothing but a curtain of billowing, black smoke and steam, he cautiously advanced, and was horrified to discover that the entire forward part of the ship was gone. Now finding himself commanding officer of the stricken *Halligan*, he swiftly organized all able-bodied personnel to search for the wounded and carry them back to the fantail. While the men were rendering whatever medical treatment was available, the repair gangs were attempting to carry out salvage operations. Coming to assist were the patrol boat *PC-1128* and the *LSMR-194*, which took on board *Halligan*'s wounded and stood by to receive the destroyer's survivors should she founder.

When it was concluded that the ship was beyond salvaging and was showing every indication of sinking, Ensign Gardner decided to abandon the battered hulk. Before leaving the ship, both ensigns and a chief petty officer made a thorough search. In doing so, they found a wounded man whose foot had been caught beneath a sheet of twisted steel. A cutting torch was quickly brought to the scene and the man was freed.

After the destroyer was abandoned, she drifted for 12 miles before piling up on a reef a short distance from the Okinawan shore. Lost with *Halligan* were 12 officers and 150 members of her crew.

Occasionally, the enemy fired upon the wreck, and throughout the years it withstood the battering of numerous storms until 1958, when her mangled, rusted remains were donated to the government of the Ryukyus Islands for scrap.

☆ ☆ ☆

USS *HALLIGAN* (DD-584)

Class: Fletcher.
Builder: Boston Navy Yard, Charlestown, Massachusetts.
Keel laid: November 9, 1942.
Launched: March 19, 1943.
Sponsor: Mrs. John Halligan, widow of Rear Admiral John Halligan, USN.
Commissioned: August 19, 1943; Commander C.E. Cortner, USN, comdg.
Date of loss: March 26, 1945; Lieutenant Commander E.T. Grace, USN, comdg.†
Location: Off Okinawa.
Awards: Six battle stars.

USS Bush

Launched October 27, 1942
Lost April 6, 1945
Off Okinawa

SECOND LIEUTENANT WILLIAM S. BUSH, USMC
(1789–1812)

William Sharp Bush was born sometime in 1789 at Wilmington, Delaware. Appointed Second Lieutenant in the United States Marine Corps on July 3, 1809, he was assigned to duty on board the frigate USS *Constitution*. While serving in her during the War of 1812, Lieutenant Bush was killed in action while boarding the HMS *Guerrière* on August 19, 1812. He was posthumously awarded a silver medal by the U.S. Congress.

After serving on escort duty between Alaska and West Coast ports, the USS *Bush* (DD-529) entered Pearl Harbor on December 4, 1943, and from there she plunged into action during the New Guinea campaign. In rapid succession, the feisty destroyer participated in nearly every major operation against Japanese forces from the Central Pacific to the shores of Okinawa.

On November 1, 1944, in the aftermath of the Leyte landings, *Bush* underwent five separate air attacks within a period of two hours while on patrol in Suragao Strait. At 0940, a torpedo plane was sighted bearing in on her, and was immediately taken under fire by the *Bush*'s sharp-shooting gunners. However, despite the fusillade of firepower that was flaying the oncoming plane, its pilot continued to slash through the wall of 20- and 40-mm shells, seemingly without harm, and unleashed his torpedo. As the plane veered to the right, it was finally blown out of the sky.

While the destroyer was evading the deadly torpedo, another intruder was seen closing in on her port side. Greeted by a maelstrom of AA fire, the pilot dropped his torpedo prematurely, thus allowing *Bush*'s skipper enough time to avoid it. In the meantime, this attacker, too, was dispatched into the sea.

At 0951, *Bush's* gunners were in action again, hammering away at a bomber that was suddenly sighted diving down on the ship. The pilot had already released his bomb, but it splashed and exploded harmlessly some 60 yards off the destroyer's starboard quarter. This plane, too, was shot down. An hour later, two more aircraft jumped the lone *Bush,* one of which was repelled; but the second plane continued to bore in. After dropping its torpedo, which was easily avoided, the plane then swept down the ship's starboard side, its rear gunner spraying the destroyer's decks with machine-gun fire that felled two of the ship's men.

After a 10-minute lull, two more bombers came screaming in. Close 5-inch bursts of flak caused the pilots to climb for the clouds. A few seconds later, one of them plunged out of the cloud bank and dropped its bomb, which *Bush's* captain dodged. Meanwhile, the ship's guns literally disintegrated the perpetrator, who crashed about 50 yards astern. At about 1110, the plucky *Bush* inflicted such heavy damage on another bomber that its pilot turned and fled for home before he could drop his torpedo.

The new year found *Bush* once more in action. On January 7, while she was screening an 850-ship convoy then en route to Lingayan Gulf, the ships were pounced upon by a flock of suicide aircraft. Owing to the heavy concentration of anti-aircraft fire from the escorts, none of the transports or cargo vessels were sunk or damaged. However, two Australian warships, plus the escort carrier *Manila Bay* and the destroyer escort *Stafford,* sustained serious damages.

On the 9th, *Bush* was lying off the northwestern coast of Luzon, providing fire support for Sixth Army as it staged its landings at Lingayan Gulf. Although the Army units landed with very little opposition, the fleet was busily employed fending off suicide aircraft, small craft and swimmers. During the initial landings, *Bush* chalked up another AA kill when she sent one of her attackers plunging into the sea. On D-Day plus two, *Bush* reunited still another suicide pilot with his ancestors.

Throughout the remainder of January, *Bush* cruised off the western coast of Luzon, during which time she sank three luggers and bombarded an ammunition depot at Rosario Harbor. At the completion of this mission, the destroyer retired to Leyte for upkeep and repairs, prior to embarking on her next objective: the landings on Iwo Jima.

During this operation, she silenced a number of gun emplacements and protected the transports against air and submarine attacks. After enemy resistance had crumbled, *Bush* was relieved and stood out for Leyte, to prepare for the assault against Okinawa.

Departing Leyte on March 27, *Bush* arrived at her radar picket station (No. 1) on the 30th, approximately 60 miles northeast of Okinawa, the first slice of the Japanese homeland to be attacked by U.S. ground forces. After being relieved by the USS *Pritchett* (DD-561), she entered Kerama Retto, a fairly safe anchorage southwest of the island, where slightly damaged ships underwent repairs. Here, *Bush* refueled, replenished stores, ammunition and carried out minor maintenance. But two days later, *Pritchett* was so badly mauled by a Kamikaze attack that Bush was hastily deployed to relieve the stricken destroyer. Then, on the afternoon of April 6, after two exhausting days and nights courageously defending herself against relentless air assaults, *Bush's* time ran out.

Earlier that morning, she had stood up to four separate air attacks, in which she shot down one of her assailants. Then, just before 1200, her vicious concentration of firepower had repulsed a fifth assault. At 1500, another flight closed in upon the *Bush* and swarmed around her like angry hornets. Fortunately, again, this attack was driven off; however, as the attackers fled, a lone fighter was sighted skimming low over the water and closing in fast on the vessel's starboard side. In spite of the intense AA fire and 5-inch shells bursting about it, this was one plane that would not be stopped.

The Kamikaze struck the ship at deck level between both stacks. Flaming gasoline shot upward with a whoosh. Firebrands showered across her whole amidships section, immolating several of the ship's crew. The aircraft's bomb penetrated into the after fire room, detonated and dislodged one of the forced draft blowers weighing over 4,000 pounds, blew it through the main deck and sent it catapulting into the air, where it smashed into the radar antenna and landed on the port wing of the bridge.

The explosion completely demolished both the after fire and forward engine rooms, resulting in the ship's losing all power. Thanks to quick action taken by her damage control parties, however, all the fires were extinguished. Meanwhile, the destroyer *Colhoun* (DD-801) and a salvage tug were on their way to lend assistance after receiving the paralyzed *Bush's* distress signal.

Upon *Colhoun's* arrival, her lookouts sighted another gaggle of fighters boring in on *Bush*. *Colhoun's* skipper, Commander George R. Wilson, swiftly interposed his ship between the disabled *Bush* and the oncoming flight of predators and scorched three of them. Then, at 1700, another horde of marauders plunged in, one of which crashed into *Colhoun*, another one slamming into *Bush*.

This second hit almost severed the *Bush* in two when the ammunition exploded in her after magazines. Right on the heels of this devastating crash, the now-reeling *Bush* staggered by a third Kamikaze. However, despite the seriousness of the blow, her captain, Commander R.E. Westholm, sincerely believed that his ship could be saved. Unfortunately, the sea, which had been steadily rising, was putting too much stress on *Bush's* already weakened hull, causing her to sag. As further swells followed, her damaged hull began to twist and corkscrew. Now knowing full well that his ship was doomed, Commander Westholm passed the order to abandon. Finally, at 1830, the valiant *Bush* split in half and slipped silently downward, out of sight. All during these attacks, *Colhoun* had stood by, taking a battering that would result in her own death.

During the night, although some of *Bush's* survivors had become separated, they were found by rescue craft on the following day. A total of 246 officers and men were rescued, of whom 42 were wounded. Lost with *Bush* were 87 officers and men, including her division commander, Commander J.S. Willis (ComDesDiv 48).

☆ ☆ ☆

USS *BUSH* (DD-529)

Class: Fletcher:
Builder: Bethlehem Steel Shipbuilding Co., San Francisco, California.
Keel laid: February 12, 1942.
Launched: October 27, 1942.
Sponsor: Miss Marion Jackson, great-great-grandniece of Second Lieutenant
    William S. Bush, USMC.
Commissioned: May 10, 1943; Commander W.F. Peterson, USN, comdg.
Date of loss: April 6, 1945; Commander R.E. Westholm, USN, comdg.
Location: Off Okinawa.
Awards: Seven battle stars.

USS Colhoun

Launched April 10, 1944
Lost April 6, 1945
Off Okinawa

REAR ADMIRAL EDMUND R. COLHOUN, USN
(1821–1897)

Edmund Ross Colhoun was born in Chambersburg, Pennsylvania, on May 6, 1821. Appointed Midshipman on April 1, 1839, he went on to serve under Commodores Connor and Perry during the war with Mexico, and participated in the attacks against Alvarado and Tobasco.

During the Civil War, he served in both the Union's North and South Atlantic Blockading Squadrons. While in command of the monitor USS *Weehawken,* he was highly commended by Admiral Farragut for his actions in the bombardment and capture of Fort Fisher, North Carolina between December 1864 and January 1865.

With the ending of the war, Commander Colhoun was advanced to the rank of Captain; from 1874 to 1875 he commanded the South Pacific Station, and later the Mare Island Navy Yard, Valejo, California (1877–81). As Rear Admiral, Colhoun retired from active service on May 5, 1883. He died on February 17, 1897.

Upon the completion of her battle-readiness exercises off the coast of California, the USS *Colhoun* (DD-801) arrived at Pearl Harbor on October 10, 1944. For the next several weeks, the destroyer carried out patrol duty thoughout the Hawaiian Islands and was often called upon to serve as plane guard for carriers as well as escort for incoming convoys.

After serving with various task forces, *Colhoun* was struck by a shell from a Japanese shore battery while bombarding Iwo Jima on March 1, 1945. One man was killed and 16 others wounded from a hit at the base of her No. 2 stack. Damage inflicted upon the destroyer included the wrecking of one of her forced-draft blowers in the after fire room, plus shrapnel puncturing her torpedo air flasks, which, in turn, exploded and caused further damage to her torpedo mount and the torpedo workshop below. Detached from her task group, *Colhoun* sailed to Saipan for repairs.

With repairs completed, *Colhoun* stood out from Saipan en route to Okinawa, where on April 1 she assisted in shore bombardment missions and served as a radar picket ship. On April 6, after successfully repulsing 11 separate air attacks without suffering any damage, she picked up the tail-end of a distress signal from the USS *Bush*, which was requesting assistance after being severely damaged by a Kamikaze.

Colhoun's skipper, Commander George R. Wilson, the same George R. Wilson who had commanded and lost the ill-fated destroyer USS *Chevalier* (DD-451) off Vela Lavella in October 1943, wasted no time and ordered full speed ahead. Digging in her heels, *Colhoun* raced to the scene, arriving just in time to interpose herself between the damaged *Bush* and a headlong rush of fresh suiciders bent on blasting the destroyer to the bottom. Thanks to the quick action taken by *Colhoun's* gunners, three of the attackers were swiftly eliminated, thus discouraging the remainder of the pilots from approaching any closer.

Then, at 1700, a swarm of 10 to 12 aircraft was sighted bolting toward the destroyers, with three planes choosing *Colhoun* as their prime target. The first attacker slashed through a wall of 20- and 40-mm fire before a 5-inch shell burst sent it crashing in between the ships in a thundering explosion. Although the other two did not attack, three additional assailants were sighted approaching at different angles, one of which was sent in flames into the sea. Off the port quarter, the second plane was hit and smacked into the water, and the third aircraft was driven off. While the sailors were fully occupied with this last assault, a fourth plane, unseen, had skimmed in low, the pilot determined to end his own life on *Colhoun's* admidships. The aircraft crashed into a 40-mm gun tub and exploded into a ball of fire, scattering wreckage and flames across the destroyer.

The aircraft's engine and bomb plunged through the deck, its bomb detonating in the after fire room, causing the boilers to explode and killing all hands in that space. Fragments from the bomb also pierced the forward bulkhead and flew into the forward engine room, causing the ship to lose electrical power and (temporarily) its steering control.

After this strike, the raiders regrouped and three more bandits plunged in for the kill. Two were quickly splashed, but the third managed to dive through the heavy mantle of AA fire and crashed into the starboard whaleboat. The aircraft's bomb then penetrated through the main deck and exploded in the forward fire room, blowing up its boilers and breaking the *Colhoun's* keel. The violent blow had torn a hole in her hull some 20 feet long and 4 feet wide below the waterline, flooding the space and starting oil and electrical fires. Swathed in a heavy cloud of smoke and scalding steam, the now-crippled destroyer sloughed to a wallowing halt. Firefighters and damage control parties rushed to the scene in an attempt to stem the flooding and douse the flames. Although the situation was quickly brought under control, another attack was in the offing, three more suiciders hurling themselves toward the now-paralyzed *Colhoun*.

With her electrical power knocked out, her gunners were compelled to fire their weapons by local, or manual, control, Yet despite this disadvantage, the gun crews succeeded in downing one plane and caused the second attacker to retire after dropping a premature torpedo. But the third aircraft succeeded in cutting through the dense fabric of AA fire and crashed his plane headlong into the base of No. 2 stack.

A deluge of flaming gasoline now showered *Colhoun's* superstructure and cascaded belowdecks, virtually cremating everyone who was unable to escape the conflagration. The plane's bomb was jarred loose and skidded across the O-1 deck, dropped onto the maindeck, fell overboard and exploded. The concussion from the detonation blasted another 3-foot hole in the ship's hull beneath the waterline, causing additional flooding in the already damaged after fire room.

Commander Wilson had faced disaster once before, on the *Chevalier*, and he was not about to lose another destroyer if he could help it! Subsequently, all hands pitched in tenaciously topside and belowdecks, applying every method available in an effort to save their ship. All topside weight was reduced by jettisoning depth charges, torpedoes and all unnecessary gear. Belowdecks, holes were plugged, weakened bulkheads were shored up and portable suction pumps—handy billies—were used to pump out flooded compartments.

Unfortunately, in spite of all the excruciating and strenuous labor that the crew could muster, the battle-ravaged and smoldering *Colhoun* was steadily settling by the stern. Then a lone aircraft was seen boring in. Quickly taken under fire, it burst into flames, but then plummeted into the bridge, thus sounding the death knell for the die-hard Tin Can. Still, Commander Wilson retained a salvage crew, even as he ordered the rest of the men and the wounded to be transferred over to the landing craft *LCS-48*.

By 1900, several rescue craft had arrived and were searching the waters for survivors from the *Bush*. The destroyer *Cassin Young* (DD-739) eased alongside *Colhoun* to render assistance and attempted to take the ship in tow. The stricken destroyer's water-logged hull put too much of a strain on the towline, however, causing it to part. To make matters much more difficult, the seas had begun to rise and were getting increasingly worse. Yet, regardless of the adverse conditions facing the repair crew, they continued to toil without letup. Working with only battle lanterns and flash lights, they continued to shore up her buckling bulkheads and strived to pump out the flooded spaces until about 2230, when a rash of electrical fires broke out. Without the means to contain them, the disheartened but brave crews were forced to give up the ghost. Reluctantly, Commander Wilson had no other choice but to order his ship abandoned.

At about 2300, the *Cassin Young* came alongside and received *Colhoun's* bedraggled and battle-weary crew. By now, the *Colhoun* was reduced to a smoldering ruin, listing heavily to starboard, the waves sizzling as they lapped alongside her white-hot hull. Shortly after her captain left the destroyer, she shuddered and screeched agonizingly as she began to break up. To speed her to the bottom, the *Cassin Young* dispatched the gallant *Colhoun* with gunfire.

Considering the extreme punishment *Colhoun* had endured, the human casualties were exceptionally light. Thirty-two officers and crewmen went down with the ship, and out of the 295 who survived only 21 were wounded, although two of them later died.

☆ ☆ ☆

USS *COLHOUN* (DD-801)

Class: Fletcher.
Builder: Todd Pacific Shipyards, Inc. Seattle, Washington.
Keel laid: August 3, 1943.
Launched: April 10, 1944.
Sponsor: Captain Kathryn K. Johnson, WAAC, great-grandniece of Rear
    Admiral Edmund R. Colhoun, USN.
Commissioned: July 8, 1944; Commander George R. Wilson, USN, comdg.
Date of loss: April 6, 1945; Commander George R. Wilson, USN, comdg.
Location: Off Okinawa.
Awards: One battle star.

USS Mannert L. Abele

Launched April 23, 1944
Lost April 12, 1945
Off Okinawa

LIEUTENANT COMMANDER MANNERT L. ABELE, USN
(1903–1942)

Mannert Lincoln Abele was born in Quincy, Massachusetts, on July 11, 1903, and enlisted in the Navy on August 12, 1920. Appointed Midshipman in June 1922, he was commissioned Ensign upon his graduation from the U.S. Naval Academy in June 1926.

After graduating from the Submarine Training School, New London, Connecticut in 1929, he went on to serve in several classes of submarines and, prior to World War II, commanded the submarines *R-13* and *S-31*. Advanced to the rank of Lieutenant Commander on December 1, 1940, he assumed command of the USS *Grunion* (SS-216) at her commissioning on April 1, 1942.

Ordered to the submarine base at Pearl Harbor, the *Grunion* departed New London on May 24. En route to the Panama Canal, she rescued 16 survivors from the U.S. Army Transport *Jack*, which had been sunk by a German U-boat. After discharging the rescued men at Coco Solo, Panama, *Grunion* transited the canal and proceeded on to Pearl Harbor. On June 30th, Lieutenant Commander Abele eased the *Grunion* out of Pearl to commence his first and last war patrol in the western Aleutians.

During his patrols off Kiska, he sank two patrol boats, but owing to the lack of enemy shipping throughout the month of July, he was ordered back to Dutch Harbor, Alaska. Unfortunately, after receiving these orders, *Grunion* was never seen or heard from again. After several intensive days of fruitless air and sea searches among the Aleutian Islands, rescue operations were canceled. On August 16, *Grunion* and her crew were listed as missing and presumed lost.

After the war, captured Japanese documents indicated that at the time of *Grunion*'s disappearance, no Japanese ASW attacks were reported off Kiska or in the area of the Aleutians. Hence, to this day, the cause of *Grunion's* loss remains a mystery. Lieutenant Commander Mannert L. Abele was posthumously awarded the Navy Cross.

The USS *Mannert L. Abele* (DD-733) arrived at Pearl Harbor on November 17, 1944, and, after the completion of an intensive, grueling two-week period of battle-readiness exercises, she stood out for the western Pacific, escorting a convoy en route. Two weeks later, she returned to the Pearl Harbor Navy Yard, where she received the latest and most highly specialized radio and radar equipment. Upon the completion of radar picket training, *Mannert L. Abele* departed Pearl on January 27, 1945, for the war zone—to participate in the invasion of Iwo Jima.

Throughout the Iwo Jima campaign, the destroyer was kept busy providing shore bombardment against enemy gun emplacements and pockets of resistance. Other assignments included radar picket patrols and protecting the supply ships and transports against air and submarine attacks. On March 10, *Abele* was relieved and proceeded on to Ulithi, where she was replenished and made preparations for the landings on Okinawa.

On March 24, *Abele* participated in the pre-invasion bombardment of Okinawa and covered UDT operations off the Okinawan beaches. After lending fire support during the initial landings on April 1, the destroyer reported to her radar picket station. On the 3rd, she was attacked by three aircraft, two of which were quickly shot down. Relieved on the 5th, she returned to the transport area and on the following day shot down a twin-engined bomber.

On the 7th, she joined up with Task Force 54 to intercept a special attack force composed of the super-battleship IJN *Yamato,* a cruiser and eight destroyers. Sighted by the task force's aircraft, the mini-armada was ripped apart by torpedoes, bombs and strafings. The enemy lost six ships, including the 72,000-ton giantess *Yamato,* and the battered remnants of the fleet barely got back to Japan.

On April 12, while on radar picket station No. 4, just 70 miles northwest of Okinawa, *Mannert L. Abele* was torn asunder by a Kamikaze and blasted to the bottom by a new weapon known as the "Oka" rocket. The missile, manned by a single pilot and carrying a warhead packed with 2,645 pounds of nitro-tri-anasol, was transported to its destination by a mother aircraft and released. The pilot then cut in the missile's three rocket engines and aimed it toward his target at a then-unheard-of speed of 500 mph. It didn't take long for the Americans to nickname these nefarious little horrors "Bakas," which, translated into English, means "crazy" or "fool."

At 1445, three dive bombers flung themselves into a vicious hail of AA fire from the *Mannert L. Abele,* and two tumbled into the sea in flames before they could inflict any damage. The third suicider, having sustained numerous hits, attempted to dive into a landing craft, but crashed several yards from the ship. Fifteen minutes later, a flock of 15 to 25 aircraft were swarming around the destroyer and her consorts, but the intense anti-aircraft fire hurled up at the assailants kept them at bay. Only one was daring enough to close in, but, after being stung by several rounds of 20- and 40-mm shells, he too cleared the area.

Then, at about 1440, three fighters dashed in, two of them soon disintegrating under fire like so much flaming confetti. But the third attacker, a Zero, continued to bore in. In spite of the maelstrom of AA fire and 5-inch shell bursts that blossomed about it, and despite transforming en route into a virtual mass of wreckage trailing a heavy plume of black smoke, the Japanese plane crashed into the starboard side of *Mannert L. Abele* abaft of No. 2 stack. The bomb it carried penetrated through the maindeck and exploded in the after engine room with a tremendous downward force, breaking the ship's keel and propeller shaft and killing nine men. About one minute later, a Baka bomb was sighted to starboard, skimming just above the water and estimated to be traveling at a speed of 400 to 450 mph. Four 20-mm cannons were still firing on the rocket when it hit the ship in the forward fire room with a thunderous explosion. The impact of the detonation, in concert with her boilers exploding, jolted *Abele* from stem to stern and broke her keel for the second time. Immediately afterwards, she began to sag and settle.

The force of the explosion had killed and maimed several of her crew and had blown many others overboard. One of them, Lieutenant George L. Way, was close to the ship, and although she was still slogging along at about seven knots, he managed to grasp hold of a length of line that was dangling over the rail to haul himself on board. In spite of his groggy condition, he rounded up several men and ordered them to cut all the life rafts, netting and boats loose and launch them into the sea. From there, he went on to search for stragglers.

By this time, *Abele's* captain, Commander A.E. Parker, had passed the order to abandon ship, which was now going under fast. Still, Lieutenant Way continued to search for any stragglers and wounded. In doing so, he discovered that the door to the piloting room had been so badly warped that it could not be opened from the inside. Finding a crowbar from a nearby repair locker, he succeeded in prying the door open, thus saving the lives of all hands trapped in that space. Then, as he was making his way down the maindeck, he heard a clanging noise coming from the forward engine room hatch. Owing to its cover being twisted, the men could not loosen the dogs. With the help of Electrician's Mate Second Class Henry S. Paulman, Lieutenant Way was able to pry the hatch cover open, and out of the flooding, dark, steam-filled depths of the engine room crawled ten oil-smeared but thankful engineers, including the Chief Engineer, Lieutenant J.J. Hoblitzell, III.

With the destroyer's main deck now well awash, these dazed and bedraggled men made a dash for the rail and dove over the side. A few moments later, the battle-damaged *Mannert L. Abele* broke in half and sank.

While the support vessels, commonly called "pall bearers," were closing in to pick up the *Abele's* survivors, a number of enemy aircraft began to drop their bombs and strafe the men in the water and the rescue craft. When the skies were clear of marauders, the *LSMs 190* and *189* resumed their rescue operations.

Out of a crew of 336 officers and men, a total of 82 perished with the *Mannert L. Abele* or were killed in the water by strafing aircraft and bombs. Of those who survived, 32 were wounded.

☆ ☆ ☆

USS *MANNERT L. ABELE* (DD-733)

Class: Allen M. Sumner.
Builder: Bath Iron Works, Bath, Maine.
Keel laid: December 9, 1943.
Launched: April 23, 1944.
Sponsor: Mrs. Mannert L. Abele, widow of Lieutenant Commander Mannert L. Abele, USN.
Commissioned: July 4, 1944; Commander A.E. Parker, USN, comdg.
Date of loss: April 12, 1945; Commander A.E. Parker, USN, comdg.
Location: Off Okinawa.
Awards: Two battle stars.

USS Pringle

Launched May 2, 1942
Lost April 16, 1945
Off Okinawa

VICE ADMIRAL JOEL R.P. PRINGLE, USN
(1873–1932)

Born in Georgetown, South Carolina, on February 4, 1873, Joel
Roberts Poinsett Pringle was appointed to the Naval Academy in
1888 and commissioned Ensign in 1892. Prior to his advancement
to Vice Admiral in 1932, he served with distinction both at sea and
ashore, as commanding officer of the destroyer *Perkins* (DD-26),
screw steamer *Dixie* and battleship *Idaho*, as well as commander of
Battleship Division 3, Battle Force.

For his outstanding performance while serving as commanding
officer of the USS *Melville* (AD-2) and as Chief of Staff of Destroyer
Flotillas during World War I, he was awarded the Distinguished
Service Medal. He then went on to serve as Commandant of
Battleships, Battle Forces and the Naval War College, Newport,
Rhode Island. After his retirement he resided in San Diego,
California, where he died on September 25, 1932.

Upon the completion of her battle-readiness exercises, USS *Pringle* (DD-
477) joined a Halifax-bound convoy in the mid-Atlantic on January 1,
1943. Upon her return to the United States, she underwent voyage repairs
and on February 6 was assigned to the Pacific Fleet.

Prior to proceeding to the South Pacific, *Pringle* carried out extensive
battle exercises off the coast of California and in Hawaiian waters until
mid-May. Arriving at Guadalcanal on May 30, the destroyer was immediately assigned to patrolling duties in the Solomons. She then went on to participate in the bombardments of the Shortland Islands (6/29), the shelling of
a Japanese airfield on Munda (7/15) and, on the night of July 17–18, while
in company with her sister destroyers *Saufley* (DD-465) and *Waller* (DD-

466), she engaged with and damaged three enemy destroyers with gunfire and torpedoes. During the shoot-out, an aircraft attempted to intervene, but was shot down by *Pringle's* AA fire.

Other actions included up to eight sea/air engagements and numerous shore bombardments against Japanese installations throughout the Solomon Islands, into early January 1944. During that period, she sank three landing barges, damaged several others and shot down one aircraft.

In late January, *Pringle* entered Sydney, Australia, where her crew enjoyed a few days of shore leave and the hospitality of the citizens of that city. From there, *Pringle* went on to carry out her operations with various task forces during their sweeps through the central Pacific, taking part in the strikes against the Marshall, Caroline and Marianas Islands. In late September, she returned stateside for shipyard repairs and alterations at the Mare Island Navy Yard, Vallejo, California. Repairs completed, *Pringle* was back in action in Philippine waters in mid-November. On the night of the 27th–28th of that month, she participated in the bombardment of Ormoc Bay, Leyte, where she splashed one aircraft.

From December 27 to 30, *Pringle* came under a series of extremely violent air attacks while escorting a resupply convoy to Mindoro. Although several ships in the convoy were sunk or damaged, *Pringle* succeeded in shooting down two planes. On the 30th, however, the destroyer was hit on her after deckhouse by a suicide aircraft that killed 11 of her crew and wounded 20 others. One 40-mm gun mount and two of her after 5-inch gun mounts were wrecked in this attack.

Upon completion of repairs, *Pringle* took part in the landings on Iwo Jima, and remained in the area, providing shore fire support and screening the transports and cargo ships against submarine and air attacks. Relieved from this assignment on March 1, *Pringle* arrived at Ulithi and made preparations for the upcoming landings on Okinawa.

After serving as a fire support ship off the Okinawan coast, the destroyer was assigned to serve as a radar picket ship on April 15. On the following day, the skies were swarming with Kamikaze aircraft. On this date, *Pringle,* in company with the destroyer/minelayer *Hobson* and two patrol craft, was on radar picket station No. 14, approximately 80 miles northwest of Okinawa. At about 0900, a "bandit" was picked up on her radar.

The plane, skimming low over the water, plunged through a vicious cyclone of hot steel and lead that nearly sheared off one of its wings, causing it to crash into the sea in a violent explosion. After a ten-minute breather, three more planes were seen cavorting about the ships, skillfully weaving and feinting about the area like elusive butterflies, hoping to confuse the ships' gunners. Eventually, one of the pilots decided to end this aerial ballet and closed in for the kill, hell-bent for the *Pringle*.

In an effort to allow most of his gunners to bear on the approaching Kamikaze, her skipper, Lieutenant Commander J.L. Kelley, Jr., attempted to change course, but the ship was unable to answer her helm fast enough. The Japanese pilot, despite his plane being virtually ripped to shreds, hurtled through a mesh of AA fire and plunged into the *Pringle*'s superstructure abaft No. 1 stack. The destroyer was rocked by a monstrous, fiery explosion.

There was hardly a second's pause before the ship was further shattered when the 1,000-pound bomb that the plane was carrying detonated in the forward fire room and engine room. Now the ship's keel was broken, both stacks were knocked askew and all power was instantly lost.

At the time of the attack, Yeoman Second Class William L. Herman was manning his battle station as a loader in No. 3 5-inch gun mount, just aft of No. 2 stack and the after bank of torpedo tubes. He vividly remembers that the shock from the plane's crashing and the violent explosion from the bomb tossed the men about in the gun mount, which resulted in his suffering a bad cut on his right thigh. Upon opening the door of the mount, many men were seen in the water; and the ship by this time was beginning to jackknife. Realizing that *Pringle* was going under, the gun crew left their mount and hastily leaped into the sea.

With the sea pouring into her forward engineering spaces, and smothered in a heavy blanket of black smoke and scalding steam, the battered *Pringle* broke in two with her engines, machinery and men spilling into the roiling waters. Emerging dazedly from the burning wreckage stumbled her maimed, burned and oil-smeared crewmen, who then jumped over the side. Five minutes after the Kamikaze struck, all that remained of the *Pringle* were her survivors thrashing about in a sea of glutinous oil, strewn with debris and flotsam.

The *Hobson* and the two patrol craft then closed in to pick up *Pringle*'s survivors and by 1200 had rescued 285 officers and men—more than half of whom were suffering from wounds and burns. A final muster revealed that 62 members of the ship's crew had perished with the *Pringle*.

☆ ☆ ☆

USS *PRINGLE* (DD-477)

Class: Fletcher.
Builder: Charleston Navy Yard, Charleston, South Carolina.

Keel laid: July 31, 1941.
Launched: May 2, 1942.
Sponsor: Mrs. John D. Kane.
Commissioned: September 15, 1942; Lieutenant Commander H.O. Larson,
    USN, comdg.
Date of loss: April 16, 1945; Lieutenant Commander J.L. Kelley, USN, comdg.
Location: Off Okinawa.
Awards: Ten battle stars.

USS Little

Launched May 22, 1944
Lost May 3, 1945
Off Okinawa

CAPTAIN GEORGE LITTLE, USN
(1754–1809)

George Little was born on April 10, 1754, in Marshfield, Massachusetts. He was appointed First Lieutenant in 1779 while serving on the Massachusetts ship *Protector*, which shortly afterwards engaged in a fierce running battle against the British ship HMS *Thames*. In a later confrontation, Little was captured and imprisoned, but soon managed to escape.

Placed in command of the Massachusetts ship *Winthrop*, he went on to capture two British privateers, the armed brig HMS *Miriam*, and several other smaller vessels. On March 4, 1799, he was commissioned Captain in the infant U.S. Navy and assumed command of the frigate *Boston*. During the quasi-war with France, his distinguished naval career was further enhanced by his capture of the French brig *Le Berceau* and seven other ships. Captain Little died after a brief illness at Weymouth, Massachusetts on July 22, 1809.

At the completion of her battle-readiness exercises off the coast of California and in Hawaiian waters, the USS *Little* (DD-803) proceeded to the western Pacific to provide shore bombardment during the Iwo Jima landings on February 19, 1945. Relieved from this assignment on the 24th, she was ordered to return March 4 to train her guns on enemy weapons emplacements that were hindering the advance of the ground forces. With Iwo Jima finally secured, *Little* departed for Saipan in order to prepare for the landings on Okinawa.

On April 1, *Little* was lying off the coast of Okinawa with her 5-inch batteries pounding enemy pockets of resistance and screening the off-loading transports and cargo vessels against Japanese air and submarine attacks.

Aside from providing shore bombardment in support of the troops, the destroyer also served as a radar picket ship (April 20–24). During those four days, she experienced one night and several daylight air attacks without sustaining any damage. On the 28th, after replenishing, *Little* arrived at her radar picket station (No. 5) about 60 miles east of Okinawa. During the last days of April and up to May 3, foul weather conditions—much to the relief of the destroyer picket crews—kept the dreaded Kamikaze pilots grounded.

Although the morning of May 3 was heavily overcast, the skies began to gradually clear and the men braced themselves for the anticipated onslaught of fanatical Kamikazes. Operating with *Little* were the destroyer minelayer *Aaron Ward* (DM-34) and four "pall bearers." Constantly on the alert, all lookouts, gun crews and non-watch standers scanned the skies and horizon hour after hour, for it would only be a matter of time before the maniacal suicide pilots would strike. At 1415, several blips began to speckle the radar scanners, but thankfully nothing materialized. Then, at 1813, about 20 Kamikazes were picked up on the radar screens and also sighted by the ships' lookouts. By 1859, the attackers were bolting headlong toward *Little* and her consorts.

Tracers stitched the skies, and several of the planes were blown out of the air by 5-inch shells armed with proximity fuses. Several others broke apart under 20- and 40-mm fire. However, the remainder of the pilots seemed undeterred and continued to throw themselves into the wall of AA fire. At 1841, *Aaron Ward* took the first Kamikaze hit, and less than a minute later a suicider struck *Little* on her port side. Four minutes later, three more planes, in rapid succession, came crashing into the destroyer's amidships section.

The volcanic eruptions crushed her superstructure, broke her keel and opened three of her engineering spaces to the sea. Men, airplane parts and a potpourri of deck gear and debris shot skyward and across the surrounding water. Smothered in a cloud of black, roiling smoke, scalding superheated steam and blazing gasoline fires, *Little* was further shattered by internal explosions. In less than two minutes, at 1855, the stalwart destroyer broke in two and slid beneath the surface, engulfed in a pillar of smoke and steam.

In the meantime, the fighting *Aaron Ward* was taking a brutal thrashing. Having been struck by five suicide aircraft, her rudder was damaged and the cable to her steam whistle severed. Consequently, the wounded vessel continued to steam in circles around *Little's* survivors, her whistle sounding off at full blast.

Considering the extensive damage that *Little* had sustained, and sinking as swiftly as she did, it was amazing that only 30 of her personnel were lost with the ship.

☆ ☆ ☆

USS *LITTLE* (DD-803)

Class: Fletcher.
Builder: Seattle-Tacoma Shipbuilding Co., Seattle, Washington.
Keel laid: September 13, 1943.
Launched: May 22, 1944.
Sponsor: Mrs. Russell F. O'Hara.
Commissioned: August 19, 1944; Commander Haddison Hall, USN, comdg.
Date of loss: May 3, 1945; Commander Haddison Hall, USN, comdg.
Location: Off Okinawa.
Awards: Two battle stars.

USS Luce

Launched March 6, 1943
Lost May 4, 1945
Off Okinawa

REAR ADMIRAL STEPHEN B. LUCE, USN
(1827–1917)

Stephen B. Luce was born on March 25, 1827, in New York City, and entered the Navy on October 29, 1841. Highly respected by his fellow officers, he was proficient in many fields, including seamanship, strategy and naval education. Prior to the outbreak of the Civil War, he assisted in astronomical work at the Naval Observatory in Washington, DC, and participated in surveying the waters of the eastern seaboard. In 1862, while serving as head of the Department of Seamanship at the Naval Academy, he authored one of the first seamanship textbooks to be studied by naval cadets.

At his request, Luce was assigned to sea duty and for a brief time served with the North Atlantic Blockading Squadron. Later, he assumed command of the monitor USS *Nantucket* and participated in the siege of Charleston, South Carolina. He went on to command the monitors *Sonoma*, *Pontiac* and *Canandaigua* and, at the end of the war, was commissioned as superintendant of the Naval Academy, a post he had held from 1865 to 1868.

Throughout the 1870s Luce organized the Navy's apprentice training program for seamen and petty officers, and served in various ships. Between 1878 and 1881, Captain Luce was inspector of training ships and, as Commodore, commanded the U.S. Naval Training Command from 1881 to 1884.

Due to the need to educate officers in naval strategy, the Naval War College at Newport, Rhode Island, was established on October 6, 1884, with Commodore Luce its first administrator. He was also instrumental in starting the U.S. Naval Institute and its *Proceedings* magazine. Commodore Luce retired on March 25, 1889. Residing in Newport, he died there on July 28, 1917.

The USS *Luce* (DD-522) departed New York on September 5, 1943, for Bremerton, Washington, arriving there on October 28. On November 1, she stood out for Pearl Harbor, escorting the carrier *Enterprise* en route. After conducting gunnery exercises in Hawaiian waters for two weeks, *Luce* left Pearl on the 24th for operations in the Northern Pacific, a tour of duty that would continue into August 1944. Here, she was primarily assigned to ASW patrols throughout the Aleutian Islands.

Within those nine months, *Luce* took part in the bombardment of Paramushiru Island in the Kurile chain on February 3, during which time she sank a 2,000-ton cargo ship. On June 13, she returned to the Kuriles and took part in a bombardment mission against the island of Matsuwa and, on the 26th, hit Paramushiru for the second time. In mid-August, *Luce* arrived at San Francisco and underwent a shipyard overhaul before reporting to the western Pacific.

Arriving at Pearl Harbor on August 31, *Luce* remained there to conduct her battle-readiness exercises and to serve as a plane guard for the new carriers that were en route to the war zone. Then, in late September, she sailed for the South Pacific, on October 1 standing out from Manus Island for the invasion of Leyte in the Philippines. On October 20, *Luce* supported the landings by providing shore fire, and screened the offloading transports against enemy air attacks.

Throughout the remainder of 1944, *Luce* served as a convoy escort between Leyte, Manus Island and New Guinea—until January 9, 1945, when she covered the landings at Lingayan Gulf, Luzon. On the 11th, while covering several LSTs, her group was attacked by a flock of aircraft, one of which was splashed by her gunners. On the 25th, she joined in the bombardment of enemy supply and ammunition dumps at San Felipe and San Antonio. From there, she sailed for Minduro for replenishment before escorting a resupply convoy to Lingayan Gulf.

On March 24, Luce departed Leyte to take part in the landings on Okinawa and to serve on radar picket duty. On the morning of May 4, she was patrolling on Radar Picket Station No. 5, approximately 50 miles east of Okinawa, when a swarm of Kamikazes rushed into her sector from the north. Despite the intervention of the combat air patrol, several of the raiders got through and made a mad, headlong dash for *Luce*.

It was about 0750 when *Luce's* guns were furiously banging away at the oncoming flock. One plane was downed close to the ship's port side forward, but the violent impact from its exploding bomb caused the ship to lose power. Immediately afterwards, a second suicider crashed into her hull on the port quarter in a thunderous explosion, knocking out her port engine, opening her after engine room to the sea and jamming her rudder. While her damage control parties were attempting to stem the inrushing flood to the engine room, the ship began to take on a precarious list to starboard. Realizing that *Luce* was beyond all hope of saving, and to save as many lives as possible, her captain, Commander J.W. Waterhouse, ordered the ship abandoned. Within a few moments after passing this order, the battered destroyer abruptly upended and plunged in a rush to her watery grave, accompanied by a tremendous explosion.

Lost with the Luce were 126 officers and men. Of the 186 survivors, 57 were severely burned and wounded, 37 others suffering from minor wounds and injuries.

☆ ☆ ☆

USS *LUCE* (DD-522)

Class: Fletcher.
Builder: Bethlehem Steel Shipbuilding Co., Staten Island, New York.
Keel laid: August 24, 1942.
Launched: March 6, 1943.
Sponsor: Mrs. Stephen B. Luce III, wife of Rear Admiral Stephen B. Luce's grandson.
Commissioned: June 21, 1943; Commander D.C. Varian, USN, comdg.
Date of Loss: May 4, 1945; Commander J.W. Waterhouse, USN, comdg.
Location: Off Okinawa.
Awards: Five battle stars.

USS Morrison

Launched July 4, 1943
Lost May 4, 1945
Off Okinawa

COXSWAIN JOHN G. MORRISON, USN
(1838-1897)

John Gordon Morrison was born in Ireland on July 13, 1838, and arrived in the United States in 1855. Although he had enlisted in the United States Army on April 24, 1861, he volunteered to serve on board the gunboat USS *Carondelet* on February 15, 1862.

Later, he was appointed Coxswain and was awarded the Congressional Medal of Honor for his exceptional courage during an engagement against the Confederate ram CSN *Arkansas* in the Yazoo River on July 15, 1862. Wounded in a later battle, he was discharged from the Navy on March 31, 1863. Residing in New York City, he died there on June 9, 1897.

Departing Seattle on February 25, 1944, the USS *Morrison* (DD-560) arrived at Manus, Admiralty Islands, in late March of that year. Joining up with Task Group 50.17, she played a part in the strikes against the Caroline Islands, and upon completion of this assignment steamed for Pearl Harbor, arriving there on May 9. Here, she underwent a period of amphibious training with the Marines in preparation for the landings in the Marianas.

From the Marianas, *Morrison* clawed her way up through the Central Pacific and took part in the strikes against the Philippines, Ryukyu Islands and Palau. On the morning of September 9, while her 5-inch guns were blasting away against enemy gun emplacements on Mindanao, a convoy of 50 Japanese freighters and sampans was sighted north of the island. Navy fighter planes were immediately dispatched to the area and succeeded in wreaking havoc among the enemy ships. *Morrison* was then ordered to lead a force of destroyers to finish off the remnants of the "armada," and, after dispatching 15 sampans to the bottom, the destroyer returned to Mindanao to resume her bombardment mission.

On October 24, *Morrison* came to the assistance of the light carrier *Princeton*, which had been severely bomb-damaged during the battle off Cape Egano. After spending over an hour picking up 400 of her survivors from the sea, she came alongside the fiercely burning flattop to help douse her fires. The moderate swells, however, caused the destroyer's mast and forward stack to become wedged into the carrier's uptakes. To avoid further damage to his ship, *Morrison's* captain pulled away, the cruiser *Birmingham* moving in to render further assistance.

Ten minutes later, tragedy struck when the carrier was rocked by a violent explosion. The disaster was devastating. In an instant, a shower of steel, rubble and debris flayed the decks of *Birmingham*, cutting down 233 officers and men where they stood and injuring over 450 others. Fearing that another explosion would endanger the lives of his own crew, and with his ship already reduced to a seething caldron, *Princeton's* captain ordered the carrier abandoned. Later, the cruiser *Reno* and the destroyer *Irwin* sent the fiery, exploding derelict to the bottom with gunfire and torpedoes. *Morrison* then proceeded to Ulithi, where she disembarked *Princeton's* survivors on the 27th and shortly afterwards departed for San Francisco for repairs.

Morrison was back in action on March 27 when she participated in the pre-invasion bombardment of enemy gun emplacements on Okinawa. On the day of the landings, April 1, 1945, she and the destroyer *Stockton* (DD-646) made a positive submarine contact and unleashed a vicious depth-charge attack against the intruder. Badly damaged, the submarine *I-8* bobbed to the surface, only to be promptly dispatched to the bottom by gunfire from both destroyers.

On the morning of May 4, after three days of foul weather (and its consequent respite from air attacks), *Morrison* pitted her guns against a bevy of Kamikazes while on picket duty some 51 miles north of Okinawa. With her were four landing craft and the destroyer *Ingraham* (DD-694, namesake of DD-444). As the flock of 25 or more aircraft closed in, they were intercepted by planes from the combat air patrol, but several of them escaped and dashed in toward *Morrison*.

Plunging through a thick curtain of 20- and 40-mm fire and flak, one plane released a bomb that splashed harmlessly off *Morrison's* starboard beam. Two more aircraft dropped one bomb each, without causing any damage. Then, at about 0825, a suicider penetrated the heavy net of gunfire and crashed into the ship's forward stack and bridge. While still reeling from this hit, *Morrison* was struck a death-dealing blow when three more Kamikazes smashed into her in rapid succession. Ironically, all three aircraft were old, slow-flying seaplanes. Swathed in a shroud of smoke, steam and roaring flames, the severely damaged *Morrison* began to take on a heavy list to starboard.

Owing to the loss of communications throughout the ship, the order to abandon did not reach those who were at their battle stations belowdecks. Then, suddenly, two thunderous internal explosions ripped through the ship's battered innards. Within a few seconds, *Morrison* raised her bow and slipped beneath the surface so swiftly that 150 of her personnel in the interior of the ship went down with her. Of the 179 officers and bluejackets who survived the destroyer's loss, 108 were wounded, with only 71 escaping unharmed.

☆ ☆ ☆

USS *MORRISON* (DD-560)

Class: Fletcher.
Builder: Seattle-Tacoma Shipbuilding Corp., Seattle, Washington.
Keel laid: June 30, 1942.
Launched: July 4, 1943.
Sponsor: Miss Margaret M. Morrison, daughter of Coxswain John G. Morrison, USN.
Commissioned: December 18, 1943; Commander W.H. Price, USN, comdg.
Date of loss: May 4, 1945; Commander J.R. Hansen, USN, comdg.
Location: Off Okinawa.
Awards: Navy Unit Citation and eight battle stars.

USS Longshaw

Launched June 4, 1943
Lost May 18, 1945
Off Okinawa

ASSISTANT SURGEON WILLIAM LONGSHAW, JR., USN
(1839–1865)

William Longshaw, Jr., was born near Richmond, Virginia, on April 26, 1839. After studying pharmacology at the University of Louisiana, he went on to receive his medical degree from the University of Michigan in 1859.

Entering the U.S. Navy as an assistant surgeon on April 25, 1862, he was serving on board the monitor USS *Lehigh* on November 16 when she ran aground while engaged with Confederate gun batteries on Sullivan's Island, South Carolina. During the height of this action, Dr. Longshaw displayed exceptional bravery under intense fire, when he threw over a hawser to the monitor USS *Nahant*, which was standing by to tow the *Lehigh* free. Despite having had two hawsers shot away, Dr. Longshaw was not deterred; he succeeded in securing a third line to the *Nahant*. For his outstanding courage, he was highly praised by Rear Admiral John A. Dahlgren and by then-Secretary of the Navy Gideon Welles.

Dr. Longshaw was killed in action on January 15, 1865, while dressing the wounds of a Marine during the attack on Fort Fisher, North Carolina.

Except for a brief shipyard overhaul at Pearl Harbor in May 1944, the USS *Longshaw* (DD-559) operated continuously with various task forces, participating in the strikes and covering the landings on New Guinea, the Marianas, the Philippines, and the destruction of airfields on Formosa and Okinawa. During a fierce sea/air engagement off Formosa on October 13, *Longshaw* shot down one plane and shared a second kill with another destroyer.

On January 9, 1945, while the landings were underway at Lingayan Gulf, *Longshaw* was operating with Task Force 38, over the next ten days covering the assaults against enemy installations in French Indo-China (today Vietnam), Hong Kong, Hainan Island and Formosa. From there, the force swept through the Balintang Channel and pounded airfields and shipping at Okinawa, before retiring to Ulithi on the 26th.

On February 17–18, *Longshaw* screened the fleet carriers while their aircraft struck important targets on the Japanese mainland, including shipping in Toyko Bay, factories in Yokohama and Tokyo and the Yokosuka Naval Shipyard. Upon retiring, the force raced southward to take part in the action against Iwo Jima. *Longshaw* rendered her services by providing shore bombardment against points of enemy resistance and by protecting the transport area against the incursion of enemy aircraft. Upon being relieved from this assignment, the destroyer stood out again for Ulithi, arriving there on March 12.

On the 21st, *Longshaw* departed Ulithi, escorting a pre-invasion bombardment force to the shores of Okinawa. Throughout the Okinawan campaign, the destroyer served alternately on radar picket duty and as a source of fire support for the forces ashore.

By mid-May, the Kamikaze blizzard had exacted an excruciating toll in both ships and men. Hundreds of sailors had died and thousands more were wounded. No vessels, except for submarines, were immune from the diabolical onslaught, and throughout the fleet nerves were frayed. Thus far, seven destroyers had been blown under by this fiery typhoon, and the 1,450-ton destroyer escort *Oberrender* was so badly mauled that she had to be written off as a total loss upon her arrival at Kerama Retto.

On the morning of May 18, after a four-day and night session of shore bombardment, in between warding off air assaults, *Longshaw* and her bleary-eyed crew were deployed to a new patrol station south of the Naha airfield. Unknowingly, the destroyer was steaming through shoal waters, and at 0719 disaster struck when her hull scraped over a reef and she found herself aground directly beneath the mouths of an enemy shore battery.

All means were employed to extradite the helpless *Longshaw*. Her 60,000-hp engines were reversed at full speed, her twin screws whipping up a muddy froth from under her stern. Anything that could lessen the weight of the ship forward was tossed over the side, while over 800 rounds of 5-inch ammunition was shifted to the fantail.

At the time *Longshaw* struck the reef, Radar Technician Second Class Leo E. Scott was preparing to take a shower. The jolt slammed him against the shower bulkhead, but despite being a bit disoriented, he quickly donned his dungarees and shoes and rushed out to the maindeck. From there, he could see that the ship's bow was pointing skyward and twisted at a crazy angle. Nearby were the salvage tug USS *Arikara* and another destroyer, and each ship passed a line over in an effort to pull the stranded *Longshaw* free, but the vessel could not be budged. Surprisingly, while this attempted rescue was in progress the enemy did not fire a shot.

Then, at 1100, as was anticipated sooner or later, the Japanese shore guns opened up. Lethal shells whistled overhead, splashing and detonating close aboard. *Longshaw* responded in turn with only a few rounds of 5-inch shells, before a direct hit smashed into one of her forward 5-inch magazines. The tremendous detonation blew the destroyer's bow completely off, deadly chunks of shrapnel and fragments of the ship being hurled upward and across the sea. The ship's bridge was virtually flattened by the force of the malevolent concussion, which transformed the entire structure into a charnel house of blood and gore.

From that time on, the situation had the makings of a massacre. There wasn't anywhere the beleaguered destroyermen could find refuge from the point-blank shelling that was systematically pounding the ship into scrap. Her decks were blown up; her superstructure was torn down. Both smokestacks were wrenched off their mountings, the forward stack leaning drunkenly against the bridge. Among the battered ruins lay the dead, the helpless wounded and the injured.

Leo Scott recalls his horrendous experience as follows: "When the shore guns began to fire, I rushed to my battle station in the radar transmission room. We could feel the shells striking the ship, which was like being in a metal barrel that was being hit with a sledgehammer. Suddenly, a violent explosion forward sent us reeling about the room. Then, amidst all the confusion and the din of the shelling, I thought I heard the order to abandon ship. It was my responsibility to see that the secret magnetrons for the radar equipment were destroyed. However, when I opened the door to the room where they were located, the space was like a blast furnace and filled with black smoke. Worse yet, I could hear the agonizing screams of the poor souls, most of whom were my friends, trapped in that inferno and I was unable to save them.

"As I was heading for the maindeck, I stumbled over the body of a man, and as I came out on deck I saw several bodies lying about in bizarre attitudes, many of them missing limbs. Most of the men's clothing was ripped to shreds and soaked with blood. Farther on, I saw a man sitting on the deck with his back against the bulkhead, his head resting on his chest. I ran over to him with the hope of trying to help him, but to my horror I found that his face was missing. I then ran aft and jumped into the sea.

"When I was about 30 yards from the ship I could see that there were still several men on deck, and in spite of the shells bursting among them, they were still trying to fight the fires. Apparently, they did not hear the order to abandon ship. Many of us in the water were tossed about whenever a shell detonated near us. One exploded so close to me that I was thrown out of the water. Although I was stunned by the blast, I did not lose consciousness, but I did suffer minor internal injuries and lost my hearing for some time after"

Realizing that the situation was hopeless and, in the absence of the captain, Commander C.W. Becker, who was last seen badly wounded and wandering about the deck with a Colt .45 automatic pistol in his hand, a senior officer ordered the ship abandoned.

After the shelling had ceased, *Longshaw*'s survivors were picked up by rescue vessels. Amazingly, 11 officers and 225 crewmen survived the savage bombardment. Of that number, four officers and 95 crewmen were wounded. Two officers and five bluejackets would die later. A final muster revealed that 11 officers, her captain and 65 crewmen had perished with the ship.

Later that day, the battered remains of the valiant *Longshaw* were obliterated by friendly gunfire, so that nothing of value would fall into enemy hands.

☆   ☆   ☆

USS *LONGSHAW* (DD-559)

Class: Fletcher.
Builder: Seattle-Tacoma Shipbuilding Corp., Seattle, Washington.
Keel laid: June 16, 1942.
Launched: June 4, 1943.
Sponsor: Mrs. E. Richards.
Commissioned: December 4, 1943; Commander D.T. Birtwell, USN, comdg.
Date of loss: May 18, 1945; Commander C.W. Becker, USN, comdg.†
Location: Off Okinawa.
Awards: Nine battle stars.

USS Drexler

Launched September 3, 1944
Lost May 28, 1945
Off Okinawa

ENSIGN HENRY C. DREXLER, USN
(1901–1924)

Henry Clay Drexler was born in Braddock, Pennsylvania, on August 7, 1901, and entered the Naval Academy in 1920. Upon graduating from the Academy in June 1924, he was assigned to the cruiser USS *Trenton*. Five months later, on October 20, while *Trenton* was conducting gunnery practice, a powder charge ignited in Ensign Drexler's gun mount. While Ensign Drexler was attempting to immerse it in a bucket of water, it exploded, killing him and several men in the mount. For his heroic attempt to save the lives of his men, Ensign Drexler was posthumously awarded the Navy Cross.

The USS *Drexler* (DD-741) reported to the Commandant of Destroyers, Pacific Fleet (ComDesPac) on February 10, 1945. After a brief layover at Pearl Harbor, she escorted a convoy to Guadalcanal, and from there steamed for Ulithi, where was she prepared to take part in the landings on Okinawa.

From the beginning of the Okinawa campaign, *Drexler* was busily engaged serving on the picket lines, and often was called upon to bombard enemy pockets of resistance. On May 4, she and the destroyer *Wadsworth* (DD-516) splashed a suicide aircraft and repelled another attacker with a violent curtain of 20- and 40-mm. fire.

The final hour of *Drexler's* short life arrived on the morning of May 28, while she was manning her picket station (No. 10), about 60 miles southwest of Okinawa. In company with the *Lowery* (DD-770), this was her fifteenth consecutive day on the picket line, and during that time she had succeeded in downing two Kamikazes and scored two or more possible kills during night attacks.

At 0700, two aircraft hurled themselves toward the *Drexler* and her sister destroyer. One of them was shot down by fire from both ships plus a combat air patrol fighter that was on the scene. Badly scorched by *Lowery*, the second plane attempted to crash into her, but lost control, flew off course and plunged into the starboard side of *Drexler* instead. Immediately, the ship's power was knocked out and several fires were started.

Then, at 0703, seemingly from out of nowhere, three more planes were seen bearing down upon the ship. Despite the damage she had sustained, and while her repair parties were trying to contain the raging fires, *Drexler's* gunners remained at their posts, banging away at her assailants and sending two of them spinning into the sea. One of the planes, however, though severely damaged, succeeded in hurtling through the vicious hailstorm of AA fire to crash into the destroyer's superstructure in a fiery explosion. One minute after the crash, *Drexler* rolled over on her starboard side and sank under a pall of smoke and steam. Owing to the swiftness of *Drexler's* sinking, 158 officers and men went down with her. Among the survivors, 52 were wounded, including her captain, Commander R.L. Wilson, USN.

☆ ☆ ☆

USS *DREXLER* (DD-741)

Class: Allen M. Sumner.
Builder: Bath Iron Works, Bath, Maine.
Keel laid: April 24, 1944.
Launched: September 3, 1944.
Sponsor: Mrs. Louis A. Drexler, mother of Ensign Henry C. Drexler, USN.
Commissioned: November 14, 1944; Commander R.L. Wilson, USN, comdg.
Date of loss: May 28, 1945; Commander R.L. Wilson, USN, comdg.
Location: Off Okinawa.
Awards: One battle star.

USS William D. Porter

Launched September 27, 1942
Lost June 10, 1945
Off Okinawa

COMMODORE WILLIAM D. PORTER, USN
(1808–1864)

William David Porter, the son of Commodore David Porter, and the older brother of Admiral David Dixon Porter, was born on March 10, 1808, in New Orleans, but spent most of his childhood years in Chester, Pennsylvania. On January 1, 1823, he was appointed Midshipman; eleven years later he was promoted to the rank of Lieutenant.

Captain Porter retired from the Navy in 1855, but in 1859 he returned to active duty and assumed command of the sloop-of-war *St. Mary's*. During the next two years, he cruised along the western coasts of Central America and Mexico, protecting American interests in those areas.

With the outbreak of the Civil War, Captain Porter was dispatched to St. Louis to assist in the establishment of the Mississippi Gunboat Flotilla in the Union's effort to seize and control that river and its tributaries. On October 3, 1861, he was placed in command of the gunboat *New Era*. Later, he changed the ship's name to *Essex*, in honor of his father's frigate, which had been defeated in a courageous battle against two British frigates off Valparaiso, Chile, during the War of 1812.

Between January and August 1862, Captain Porter served with distinction and bravery up and down the Mississippi, engaging with Confederate gunboat flotillas and wreaking havoc and destruction upon Rebel fortifications. On January 10, while in company with the gunboat *St. Louis*, he engaged three Confederate gunboats and forced them to retreat. On February 6, Porter, now holding the rank of commander, pitted *Essex* against the guns of Fort Henry, during which the ship sustained 15 hits before a 32-pound shell struck her boilers.

The explosion scalded and severely burned 28 members of the crew, including Commander Porter. Although blinded, he managed to conn his ship until she was out of the range of the Confederate shore batteries.

Upon recovering from his wounds, Commander Porter resumed command of *Essex,* and in July engaged the Confederate ram *Arkansas.* During the slugfest, Porter attempted to ram the ironclad, but only struck her with a glancing blow, causing *Essex* to run aground. However, he was able to back clear and retire. From then on, *Essex* continued to patrol the Mississippi between Vicksburg and Baton Rouge.

Then, on August 6, while assisting Union forces in repelling a Confederate land assault at Baton Rouge, Commander Porter once again tangled with *Arkansas.* During the heated confrontation, Porter employed incendiary shells that he had invented, and twenty minutes later the *Arkansas* was aflame from bow to stern; shortly afterwards, she blew up. Not only was Commander Porter highly praised by the U.S. Congress for this outstanding victory, but he and his crew were awarded a sum of $25,000 in prize money.

Commander Porter's last action of the Civil War occurred in September 1862, when *Essex* participated in the bombardment of Natchez, Mississippi, and the gun batteries at Port Hudson. Advanced to the rank of Commodore, Porter was then assigned to New York City, serving in various capacities until he was hospitalized for a heart problem in April 1864. On May 1, Commodore Porter died at St. Luke's Hospital in New York and was buried in Greenwood Cemetery. His remains were later removed and laid to rest beside those of his famous father.

Upon the conclusion of her shakedown trials and battle-readiness training in Caribbean waters, the USS *William D. Porter* (DD-579) entered the Charleston Navy Yard in early September for post-shakedown repairs. At the end of the month, she got underway for Norfolk, and in mid-November conducted her operations off the eastern seaboard with the carrier *Intrepid.*

On November 13, *William D. Porter* and her division rendezvoused with the battleship *Iowa,* which was en route to North Africa, embarked with President Franklin D. Roosevelt, who was to attend the Cairo and Tehran Conferences. On the following day, during battle drills, the *William D. Porter* accidentally fired a live torpedo toward *Iowa.* An immediate signal was flashed to the battleship, warning her of the oncoming torpedo. Evading just in time, the weapon exploded some several yards astern of the mighty battlewagon. When the destroyer completed her part in escorting *Iowa*, she steamed on to Bermuda, arriving there on the 16th.

Back in Norfolk a week later, *William D. Porter* received her orders to report to the Pacific Fleet. Upon her arrival at San Diego on December 19, she replenished fuel and stores and was issued cold-weather clothing. On the 20th, she sailed for the North Pacific, arriving at Dutch Harbor, Alaska, on the 29th. Here, she was assigned to Task Force 94 and operated off the Aleutian Islands throughout the rest of 1943 and into September 1944..

Except for three bombardment missions against enemy positions in the Kurile Islands (Matsuwa on June 13 and Paramushiro on June 26 and August 1), *William D. Porter* was primarily consigned to monotonous ASW patrols throughout the frigid waters of the North Pacific until she was ordered to San Francisco for a shipyard overhaul.

On September 27th, she departed San Francisco for Pearl Harbor, and after carrying out advanced battle exercises in Hawaiian waters for two weeks, she sailed to the western Pacific. Although *William D. Porter* arrived too late to play a part in the initial landings on Leyte in October, she was kept busy screening resupply ships against enemy air attacks, and shared a kill in shooting down a plane with a nearby destroyer.

For the remainder of the year, *William D. Porter* served on escort duty, screening troop and supply ships between Leyte, Manus, Hollandia, Minduro and Bougainville. On December 12, her convoy came under two air attacks, the first being easily repulsed. But later that day another attempt was made, and only after several Japanese planes had been shot down—one splashed by *William D. Porter*—did they swiftly retire. On the following morning, the destroyer sank an abandoned landing barge that was heavily laden with supplies.

On January 6, 1945, the destroyer was lying off Lingayan Gulf taking part in a pre-invasion shore bombardment mission when she shot down a lone fighter, and then 20 minutes later downed a twin-engined "Betty" bomber. Between January 9 (the day of the landings on Lingayan Gulf) and February 15, *William D. Porter* protected the transport areas against enemy aircraft, and often was called upon to seek out and bombard enemy supply and ammunition dumps.

Prior to the landings on Okinawa, the destroyer assisted in the assault and occupation of Kerama Retto Island. From the day of the landings on Okinawa (April 1) to May 5, *William D. Porter* expended well over 8,500 rounds of 5-inch shells against aircraft and shore installations. During that time, she added five more aircraft kills to her war record, and splashed another plane while serving on picket duty between May 5 and June 9.

On June 10, at 0815, she was attacked by an obsolete "Val" dive bomber. Plunging down out of a cloud bank, the plane dove directly at the destroyer, whose gunners greeted it with a vicious fusillade of anti-aircraft fire. Although set aflame and trailing a plume of black smoke, the aircraft continued to bear down on the ship, whose captain had taken evasive action, causing the plane to crash into the sea with a tremendous, fountaining explosion off her port side. The plane's bombs, however, detonated beneath the destroyer's keel, lifting her out of the water and splitting her hull open in several places. The terrific concussion tossed several of her crew off their feet and into the air. All power, both electrical and propulsion, was lost because her steam lines had been ruptured by the blast.

Although several small fires had broken out, these were quickly extinguished. During the next three hours, the destroyer's repair parties worked strenuously to plug the numerous leaks that had broken out throughout her frail hull. Unfortunately, despite assistance that was rendered by the crews of four landing craft, the ingress of the sea could not be stemmed. When the ship began to take on a precarious list to starboard, her captain, Commander C.M. Keys, passed the order to abandon. Twelve minutes after the order was given, and seven minutes after Commander Keys left the ship, she rolled completely over on her beams end and, at 1119, slipped beneath the surface, stern first.

William D. Porter was the only ship to be sunk by a Kamikaze without suffering a fatality. Of the 61 members of her crew who were wounded, all of them subsequently recovered without serious complications.

☆ ☆ ☆

USS *WILLIAM D. PORTER* (DD-579)

Class: Fletcher.
Builder: Consolidated Steel Co., Orange, Texas.
Keel laid: May 7, 1942.
Launched: September 27, 1942.
Sponsor: Miss Mary E. Reader, great-great-granddaughter of Commodore William D. Porter, USN.
Commissioned: July 6, 1943; Commander W.A. Walter, USN, comdg.
Date of loss: June 10, 1945; Commander C.M. Keys, USN, comdg.
Location: Off Okinawa.
Awards: Four battle stars.

USS Twiggs

Launched April 7, 1943
Lost June 16, 1945
Off Okinawa

MAJOR LEVI TWIGGS, USMC
(1793–1847)

Levi Twiggs was born on May 23, 1793, in Richmond County, Georgia. Commissioned Lieutenant in the U.S. Marine Corps on November 10, 1813, he was assigned to the frigate USS *President*. He was still serving on her when she was defeated in an engagement against four British warships on January 15, 1815. Taken prisoner, Lieutenant Twiggs was released after peace was declared.

In 1836 and into 1837 he fought in the Indian Wars in Florida and Georgia. At the outbreak of the Mexican War, now-Major Twiggs was attached to the Marine Battalion in New York City. Requesting permission to take part in the war, his battalion left New York in June 1847. On September 13, 1847, Twiggs was killed by enemy fire while leading a landing party against the town of Chapultepec, Mexico.

After transiting the Panama Canal and a short layover at San Diego, the USS *Twiggs* (DD-591) arrived at Pearl Harbor on June 6, 1944. Departing from Pearl on the 16th, she sailed for Eniwetok and was based there between the strikes against Saipan and Tinian. August 19th found the *Twiggs* back in Pearl Harbor for voyage repairs and additional battle exercises in Hawaiian waters.

Returning to the western Pacific in late September, she was deployed to Seeadler Harbor, Manus Island, on October 14, where she made preparations for the upcoming invasion of Leyte. Here, she provided shore bombardment as the ground forces stormed the beaches at Dulac and Tacloban. With enemy air power still in evidence, *Twiggs* was kept busy fending off swarms of aircraft that were harassing the landing operations. On one occasion, she picked up a downed pilot from the light carrier *Petrof Bay*. Hearing news of an imminent attack by a massive enemy naval force, *Twiggs* and several other destroyers were hastily ordered to weigh anchor and escort the empty and virtually defenseless transports and supply ships to Manus.

On December 13, while *Twiggs* was attatched to Task Group 77.12, then en route to support the landings on Mindanao, the ships were attacked by four enemy fighters. Though all of the assailants were hit by AA fire, one succeeded in crashing into the destroyer *Haraden* (DD-585), causing severe damage and leaving 14 members of her crew killed and 24 wounded. *Twiggs* was detached from the task group to escort the crippled destroyer to San Pedro, Leyte, before rejoining her task force on the 14th, in time to lend fire support for the landing operations. On the 16th, the destroyer returned to San Pedro, and from there departed for Manus for a brief rest and to make preparations for her next deployment.

On January 1, 1945, *Twiggs* joined Rear Admiral Jesse B. Oldendorf's Task Group 77.2 and steamed northward to cover the landings at Lingayen Gulf. While forging up the coast of Luzon, the force was attacked by aircraft, one of which crashed into the escort carrier *Ommaney Bay*, only a short distance from the *Twiggs*. Within a short time, the baby flattop was wracked with volcanic eruptions and swathed in a pillar of smoke and roaring flames. Without hesitation, *Twiggs'* skipper raced to the carrier's side in an effort to rescue her crew. Moments after picking up all the men she could find, the after section of the now furiously burning carrier exploded, flaying *Twiggs* with a rain of debris. Fortunately, none of her crew were injured, nor was serious damage inflicted on the ship. The carrier now abandoned, she was given the coup de grâce by gunfire and torpedoes from the destroyer *Burns* (DD-588). All told, *Twiggs* managed to rescue 200 survivors from the carrier and transferred them to the battleship *West Virginia*.

On January 9, while the landings were underway at Lingayen Gulf, *Twiggs* and her task group were patrolling in the South China Sea to intercept any aircraft or naval units that might have intentions of disrupting the landings. She remained in these waters until relieved on the 19th, when she then stood out for Ulithi, via San Pedro. After effecting minor repairs and general upkeep, the destroyer was prepared for the invasion of Iwo Jima.

Arriving off that volcanic island on February 17—D-Day, minus two—she covered several landing craft as they surged toward the beaches. Later in the day, *Twiggs* shot down a suicider, which crashed close aboard, but did not inflict any damage or casualties. She continued to support the ground forces until she was relieved on March 10.

After a short layover and replenishment at Ulithi, *Twiggs* arrived off Okinawa on March 25 to participate in the pre-invasion bombardment of the proposed landing sites. Throughout the Okinawan campaign, *Twiggs* pulled her share of the load, and then some, in her efforts to support the ground forces in one of the most grueling operations of the Pacific war.

On April 28, the Kamikazes were swarming across the skies in droves. On that date, 12 planes were shot down in *Twiggs'* sector, two of which fell under her 20- and 40-mm fire. However, one plane succeeded in slicing through the destroyer's thick barrier of AA fire and bursting 5-inch shells. Despite his plane being reduced to a mass of flaming wreckage, the suicide pilot managed to hook its wing on the searchlight platform on the forward stack. The aircraft then spun about, smashed into the bridge, wrecked the captain's cabin, flipped over and splashed into the sea on the starboard side of the ship. The 500-pound bomb it was carrying had meanwhile dislodged and exploded beneath the bridge, blowing a large hole in the deck and killing nine men. Relieved from her station, the wounded *Twiggs* steamed on to Kerama Retto, where she was hastily patched up and put back on the picket line.

After experiencing several more narrow escapes, *Twiggs'* luck finally ran out on the night of April 16. Throughout the day, she had been lying off Senaga Shima, bombarding enemy concentrations before returning to her picket station. At about 2030, a low-flying torpedo bomber, which had eluded the radar net, was seen too late bearing in on the lone destroyer. In spite of all the guns that *Twiggs* could bring to bear, the destroyer was already doomed, for the plane had dropped its torpedo, which was now spearheading toward the ship.

The black night was split asunder with an ear-shattering roar and a split-second flash of glaring orange light, as the lethal torpedo struck *Twiggs* in her No. 2 magazine. A towering column of fire, debris, water and oil bolted some 100 feet into the air, and, when it settled, the ship's entire bow as far aft to the bridge had completely disintegrated. What remained of the forward section of the ship was now a mass of flames and tangled wreckage. Among the shattered ruins of her bridge lay the bodies of the dead and mortally wounded, including her captain, Commander George Philip.

While the ship's repair parties were struggling to fight the fires forward, the same plane—which had escaped the wrath of *Twiggs'* gunfire, yet was still intent on suicide—had circled about and now dove headlong into the after section of the ship. Another devastating explosion followed when the 5-inch ammunition exploded, causing more fires to break out. Now the

Twiggs had only 30 minutes to live.

Within that short time, all efforts by the damage control parties to snuff out the raging conflagration failed. The ship was constantly assailed by internal explosions as more ammunition detonated in her after magazines. The intense heat and lung-searing smoke drove the crewmen from all four engineering spaces, and without steam power to operate her fire pumps there was no way the fires could be extinguished.

Caught between the fires forward and exploding ammunition aft, there was nowhere to go but over the side. Less than 12 minutes after the last man left the ship, *Twiggs'* No. 5 magazine blew up with a tremendous roar and, a few seconds later, the fire-gutted and explosion-wracked vessel dipped her stern under and settled to the bottom.

Though 180 sailors managed to survive the disaster, lost with the *Twiggs* were her captain and 152 officers and men.

☆ ☆ ☆

USS *TWIGGS* (DD-591)

Class: Fletcher.
Builder: Charleston Navy Yard, Charleston, South Carolina.
Keel laid: January 1, 1943.
Launched: April 7, 1943.
Sponsor: Mrs. Roland S. Morris; great-granddaughter of Major Levi Twiggs, USMC.
Commissioned: November 4, 1943; Commander J.B. Fellows, USN, comdg.
Date of loss: June 16, 1945; Commander G. Philip, USN, comdg.†
Location: Off Okinawa.
Awards: Four battle stars.

USS Callaghan

Launched August 1, 1943
Lost July 29, 1945
Off Okinawa

REAR ADMIRAL DANIEL J. CALLAGHAN, USN
(1890–1942)

Daniel Judson Callaghan was born in San Francisco on July 26, 1890. After graduating from the Naval Academy in 1911, he went on to serve in various ships and shore facilities. In 1915, he assumed command of the torpedo boat destroyer USS *Truxtun*.

In the late 1930s, he served as naval aide to President Franklin D. Roosevelt and as commanding officer of the cruiser *San Francisco* from May 1941 to May 1942. Upon being promoted to Rear Admiral, he was assigned as Chief of Staff to the Commander of the South Pacific Naval Forces.

Later, Callaghan was appointed Commander of Task Force 67.4, and hoisted his flag on board his former command *San Francisco*. On the night of November 12–13, 1942, his meager force of five cruisers and eight destroyers intercepted and engaged a much larger Japanese battle group off Savo Island in the Solomons. During this confused night battle the Americans lost four destroyers and two cruisers. The Japanese fleet commander, however, whose primary mission was to bombard the Marine garrison on Guadalcanal, broke off the action and fled.

Rear Admiral Callaghan was killed during this violent slugfest, and was posthumously awarded the Congressional Medal of Honor.

The USS *Callaghan* (DD-792) joined the fast and hard-hitting Fifth Fleet in early March 1944 as it pummeled enemy installations on Palau, Ulithi, Yap and Woleai from March 10 through April 1. Later that month, she supported the operations against Hollandia, New Guinea, and assisted in the bombardments of Truk, Ponape and Satawan into early May.

From June 15 to July 13, *Callaghan* was also on hand to support the landings on Saipan, during which time she shot down a torpedo bomber. She then came to the assistance of the bomb-damaged escort carrier *Fanshaw Bay* and escorted her safely to Eniwetok. *Callaghan* also participated in the landings on and eventual capture of Guam between July 22 and August 2.

On October 20, *Callaghan* supported the initial landings on Leyte and, on the 25th, raced northward with Task Group 38.3 to mop up the remnants of the crippled enemy battle force that had been decimated by Rear Admiral Halsey's Third Fleet. En route, a pillar of black smoke billowing over the horizon led the task group to an abandoned, burning enemy destroyer, which the destroyer *Porterfield* (DD-682) was directed to dispatch to the bottom. However, as she approached the derelict, it blew up and sank.

On November 1, while the task group was returning to Eniwetok, the enemy stepped up its air assaults against the naval and ground forces at Leyte. Consequently, the task group was ordered to return to the Philippines. En route, the cruiser *Reno* was struck by a torpedo and *Callaghan* was detached from the group to screen the damaged vessel to Eniwetok.

After refueling there, the busy destroyer rejoined her task group and took part in the strikes against Manila and enemy airfields throughout the Philippines—a task that continued into late December. On Christmas day, *Callaghan* was placed in drydock for voyage repairs. Five days later she was again underway, en route to the South China Sea with her task force to carry out air attacks against enemy installations in French Indo-China, Hong Kong and Formosa, as well as industrial targets on the Japanese homeland.

Throughout January and to mid-February 1945, *Callaghan* was constantly on the move, screening various task forces during their strikes on targets of opportunity on Iwo Jima, Formosa, Okinawa and Japan. On February 18, she assisted in sinking an enemy picket ship, and in late March joined a battleship force to participate in the pre-invasion bombardment of Okinawa. While taking part in the initial landings on Okinawa, she, with an assist from the *Porterfield,* sank a midget submarine and shot down three dive bombers.

Up to this time, *Callaghan* had been operating in the Western Pacific for 17 months. During that period she had played a role in just about every major operation from the Central Pacific up to the front door of the Japanese homeland. Twelve aircraft had fallen under the wrath of her sharpshooting gunners, and several others had been damaged.

It was now late July and, needless to say, her crew was battle-weary, their nerves rubbed raw. Her guns were virtually worn-out; her machinery and boilers were long overdue for an overhaul and cleaning; and her fire control directors and radar components had seen better days, lacking the accuracy of when they were new.

Callaghan had been back on the picket line since July 19, but on the 27th, a whoop of joy resounded throughout the ship when a message was received informing her captain, Commander C.M. Bertholf, that she was to proceed to San Francisco in two days upon being relieved by the destroyer Laws (DD-558).

Consequently, hardly a man could sleep on the night of July 28–29. Laws was expected to arrive on station at 0200, and the anticipation of this long-awaited event was beyond comprehension. Then, at 0030, the crew were shocked out of their reverie when the Callaghan's radar operator reported the presence of a single plane bearing down on the ship from out of the night sky.

Within a minute, all of the destroyer's guns that could bear were firing away upon the intruder. The night was torn apart with the thundering of her 5-inch guns and the chattering and thumping of her 20- and 40-mm cannons. Incandescent tracers stitched through the darkness like angry, fiery bees. The split-second gun flashes revealed an unusual target: a rickety-appearing biplane from a bygone era; probably a training relic dating back to the 1930s that was sporting the Japanese "meatball" insignia. The furious barrage from the Fletcher-class destroyer seemed to discourage the pilot from approaching any closer, and he abruptly turned away and clattered off into the darkness.

Ten minutes later, however, a lookout on the bridge shouted: "Aircraft off the port quarter!" Unfortunately, the warning came too late to allow Callaghan's captain to take evasive action, for the aircraft was less than 1,000 yards away and it was none other than the same old plane that had just been driven off. Undetected by radar and human eyesight, the pilot had circled around, shut off the plane's engine and glided in silently under the radar's probing beam. At 0041, the plane crashed into Callaghan's after deck house and into her No.3 5-inch gun's upper handling room.

A 150-foot geyser of fire shot skyward, followed by a devastating explosion as the aircraft's bomb detonated in the after engine room. All hands in that space were instantly killed, and the thin hull plating split open. Callaghan was rocked by a second explosion when burning gasoline cascaded into her No. 3 magazine and ignited her 5-inch shells and powder cases. The violence from the concussion felled several more men and split open the hull plates in the after section of the ship.

Callaghan's stern was now a mass of roaring flames and wreckage. Exploding 20- and 40-mm ammunition added to the carnage, forcing the firefighters to retreat before the storm of fiery shells and shrapnel. A third explosion shattered the ship when No. 4 magazine let go and rumbled through her inferno-ravaged hull. As more and more of her compartments began to flood, *Callaghan* started to settle by the stern.

Not ten minutes after the plane had crashed into the now-foundering destroyer, the captain ordered the "pall bearers" alongside to receive the wounded and most of his crew, while he remained on board with a salvage party, hoping for a chance to save his ship. During this time, one of the rescue vessels was vainly attempting to quell the fires on her fantail. But, when another explosion tore through the ship, spewing additional death and destruction in every direction, Commander Bertholf had no other choice but to concede to the inevitable, and ordered the *Callaghan* abandoned.

At 0235, the gallant *Callaghan,* her insides gutted by fire and devastated by thunderous explosions, dipped her stern into the sea and vanished beneath the surface under a foggy haze of smoke and steam. One officer and 46 men went down with the ship. Of her survivors, two officers and 71 of her crewmen suffered wounds, injuries or burns.

Callaghan was the last American destroyer to be lost in World War II and the thirteenth to die off Okinawa.

☆　☆　☆

USS *CALLAGHAN* (DD-792)

Class: Fletcher.
Builder: Bethlehem Steel Shipbuilding Corp., San Pedro, California.
Keel laid: February 21, 1943.
Launched: August 1, 1943.
Sponsor: Mrs. Daniel J. Callaghan, widow of Rear Admiral Daniel J. Callaghan, USN.
Commissioned: November 27, 1943; Commander F.J. Johnson, USN, comdg.
Date of loss: July 29, 1945; Commander C.M. Bertholf, USN, comdg.
Location: Off Okinawa.
Awards: Eight battle stars.

APPENDIX A
American Destroyer Classes of WWII

WICKES/CLEMSON CLASS (1917–1922)
DD NOS. 7–347

Normal displacement: 1,090 tons[1]
Standard displacement: 1,154 tons (ready for sea)
Length overall: 314'5"; Maximum width: 31'8"; Mean draft: 8'8"
Designed complement: Officers: 5; Enlisted: 95[2]
Armament—
Primary: four 4-inch/50-cal. guns
Secondary: one 1-pounder, two 3-inch/23-cal.(AA battery), three 30-cal. machine guns[3]
Torpedo tubes: twelve 21-inch
Designed speed: 32–35 knots
Engines: two geared turbines; Screws: two; Shaft horsepower: 26–28,000
Fuel capacity: 275 tons (Wickes); 375 tons (Clemsons)
Cruising range @ 15 knots: 4,300 miles[4]
Number built: 273[5]
Number lost in World War II: twelve[6]

---

(1) "Clemsons" approximately 100 tons heavier; (2) Peacetime complement; wartime up to 12 officers; 140–50 enlisted; (3) .50-cal. machine guns installed later, with 20–40 mm cannons installed in 1942; (4) Approximately 5,400 miles for "Clemson's"; (5) DDs Nos. 200 through 205 canceled on February 3, 1919; (6) Does not apply to destroyers converted to high-speed transports (APD), high-speed minesweepers (DMS), seaplane tenders (AVD), etc.

FARRAGUT CLASS (1931–1932)
DD NOS. 348–355

Normal displacement: 1,375 tons; Standard displacement: 1,700 tons
Length overall: 341"3'; Maximum width: 34'2"; Mean draft: 15'5"

Designed complement: Officers: 10; Enlisted: 150[1]
Armament—
Primary: five dual-purpose 5-inch/38-cal.
Secondary: four .50-cal. 20–40mm cannons installed 1942
Torpedo tubes: eight 21-inch
Designed speed: 36.5 knots
Engines: two geared turbines; Screws: two; Shaft horsepower: 42,800
Fuel capacity: 600 tons; Cruising range: 6,000 miles @ 15 knots
Number built: eight
Number lost in World War II: three

---

(1) Peacetime complement.

PORTER CLASS[1] (1933)
DD NOS. 356–363

Normal displacement: 1,850 tons; Standard displacement: 2,130 tons
Length overall: 381'1"; Maximum width: 36'11"; Mean draft; 10'4"
Designed complement: Officers: 9; Enlisted: 185[2]
Armament—
Primary: eight 5-inch/38-cal.[3]
Secondary: eight 1.1-inch/75 (AA batteries); 20–40 mm.cannons. installed
    1942
Torpedo tubes: twelve 21-inch
Designed speed: 37 knots
Engines: two geared turbines; Screws: two; Shaft horsepower: 50,000
Fuel capacity: 636 tons; Cruising range: 6,140 miles @ 15 knots
Number built: eight
Number lost in World War II: one

---

(1) Designated as destroyer squadron leaders; (2) Peacetime complement; (3) Twin mounts were unsuitable for anti-aircraft defense.

MAHAN CLASS (1933)
DD NOS. 364–379

Normal: 1,500; Standard displacement: 1,726 tons
Length overall: 341'3"; Maximum width: 34'8"; Mean draft: 17'0"
Designed complement: Officers: 8; Enlisted: 150[1]
Armament—

Primary: four dual-purpose 5-inch/38-cal.
Secondary: two .50-cal. machine guns; one 1'/75-cal., 20–40 mm cannons
  installed 1942
Torpedo tubes: twelve 21-inch
Designed speed: 35.5 knots
Engines: two geared turbines; Screws: two; Shaft horsepower: 42,800
Fuel capacity: 525 tons; Crusing range: 5,750 miles @ 15.5 knots
Number built: 16
Number lost in World War II: six

---

(1) Peacetime complement. *Note:* Two modified "Mahans," classified as Fanning Class of 1934, USSs *Dunlap* (DD-384) and *Fanning* (DD-385), were commissioned on June 12, 1937, and October 8, 1937, respectively. Statistical data similar to Mahan Class. Both destroyers survived the war.

CRAVEN/GRIDLEY CLASS (1934–1935)
DD NOS. 380–393

Normal displacement: 1,500 tons; Standard displacement: 2,395 tons
Length overall: 341'3"; Maximum width: 34'8"; Mean draft: 17'0"
Designed complement: Officers: 8; Enlisted: 150[1]
Armament—
Primary: five dual-purpose 5-inch/38 cal.
Secondary: two .50-cal. machine guns, one 1'/75-cal., 20 mm installed 1942[2]
Torpedo tubes: sixteen 21-inch
Designed speed: 35–40 knots
Engines: two geared turbines; Screws: two; Shaft horsepower: 50,000
Fuel capacity: 525 tons; Crusing range: 5,750 miles @ 15.5 knots
Number built: ten
Number lost in World War II: three

---

(1) Peacetime complement; (2) Owing to instability problems, 40-mm guns were not installed on the Craven/Gridley Classes.

SOMERS CLASS[1] (1935–1936)
DD NOS. 381–396[2]

Normal displacement: 1,850 tons; Standard displacement: 2,905 tons
Length overall: 381'0"; Maximum width: 36'2"; Mean draft: 16'6"
Designed complement: Officers: 10; Enlisted: 225[3]

Armament—
Primary: eight 5-inch/38 cal.
Secondary: two .50-cal. machine guns, 20–40 mm. cannons installed 1942
Torpedo tubes; twelve 21-inch
Designed speed: 37.5 knots
Engines: two geared turbines; Screws: two; Shaft horse power: 50,000
Fuel Capacity: 619 tons; Cruising range: 6,490 miles @ 15.5 knots
Number built: five
Number lost in World War II: one

(1) Designated as destroyer squadron leaders; (2) DD-382 was assigned to the USS *Craven* (Craven/Gridley Class); (3) Peacetime complement.

BENHAM/MCCALL CLASS (1935)
DD NOS. 379–408

Normal displacement: 1,500 tons; Standard displacement: 1,725 tons
Length overall: 341'3"; Maximum width: 34'8"; Mean draft: 17'0"
Designed complement: Officers: 10; Enlisted: 225[1]
Armament—
Primary: five 5-inch/38-cal.
Secondary: two .50-cal. machine guns, 1.1/75 cal., 20–40 mm. cannons
    installed 1942
Torpedo tubes: twelve 21-inch
Designed speed: 37.5 knots
Engines: two geared turbines; Screws: two; Shaft horsepower: 52,000
Fuel capacity: 619 tons; Cruising range: 5,220 miles @ 15 knots
Number built: 12
Number lost in World War II: two

(1) Peacetime complement.

SIMS CLASS (1936)
DD NOS. 409–420

Normal displacement: 1,570 tons; Standard displacement: 1,770 tons
Length overall: 347'11"; Maximum width: 35'7"; Mean draft: 11'9"
Designed complement: Officers: 10; Enlisted: 182[1]
Armament—
Primary: four 5-inch/38-cal.

Secondary: four .50-cal. machine guns; 20–40 mm. cannons installed 1942
Torpedo tubes: eight 21-inch
Designed speed: 35–37 knots
Engines: two geared turbines; Screws: two; Shaft horsepower: 50,000[2]
Fuel capacity: 457 tons; Cruising range: 5,420 miles @ 15 knots
Number built: twelve
Number lost in World War II: five

(1) Peacetime complement; (2) Sims class destroyers destroyers had three boilers instead of the customary four.

BENSON/LIVERMORE CLASS (1937–1941)
DD NOS. 421–648

Normal displacement: 1,620 tons; Standard displacement: 2,030 tons
Length overall: 347'4"; Maximum width: 35'6"; Mean draft: 11'10"
Designed complement: Officers: 10; Enlisted: 182[1]
Armament—
Primary: five 5-inch/38
Secondary: four .50-cal. machine guns, 20–40 mm. cannons installed 1942
Torpedo tubes: ten 21-inch
Designed speed: 37.5 knots
Engines: two geared turbines; Screws: two; Shaft horsepower: 50,000
Cruising range: 5,430 miles @ 15 knots
Number built: 96
Number lost in World War II: fifteen

(1) Wartime complement.

FLETCHER CLASS (1940–1942)
DD NOS. 445–644

Normal displacement: 2,100 tons; Standard displacement: 2,700 tons
Length overall: 376'4"; Maximum width: 39'8"; Mean draft: 13'0"
Designed complement: Officers: 15; Enlisted: 235[1]
Armament—
Primary: five 5-inch/38 cal.
Secondary: six 20-mm, eight 40-mm cannons
Torpedo tubes: ten 21-inch
Designed speed: 35.5 knots

Engines: two geared turbines; Screws: two; Shaft horsepower: 60,000
Fuel capacity: 525 tons; Cruising range: 4,790 miles @ 15.5 knots
Number built: 175
Number lost in World War II: nineteen

(1) Wartime complement. Note: Fifty-six "late" high-numbered Fletchers (DDs 649–804) were constructed between 1942 and 1944.

ALLEN M. SUMNER CLASS (1942–1943)
DD NOS. 692–857

Normal displacement: 2,200 tons; Standard displacement: 3,035 tons
Length overall: 376'6"; Maximum width: 40'0"; Mean draft: 15'8"
Designed complement: Officers: 15; Enlisted: 235[1]
Armament—
Primary: six 5-inch/38-cal.
Secondary: ten 20-mm, twelve 40-mm.
Torpedo tubes: ten 21-inch
Designed speed: 34 knots
Engines: two geared turbines; Screws: two; Shaft horsepower: 60,000
Fuel capacity: 500 tons; Cruising range: 5,010 miles @ 15.8 knots
Number built: 70
Number lost in World War II: four

(1) Wartime complement.

Appendix B
The Honor Roll

Below is a roster of destroyers and destroyer escorts that have been named in honor of officers and enlisted men who died in WWII actions described in this book. Regrettably, lack of space prohibits description of their individual exploits.

USS **Atherton (DE-169):** Ens. John McDougal Atherton of the *Meredith* (DD-434).

USS **Black (DD-666):** Lt. Cdr. Hugo D. Black, Commanding Officer of the *Jacob Jones* (DD-130).

USS **Bronstein (DE-189)/(FF-1037):** Lt.(j.g) Ben R. Bronstein (MC), Medical Officer of the *Jacob Jones* (DD-130).

USS **Carlson (DE-9):** Chief Machinist's Mate Daniel W. Carlson of the *Hammann* (DD-412).

USS **Cockrill (DE-394):** Lt. Dan R. Cockrill of the *Meredith* (DD-434).

USS **Cofer (DE-208):** Seaman First Class John J. Cofer of the *Aaron Ward* (DD-438).

USS **Douglas H. Fox (DD-779):** Lt. Cdr. Douglas H. Fox, Commanding Officer of the *Barton* (DD-599).

USS **Durik (APD-68) (ex-DE-666):** Apprentice Seaman Joseph E. Durik of the *Meredith* (DD-434).

USS **Edgar R. Chase (DE-16):** Lt. Edgar R. Chase, Executive Officer of the *Meredith* (DD-434).

USS **Elden (DE-264):** Lt. Ralph W. Elden, Executive Officer of the *Hammann* (DD-412).

USS **Enright (APD-66) (ex-DE-216):** Ens. Robert P.J. Enright of the *Hammann* (DD-412).

USS **Fowler (DE-222):** Lt. (j.g.) Robert L. Fowler of the *Duncan* (DD-485).

USS **Gustafson (DE-182):** Lt. Arthur L. Gustafson of the *Peary* (DD-226).

USS **Hank (DD-702):** Lt, Cdr. William D. Hank, Commanding Officer of the *Laffey* (DD-459).

USS **Harry E. Hubbard (DD-748):** Cdr. Harry E. Hubbard, Commanding Officer of the *Meredith* (DD-434).

USS Haynsworth (DD-700): Cdr. William McCall Haynsworth, Commanding Officer of the *Ingraham* (DD-444).

USS Heywood L. Edwards (DD-663): Lt. Cdr. Heywood L. Edwards, Commanding Officer of the *Reuben James* (DD-245).

USS Hickox (DD-763): Lt. Cdr. Ralph Hickox, Commanding Officer of the *Truxtun* (DD-229).

USS Hyman (DD-732): Lt. Cdr. Wilford M. Hyman, Commanding Officer of the *Sims* (DD-409).

USS James E. Kyes (DD-787): Cdr. James E. Kyes, Commanding Officer of the *Leary* (DD-158).

USS Jansson (DE-396): Lt. Ralph W. Jansson of the *Porter* (DD-356).

USS John M. Bermingham (DE-530): Lt. Cdr. John M. Bermingham, Commanding Officer of the *Peary* (DD-226).

USS Joyce (DE-317): Ensign Philip M. Joyce of the *Peary* (DD-226).

USS Knudsen (APD-101) (ex-DE-591): Seaman First Class Milton L. Knudsen of the *Laffey* (DD-459).

USS Lovering (DE-39): Lt. (j.g.) William B. Lovering of the *Hammann* (DD-412).

USS Marshall (DD-676): Lt. Cdr. Thomas W. Marshall, Executive Officer of the *Jacob Jones* (DD-130).

USS Martin H. Ray (DD-338): Lt. Martin H. Ray of the *Hammann* (DD-412).

USS Naifeh (DE-352): Lt. (j.g.) Alfred Naifeh of the *Meredith* (DD-434).

USS Odum (APD-71) (ex-DE-670): Fireman First Class Joseph Odum of the *Meredith* (DD-434).

USS Purdy (DD-743): Lt. Cdr. Frederick W. Purdy, Executive Officer of the *Strong* (DD-467).

USS Rizzi (DE-537): Coxswain Rosalio M. Rizzi of the *Duncan* (DD-495).

USS Sarsfield (DD-837): Lt. Cdr. Eugene S. Sarsfield, Commanding Officer of the *Maddox* (DD-622).

USS Silverstein (DE-534): Lt. Max Silverstein of the *Sims* (DD-409).

USS Stormes (DD-780): Cdr. Max C. Stormes, Commanding Officer of the *Preston* (DD-379).

USS Thomas E. Fraser (DD-737): Cdr. Thomas D. Fraser, Commanding Officer of the *Walke* (DD-416).

USS Tolman (DD-740): Cdr. Thomas E. Tolman, Commanding Officer of the *De Haven* (DD-469).

USS Vance (DD-387): Lt. (j.g) Joseph W. Vance of the *Parrott* (DD-218).

Appendix C
U.S. Destroyer Losses in World War II
(Alphabetical Listing)

[A] Aircraft; [C] Collision; [EA] Enemy Action; [EX] Explosion; [G] Grounding;
[K] Kamikaze; [M] Mine; [S] Storm; [SC] Scuttled; [T] Torpedo; [USN] Sunk by USN.

USS	Cause	Location	Date
Aaron Ward (DD-483)	[A]	Guadalcanal	4/07/43
Abner Read (DD-526)	[A]	Leyte Gulf	11/01/44
Barton (DD-599)	[EA]	Guadalcanal	11/13/42
Beatty (DD-640)	[A]	Mediterranean	11/06/43
Benham (DD-397)	[EA]	Guadalcanal	11/15/42
Blue (DD-387)	[T]	Guadalcanal	8/22/42
Borie (DD-215)	[USN]	North of Azores	11/02/43
Bristol (DD-453)	[T]	Mediterranean	10/13/43
Brownson (DD-518)	[A]	Cape Gloucester	12/26/43
Buck (DD-420)	[T]	Salerno Gulf	10/09/43
Bush (DD-529)	[K]	Okinawa	4/06/45
Callaghan (DD-792)	[K]	Okinawa	7/29/45
Chevalier (DD-451)	[EA]	Vella Lavella	10/07/43
Colhoun (DD-801)	[K]	Okinawa	4/06/45
Cooper (DD-695)	[EA]	Ormoc Bay, Philippines	12/03/44
Corry (DD-463)	[M]	Off Normandy	6/06/44
Cushing (DD-376)	[EA]	Guadalcanal	11/13/42
De Haven (DD-469)	[A]	Guadalcanal	2/01/43
Drexler (DD-741)	[K]	Okinawa	5/28/45
Duncan (DD-485)	[EA]	Cape Esperance	10/12/42
Edsall (DD-219)	[EA]	South of Java	3/01/42
Glennon (D-620)	[M]	Off Normandy	6/10/44
Gwin (DD-433)	[EA]	Kolombangara	7/13/43
Halligan (DD-584)	[M]	Okinawa	3/26/45
Hammann (DD-412)	[T]	North of Midway Island.	6/06/42
Henley (DD-391)	[T]	South Pacific	10/03/43
Hoel (DD-533)	[EA]	Samar Island, Philippines	10/25/44
Hull (DD-350)	[S]	Philippine Sea	12/18/44
Ingraham (DD-444)	[C]	North Atlantic	8/22/42
Jacob Jones (DD-130)	[T]	Cape May, N.J.	2/28/42

Jarvis (DD-393)..................[A] ....Guadalcanal.............................8/08/42
Johnston (DD-557) ....[EA] ....Samar Island, Philippines 10/25/44
Laffey (DD-459) ....[EA] ....Guadalcanal.............................11/13/42
Lansdale (DD-426)..............[A] ....Off Algeria 4/20/44
Leary (DD-158)...................[T] ....North Atlantic 12/24/43
Little (DD-803) ....[K] ....Okinawa...................................5/03/45
Longshaw (DD-559)............[G] ....Okinawa...................................5/18/45
Luce (DD-522)....................[K] ....Okinawa...................................5/04/45
M. L. Abele (DD-733) ....[K] ....Okinawa...................................4/12/45
Maddox (DD-622)...............[A] ....Sicily 7/10/43
Mahan (DD-364).................[A] ....Leyte, P.I. 12/07/44
Meredith (DD-434) I...........[A] ....South of Solomons 10/15/42
Meredith (DD-726) II..........[M] ....Off Normandy........................6/09/44
Monaghan (DD-354)...........[S]...........Philippine Sea 12/18/44
Monssen (DD-436)..............[EA] ....Guadalcanal.............................11/13/42
Morrison (DD-560) ....[K] ....Okinawa...................................5/04/45
O'Brien (DD-415).................[T] ....Off Samoa 9/15/42
Parrott (DD-218)..................[C] ....Hampton Roads, VA 5/02/44
Peary (DD-226)....................[A] ....Darwin, Australia 2/19/42
Perkins (DD-377).................[C] ....Off New Guinea 11/29/43
Pillsbury (DD-227)..............[EA] ....South of Java 3/01/42
Pope (DD-225)....................[EA] ....Java Sea 3/01/42
Porter (DD-356)..................[A] ....Santa Cruz Is...........................10/26/42
Preston (DD-379)................[EA] ....Guadalcanal.............................11/14/42
Pringle (DD-477) ....[K] ....Okinawa...................................4/16/45
Reid (DD-369) ....[A] ....Ormoc Bay, Leyte 12/11/44
Reuben James (DD-245)......[T] ....North Atlantic 10/31/41
Rowan (DD-405)..................[T] ....Off Salerno 9/11/43
Sims (DD-409)....................[A] ....Coral Sea 5/07/42
Spence (DD-512) ....[S]...........Philippine Sea 12/18/44
Stewart (DD-224)................[SC] ....Surabaya, Java 3/02/42
Strong (DD-467) ....[T] ....New Georgia Island 7/05/43
Sturtevant (DD-240) ....[M] ....Off Florida Keys 4/26/42
Truxtun (DD-229)...............[G] ....Newfoundland 2/18/42
Tucker (DD-374).................[M] ....Espiritu Santo.........................8/04/42
Turner (DD-648) ....[EX] ....Sandy Hook, NJ 1/03/44
Twiggs (DD-591)................[K] ....Okinawa...................................6/16/45
W. D. Porter (DD-579) ....[K] ....Okinawa...................................6/10/45
Walke (DD-416)..................[EA] ....Guadalcanal.............................11/14/42
Warrington (DD-383)..........[S]...........Atlantic....................................9/13/44
Worden (DD-352) ....[G] ....Amchitka Island 1/12/43

Appendix D
The "Divine Wind"

Of the 88 destroyers and 30 destroyer escorts that were damaged during the battle for Okinawa, many were struck by "Bakas," suicide boats, friendly and enemy gunfire, or mauled by collisions and storms. A total of 47 destroyers and 10 destroyer escorts, however, suffered firsthand from the wrath of the Kamikazes. Several of them were eventually removed from the active list and scrapped when they were considered beyond economical repair.

Below is a listing of the ships which, although bloodied, battered and bruised, withstood the ravages of the "Divine Wind."

No. USS	Date	Damage	Killed	Wounded
521—Kimberley	3/26	Minor	4	54
682—Porterfield	3/27	Minor	0	1
576—Murray	3/27	Major	1	4
725—O'Brien	3/27	Major	50	76
633—Foreman (DE)	3/27	Minor	0	1
	4/03	Major	0	0
554—Franks	4/02	Major	0	2
561—Prichett	4/03	Major	0	0
	7/29	Minor	2	1
586—Newcomb (S)	4/06	Major	40	51
481—Leutze	4/06	Major	8	30
528—Mullany	4/06	Major	30	36
529—Howorth	4/06	Major	9	14
732—Hyman	4/06	Major	11	41
417—Morris	4/06	Major	12	45
573—Harrison	4/06	Minor	0	0
700—Haynsworth	4/06	Major	12	27
640—Fieberling (DE)	4/06	Minor	0	0
476—Hutchins (S)	4/06	Minor	1	3
	4/27	Major	0	18
184—Wesson (DE)	4/07	Major	8	25
473—Bennett	4/07	Major	3	18
802—Gregory	4/08	Major	0	2
802—Gregory	4/08	Major	0	2
657—Charles J. Badger	4/09	Major	0	0
36—Manlove (DE)	4/11	Minor	1	10

661—Kidd	4/11	Major	38	55
702—Hank	4/11	Minor	3	1
642—Hale	4/11	Minor	0	2
643—Whitehurst (DE)	4/12	Major	37	37
662—Bennion	4/12	Minor	1	6
	4/30	Minor	0	0
478—Stanly	4/12	Medium	0	3
185—Riddle (DE)	4/12	Medium	1	9
793—Cassin Young	4/12	Major	1	59
304—Rall (DE)	4/12	Major	21	38
743—Purdy	4/12	Major	13	58
502—Sigsbee	4/14	Major	3	75
677—McDermut	4/16	Major	2	33
724—Laffey	4/16	Major	32	71
737—Bowers (DE)	4/16	Major	48	59
665—Bryant	4/16	Major	34	33
527—Ammen	4/21	Minor	0	8
475—Hudson	4/22	Minor	0	1
	5/04	Major	0	0
516—Wadsworth	4/22	Minor	0	0
520—Isherwood	4/27	Major	42	41
390—Ralph Talbot	4/27	Major	5	9
519—Daly	4/28	Minor	3	33
591—Twiggs	4/28	Major	(unknown)	
555—Haggard (S)	4/29	Major	11	40
531—Hazelwood	4/29	Major	46	36
635—England (DE)	5/09	Major	34	36
344—Oberrender (DE) (K)	5/09	Major	(unknown/many fatally)	
552—Evans (S)	5/11	Major	31	29
744—Hugh W...Hadley (S)	5/11	Major	28	67
470—Bache	5/13	Major	41	32
779—Douglas H. Fox	5/17	Major	9	35
339—John C. Butler (DE)	5/20	Minor	0	3
547—Cowell	5/25	Minor	0	2
780—Stormes	5/25	Major	21	16
515—Anthony	5/27	Minor	0	0
	6/07	Minor	0	5
630—Braine	5/27	Major	50	78
639—Shubrick (S)	5/29	Major	32	38

(S) Scrapped in USA.; (K) Scrapped at Kerama Retto. Cannibalized for spares.

Appendix E
Destroyer Escorts

Destroyer escorts are mentioned throughout this book, however some readers may be unclear as to the exact nature of this type of ship. The primary function of the destroyer escort was to screen slow merchant convoys, primarily against enemy submarines. However, they were quite often allocated to perform other tasks, such as teaming up with "baby flattops" (CVE's), whose specific roles were to hunt for and kill submarines.

Smaller than a destroyer (average length: 290 to 305 feet; width: 35 to 37 feet with a standard displacement of 1,140 to 1,400 tons), armament varied as the war progressed. Earlier classes (Evarts) were equipped with three 3-inch/50 cal. guns (main battery), with their secondary armament consisting of one quadruple 1.1-inch anti-aircraft battery (due to maintenance problems and breakdowns, these weapons were replaced by 20 and 40 mm. cannons). The newer vessels were equipped with two 5-inch/38 cal. dual purpose guns. Anti–submarine weapons consisted of depth charges and the newer "hedgehog" rocket projector. The former could be rolled off the stern or lobbed over both sides of the ship by a weapon commonly known as the "K-gun."

The "hedgehog," developed by the British, consisted of a steel cradle in which were planted four rows of spike-like spigots (hence the term "hedge-hog"). Consequently, this projector served as a rocket launcher, however they were not conventional rockets. The launcher could fire a brace of 24 projectiles several yards ahead of the ship, however they would not explode unless they made a direct hit upon the target. The later classes of DE's, after the Evarts, were equipped with three 21-inch torpedoes in triple mounts.

The main propulsion machinery varied between diesel and steam engines. Since they were intended to accompany slow-moving vessels, their average top speed was from 21 to 24 knots. Their designed complement could range from between 6 to 8 officers and up to 180 enlisted personnel.

Under the terms of the Lend-Lease Bill, 84 DE's were delivered to Allied Navies: 78 to Great Britain (of which 4 were lost) and 6 to France. During 1944, 6 were loaned to Brazil.

Over the years 101 DE's were converted to APD's with each carrying 4 LCVP's. Thirteen were recipients of the Presidential Unit Citation and 11 were war losses.

Destroyer Escort Losses in WWII

[A] Aircraft; [K] Kaiten*; [M] Mine; [S] Surface Action; [T] Torpedo

USS	Cause	Date	Location
Bates (APD-47)**	(A)	5/25/45	Okinawa
Eversole (DE-404)	(T)	10/24/44	Philippines
Fechteler (DE-157_	(T)	5/04/44	Mediterranean
Fisk (DE-143)	(T)	8/02/44	Atlantic
F.C. Davis (DE-136)	(T)	4/24/45	Atlantic
Holder (DE-401)	(A)	4/11/44	Mediterranean
Leopold (DE-319)	(T)	3/10/44	Atlantic
Rich (DE-695)	(M)	6/08/44	Normandie
S.B. Roberts (DE-413)	(S)	10/25/44	Leyte Gulf
Shelton (DE-407)	(T)	10/03/44	New Guinea
Underhill (DE-682)	(K)	7/24/45	Philippines

*   Japanese suicide midget submarines
** Formerly, DE-68

GLOSSARY

AD	Destroyer Tender
Adm.	Admiral
AE	Ammunition Ship
AK	Cargo Ship
AKA	Attack Cargo Ship
AKS	Stores Cargo Ship
AO	Fleet Oiler
APD	High-Speed Transport (converted WW-I Destroyer or Destroyer Escort)
ASW	Anti-Submarine Warfare
AVD	Seaplane Tender (converted WW-I Destroyer)
BB	Battleship (26,000 to 45,000 tons)
CAA	Anti-Aircraft Cruiser (6,000 tons)
CA	Heavy Cruiser (9,000 to 13,000 tons)
Cdr.	Commander
CL	Light Cruiser (7,000 to 10,000 tons)
Co DesDiv	Commander, Destroyer Division (Four destroyers form one division)
ComDesLant	Commander, Destroyers, Atlantic Fleet
ComDesPac	Commander, Destroyers, Pacific Fleet
ComDesRon	Commander, Destroyer Squadron (Thirteen Destroyers form one Squadron, one of which is ConDesRon's flagship)
CV	Aircraft Carrier (27,000 to 33,000 tons)
CVE	Escort Aircraft Carrier (Built from merchant ship hull)
CVL	Light Aircraft Carrier (Built from light and heavy cruiser hulls)
DD	Destroyer (1,200 to 2,200 tons)
DE	Destroyer Escort (1,200 to 1,400 tons. Utilized primarily as an escort for slow merchant convoys and ASW defense)
DM	Minelayer Destroyer
DMS	Minesweeper Destroyer
Ens.	Ensign
Hedgehog	Anti-Submarine Weapon
HMAS	His or Her Majesty's Australian Ship
HMNZS	His or Her Majesty's New Zealand Ship
HMS	His or Her Majesty's Ship

345

IJNS	Imperial Japanese Navy Ship
K-Gun	Depth Charge Projector (DCR)
LCS	Landing Craft, Support
LSMR	Landing Ship Medium (Armed with rockets)
Lt.	Lieutenant
Lt.Cdr.	Lieutenant Commander
Lt.(j.g.)	Lieutenant (junior grade)
PBY	Consolidated Patrol Bomber (Commonly known as the "Catalina.")
RAdm.	Rear Admiral
TF	Task Force
TU	Task Unit
USMC	United States Marine Corps
USN	United States Navy
USNR	United States Navel Reserve
VAdm.	Vice Admiral

Note: All tonnages are WW-II configurations.

* Heavy cruisers carried nine to ten 8"/55 cal.. guns; light cruisers ten to twelve 6"/47 cal. guns; anti-aircraft cruisers, ten to twelve 6"/47 cal. guns, anti-aircraft cruisers twelve 5"/37 cal. guns.

SELECT BIBLIOGRAPHY

Abbazia, Patrick. *Mr. Roosevelt's Navy: The Private War of the U.S. Atlantic Fleet.* Annapolis, Md.: United States Naval Institute, 1975.

Alden, John, CDR., USN. *Flush Decks and Four Pipes.* Annapolis, Md.: United States Naval Institute, 1965.

Belote, James H., and William M. Belote. *Typhoon of Steel: The Battle for Okinawa.* New York: Harper and Row, 1970.

Brown, Cassie. *Standing into Danger.* Doubleday of Canada, Ltd., 1979.

Clagett, John. *The U.S. Navy in Action.* Derby, CT: Monarch Books, 1963.

D'Este, Carlo. *Bitter Victory: The Battle for Sicily, 1943.* New York: E.P. Dutton, 1988.

Dictionary of American Fighting Ships. Vols. I–VIII. Washington, D.C.: U.S. Government Printing Office, 1959–81.

Fahey, James C. *Ships and Aircraft of the U.S. Fleet.* Vol. I (1939); Vol. II (1940); Vol. III (1942); Vol. V. (1945). New York; reprinted by United States Naval Institute, 1976.

Floating Drydock. Kresgeville, PA, n.p., n.d.

Frank, Richard B. *Guadalcanal.* New York: Random House, 1990.

Hailey, Foster, and Milton Lancelot. *Clear for Action.* New York: Bonanza Books, 1975.

Hoyt, Edwin P. *The Lonely Ships: The Life and Death of the U.S. Asiatic Fleet.* New York: David McKay Company, 1976.

Hughes, Terry, and John Costello. *The Battle of the North Atlantic.* New York: Dial/John Wade, 1977.

Karig, Walter, Capt., USNR. *Battle Report: The Atlantic War.* New York: Farrar & Rinehart, 1946.

Lord, Walter. *Incredible Victory.* New York: Harper & Row, 1967.

McIntire, Donald. *The Naval War Against Hitler.* New York: Charles Scribner's Sons, 1970.

Messimer, Dwight R. *Pawns of War: The Loss of the USS Langley and USS Pecos.* Annapolis, Md.: United States Naval Institute, 1983.

Morrison, Samuel Eliot. *The Two Ocean War.* Boston: Little, Brown, Co., 1963.

National Archives. Washington, D.C.

Preston, Antony. *Destroyers.* Englewood Cliffs, NJ: Prentice-Hall, 1977.

Rattray, Jannette E. *The Perils of the Port of New York.* New York: Dodd, Mead & Co., 1973.

Reilly, Jr., John C. *United States Destroyers of WWII*. Dorset, U.K.: Blandford
    Press, 1983.
Roscoe, Theodore. *United States Destroyer Operations in WWII*. Annapolis, MD:
    United States Naval Institute, 1953.
Schofield, William G. *Destroyers—60 Years*. Boston: Burdette & Co., 1962.
Sharkhunters U-Boat History Group, Hernando, FL.
Smith, E. *The United States Navy in World War II*. New York: Ballantine Books,
    1966.
U.S. Naval Historical Center. Washington, D.C.
U.S. Naval Imaging Command. Washington, D.C.
War Reports of General George C. Marshall, USA; General H.H. Arnold, USAAF;
    and Admiral Ernest King, USN. Philadelphia: J.B. Lippincott, 1947.
Watts, John A. *Warships of the Japanese Navy in WWII*. New York: Doubleday,
    1967.
Watts, John A., and Brian A. Gordon. *The Imperial Japanese Navy: 1898–1945*.
    New York: Doubleday & Co., 1971.

ILLUSTRATION ACKNOWLEDGMENTS

The publishers are indebted to the courtesy of the United States National
Archives and the United States Navy for the majority of the photos used in this
book. Special thanks are also due the Naval Institute Press in Annapolis, MD,
for the photo of the surfaced U-boat, the double-spread of the Battle off Samar
Island, and the damaged USS *Selfridge*. In addition, sincere gratitude is hereby
expressed to John S. Desiderio for the *Truxtun* salute, Ernest Graham for his
series of photos of the USS **Meredith**, and AP-Wide World Photos for the *Stewart*
series. The original maps on pages ix, x and xi were created by Julius Weil.

INDEX